Ql

MODERN EUROPE

QUEENSHIP IN EARLY MODERN EUROPE

Charles Beem

 macmillan international HIGHER EDUCATION

 RED GLOBE PRESS

First published 2020 by
RED GLOBE PRESS

Red Globe Press in the UK is an imprint of Springer Nature Limited, registered in England, company number 785998, of 4 Crinan Street, London N1 9XW.

Red Globe Press® is a registered trademark in the United States, the United Kingdom, Europe and other countries.

ISBN 978–1–137–00508–3 hardback
ISBN 978–1–137–00507–6 paperback

This book is printed on paper suitable for recycling and made from fully managed and sustained forest sources. Logging, pulping and manufacturing processes are expected to conform to the environmental regulations of the country of origin.

A catalogue record for this book is available from the British Library.

A catalog record for this book is available from the Library of Congress.

Contents

Acknowledgements

This volume was inspired in part by Theresa Earenfight's *Queenship in Medieval Europe* (2013), which synthesized older scholarship with more recent feminist-inspired works to both identify and explain how royal women created the many forms of queenship that appeared across Europe over the course of the medieval millennium. As a survey, rather than a work of original scholarship, I have read countless books and articles in the research for this project. Accordingly, I wish to thank the staff of the Livermore Library at the University of North Carolina at Pembroke (UNC Pembroke) for all their assistance in the research of this book. I also wish to thank the staffs of the various libraries of North Carolina State University, who have also been so helpful in obtaining the resources needed for the researching of this volume. I am also much beholden to UNC Pembroke's Teaching and Learning Center for grants and academic leaves which made the writing of this book possible. I also wish to thank Charles Harrington and Kenneth Kitts, former UNC Pembroke provosts, for their support to this project. I am grateful to Carole Levin, Elaine Kruse, Elena Woodacre, Bruce Dehart, Anthony Johnson, and anonymous readers for Red Globe Press for reading and offering commentary on various drafts of my manuscript. Finally, I am much beholden to the many authors and contributors to the Queenship and Power book series, whose scholarship has provided me with so much insight in the writing of this book. As this work is a survey, the specialist must necessarily venture beyond their disciplinary comfort zone. In this context, I wish to acknowledge all errors, both factual and interpretive, that may exist in this volume.

NOTE ON NAMES

I have taken a common sense approach to the use of names in this book. The guiding rule is to assign the name most readily identified with a particular individual, i.e. Isabella and Ferdinand of Spain, rather than Isabel and Fernando, and Anne of Austria, rather than Anne d'Autriche. But by the same rule I use the name Juana, rather than Joanna, for Isabella and Ferdinand's eldest surviving daughter. Because of a plethora of Iberian queens named Isabella, I have termed Charles V's consort as Isabel of Portugal simply to avoid confusion. I have also used Elisabeth, rather than Elizabeth, for various Spanish queens of French and Italian origin.

1 Introduction to Early Modern European Queenship

When we think of a queen, dressed in lavish robes, dripping in jewels, wearing a crown, and sitting on a throne, we often conjure up images of Europe's early modern queens. At the beginning of this era was the formidable Isabella of Castile, who reigned jointly with her husband Ferdinand of Aragon, conquered the Spanish Muslims, and funded Christopher Columbus's initial voyage to the new world. Or, perhaps the most famous queen *of all time*, Elizabeth I of England, who reigned confidently as an unmarried virgin queen and gave her name to a particularly illustrious age of English history. More than any other queen in history, Elizabeth's historical image has been perennially reproduced in countless popular histories, novels, and feature films.

Almost as famous was Elizabeth's cousin and bête noire, Mary Queen of Scots, whose queenship has for centuries served as a historical counterpoint to Elizabeth's allegedly much more successful reign. For generations of historians and novelists, the Mary Queen of Scots story was the cautionary tale of a tragic queen destroyed by her passionate romantic nature. And, at the end of the early modern era, we have the regal mastery of Catherine II of Russia, known during her lifetime as "the Great," who deposed her husband and assumed his place on the throne as she furthered Russia's progress towards modernity with firm yet enlightened imperial majesty.

Today, the queens of Early Modern Europe capture our popular imaginations in films and in cable television series like *Reign, Ekaterina, Versailles*, and *Isabel*, where they are usually cast as sexualized and romanticized heroines and villainesses.[1] In the history of Early Modern Europe, however, queenship was not quite as exciting; there was very little that was *romantic* about queenship, while actual and consummated romantic love was a physical and emotional luxury that few queens ever enjoyed unless it happened within the context of their marriage. Queenship was in fact a vocation, in the sense that there were responsibilities to perform, such as being a wife, a mother, and a household and estate manager. This book seeks to uncover the processes behind being a queen in Early Modern Europe, to flesh out the possibilities of what a queen could accomplish, and to measure the performances of Europe's early modern queens as a uniquely *trans-European phenomenon*.[2] While most Early Modern European kings remained in their kingdoms for the duration of their reigns, leaving only to fight wars or go on pilgrimages, their queens were drawn from a peripatetic class of women who functioned as the great pollinators of European culture and society, adapting to new homes in foreign kingdoms yet bringing their native cultures with them.[3]

What emerges from the analysis of queenship in this book is a form of template that identifies certain trends and behaviors that proved to be identifiable strategies for queenly success and failure. As historian Clarissa Campbell Orr has noted, there is a difference between studying queens individually and studying the forms and means by which women exercised queenly power.[4] Indeed, in Early Modern Europe there were numerous types of queens (to be discussed below) who exercised myriads of forms of power and influence within a variety of dynamic social, cultural, and political contexts.[5] As Early Modern European monarchies "progressed" through the early modern era, so did forms of queenship, which played an integral role in Europe's political, religious, and cultural life.

WHAT IS QUEENSHIP?

In their general usage, the terms "king" and "queen" are a binary construction, assigned to individuals like King Louis XIV of France or his Queen Maria Theresa of Spain. Most students of Early Modern European history tend to study the reigns of *individual* kings and queens, outlining their differences from one another in terms of intelligence, aptitude, accomplishments, and leadership ability. But there is also the study of *kingship*; the act of being a king, of inhabiting the role and exercising its powers. For the historian, this involves measuring and evaluating kingly strategies as they developed through time in response to the dynamic social and historical forces that shaped the history of Early Modern Europe.[6] The study of kingship, rather than the study of individual kings, looks for similarities and patterns in the ways in which kings governed their kingdoms, rather than the differences between individual kings. Similarly, this book seeks to uncover the defining features of queenship. What were standard practices, if any, that most queens followed? Which strategies, observed over a three-century period, periodically led to queenly success or failure? How did queenship evolve over the early modern period in response to societal and religious pressures? Thus queenship, in the context of this book, is that collective body of experiences that European queens shared, which are reflective of or reactive to a pan-European template of queenship that possessed certain universal characteristics but was subject to regional variations.

WHAT IS A QUEEN?

As a descriptive term, "queen" is a bit more complicated than "king," which does not need to be qualified to understand its meaning, unless of course the king is a consort, which was for the most part an anomalous, restrictive, and ambiguous male role.[7] In contrast, in Early Modern Europe there were several different types of queens. The most prevalent form was a *queen consort*, a queen who enjoyed her title and position because she was married to a king, such as the French queens Catherine de Medici, Anne of Austria, and Marie Antoinette, and the six women whose fate it was to be married to Henry VIII of England. Most Early Modern European queens were this type of queen, and *all* the queens of monarchies that did not allow a female succession, such as France and the Holy Roman Empire, were consorts. In theory, European queen consorts were recognized as reigning alongside or in conjunction with kings, and they were often crowned and anointed either alongside their husbands or in separate ceremonies, which conferred even greater dignity as well as sanctity upon their queenships.[8]

The notion that the wives of male monarchs should enjoy formal recognition of their status alongside their husbands has been well entrenched in virtually every human culture and has made the transition to modern, republican forms of government in the concept of a *first lady*. Like contemporary first ladies, queen consorts functioned as social helpmates to their husbands while presiding over the administration of their own royal household.[9] As the premier married couple in their kingdoms, the most successful kings and queens were able to provide a positive example of domestic marital harmony and stability for their subjects to emulate, regardless of dynastic considerations that did not always consider compatibility a primary factor in the making of royal marriages.

If kings were idealized as the ultimate role model for their male subjects, emulating male gendered virtues such as leadership, martial virility, courage, rationality, and paternal care and protection, queens were expected to do the same thing for their female subjects, as the most successful of early modern consorts embraced Christian piety and chastity, compassion, charity, obedience to male authority, and motherhood while serving as intercessors between a king and his subjects.[10] But kings and queens also worked together for their mutual benefit. As Joseph F. O'Callaghan has argued, a successful royal marriage bolstered the power of kingship: "the queen who was honored, loved, and protected by her husband would love and honor him, and thus would offer a good example to all the people of the realm."[11]

But consorts also played more overtly political roles. As the wife of a king, they had access to their husband's ear, especially in the royal bedchamber, away from the constraining influence of male advisors and the public and formal institutions of royal government. Consorts also possessed the ability to influence the distribution of patronage, an integral facet of royal power, and participate in the raising and education of their children. Some consorts were actively recruited for their potential to wield political power, like Louisa Ulrika, sister of Frederick the Great of Prussia, who was the power behind the throne of her weak-willed husband, Adolph Frederick of Sweden.[12] But the most talented and politically adept consorts shared their husband's royal power in various capacities and degrees, such as serving as regents for their husband when they were temporarily out of their kingdoms, usually to fight wars, or when there were multiple dominions under one crown, such as that of the sixteenth-century peripatetic Holy Roman Emperor Charles V, who employed his empress, Isabel of Portugal, as his regent in Spain. Additionally, queens often filled the political vacuum created when husbands were either incapacitated or unable to perform their duties as kings, such as the seventeenth-century Catherine of Braganza, who served as regent in Portugal for her brother, and the eighteenth-century Maria Carolina of Naples, who wielded a kingly authority in place of her husband Ferdinand IV during the years of revolutionary tumult and the Napoleonic Wars.[13]

Yet even though Maria Carolina reportedly loathed her husband, it did not stop her from propagating the dynasty, which has always been the benchmark for queenly success. In fact, the production of heirs was the essential prerequisite for Maria Carolina's assumption of regal power, as dynastic reproduction was the primary task of queenship in hereditary monarchies. Often queens were married soon after the onset of puberty, beginning annual reproductive duties for the duration of their childbearing years. Because of dynastic inbreeding, many queens were physically frail. Nonetheless, many spent much of their married lives pregnant, while death in childbirth was the leading cause of queenly mortality, as many early modern queens were literally bred to death, like Queen Claude, consort of Francis I of France, who died at age twenty-five after seven grueling pregnancies, which ruined her health. Conversely, several Holy Roman Empresses from Maria of Spain to Maria Theresa delivered upwards of a dozen children, most of whom survived to maturity.

Despite the dangers, pregnancy was always a welcome development, as even the most capable and popular of queens could find themselves sidelined by their inability to bear children, as the matrimonial career of Henry VIII of England aptly demonstrates. Other queens, however, such as Irina Godunovna, consort of Feodor I of Russia, overcame the handicap of childlessness to enjoy successful and productive queenships. Conversely, queens who suffered marginalization at the hands of their husbands, such as the French queens Catherine de Medici and Anne of Austria and Juliana Maria of Brunswick-Wolfenbuttel, queen of Denmark, later enjoyed enhanced political power following their husband's deaths during the reigns of their underage sons.

Most early modern queens also strove to create a reputation for religious devotion. The most successful of early modern queens were also the most pious, a pan-European method of earning queenly prestige. This took several forms, such as attending church services regularly, dispensing charity to the poor and to religious houses, going on ritualistic pilgrimages to religious sites, often to pray for fertility, and setting an example of moral probity. Emulating the Virgin Mary, queens served as intercessors between king and subjects, as Catherine of Aragon famously did for the evil May Day rioters of 1517. The most ambitious of queens also founded and built monastic establishments, churches, hospitals, schools, and orphanages, while exhibiting Christian care for their subjects. Even secular-minded queens such as Catherine II of Russia were ostentatiously devoted to their religious observances and responsibilities.

With the notable exception of Catherine II's Russia, guaranteeing the legitimacy of heirs was considered extremely important in hereditary monarchies. While kings were free to engage in extramarital sexual activities, queens needed to guard their chastity, both before and after marriage. Most European queens were surrounded in their own households by ladies who constituted a twenty-four-hour per day chaperone service, with the queen's sexuality highly regulated within the structures of the royal court and her personal relationship with the king. On those occasions when the paternity of a royal heir was suspect, queens were subject to divorce or exile, such as Carolina Matilda of Denmark. Conversely, many queens had to accept the presence of royal mistresses and their progeny within the spaces of the royal court.

For the most part, with a few exceptions, royal and aristocratic women, and occasionally daughters of wealthy merchants, became queens because of arranged marriages which formed part of a treaty or diplomatic alliance, the way in which women from Catherine of Aragon to Marie Antoinette became queens. Indeed, the conduct of pan-European marriage brokering was a key factor in the making of Early Modern European dynastic alliances, as well as a powerful source of queenly power. Negotiations, often conducted between royal and aristocratic women through kinship networks, included provisions for the dowry, the money and/or property the bride brought to the marriage from her family, as well as the dower, or jointure, which a king provided for his queen should she outlive him. The ability to broker the marriages of children and close relatives was the final benchmark for queenly success.

Once the marriage had been negotiated, a consort needed to walk the delicate line between loyalty to their homelands and their adoptive kingdoms. Thus, most consorts were foreigners in their kingdoms and were expected to learn the language and adopt the customs of their kingdom; not surprisingly, some of the more successful Early Modern European queens were brilliant linguists, which proved beneficial in relations with ambassadors as well as the conduct of marriage brokering. Second to their ability to perpetuate the succession, negotiating this process was a key element, whether to becoming a popular queen, like Caroline of Ansbach, who took a crash course in English language and customs prior to her arrival in England, or a detested one, like Elisabeth Farnese of Spain, vilified for her perceived contempt for the Spanish people. It was also advantageous for a queen to create a companionate marriage, which, along with the production of heirs, was the surest route to queenly power and influence.

For those consorts who survived their husbands into the reign of the next monarch, their status changed from *consort* to *dowager*. Dowager queens often retained much of the political and economic power they wielded as consorts if they were the mother to the next monarch. And, in the case of a royal minority, dowagers could function as regents for their underage sons, such as the French dowager queens Catherine de Medici, Marie de Medici, and Anne of Austria.[14] Most dowagers gave up queenly apparel for widow's weeds, signifying their devotion to their dead husband and legitimizing the power they wielded on their children's behalf. Some dowagers, however, remarried, like Margaret Tudor, who married Archibald Douglas, Earl of Angus after the death of her husband, Scottish king James IV, or found a powerful male advisor to assist them in their minority governments, as Anne of Austria did with Cardinal Mazarin. But for dowagers who were unable to perpetuate a hereditary succession, like Catherine of Braganza, the consort of Charles II of England, their widowhoods were often spent in obscurity, as their queenly power and influence was assumed by the next queen consort.

But the next form of queenship is fundamentally different from either consorts or dowagers. *Queens regnant*, women who in hereditary monarchies inherited the kingly office usually because of a temporary lack of viable male heirs, occupied an anomalous position in Early Modern Europe. They were, in form and function, *female kings*, women who inherited the estate and occupied the office of king.[15] As such, they possessed the eternal body politic of kingship, as conceptualized in many European monarchies, but they bore the responsibilities of both kingship and queenship, as they were responsible for wielding kingly power as well as the queenly responsibility of providing for a hereditary succession.[16] However, several early modern queens regnant, such as Elizabeth I of England and Christina of Sweden, came to their thrones unmarried but then declined to marry and instead provided for the succession through collateral male members of their ruling dynasties.

In comparison to their male counterparts as kings, queens regnant often faced significant obstacles to maintaining their authority. The most formidable problem that all regnant queens faced was that they were performing the male gendered role of king as women, a gender-bending role fraught with difficulties. Female rulers rarely played the role of military leader, one of the more visceral functions of kingship, with women limited to playing a military role in purely symbolic or allegorical terms. Female authority also ran counter to prevailing notions of female inadequacy and subordination grounded in biblical and classical texts.[17] By and large, female rulers succeeded by demonstrating to their contemporaries that they were exceptions to these rules, rather than arguing against their veracity.

But since most Early Modern European queens were consorts, describing female kings as *queens* is theoretically analogous to describing contemporary female chief executives as *first ladies*, which both mislabels and obscures the actual political role they performed. In both English and the Romance languages, the terms *king* and *queen* are gender specific, which has meant that the female kings of Early Modern Europe have always been identified as queens. But despite the fundamental differences between consort and regnant queens, there was some permeability between these two seemingly distinct roles; while regnant queens frequently performed the office of king, they also performed the same queenly duties as queen consorts. Isabella of Castile was simultaneously a consort, as the queen of Ferdinand of Aragon, as well as regnant Queen of Castile. Mary Queen of Scots was born a regnant queen of Scotland but also served as a queen of France as the consort of King Francis II, only returning to Scotland to rule as queen after his death. Following her forced abdication and flight to England, Mary endured nearly twenty years of imprisonment as an exiled Scottish dowager queen. Perhaps the most striking example of a simultaneous consort and regnant was Maria Theresa of Austria. Unable to be elected Holy Roman Empress in her own right because of her gender, she nonetheless facilitated the election of her husband, Francis Stephen, who functioned as her *de facto* consort.

Another responsibility shared by queens, consort and regnant alike, was in personal adornment. Indeed, one of the easiest ways to chart the evolution of styles of clothing, hairstyles, shoes, and various queenly accessories, including coaches and jewels, is from early modern royal portraiture and material culture. Many queens took seriously the challenge to be the best coiffed, best dressed, and most bejeweled woman in their royal court, to bolster their influence as well as create their queenly legacy, which meant that queenly patronage extended to jewelers, wig makers, cobblers, clothiers, perfume makers, furriers, and purveyors of cosmetics. This was true of even the most devoutly religious queens, who also recognized that their role was to project the majesty of their kingdoms, particularly in religious spectacles such as coronations, christenings, and rituals surrounding the clerical holiday calendar. Purchasing jewels was a common pastime among Early Modern European queens, but jewels were not only for adornment; they also represented liquid assets when the monarchy was in trouble and needed quick cash. Isabella of Castile, Henrietta Maria of England, and a host of other queens routinely pawned their jewels to obtain emergency funds.

Personal adornment carried enormous weight in constructing an image of monarchy, not only for the royal court but also for the monarch's subjects who, by and large, grew progressively more literate and aware of the functions of monarchy, including that of queenship, over the course of the early modern era. Queens not only appeared in court and went on procession through their kingdoms; they also were painted, often with their children, and if widowed in their widow's weeds, to create an image of queenship for public consumption. The ability to create representations of their queenships was a form of "soft power" in which subjects were persuaded to support the regime by the messages embedded in commissioned works of art and building projects such as churches and monasteries.[18] Queens also worked to make Europe increasingly more cosmopolitan. Adam Morton has discussed how queens across the continent of Europe created "cultural encounters" by patronizing foreign artisans, musicians, writers, and scientists, stimulating the export of both the Renaissance and the later Scientific Revolution and the Enlightenment to Central, Eastern, and Northern Europe.[19]

QUEENSHIP AND EARLY MODERN EUROPE

The early modern era in Europe (circa 1500–1800) bridged the medieval and modern epochs. This was a period when many aspects of what can be termed as modernity crept into the many differing facets of European culture, society, economics, and politics, represented by the Renaissance and Reformation, the European Enlightenment and Scientific Revolution, and the transition from *providential* to *material* world views. We generally consider the epoch to properly begin with the spread of the Italian Renaissance to Western, Central, and Northern Europe at the end of the fifteenth century and to end with the outbreak of the French Revolution in 1789. At the beginning of this period, the rebirth of classical civilization reinvigorated European culture both intellectually and artistically, as medieval queenship gave way to a more literate and worldlier Renaissance queenship; queens such as Elizabeth I of England and Christina of Sweden rank among the most educated rulers of the entire early modern epoch. Queens with access to patronage, such as Marie de Medici of France and Catherine II of Russia, were great art collectors and patrons of Renaissance artists from Titian to Rubens and Velasquez, an important component of queenly legacy building.

The discovery of the new world and the formation of global empires broadened the perspective of queenship as early modern queens consort and regnant emerged as global figures on the world stage. Isabella of Castile, noted for her Christian piety, a textbook strategy for successful queenship, initiated the conversion to Christianity of the indigenous peoples of the New World. Elizabeth I of England hid behind the screen of plausible deniability while rewarding pirates like Francis Drake and John Hawkins for their audacious attacks on trans-Atlantic Spanish shipping, while at the end of her reign Elizabeth granted a charter to the East India Company, heralding the beginning of the British Empire. A century later, Queen Anne of Great Britain presided over her empire's participation in the War of the Spanish Succession, the first truly globalized European war, and at the end of her reign pushed through the ratification of the Peace of Utrecht (1713) in the face of significant domestic opposition. In Eastern Europe, Catherine II of Russia brought increasing numbers of Muslims and other ethnic minorities under the rule of an imperial Russian empire.

Queens also played significant roles in the religious changes that swept the early modern period. The Protestant Reformation, which shattered the medieval unity of the medieval Christian Church, and the Counter-Reformation, in its efforts to revitalize the Roman Catholic Church, provided the context for European queens of the sixteenth and seventeenth centuries to play pivotal roles on the European stage. Isabella of Castile played a central role in initiating the Spanish Inquisition, founded to root out Jewish and Muslim *conversos* in Spain. In Scotland and in France, Mary of Guise and Catherine de Medici played the queenly role of peacemaker in their attempts to mediate the religious polarizations of sixteenth-century Europe. In England, the

Tudor half-sisters Mary I and Elizabeth I, operating from opposite poles of Christian belief, played significant roles in the religious history of their kingdom, while Stuart queen consorts of the seventeenth century practiced a Catholicism at odds with the religious beliefs of most of their subjects, contributing to the causes of both the English Civil War and the Glorious Revolution.

Elsewhere in Europe, Christina of Sweden, who strove to achieve the platonic model of a philosopher king, converted to Roman Catholicism, which led to her abdication. Conversely, Catherine II of Russia, a Protestant German by birth, shed her native Lutheranism to embrace the Russian Orthodox religion that served as a powerful bolster to her power as empress and tsarina. In a much broader sense, Holy Roman Empresses Consort practiced a form of religious devotion known as the *pietas austriaca* to bolster the power and influence of their queenships, while also serving as patrons of baroque artists to create visual representations of their queenships. While the Protestant Reformation created a confessional divide between Catholic and Protestant kingdoms that restricted the pre-Reformation pan-European kinship network, the breach was not insurmountable, with several queens converting to Catholicism and vice versa, while others, such as England's seventeenth-century Catholic queens, maintaining their religion despite the hostility of their adopted country.

The development of Protestant denominations and the continued rise of European literacy, a direct result of the invention of the printing press, brought Early Modern European queenship under increased critical scrutiny, symbolized by the 1558 publication of John Knox's notorious treatise, *First Blast of the Trumpet Against the Monstrous Regiment of Women,* which cited classical and scriptural evidence to argue against female rule.[20] For the remainder of the early modern era, European queens often faced pressure and resistance to their authority and their influence from the increasingly literate societies over which they reigned. Consorts who failed to culturally adapt to their adopted homelands were often lampooned or attacked in various forms of print media, as Marie Antoinette and the Catholic queen consorts of seventeenth-century England learned to their detriment.[21]

The early modern era also witnessed the increasing sophistication and secularization of European economies and the rise of monarchical absolutism, which placed considerably more power in the hands of early modern queens than their medieval counterparts. Royal women all over Europe played the role of dynastic marriage brokers, influencing the balance of power between France, Britain, and Spain, the principalities of Italy and the Holy Roman Empire, and the Baltic regions and the Russian Empire. Other queens, such as

Bona Sforza of Poland and Sophie of Mecklenburg-Güstrow of Denmark, set examples as sound business and estate managers.

Over the course of the eighteenth century, the transition from providential to material world views and the development of the Enlightenment and the Scientific Revolution all affected the evolution of Early Modern European queenship, as Christina of Sweden, Maria Theresa of Austria, and Catherine the Great of Russia endeavored to present themselves to their subjects as enlightened monarchs. Conversely, Marie Antoinette of France found herself the victim of increasingly modern notions of statehood that were at odds with the public's perceptions of her as queen, as the French Revolution put into action the ideologies of the eighteenth-century Enlightenment. Nonetheless, the forms and functions of medieval queenship continued to inform how the queenly role was performed throughout the early modern era, especially in the continued emphasis on wifely chastity, queenly religiosity, the intercessory role, and the raising of royal children and the brokering of royal marriages.[22]

EARLY MODERN EUROPEAN QUEENSHIP IN HISTORY

Most Early Modern European queens did not enjoy the luxury of controlling the narratives of their queenships, which were usually created by contemporary male commentators, who were usually more focused on describing kingly rather than queenly activities. Conversely, women historians were often drawn to the subject of queens, perhaps most strikingly in Agnes Strickland's sprawling eight-volume mid-nineteenth-century *Lives of the Queens of England*.[23] This work, influenced by the social mores and gender stereotypes of early Victorian Britain, presented its queens as individualized studies who did not necessarily have any historical relationship with each other, nor did Strickland suspect that their collective experiences might add up to something called English queenship. Most historians have followed this model in their respective studies of European queens.

Studies of continental queens also mostly appear as individualized studies. The most recognizable, Isabella of Castile, Catherine de Medici, Marie Antoinette, Christina of Sweden, and Catherine II of Russia, have long been the subjects of historical inquiry and have captured the lion's share of historical attention directed towards early modern continental queenship. In the cases of Isabella and Catherine II, conventional biographical studies usually consider these queens as exceptional women whose achievements are considered unusual for the female sex, while assessments of Mary Queen of Scots and Marie Antoinette inevitably lead to the trope of a tragic queen, unable to cope with the harsh realities of royal politics. Then there are the rest of the early modern queens, whose reigns are usually considered unimportant sideshows to the reigns of their husbands, but whose collective experiences are, like those of their more famous colleagues, also critical in assessing early modern forms of queenship.

Most of the recent comparative work on early modern queens has concentrated on either regnant or consort queenship. Studies of consorts, despite their obvious strengths, usually exist in splendid isolation from each other, although Clarissa Campbell Orr published a pair of well-received volumes on both early modern British and European consorts in the first few years of this new century, while Helen Watanabe O'Kelly and Adam Morton published a wide-ranging volume on early modern consortship in 2016. These and other recent studies have employed the strategies of gender studies, which have done much to transform our understanding of women in history, particularly queens. As social historians integrated studies of race and class to broaden our historical perspective from "the bottom up," feminist scholars have deployed gender analysis as a mean to understand how women staked out and contested forms of power and influence in Early Modern European societies. As Joan Scott made clear in a groundbreaking article from the 1980s, the social construction of gender roles for men and women was the construction of systems of power.[24]

As feminist-oriented scholars have rightly pointed out, queenly power and influence is often obscured in conventional histories. To quote a much-abused cliché, most histories that discuss women were written by men for other men with a narrow definition of what constituted queenly power. While historians, most of them men, in the past identified narrow parameters in their definitions of queenly power, feminist historians have broadened this scope, rejecting more traditional notions that only located the exercise of power within the public and formalized spaces of royal government and administration. Instead, feminist historians have identified those more informal or private spaces where queenly power and influence was routinely exercised, in terms of marriage brokering, educating their children, running their royal households, managing their estates, directing the distribution of patronage, patronizing prominent artists and scholars who created forms of material culture with visual and literary representations of queenly power, and setting examples of queenly piety and charity.

The following chapters comprise a set of comparative case studies which conceptualizes a series of four concentric circles emanating out of Europe's major kingdoms – England, Scotland, and Great Britain; Iberia and Spain; the Holy Roman Empire and the Habsburg dominions; and Denmark, Sweden,

Poland/Lithuania, Prussia, and the Russian Empire – which illustrate the trans-European character of European queenship. Each chapter begins with an introductory discussion of a queen whose queenship was emblematic of that region before moving on to a broader chronological discussion of queenship within that geographical area.

ISABELLA OF CASTILE: BRIDGING THE MEDIEVAL AND THE EARLY MODERN

As the following chapters all open with a historical description of a queen emblematic to that region, this introduction concludes with an examination of one of Europe's most influential queens, Isabella of Castile (1451–1504), whose Janus-like figure straddled the medieval and early modern epochs. The daughter of King Juan II of Castile (r. 1406–1454) and his second wife Isabella of Portugal, Isabella was recognized as heir to her elder half-brother Enrique IV (r. 1454–1474), after the death of her younger brother Alfonso in 1568. We know very little of Isabella's actual education, other than that her father had assigned courtier Gonzalo Chacon as her tutor. Isabella also received a form of queenly tutelage from both her Portuguese grandmother, Isabella de Barcelos, and her own mother, who suffered from mental illness during her widowhood. Isabella's own sense of royal deportment and destiny was undoubtedly instilled in her by these women. Isabella was also trained in the domestic arts, like all the queens of Early Modern Europe. This is exemplified by her skill at needlework, which she displayed throughout her life, making her husband Ferdinand's shirts for him, a skill passed down to her daughter Catherine of Aragon, who performed the same task for her husband Henry VIII of England. Isabella was also exposed to and trained in the ideals of chivalry, especially cherished by a Crusader kingdom determined to expel the Moors from Spain.

As a Castilian female heiress, marriage was an inescapable part of Isabella's future, as it was for nearly all Early Modern European queens. But as a woman who was heir to the powers and prerogatives of Castilian kingship, how this would be affected by marriage remained to be decided. Just prior to her marriage to Ferdinand of Aragon, Martin de Cordoba, an Augustinian friar, presented Isabella with a copy of *A Garden of Noble Maidens,* a treatise on Eve and original sin, whose fundamental message was that a woman could be an effective leader provided she avoided the pitfalls of her feminine nature, by acknowledging her shortcomings and having checks, like a husband, on their power.[25]

Nonetheless, Isabella was determined to be her own woman within the context of her marriage. In direct defiance of both her brother Enrique IV and wider European social mores which dictated that unmarried women submit to the will of their male guardian, Isabella chose as her husband her cousin Ferdinand, heir to the Aragonese and Sicilian thrones, a distant cousin whose royal line was a cadet branch of the Trastamara dynasty. It appears that Isabella selected Ferdinand of her own free will, and married him in haste in Valladolid on October 19, 1469, when she was eighteen and he one year younger.

While Isabella unquestionably developed a genuine love for her husband, the marriage also made sense dynastically, uniting Castile and the various states under the crown of Aragon, and in the long term, resulting in the eventual political unification of Spain. In terms of land and resources, Castile was by far the larger, wealthier, and more powerful kingdom; Ferdinand possessed little leverage in the marriage negotiations. But just as important were Isabella's intelligence and force of character, which compelled her to clearly outline her expectations for the power sharing that would ensue when she became Queen of Castile. In acquiescing to the terms of the *Capitulaciones,* a form of pre-nuptial agreement, Ferdinand gained Isabella's hand by recognizing her position as sole proprietress of the Castilian crown and its powers and prerogatives. He also agreed to obey Castile's laws and pledged to not take Isabella or their future children out of the kingdom.

At the same time, Isabella couched other aspects of the agreement firmly within acceptable gendered parameters. Ferdinand would take precedence over her and they would sign everything jointly and share all titles. This agreement set a European precedent for future queens regnant; Isabella and Ferdinand's great grandson Philip II agreed to all these stipulations in a marriage contract ratified as a parliamentary statute prior to his marriage to Mary I of England in 1554, which was used as the prototype during various marriage negotiations for Elizabeth I of England.[26] While it may partially be the result of a highly successful hegemonic hagiography surrounding their marriage, contemporaries and subsequent scholars have agreed that Ferdinand and Isabella were entirely successful at creating the perception that they loved and respected one another, the cornerstone of their public images as monarchs. Their successful marriage also created a positive example for their married subjects to emulate, an archetypal function of monarchy.

Although the marriage was successful as royal marriages go, Isabella demonstrated her monarchical independence following her brother's death on Dec. 11, 1474. Unlike other Western European states such as England and France, kings of Castile were not crowned, but underwent a form of inauguration, usually an acclamation, that signified their accession to the throne.

Isabella wasted no time by literally proclaiming herself Castile's next sovereign in Segovia before Ferdinand could join her and participate in her accession. Ferdinand was somewhat alarmed; Isabella had borne before her the sword of justice, which had previously only been done for Castilian kings, which, on paper, Ferdinand now was.

But Isabella knew exactly what she was doing. Early on, she realized that if she were to be a successful queen, her marriage must be perceived as harmonious. Although they had been married for five years prior to Isabella's accession, her new status as queen inaugurated an initial period of adjustment as the issues of joint sovereignty were negotiated between the pair. In his acquiescence to Isabella's sole proprietorship of the Castilian throne, Ferdinand shared jointly in aspects of his wife's royal prerogative, serving as her military commander in Castile. In time, Isabel relaxed the restrictions of the *Capitulaciones,* allowing Ferdinand wider latitude in his position as a representation of their joint selves, symbolized by the motto, "Tanto monta, monta tanto" ("It's one and the same, Isabella the same as Ferdinand").

As Christian belief comprehended marriage as being of one flesh, Isabella and Ferdinand gave this concept a tangible political dimension by the way in which their joint power flowed between them and out into their kingdom, which allowed Isabella to enjoy her sovereign rights as queen without damage to Ferdinand's masculine reputation as king consort.[27] While she herself exercised the prerogatives of kingship within her council chamber, for public consumption Isabella inhabited the more recognizable role of *queen,* even though she was, for all intents and purposes, Castile's ruling prince, while Ferdinand inhabited the recognizable male gendered role of king. By playing public roles that outwardly conformed to gendered expectations for kingly and queenly behavior, Isabella never became the target for the kind of theoretical challenges to female rule that plagued later sixteenth-century regnant queens.

Isabela was also able to reap the final benefit of a long-lived queenship by playing the role of dynast and marriage broker. While Isabella's success as queen was not questioned, Castile remained a kingdom, which required heirs, preferably male, to perpetuate the dynasty. Isabella gave birth to her namesake daughter in 1470 but her next pregnancy did not occur until 1475, during the succession war with Afonso V of Portugal and Juana *La Beltraneja*, the daughter of Enrique IV. This pregnancy resulted in the stillborn birth of a son, which represented a clear conflict between Isabella's kingly and queenly imperatives. Only with the conclusion of this war did Isabella conceive again, giving birth to her son and heir Juan in Seville in 1478. Three more daughters followed, Juana in 1479, Maria in 1482, and Catalina (or Catherine of Aragon) in 1485. The birth of Isabella and Ferdinand's male heir was wildly celebrated in the Spanish kingdoms as it conferred even greater legitimacy upon Isabella's queenship, which was interpreted not only as a sign of God's approval but as an assurance that the dynasty would revert once again to a line of male kings. But Juan's untimely death in 1497, at age 19, after his marriage to the Habsburg Archduchess Margaret of Austria, the daughter of Holy Roman Emperor Maximilian I, meant that Isabella would be succeeded by one of her daughters.

It was in the raising of her four daughters that Isabella displayed her flair for *queenship*, as opposed to the kingly prerogative she exercised as a queen regnant. Rodrigo Maldonaldo de Talavera, in the printed version of a 1475 sermon, counseled her to raise her children in good works and emulate the noble customs of Old Testament matriarchs, citing the chastity of Sarah, the modesty and diligence of Rebecca, Leah's hard work, and the discretion and judgment of Deborah. Above all, de Talavera emphasized the virtues of the Virgin Mary, whose perfect humility and compassion served as a contrast to the laziness, chatter, and light life of Eve, that Old Testament archetype of failed womanhood.[28] Isabella's daughters also received Renaissance humanist educations. Isabel herself lamented her own relative lack of scholarship, and in the middle of her life painstakingly learned Latin not only to demonstrate her intellectual equality with other Renaissance princes, but as an example for her own daughters, all of whom would shoulder the burdens of Renaissance queenship themselves.

Isabella's daughters were raised to be queens, and the marriages Isabella brokered for them balanced intra-Iberian and wider European dynastic concerns. The eldest, Isabella, had been recognized as her mother's heir in Castile until the birth of her brother, and was married to Afonso, Prince of Portugal, in 1490. Following her husband's death in 1491 and her brother's in 1497, which made her once again Castile's heir, Isabella married Manual I of Portugal, and died in childbirth. Following the death of Isabella's infant son Miguel in 1500, Isabella's oldest surviving daughter, Juana, married to Philip the Handsome of Burgundy, Margaret of Austria's brother, became Castile's heir. Juana was allegedly mentally unstable, although she had produced a bumper crop of male and female heirs who would continue the Habsburg line in both Spain and the Holy Roman Empire.

ISABELLA'S QUEENLY LEGACY

Early on in her reign, like other Renaissance monarchs, Isabella recognized the power and utility of the written word to create both her public image and her historical legacy.[29] Over the course of her reign, Isabella patronized a team of influential hagiographers, Fernando del Pulgar, Alonso de Palencia, and Elio Antonio de Nebrija, whose works extolled her legitimacy, her virtues, and her accomplishments, as well as the success of her marriage, laying the historical cornerstones of her reputation as a good queen who engineered the moral and religious regeneration of Spain.[30]

Isabella also recognized the power of material culture in the creation of her public image, another form of "soft power" that persuaded her subjects of the righteousness of her queenship. In the public spaces of her royal court, Isabella displayed her skill in adorning herself with rich fabrics and jewels that represented the wealth and prosperity of her kingdom. Because Ferdinand outlived her, Isabella never had to resort to dressing in the spare and somber widow's weeds adopted by Mary of Guise, Anne of Austria, and Maria Theresa, queens who experienced lengthy widowhoods. Instead, like her granddaughter Mary I of England, Isabella was free to drape herself in dazzling apparel and jewels within the spaces of a royal court that practiced ritual and spectacle to project queenly power and majesty. One contemporary, Rodger Machado, claimed he never saw the Queen in the same outfit twice.[31]

But what worked for the present did not necessarily work for creating her legacy. As Marvin Lunenfeld has noted, Isabella preferred to be depicted in portraiture in conservative dress, often veiled and kneeling in prayer or with her eyes downcast, quite unlike Elizabeth I of England and Catherine II of Russia, who both represented themselves in portraiture in lavish dress, wearing wigs, and dripping in precious stones as they make eye contact with the painting's audience.[32] A similar dichotomy existed in Isabella's behavior at court. While Ferdinand had a wandering eye, eventually siring three illegitimate children, a son and two daughters, whom he acknowledged, Isabel recognized that her own wifely chastity was crucial to maintaining her authority, refusing even to dance at court with other men if her husband was not present, despite the gaiety and splendor of her courtly entertainments. At the same time, Isabella encouraged a dialogue that employed gallantry, flowery praise, and the language of courtly love, a form of discourse Elizabeth I of England would later develop to dazzling heights. Isabella's confessors had a difficult time adjusting to such Renaissance forms of courtly life, which Isabella assured them was part and parcel of maintaining a successful queenship. But nearly all contemporaries who described her reign downplayed this aspect of her queenship, emphasizing her virtues and piety rather than the racy dialogue of courtly love.

Isabella also erected architectural monuments to celebrate the many facets of her queenship, one of the most durable forms of queenly image-making. In Miraflores, just outside Burgos, Isabella commissioned a magnificent tomb for her parents Juan II and Isabella of Portugal within the Carthusian monastery that had originally been built as a royal palace. As a good daughter, Isabella elevated her parents to a place they had not achieved in their own lifetimes, as symbols of the power and prestige of the Castilian monarchy, with their effigies flanked by Old Testament prophets and angels guarded by the four evangelists. More than anything, the tomb's iconography emphasized the complementary functions of kingship and queenship that Isabella and Ferdinand's reign personified. The same message can be found in the church of San Juan de los Reyes in Toledo, which was adorned with eagles, sibyls, and images of St. John the Evangelist, Isabel's patron saint. Like her parent's tomb, the church's iconography is a powerful testament to the indivisibility and success of Isabella and Ferdinand's marriage and the strength and durability of the Castilian monarchy.

Isabella and Ferdinand's own tomb at the chapel royal in Granada remains her final material testament. Isabella considered the conquest of Granada her greatest achievement, and in her final months she and Ferdinand made the decision that a joint tomb be built for them within the Alhambra. Isabella had requested that the tomb be humble, rather than ornate, in keeping with her attitude towards the construction of her historical legacy. Because the decision to construct the tomb had been made just a few months prior to her own death in November 1504, Isabella was not able to supervise its construction, which Ferdinand completed. The tomb turned out much grander than she had envisioned, with two gold sarcophagi sitting center stage in a marble mausoleum decorated with cherubs. But on the altar is a polychrome wood carving of Isabella, which depicted her in somber Franciscan dress, with her hair in a wimple and her eyes downcast, reflective of the piety and the austerity of her life that she wished her queenship to be remembered for.

Isabella's reign makes an instructive beginning for this study of Early Modern European queenship, as her reign virtually defined the template of Early Modern European queenship. At the end of her life, Isabella was recognized throughout Europe as a legendary queen as well as a Catholic king, who transcended the gendered differences between men and women, as Pedro Martir noted in 1502, two years before her death, "stronger than a strong man, more constant than any human soul, a marvelous example of honesty and virtue; nature has made no other woman like her."[33]

2 Mary Queen of Scots and Early Modern British Queenship

On the morning of February 8, 1587, Mary Stewart (or Stuart), dowager queen of France and deposed queen of Scotland, was led into the great hall of Fotheringay Castle to be beheaded for conspiring to kill Elizabeth I of England. Protesting her innocence to the last, and fully cognizant of the significance of her final moments on earth as a queen, Mary invested her execution with as much symbolic meaning and iconic representation as she could muster. Her performance was flawless. Literally dressed to die, she wore, as a thrice-widowed woman, black satin and a veil, with an abundance of accessories that proclaimed her devotion to the Roman Catholic faith. After ostentatiously reciting loud prayers to drown out the words of a Protestant clergyman, her attendants peeled off layers of clothing that revealed her bright crimson red petticoats, symbolizing the martyrdom she was claiming as the cause of her death. All accounts agree that she met her death both bravely and serenely, a final display of queenly courage and fortitude. Twenty-five years later, Mary's son James VI & I reinterred her in a marble tomb inside the Henry VII Chapel in Westminster Abbey, where her remains rest with those of the Tudor Queens Elizabeth of York, Mary I, and Elizabeth I.

Known during her lifetime as "the daughter of debate," Mary has always proved a daunting interpretive challenge for historians. As contemporaries and cousins, the histories and reputations of Mary and Elizabeth I of England have lent themselves to contrasting tropes and understandings of queenship in works of scholarship, historical fiction, and film.[1] These are centered upon the basic idea that Mary's failures were the result of her feminine emotions and her womanly lack of leadership ability, while Elizabeth is contrasted with her as a superbly educated woman who tamed her feminine nature and kept her womanly emotions in check to successfully rule England.[2] This dichotomy took shape during their lifetimes, as John Lesley and George Buchanan began the process of shaping the narratives of Mary's queenship, which in turn influenced generations of subsequent historians, who usually identify Mary as villain, victim, or tragic heroine.[3] As a queen who is emblematic of the many different facets of early modern British queenship, the introductory section of this chapter seeks to analyze Mary's performance of her *queenship*, which went through several distinct phases, from minority queen to consort of France, then ruling queen of Scotland, and lastly, an exiled and imprisoned dowager queen.[4]

THE QUEENSHIP OF MARY QUEEN OF SCOTS

Mary Queen of Scots became a queen regnant at the age of six days upon her father James V's death (December 14, 1542). The only other instance of a minority queen regnant was Christina of Sweden (r. 1632–1654), who became queen at the age of six. But unlike Christina, who was trained to be a king (see Chapter 5), Mary was trained from birth to be a queen consort. When Mary was a young child, her great uncle Henry VIII of England wanted her as a bride for his son and heir, the future Edward VI (r. 1547–1443), negotiating the Treaty of Greenwich in 1543. But after the Scots repudiated the treaty, Henry responded with the "rough wooing" invasions, which continued past his death in January 1547, that attempted to take possession of Mary by force. To guarantee her daughter's safety, Mary of Guise, Dowager Queen of Scotland, transported Mary to France in 1548, where she would live for the next twelve years. While in France, Mary was betrothed to the Dauphin Francis. In 1558 they were married, but with the death of Henri II in July 1559, Mary became queen consort of France.

Much like Isabella of Castile, whose earlier education had trained her for the role of consort, Mary was well trained to be a queen, excelling in the usual domestic arts like sewing and needlework, music, and other leisure activities such as dancing and hunting. She was also a skilled linguist. With this training, Mary had all the makings of a successful French consort; she was conversant in and identified with French culture, avoiding the taint of being a foreign queen like her mother-in-law the Italian Catherine de Medici. Physically, Mary was tall as well as charismatic, possessing all the talents and graces requisite of a queen. But Francis II, never robust, died on December 5, 1560, after an eighteen-month reign, leaving Mary an eighteen-year-old dowager queen of France as well as the sole proprietress of the Scottish crown. With the accession of the underage Charles IX, and the accompanying ascendancy of dowager queen Catherine de Medici, Mary made the fateful decision to return to Scotland to rule as a queen regnant. During the period of Mary's residence in France, Scotland had undergone a full-blown Calvinist

Reformation. Following Mary of Guise's death in June 1560 the Protestant Lords of the Congregation negotiated both peace with England and the terms of Mary's return as Queen of Scotland, in which she agreed to accept the political legitimacy of the Protestant ascendancy in return for her right to worship as a Roman Catholic.[5]

Mary's return to Scotland was a form of culture shock, akin to the challenges queen consorts often experienced when they journeyed to their newly adoptive kingdoms. Raised primarily in France, Mary was very much a foreign queen, in terms of her world view and cultural identification. Neither her tutelage nor her varied skills as a French queen consort adequately prepared her for the role of regnant queen of what was generally regarded as a difficult kingdom to govern. Compounding these challenges was her Catholicism, which fiery Protestant preacher John Knox continually denounced in audiences before the Queen that brought her to tears on more than one occasion.[6]

Nevertheless, for six years, from 1561 to 1567, Mary attempted to rule Scotland. As she stepped into the role of Scottish ruling queen, she did so through the rubric of the consort, the type of queenship she had been trained for. Quite unlike European male heirs to thrones, who often receive a thorough tutelage in statecraft and military training, female heiresses like Mary and her English cousins Mary I and Elizabeth I had to make do with on-the-job training to learn how to successfully wield royal authority. Historians in general do not give high marks to Mary in her efforts to inhabit the role of queen regnant; she was not particularly concerned with formulating and executing policy; she rarely attended council meetings, and when she did so she remained a mostly passive participant doing her needlepoint, allowing her illegitimate half-brother James Stewart, Earl of Moray, to formulate policy.[7]

What did interest Mary was her claim to the English throne, which derived through her grandmother, Margaret Tudor, Henry VIII's elder sister.[8] By hereditary right, as the childless Elizabeth I was the last of the Tudors, Mary was her closest heir. Soon after her return to Scotland, Mary dispatched William Maitland of Lethington to England to negotiate with Elizabeth on her English succession rights. But Elizabeth I had no interest in recognizing Mary's hereditary claims upon the English throne; Mary's position as a Catholic queen was only one of several complications that prevented her and Elizabeth from establishing a workable relationship. In July 1565, Mary countered by taking a husband of her own choosing, the exclusive right of regnant queens, choosing a man resident in her own court, nineteen-year-old Henry Stewart, Lord Darnley, her Catholic cousin, whose mother was Margaret Douglas, the daughter of Margaret Tudor.

As a regnant queen, Mary Queen of Scot's approach to marriage was far different than that of Isabella of Castile. While still Castile's heir, Isabella had decided that Ferdinand was the best fit dynastically for her. She and Ferdinand had corresponded prior to their marriage in 1569, but they first met face to face only a few days before their marriage. But both realized that their future success as monarchs depended upon the success of their marriage, so they set out to create the perception and reputation of enjoying a loving and companionate marriage.[9] This would be a model for numerous kings and queens of the early modern era, who saw marriage as a duty, if not a sacred trust, and considered creating a companionate marriage an important part of their royal duties. As did Isabella with Ferdinand, Mary chose Darnley partly for his dynastic luster. Contemporaries tend to agree that Mary fell quickly and very publicly in love with Darnley, which has easily lent itself to interpretations of Mary as the victim of her sexual appetites.[10] But Darnley failed to play the role of loving husband, dissatisfied with his courtesy title of king consort, rather than the crown matrimonial enjoyed by Mary's first husband. His Catholicism also upset the fragile equilibrium within the Scottish Protestant nobility that Mary had established in the first years of her personal reign, causing Moray to rebel and flee to England.

At this point, Mary's queenship spun out of control. Following the savage murder of her Italian secretary David Rizzio (March 9, 1566), in which Darnley was a participant, a heavily pregnant Mary was compelled to flee from Edinburgh. Mary returned a week later with an army commanded by the renegade Protestant James Hepburn, Earl of Bothwell, reconciling with Moray before giving birth to the future James VI in June 1566, fulfilling the fundamental duty of queenship. The birth of a male heir should have stabilized Mary's queenship, but instead it provided the focus for efforts to depose her, as her loathing for her worthless and violent husband was well known within the Scottish court. But in the aftermath of Darnley's murder (February 10, 1567), Mary was widely perceived as colluding with the lead suspect, the Earl of Bothwell, who was acquitted in a private prosecution on April 12. These events caused Moray to break with Mary again and flee once more to England, while Bothwell took custody of Mary, willingly or not, when she was leaving Stirling Castle after visiting her son. Whether Bothwell raped her or she consented, an already pregnant Mary married him on May 15 with Protestant rites.

It is impossible to say what Mary's actual motivations were in this largely inexplicable chain of events, whether she had fallen in love with Bothwell, the usual trope deployed, or wished to protect the legitimacy of any further children, or whether she simply desired a powerful ally to help her rule a decidedly fractious kingdom. But the result was that the death of the hitherto univer-sally despised Darnley provided the pretext for efforts to depose the Queen and replace her with her infant son. On June 15, a group of Scottish nobles, the Confederate Lords, successfully defeated Mary and Bothwell's forces at Carberry Hill, and imprisoned the Queen on Loch Leven. On July 24, after miscarrying twins the day before, Mary was threatened with physical violence and forced to abdicate her throne in favor of her one-year-old son. Through the assiduous use of her charm, Mary engineered her escape from imprison-ment. Following the defeat of her Scottish military forces, Mary made the fateful decision to flee to England in May 1568, presumably to gain assistance from her cousin Elizabeth I.

Whatever goodwill Mary had created for her queenship in Scotland had dissipated in the aftermath of Darnley's death, while the Protestant Lords actively promoted the spread of her reputation as an adulterous and homicidal queen. Moray's discovery of the so-called Casket Letters, which allegedly proved Mary's guilt in Darnley's murder, provided the pretext for Elizabeth I to appoint a commission of inquiry to examine Mary's possible guilt, which met from October 1568 to January 1569. Mary, as a sovereign queen, refused to recognize the commission's authority, insisting she was not subject to English law.[11] The authenticity of the letters is impossible to ascer-tain, although scholars still try, and Elizabeth refused to either vindicate or condemn Mary. She did assign Mary to the custody of George Talbot, Earl of Shrewsbury, and his wife, Bess of Hardwick, at Tutbury Castle, where Mary lived off and on for a decade and a half in a form of protective custody. But as a Catholic monarch who was the focus of a series of plots to depose Elizabeth, Mary's continual presence in England was destabilizing. In early 1570, Pope Pius V issued the bull *Regnans in Excelsis*, which declared Elizabeth a heretic and released her subjects from their allegiance to her. It was within the con-text of this volatile domestic and international situation that Mary continued her quest to gain support to free herself from imprisonment, which eventually led her to become willing to entertain all manner of strategies to achieve her freedom.

As international tensions increased, particularly with Spain, Elizabeth's councilors spearheaded the Bond of Association in 1584, a form of lynch law that stated that any individual who attempted to assassinate Elizabeth should be executed. Although Mary herself subscribed to the bond, she remained cut off from the outside world as Elizabeth's spymaster Francis Walsingham concocted a scheme to entrap her. Creating a system where he could monitor her secret correspondence, Walsingham produced evidence that Mary had given her consent to the Babington Plot, uncovered in September 1586, which was yet another plot to kill Elizabeth and replace her with Mary.[12] Soon after, Mary was arrested and removed to Fotheringay Castle in Northamptonshire, where in October she was tried under the Statute for the Queen's Safety, which was essentially the Bond of Association enacted as law. As she had during the inquest over the Casket Letters, Mary refused to recognize the authority of any legal tribunal in England to try her. Nevertheless, she offered a spirited defense at her trial, denying the charges as she had done so many times in the past. After Mary was convicted and sentenced to death, Elizabeth hesitated, waiting until February 1, 1587 to sign the warrant, which members of Elizabeth's Privy Council spirited up to Fotheringay. Confronted on February 7 with the news of her impending execution, Mary had less than twenty-four hours to prepare herself for her final moments as a queen, which, as we have seen, she invested with the visual trappings of Catholic martyrdom.

Mary's tenure as queen consort of France was the most successful facet of her queenship. She spent her formative years in France and was completely acclimated to French culture before she became queen, when she enjoyed a reputation as a loving and faithful wife to her first husband. While Mary was ill-prepared for her tenure as queen regnant of Scotland, the same can be said of nearly all the ruling queens of Early Modern Europe, from Isabella of Castile to Catherine II of Russia. What makes Mary Queen of Scots unique is that most regnant queens were native to the kingdoms they came to rule, which did not require a process of acculturation. Mary arrived as a virtual stranger in Scotland in 1560 at the age of eighteen, much as queen consorts did when journeying to their adoptive kingdoms. As both Kristen Post Walton and Jenny Wormald have argued, Mary never pursued a viable strategy for securing her authority in Scotland, focusing on pursuing her English inheritance rights instead.[13] Mary also draws a sharp contrast with Isabella and Ferdinand of Spain, in that she was unable to create a companionate marriage, choosing two ill-suited male consorts, which proved to be her undoing as Queen of Scotland. Even her fervent Catholic religiosity, normally a strategy that bolstered queenly popularity, worked against her in Protestant Scotland and England.

The story of Mary Queen of Scots makes an apt beginning for this chapter on early modern British queenship. The story of her queenship draws into sharp focus the complicated historical relationship between the two British kingdoms of England and Scotland, which became inextricably tied dynastically at the dawn of the early modern era, while both kingdoms experienced parallel Protestant Reformations that had a major impact on the evolution of British queenship. Mary's devotion to the Catholic religion is also emblematic of larger patterns of early modern Catholic queenship, in which Catholic queens marrying Protestant kings refused to convert, a pattern followed by nearly all the Stuart consorts of the seventeenth century in England and in Scotland.

ELIZABETH OF YORK AND EARLY TUDOR QUEENSHIP

All the seventeenth- and eighteenth-century Stuart and Hanoverian monarchs of England, Scotland, and Great Britain were the direct descendants of Mary Queen of Scots, fulfilling her own epitaph, "in the end is my beginning."[14] She herself was the great-granddaughter of Elizabeth of York (1464–1503), the queenly progenitor of *all* the British royal houses of the early modern era. Quite unlike most of the European monarchies at the dawn of the early modern era, English kings of the Yorkist and Tudor dynasties preferred native-born royal and aristocratic women to foreign born royal heiresses. Elizabeth was the eldest daughter of the Yorkist Edward IV (r. 1461–83), and the queen of Henry VII (r. 1485–1509), the first Tudor king. Henry gained his throne after defeating the final Yorkist king, Richard III, at the Battle of Bosworth (August 22, 1485), which concluded the "Wars of the Roses," the dynastic rivalry between Lancaster and York.[15] Henry VII's hereditary claim was dubious, and passed to him from his still-living mother, Margaret Beaufort, while his possession of the throne was based largely on recognition of his victory at Bosworth as the providential verdict of God. Only after Henry was anointed and crowned, and the English Parliament had recognized his title, did he marry twenty-year-old Elizabeth of York, after obtaining the necessary papal dispensations, which was usually a routine matter in royal and aristocratic marriages. For Henry VII, as a usurper with a dubious hereditary title, the advantages of marrying a native-born daughter of an English king with a powerful dynastic pedigree outweighed the advantages of a foreign match that could have brought a sizeable dowry and strategic and commercial advantages.

Thus, Tudor queenship started off as an entirely domestic affair. Unlike the Francophile Mary Queen of Scots, who needed to gain the trust and affection of her subjects when she arrived in Scotland in 1560, Elizabeth was a native-born daughter of a popular king, bringing considerable reserves of political capital as a dowry to her marriage, which, by all accounts, developed into a companionate and loving relationship. If there was any discord in their marriage, it was skillfully kept from contemporary eyes. Instead, Henry VII quite visibly if not ostentatiously paid his queen the highest courtesy and respect. The description of how the king and queen comforted each other upon the death of their eldest son, Arthur, in 1502, as recorded by an anonymous court scribe, is a striking example of the positive press that the first Tudor king and queen enjoyed over the course of their marriage.[16]

Elizabeth of York succeeded admirably in the most important facet of her queenship, which was propagating the dynasty. Elizabeth gave birth to her first child, Arthur, in late 1486, the same year as her marriage. Several pregnancies over the following sixteen years resulted in three children who survived to adulthood. As it did for Isabella of Castile, the birth of a male enhanced the prestige of Elizabeth's queenship as it buttressed the stability of the Tudor dynasty. In many ways, Elizabeth's subsequent 1487 coronation was the reward for a job well done. The births and christenings of her children, and their later betrothals and marriages, provided the context for Elizabeth to participate publicly in ritualistic court spectacles that showcased her beauty, her grace, and her obvious love of music and pageantry.[17] Henry and Elizabeth foreshadowed the Renaissance courts of Henry VIII and Elizabeth I in their court entertainments, which featured disguising, masques, and tournaments, as well as elaborate Christmas festivities that often included a Lord of Misrule. Music was ubiquitous at their court, with the Queen herself a participant in both singing and the playing of instruments.

Elizabeth also created a reputation as a charitable queen. Her generosity, to needy members of her family, but especially to the poor and needy, as well as to monastic houses, established her reputation as a good queen. Gift giving at court reached dizzying new heights under Elizabeth's queenship, particularly at New Year's, when the Queen exchanged gifts with the noblewomen of her court as well as foreign potentates, a standard form of queenly power that reinforced relationships with the upper echelons of Tudor political society, and her dynastic counterparts in the royal courts of Europe.[18] Elizabeth also generated a constant flow of gifts to her servants and subjects at large, especially when a story of unfortunate circumstances reached her ears. At the same time, she largely avoided any accusations of profligacy or acquisitiveness.

These actions, while undoubtedly sincere, given what we know about her character, represent a skillful use of political capital, which accrued to her husband's kingship and to the Tudor dynasty in general. Elizabeth was frequently by her husband's side at court, participating in Knight of the Garter ceremonies, the most prestigious of English chivalric orders, projecting themselves as models of kingly and queenly behavior and domestic tranquility, mirroring the reputations of Isabella and Ferdinand in Spain. As Isabella did for Ferdinand, Elizabeth made garments for her husband, such as his garter mantle, by hand, a powerful model of queenly fidelity and obedience. Elizabeth also cultivated a conventional piety that was the cornerstone of nearly all successful queen-ships, which included periodic pilgrimages to the Shrine of Our Lady of Walsingham in Norfolk, as well as gifts to monastic houses, particularly the Carthusians, a strict ascetic order also favored by her mother.

Elizabeth shared the stage at court with her formidable mother-in-law Margaret Beaufort, countess of Derby and dowager countess of Richmond. A formidable, well-educated, and ostentatiously pious woman, Beaufort emerged as an intimate and powerful advisor to her son. This may have caused a conflict of interest with Elizabeth Wydeville, the actual dowager queen, who retired to Bermondsey Abbey, willingly or not, in 1487. In her place, Margaret emerged as "My Lady the King's Mother," a title which con-ferred upon her a sort of semi-regal status. To facilitate her position as an active and engaged member of the Tudor dynasty, her son conferred on his mother the status of *feme sole*, which allowed her to own property and enter into contracts in her own name, which she signed as "Margaret R." In this capacity, she served as the benefactress of numerous monastic houses as well as the founder of two colleges at Cambridge, Christ's and St. John's.

Elizabeth kept pace with her mother-in-law, continuing to expand the scope and function of her queenship for the duration of her life.[19] In 1500, Elizabeth accompanied Henry VII to Calais, one of the few occasions in the sixteenth century when an English queen left the island of Britain. Two years later, she played a major role in the festivities surrounding the marriage of her eldest son, Arthur, to Catherine of Aragon, as well as the events preceding her eldest daughter Margaret's journey to Scotland to wed James IV. Elizabeth also underwent a progress through Wales in the summer of 1502, two months after Arthur's death and shortly after she conceived her final child. This final dynastic endeavor cost Elizabeth her life as well as that of the infant daugh-ter she gave birth to, dying on February 13, her thirty-seventh birthday. Elizabeth of York was successful in creating the perception of a popular and well-rounded queen consortship, the likes of which had not been seen in England since Philippa of Hainault, the consort of Edward III (r. 1327–1377), and would not be duplicated until the eighteenth-century queenships of Caroline of Ansbach and Charlotte of Mecklenburg-Strelitz.

THE SIX WIVES OF HENRY VIII

Henry VIII (r. 1509–1547), along with several of the Vasa kings of Sweden and the Rurik and Romanov tsars of Russia, was unique among Early Modern European monarchs in that he preferred to find his queens within his royal court. This predilection did much to further shape the contours of Tudor queenship, casting it as something much more domesticated than continental European queenship, in which kings routinely married foreign royal heiresses for diplomatic, economic, and territorial gains. Henry's first queen, Catherine of Aragon, though foreign born, had been resident in England for eight years prior to her second marriage, and largely avoided the challenges common to newly arrived foreign queens as she had acclimated to English culture and customs. Because she had been previously married to Henry's elder brother Arthur, a papal dispensation was acquired after Arthur's death so she could marry his younger brother, the future Henry VIII. But Henry VII preferred to keep his heir's marriage prospects open, leaving Catherine to live rather precariously on his charity for the duration of his reign. During this period, Catherine endured the seven years of her widowhood as she negotiated a rough tutelage in Tudor court politics, becoming astute enough to become accredited as ambassador of her father, Ferdinand, to Henry VII in his final years.[20]

Once he became king, however, the soon to be eighteen-year-old Henry VIII swiftly married Catherine, six years his senior, in time for her to be crowned alongside him on June 24, 1509, twelve days after their marriage. The marital bond between Catherine and Henry, symbolized by their dual coronation, translated into an active and engaged queenship. Catherine had received a thoroughly humanist Renaissance education and possessed the example of her mother's own queenly style, rendering her a powerful and influential consort, at least until Thomas Wolsey emerged as Henry's dominant councilor and advisor. During these early years of the reign Catherine deftly walked the fine line of an outwardly deferential wife, making Henry's shirts for him by hand, and an indefatigable advocate of a pro-Spanish foreign policy until her father's duplicity undermined her credibility. Prior to this, however, Henry demonstrated the confidence he had in his queen, leaving her as regent in 1513 during his invasion of Tournai.

Catherine's queenship built upon the stability that was Elizabeth of York's legacy. Like Elizabeth of York, Catherine was frequently described as a smiling and gracious queen. In her royal demeanor she was cognizant and proud of her Spanish pedigree without any trace of haughtiness; the pomegranate of Granada, a reminder of her parent's greatest victory, was prominently displayed on her heraldic badge. While it may not have been her natural inclination, Catherine recognized the political economy behind actively participating in the virtually nonstop court entertainments and recreations that characterized Henry VIII's early court, playing the role of the king's damsel in distress who was saved countless times by her royal knight in shining armor.

This style of royal extravagance reached its summit in the Field of Cloth of Gold of June 1520, when Henry and Catherine met their French counterparts Francis and Claude for a series of celebrations in the pale of Calais that were memorable only for their ostentatious displays of conspicuous royal consumption.[21]

Catherine also built up a reputation for piety and chastity, liberally distributing alms and, like Elizabeth of York, making periodic pilgrimages to the shrine of the Virgin Mary at Walsingham.[22] Catherine also possessed a well-advertised intellectual curiosity that brought her to Oxford University to converse with the leading scholars of the day. In a more traditional queenly vein, she also played the role of intercessor, as so many of her predecessors had done, most famously saving the "prentices" who had participated in the May Day riots of 1517 from hanging, after Henry acceded to her request in a time-honored display of royal theatre.

While Catherine pursued all the key strategies for a successful queenship, she failed in the one area she is most known for, the ability to perpetuate the dynasty. Catherine's six pregnancies resulted in just one child to survive infancy, Mary (later Queen Mary I), born 1516.[23] Nevertheless, Henry VIII remained ambivalent about a female succession. By 1527, nine years after Catherine's final pregnancy, Henry decided he needed a male heir, initiating proceedings to obtain an annulment of his marriage, based upon his reasoning that by marrying his brother's widow he had violated scriptural law.

European kings had been getting out of their marriages for dynastic reasons for centuries. Generally, after an annulment was obtained from the papacy, European kings would use such an occasion to negotiate a new marriage that would provide an alliance or even to gain territory, as Henry's contemporary Louis XII of France did, when his first marriage was annulled so he could marry the heiress of Brittany and annex her duchy to the French crown. But the advent of the Protestant Reformation, which erupted in 1517, complicated Henry's request. As Martin Luther condemned practices such as the selling of indulgences and called into question claims of papal infallibility, Henry and Wolsey challenged the pope's dispensing power in their quest for an annulment. Wolsey initially anticipated Henry would choose a French princess as his next queen, but by 1527 Henry had decided to marry Anne Boleyn, one of Catherine's ladies in waiting, whose elder sister Mary had once been Henry's mistress. Trained in the princely courts of Burgundy and France, Anne Boleyn proved to be a tenacious courtesan, keeping Henry's interest for the six long years it took him to obtain an annulment.

Henry and Anne's most formidable opponent was Catherine, who refused to step aside as queen. She initially reacted to the news with tears, but she soon formulated her strategy, in keeping with her queenly character, comporting herself with her usual dignity and smiling countenance within the public spaces of the royal court, while projecting an outward wifely obedience even as Wolsey worked to isolate her politically. But behind closed doors, Catherine emerged as an indefatigable defender of her queenship. Catherine had always considered herself an equal stakeholder in her husband's kingship, and she rejected the idea of taking the veil, which would have released Henry from his wedding vows while maintaining Mary's legitimacy. Instead, Catherine maintained that she had married Henry as a virgin, rendering the prohibition in Leviticus moot.

But the inability of a legatine court in England to reach a decision, which revoked the case back to Rome, precipitated Wolsey's fall. By 1533, the year parliament passed the Act in Restraint of Appeals, a statue which allowed an English ecclesiastical court to annul her marriage, Catherine had already been living apart from Henry for two years, completely isolated from court and forbidden from seeing her daughter. As parliament legislated the royal supremacy of the church and deprived Mary of her succession rights, Catherine refused to acknowledge her degraded status as Dowager Princess of Wales, despite the efforts of Henry's privy council to force her to submit. She died in January 1536 as Catherine the Queen, as she signed herself in her final letter to Henry, which was filled with the filial devotion and obedience that she wished her queenship to be remembered by.

But Catherine's widely professed wifely devotion was at odds with the imperatives of her queenship. During the first decade of Henry's reign, Catherine's had been an active and engaged queenship; she shared both her husband's bed and his intellectual and artistic pursuits. But by 1531 all that was left for Catherine to do was make Henry's shirts and defend both her queenly honor and the estate of her queenship, including jewels and other items related to royal christenings, as well as the succession rights of her daughter. She spent her final years defending these as best she could, but not even her nephew the Emperor Charles was willing to defend her honor or help her daughter, as parliament placed control of an independent English Church under a king who was also its supreme head.

For the rest of his reign, with one exception, Henry VIII chose English noblewomen and gentry women for his wives. One of the first acts of an independent English Church was to declare Henry's marriage to Catherine null and void and recognize the validity of his marriage to Anne Boleyn, which had taken place in January 1533. Henry's choice of a noblewoman without a significant dowry, royal lineage, or any of the other usual advantages of a royal marriage was a testament to Henry's emotional attachment, while Anne

Boleyn's ability to keep Henry's interest for well over six years is equal testimony to her charm and tenacity. In the thousand days of her reign, Anne Boleyn brought an entirely different dynamic to Tudor queenship, providing a startling contrast with the reigns of Elizabeth of York and Catherine of Aragon. Reminiscent of the transition from Mamie Eisenhower to Jacqueline Kennedy in 1961, Anne brought an early modern form of glamour and sophistication to her queenship with her French fashions and manners.[24]

Anne was intelligent, charismatic, and politically engaged. She inserted herself directly into her husband's affairs, both domestic and foreign, and influenced the flow of patronage and grants, principally to her family and court circle, such as her father Thomas Boleyn, ennobled as Earl of Wiltshire years before she became queen. In this position, she emerged as the most influential royal mistress since the fourteenth-century Alice Perrers, the mistress of Edward III in his final years. Henry had in fact ennobled Anne herself in 1532, as lady Marquess of Pembroke, as a prelude to her elevation as queen. Once crowned, Anne viewed her queenship as a partnership, much as Catherine had done in the early years of her marriage to Henry, but in a much more ostentatious fashion, far and beyond the scope enjoyed by her recent predecessors, who had outwardly played the role of deferential and obedient wives.

These qualities have rendered Anne a perennially popular biographical subject, but they did not make her a successful queen. Anne's eschewing of the traditional approach to queenship, which championed the maintenance of queenly chastity and moral probity, proved crucial to her downfall. While Anne had been tutored in the usual domestic arts and aristocratic pursuits, she had not received the kind of queenly training of her predecessors that emphasized wifely obedience and creating the perception of domestic tranquility, nor did she take pains to comport herself with scrupulous attention to wifely chastity within the public spaces of the royal court.

There has always been a double standard for acceptable moral and sexual behavior for kings and queens. Like many early modern kings, Henry VIII was prone to occasional sexual dalliances with the women who populated his royal court, as were his contemporaries Charles V and Francis I of France. Henry's extra-curricular sexual activities were mild on a European-wide scale, although his affair with Bessie Blount produced a son, Henry Fitzroy, born 1519, whom Henry acknowledged and later created Duke of Richmond. Catherine had endured Henry's infidelities with queenly dignity, as her mother had with Ferdinand's dalliances, and walked a fine line between being an active participant in court activities and guarding her reputation against any hint of indiscretion. But Anne Boleyn chose not to play by these well-established rules of queenly conduct, openly flirting with the men of Henry's

Privy Chamber, as well as court musician Mark Smeaton, and reproaching Henry for his sexual indiscretions in the public spaces of the court.

Anne's behavior might have been mitigated by the production of a male heir. The birth of the future Elizabeth I, in September 1533, did little to further establish her legitimacy as queen. But Anne only conceived twice after Elizabeth, suffering a miscarriage in 1534 and in January 1536 a premature birth shortly after Catherine of Aragon's death. By this time, Henry had transferred his affections to Jane Seymour, daughter of a Wiltshire gentleman and one of Anne's ladies in waiting. Like Wolsey before her, ultimately Anne was the king's creature; when he withdrew his favor, her court faction fell apart. Although chief minister Thomas Cromwell had previously been Anne's ally, he engineered her fall, undoubtedly at the King's request, although this point continues to be debated by scholars.[25] While few historians believe Anne was guilty of the crimes she was convicted of, including adultery, incest, and treason, her lack of queenly discretion greased the wheels of what is universally considered a judicial murder.[26] After Anne's conviction by a jury of peers on May 15, 1536, Cranmer pronounced the marriage null and void on May 17. Two days later Anne was beheaded by a French swordsman in the Tower of London.

The execution of a crowned queen was unprecedented in English history, with the news causing a sensation within a Europe fast becoming polarized along confessional lines between Protestants and Catholics, who considered Anne a heretic concubine and her daughter Elizabeth a bastard. The day after Anne's execution, Henry was betrothed to Jane Seymour. Ten days later they were married in Whitehall Palace. By all accounts she was shy, demur, charming but perhaps barely literate, yet she excelled at the skills typical of the daughters of country gentry, particularly embroidery, for which she was noted. It is not clear whether she was complicit in the plot to remove Anne Boleyn, although her brothers Edward and Thomas were ambitious courtiers, nor is it possible to gauge her feelings towards Henry, although her motto "bound to obey and serve" suggests a conventional attitude towards the marriage that had been arranged for her.

Jane became pregnant in early 1537. The birth of her son the future Edward VI in October was the crowning achievement of Jane Seymour's queenship. Lacking the pedigree of Elizabeth of York or Catherine of Aragon, or the wit and style of Anne Boleyn, Jane succeeded as queen in the most conventional way possible, by propagating the dynasty. Edward's birth, unfortunately, cost Jane her life, she died of complications barely one week after participating in Edward's christening, which may have hastened her death. She received a splendidly queenly funeral, quite unlike either Catherine or Anne, and was laid to rest in the Chapel of St. George at Windsor Castle, where Henry would join her at the end of his own life.

For his fourth wife, Henry chose a much more conventional path that was reflective of his immediate strategic concerns. By the late 1530s, Thomas Cromwell was able to convince Henry of the efficacy of a matrimonial alliance with a northern German Protestant prince. This meant that Henry, for the first time, wed a woman he had not actually met. Henry had sent his court painter Hans Holbein the Younger to paint Anne of Cleves, the sister of Duke William of Cleves, and allowed Cromwell to negotiate the contract, which included a mutual defense agreement against the Emperor Charles V, as well as a handsome dowry and an assurance of Anne's succession rights in Cleves.[27]

But when Anne arrived in England in early 1540, Henry did not like her looks or her charms and went through with the marriage only under protest. While contemporary commentators like chronicler Edward Hall praised her looks and manners, Henry was unable or unwilling to consummate the marriage, which created the conditions for an annulment, obtained in July of 1540. Like Jane Seymour's, Anne's education was rudimentary, and only in German, but contemporaries described her as gentle and docile and reputedly also an excellent embroiderer, but woefully out of step with English fashions and court culture. She possessed common sense, however, accepting in the annulment of her marriage to the king a generous severance package that included houses, income, and a filial relationship with the royal family. She remained on good terms with Henry for the rest of her life and was last seen at the coronation of Mary I in 1553, glittering in her jewels.[28]

It remains curious that a king who so ardently desired male heirs would pass on the opportunity to beget children with Anne, testimony ultimately to Henry's own sexual vanity and narcissism, which was aptly played out with Anne's successor Catherine Howard, one of Anne's ladies in waiting, who married Henry VIII on July 28, 1540, soon after the Cleves' marriage was annulled. By this time Tudor queenship had degenerated from the prestigious queenships of Elizabeth of York and Catherine of Aragon, queens noted for their grace, intellect, and piety, to the point that a nearly fifty-year-old Henry VIII was willing to marry a teenaged gentlewoman because he desired her sexually. In comparison to his contemporaries in Europe, kings who generally made a distinction between the dynastic responsibilities of marriage and their sex lives, Henry was much ruled by his emotions rather than his intellect in the choice of his fifth queen, who, while of noble lineage, lacked education, refinement, or any other of the qualities previously associated with Tudor queenship.

Generally, on a European-wide scale, royal marriages were negotiated, as candidates for the role of queen consort were usually thoroughly vetted for their suitability. It appears, though, that neither the king nor his advisors thought to do so for Catherine Howard, who had been sexually active since her early teens, willingly or not, having been raised in the lax atmosphere of the household of her step-grandmother, the dowager duchess of Norfolk, where young men were frequent nighttime guests. While sexual promiscuity was rampant among the male members of early modern English royalty and aristocracy, for potential queens it was the deadliest of sins to commit, raising issues of paternity. When the revelations of Catherine's indiscretions came to light, Henry may have been relieved that she never conceived while they were married, but he was suitably heartbroken, delegating the tasks of dealing with her attainder and execution to a specially created royal commission, which carried out the execution on February 13, 1542.[29]

The prestige of Tudor queenship could not have sunk any lower when the king decided to marry the twice-widowed Catherine Parr, the fourth and final English gentlewoman to be his queen. Like Elizabeth of York and Catherine of Aragon, Catherine comported herself with dignity coupled with a care for her reputation within the spaces of the royal court, which was good policy considering her predecessor's fate. At the same time, she was both a patron of scholars as well as a scholar herself, while possessing considerable managerial skills as a widow of a peer with experience running a noble household. Her skills were such that when Henry went on the last of his French invasions in 1544, he left Catherine as formal regent, as he had Catherine of Aragon in 1513, a post she acquitted with skill, issuing proclamations, allocating wartime resources, and keeping in contact with her commanders in the field in Scotland, where Henry's "rough wooing" was attempting to secure the person of Mary Queen of Scots as wife for his son Edward. Catherine also successfully created an image for herself as both a devoted wife and a doting stepmother, as she was to her first two husbands' children, whom she favored for the rest of her life. During her queenship, Catherine managed to gain the affection of all three of Henry's children, no mean feat, bringing them all together at court for the closest that Henry ever came to enjoying a reasonably sedate family life, earning for her also the reputation of the good stepmother, one of the more conventional paths to earn queenly prestige.[30]

Catherine Parr's intelligence and skill in debating religious issues nearly cost her queenship. In 1546, after debating with Henry over matters of doctrine, the leaders of the conservative faction at court, Bishop Stephen Gardiner of Winchester and Lord Chancellor Thomas Wriothesley, obtained a warrant to arrest the queen for heresy. But in a chain of events recounted in a passage of John Foxe's *Actes and Monuments* that reads like fiction, Catherine was warned, throwing herself on the king's mercy and playing to his vanity by explaining that she had only debated with him to divert his attention from his health issues, and that it was the woman's proper role to be instructed by her husband.[31] The reconciliation was undoubtedly sincere; when Henry died on January 31, 1547, he left Catherine a £7,000 per annum annuity, but no formal role in the minority government of her stepson, nine-year-old Edward VI (r. 1547–1553).

REGNANT QUEENSHIP UNDER MARY I

Mary I (r. 1553–58), the daughter of Catherine of Aragon and Henry VIII, was England's first regnant queen. Within patriarchal, male-dominant cultures such as that of early modern England, the notion that a woman could inherit the office of king developed out of an essentially feudal conception of constitutional and political theory, which viewed kingship primarily as an estate to be inherited, a conception of royal government not finally put to rest in England until the Glorious Revolution of 1688–89.[32] England never enacted any form of Salic law to bar women from the throne within its medieval succession patterns, while many feudal tenancies allowed the transmission of property and titles to women, whose husbands would assume the title and manage the estate. But England's only prior experience of a formal female ruler was that of the twelfth-century Empress Matilda, while of the six royal minorities that occurred between 1216 and 1553 only the fourteenth-century Isabella, mother of teenaged Edward III, exercised political control during a minority reign, to less than favorable contemporary commentary. Medieval England did have a series of capable and engaged consorts, most notably the eleventh-century Matilda of Flanders, the twelfth-century Eleanor of Aquitaine, the thirteenth-century Eleanor of Castile, and the fourteenth-century Philippa of Hainault.[33] Later, in the sixteenth century, both Catherine of Aragon and Catherine Parr served as formal regents.

But in hereditary monarchies the ability to rule was tangential to the ability to inherit; Mary I succeeded to the English throne because of both statutory and hereditary right, but also because there were no viable male challengers to her right to inherit. Contributing to this issue was Henry VIII's policy of eliminating possible collateral male Plantagenet heirs within the ranks of the nobility, leaving no one after his son Edward but a literal parade of possible female inheritors, beginning with his two daughters.[34] During Edward VI's reign Mary emerged as a powerful independent female magnate, even though she was denied any formal role in their brother's government, which the male relatives of kings had performed in previous minority reigns.[35]

Ironically, Mary's status as heir complicated her ability to marry. This was an anomalous situation; the daughters and sisters of kings usually ranked among the most eligible brides of medieval and Early Modern Europe. But religious polarizations between Catholics and Protestants complicated the European royal-marriage market. The uncertainties of a royal minority also explain why Mary and Elizabeth remained unmarried, as both women were a heartbeat away from possessing the throne. Obviously, whoever married either of them would be well positioned to demand a powerful political role as the potential consort of a reigning queen. For this reason, more than any other, both sisters remained unmarried for the duration of Edward VI's reign.[36]

This meant that upon Edward's death (July 6, 1553), Mary, as both the statutory and the "natural" hereditary heir of her brother, swiftly identified herself in her accession proclamation as a "sovereign lady," no longer bound by the structural and legal forms of female subordination and coverture. Her claim to the throne did not go unchallenged, however, as Edward had a different candidate in mind for England's first regnant queen, nominating his Protestant cousin Lady Jane Grey, the granddaughter of Mary Tudor, the French Queen, in place of Mary and Elizabeth, and compelling his Privy Council and other notables to subscribe to his "device for the succession" a form of will that attempted to derail the statutory succession as laid out in Henry VIII's will. But Henry's will possessed statutory force, while Edward's did not; Jane Grey's reign only lasted nine days, as Mary forcefully declared her candidacy. On August 3, 1553, Mary rode into London on a wave of hereditary and statutory legitimacy that had the backing of a sizeable armed force that had come together quite spontaneously under her banner as she journeyed from East Anglia to London.

Once installed as England's first regnant queen, Mary I created the first model for what John Knox, the notorious author of the 1558 treatise, *First Blast of the Trumpet Against the Monstrous Regiment of Women*, termed *gynecocracy*, or female rule, in England.[37] This was perhaps the most durable achievement of her five-year queenship. But Mary's task was twofold; as an unmarried woman who inherited the estate and office of kingship, she was king and queen simultaneously, inhabiting and exercising both roles, a point bishop John White of Winchester made clear in Mary's funeral oration.[38] While Mary had unmistakably inherited what Ernst Kantorowicz has identified as the eternal "body politic" of kingship, she did so as a woman, her contemporaries identified her as a queen, which in English usage had previously only referred to a consort or dowager.[39] Over the course of her five-year reign, Mary broadened both the scope and the meaning of English queenship; she performed the essentially male-gendered role of king as a woman who, by and large, exhibited queenly, rather than kingly, qualities.

Only recently, however, has Mary's queenship been identified as something creative or even competent. For centuries, historians followed John Foxe's lead, who created the enduring image of "Bloody Mary" persecuting Protestants in the face of an inevitable rise of a Protestant England. By the later twentieth century, the historiographical certainties of the Whig interpretation of British history, which identified an inevitable trend towards a Protestant polity and parliamentary supremacy, gave way to more nuanced and document-based assessments of Mary's reign.[40] Nevertheless, scholars such as Geoffrey Elton, David Loades, and John Guy have considered Mary's performance as queen sterile, lackluster, and unproductive.[41] With the more recent rise of feminist-inspired approaches to queenship studies, however, scholars such as Judith Richards and Sarah Duncan have focused on how Mary adapted the roles and functions of both English kingship *and* queenship in the execution of her office.

Mary also recreated the dichotomy between royal spectacle and queenly piety practiced by her grandmothers, Isabella of Castile and Elizabeth of York, and her mother, Catherine of Aragon. Like all these queens, Mary recognized the political value of royal splendor, presiding over an extravagant court and wearing sumptuous clothing and jewels as she hosted a variety of musical and dramatic productions over the course of her reign. At the same time Mary lived an ostentatiously pious life, viewing her coronation, the first of its kind, as a form of wedding to her realm, a representational device that reconciled the anointing of a now genderless body politic of kingship within the body natural of a woman.[42] For representational purposes, Mary advertised herself as England's first virgin queen since Edith, the consort of the saintly eleventh-century Edward the Confessor. As orthodox Catholic teaching had long stressed chastity as the highest of human callings, this represented a particularly female-gendered way for Mary to create prestige for her queenship.

Mary's queenly sanctity, based upon her virginity as well as her status as an anointed monarch, provided the beachhead for her to appropriate the previously male-gendered kingly acts such as the washing of feet on Maundy Thursday and touching for scrofula, the "king's evil," sacerdotal actions previously performed by kings.[43] Mary was also particularly scrupulous about performing the charitable acts of queenship and was noticeably merciful to many of the participants of the plot to crown Jane Grey as well as the Wyatt Revolt that erupted at the end of January 1554, in marked contrast to the reaction of her father to the rebels of the Pilgrimage of Grace rebellion of 1536 and her sister Elizabeth's to the 1569 Revolt of the Northern Earls.

In keeping with the conventional forms of queenly, consort-like performance, Mary also adopted a form of female-gendered deference in the performance of some of her kingly imperatives. While Mary had an ambitious agenda to pursue, most importantly reversing the religious changes of her father and brother, she scrupulously avoided any identification as a virago. Instead, she disseminated an official position to her metaphorical husband, the realm, represented by her councilors and members of parliament, that she would be guided by their counsel. As a woman, Mary may have felt the need to present herself publicly as a more obedient monarch than her male predecessors as kings.[44] Only rarely did Mary deviate from this policy. In this capacity, as Alice Hunt has argued, Mary's was very much a collaborative queenship, in terms of using parliamentary statutes to push forward her religious changes, but also to preserve her royal power against the possible encroachment of her husband, calling this a form of "monarchical republic" that served to reconcile widely prevalent views of feminine deficiency with the reality of female rule.[45]

As a queen, Mary endeavored to fulfill the number one requirement of successful queenship, propagating the dynasty, by beginning the search for a husband soon after her accession. Mary's chancellor, Stephen Gardiner, Bishop of Winchester, and other members of her Privy Council favored a native English candidate, Edward Courtenay, Earl of Devon, a descendant of the Plantagenet royal house, but Mary herself favored marrying a foreign Catholic prince. Mary also took counsel from the imperial ambassador Simon Renard, whose lively descriptions of Mary's supposed deficiencies as queen still occupy a prominent place in historical assessments of her queenship. Mary's approach to the negotiations strongly resembles her mother's queenly method of operation, outwardly projecting the image of a deferential and obedient queen while forcefully defending her queenly prerogatives behind closed doors. Mary pursued a similar strategy, insisting publicly that her councilors were negotiating the marriage for her, while privately Mary compelled her privy council to fall in line behind her choice, her cousin Prince Philip of Spain. During the negotiations Mary wrote letters to Philip insisting she would be an obedient wife, yet at the same time she insisted that her royal prerogative was not on the bargaining table during the negotiations with Philip's father, Holy Roman Emperor Charles V.

While most accounts consider the marriage an abject failure, on paper the marriage had much to commend it for Mary's queenly agenda. Philip was the heir of Mary's cousin, Charles V, and stood to inherit the duchy of Burgundy and the crowns of Castile, Aragon, and Naples, as well as a vast new world empire, bringing with him a powerful block of power to bolster his wife's queenship.[46] It is hard to imagine how Mary could have anticipated that Philip could be anything more than a part-time king of England, which was a typical scenario when a royal couple had several crowns in their possession; Charles V himself was never more than a part-time husband to his empress Isabel, who served as his regent in Spain while he directed his imperial affairs from Brussels. In all likelihood, such a scenario was an attractive proposition, given that Mary's official chief reason for marrying was to produce, as she stated it, "some fruit of my body to leave as your governor," rather than share her prerogative with her husband. The marriage also resurrected the old Hispano-Burgundian alliance that dated back to the reign of Edward IV, which was the main reason why Holy Roman Emperor Charles V, Philip's father, pursued the negotiations.

But the downsides were English xenophobia as well as the age difference; Philip was eleven years younger than Mary. Much of the hostility surrounding the marriage stemmed from the fear that Philip would usurp Mary's royal prerogative and use the resources of the kingdom against the national interest. This was coupled with a fear of a return to Catholicism, which prompted Wyatt's revolt of early 1554. While the revolt was put down, and Mary made a quite memorable show of bravery in her rallying speech at London's Guildhall, she subsequently called a parliament to resolve the issues stemming from her proposed marriage to a foreign prince, as common-law lawyers began to make the claim that as soon as they were married Philip would be entitled to Mary's royal prerogative.

Mary's April-May 1554 parliament addressed these uncertainties, ratifying the marriage treaty in statutory form, to allay fears that Philip would not adhere to the terms after he arrived in England. The treaty's terms were highly reflective of the *capitulaciones* that Isabella of Castile had compelled her husband Ferdinand to agree to, a form of pre-nuptial agreement that preserved the gendered conventions of marriage, by assigning Philip the title of king with precedence over his wife; on paper, Philip reigned alongside his wife. But the treaty limited Philip's reign to the natural life of his wife and prohibited him from having any direct influence over English government. Parliament also passed the Act for the Queen's Regal Power, a declaratory act which made clear that the royal prerogative of a queen regnant was the same as that of a king and could not alienated by marriage.[47] Coupled with the marriage treaty, the act severely circumscribed Philip's room to maneuver as England's only king consort.

In practice, the marriage was a long-distance relationship. Philip spent a total of eighteen months in England, from July 1554 to August 1555 and from March to July 1557. In contrast, Mary was a totally absentee Queen of Naples and Spain, after Philip inherited his father's Spanish crowns in 1556.

The marriage was as companionate as it could be under the circumstances; Philip endeavored to make a favorable impression, treating Mary with the utmost respect. Most accounts agree that Mary was quite enamored with Philip, who was reputed to be handsome, while Philip approached his marriage with the business-like attitude of fulfilling the terms of the marriage treaty, most importantly propagating the dynasty. But Mary never seriously considered any attempt to create some form of crown matrimonial for Philip, or have him crowned, as female consorts usually were, although the terms of the marriage treaty guaranteed Philip an English regency if Mary died in childbirth leaving a living heir.

The production of an heir certainly could have helped Philip's chances for a more substantial form of English kingship. In September 1554, Mary announced she was pregnant, exhibiting all the signs for nearly a year, when it became clear she had experienced a false pregnancy. Philip left England in 1555 for Flanders, while Mary very publicly mourned the loss of a husband who was never expected to be permanently resident in England. Philip returned to England in March 1557, ostensibly to convince Mary to join him in a war against France, which was expressly forbidden in the marriage treaty, but also as a last-ditch effort to get Mary pregnant again. This resulted in another embarrassing false pregnancy, although the symptoms might instead have been caused by the advance of terminal ovarian cancer.

Philip was more helpful in Mary's most ambitious legislative program, which was reuniting England with the Church of Rome, which was accomplished during Mary's third parliamentary session (November 1554–January 1555). Parliament also revived the heresy laws, and nearly 300 heretics were subsequently executed, including such high-profile figures as Thomas Cranmer, Archbishop of Canterbury, who was burned at Oxford in 1556 after recanting his recantation, becoming the most famous of the Protestant martyrs chronicled in John Foxe's decidedly anti-Marian *Actes and Monuments*. Mary also sought many other means to bring about a Catholic revival, focusing on priestly education and the re-endowment of monastic institutions, which had been confiscated by the crown during her father's reign, actions which reinforced her queenly persona as a pious and obedient daughter of holy mother church. While several hundred die-hard Protestants left England for exile on the continent, the majority of Mary's subjects outwardly conformed to her official religious policy, including many men, such as William Cecil and William Fleetwood, who later served Elizabeth I, and Nicholas Udall and William Baldwin, who created her court entertainments, all of whom were well known as Protestants during Edward VI's reign.[48] It remains an historical irony that a queen whose queenly style was for the most part mild mannered and merciful should have such an enduring popular reputation as a supposedly blood-thirsty monarch for her religious policy.

Nevertheless, Mary considerably broadened the scope of the religious functions of English queenship, using parliamentary statutes as the means to implement her religious changes, as would her sister Elizabeth in the next reign. Because Mary reigned for only five years, the initial histories of her reign were written during the reign of her sister Elizabeth, mostly by Protestant polemicists, who, coupled with Simon Renard's observations, created the enduring image of a mediocre, if not blood-thirsty, queen. Her religious persecutions aside, which must be assessed in the context of their times, Mary deployed the rubric of queenship to create an acceptable model of female rule much more successfully than Mary Queen of Scots had in Scotland. This legacy she left for her half-sister and successor Elizabeth I (r. 1558–1603) to build upon.

THE QUEENSHIP OF ELIZABETH I

Over the course of her forty-four-year reign, Elizabeth I built upon Mary's more successful queenly strategies, such as identifying herself as both a virgin queen and her kingdom's wife, and rejected those that were not, such as declining to take a husband. Elizabeth's ability to reign without a husband or a recognized successor was just one facet of her arsenal of queenly strategies that has rendered her a perennially fascinating historical figure. Her name is equated with a "golden age" of English history, which experienced the full flowering of the English Renaissance in works of Shakespeare and Marlowe, while English seafarers like Francis Drake and Walter Raleigh laid the groundwork for the emergence of the British Empire. She ranks among the most famous queens in history, and is instantly recognizable, in images and in films, as a vivacious, flirtatious, beautifully dressed, bejeweled, and bewigged queen, negotiating her way through the second half of the sixteenth century with regal poise, confidence, and the strategically deployed temper tantrum when it suited her purpose. In contemporary popular culture she is often uncritically considered a model of queenly achievement who defied the odds to provide leadership and wield power within the confines of a well-entrenched patriarchal political culture. As the BBC History internet page for Elizabeth states,

Elizabeth I is considered one of the country's most successful and popular monarchs. Clever, enigmatic, and flirtatious, she re-wrote the rules of being Queen. But what was Elizabeth really like?[49]

This, of course, is the million-dollar question that countless historians have wrestled with for five centuries. Most biographers, from the early seventeenth-century William Camden to the twentieth-century J.E. Neale, considered Elizabeth to be a singular type of queen, whose achievements seem extraordinary for her gender and without any discernible relationship to previous forms of English queenship.[50] In more recent times, scholars have challenged this conventional interpretation of Elizabeth in a variety of ways, such as Carole Levin, whose work revealed deep-seated gendered uncertainties surrounding Elizabeth's role as an unmarried queen, and Susan Doran, who has questioned the widely held belief that Elizabeth was always determined to remain unmarried.[51]

The future Elizabeth I was born September 7, 1533, the daughter of Henry VIII of England and his second wife, Anne Boleyn. Her birth was a dynastic disappointment; Henry had moved heaven and earth to get out of his first marriage to Catherine of Aragon, the mother of his elder daughter, the future Mary I, so that he could obtain a male heir. After Anne Boleyn was executed in May 1536, parliament removed Elizabeth from the succession as they had previously done to her elder half-sister Mary. Following the 1537 birth of her half-brother, the future Edward VI, Elizabeth endured the anomalous position of a statutorily bastardized daughter of a king, although Parliament later restored both of Henry VIII's daughters to the succession in 1543, reinforced by the King's will, also ratified by parliament, with stipulations concerning their marriages, but without restoring their legitimacy.

By all accounts Elizabeth was highly intelligent, and she and her brother Edward VI were among the best-educated monarchs in the history of Early Modern Europe. During her brother's reign, Elizabeth's education took on a life of its own, as Roger Ascham emerged as a challenging and rigorous primary tutor, who happily described his charge as possessing a "masculine" intellect. It was her place in the succession, not her intelligence nor her education, that made Elizabeth an enticing marriage prospect. But following her father's death in 1547, the Protestant minority governments of Edward VI declined to find Elizabeth a husband, leaving her an unmarried heiress presumptive when her sister Mary I ascended the throne in July 1553. Unlike her predecessor, the Protestant Edward, Mary was dogmatically Catholic, and suspected Elizabeth of secretly harboring heretical religious views. Following Wyatt's revolt at the end of January 1554, which sought to prevent Mary from marrying a foreign price as well as to depose her, Elizabeth was suspected of complicity in the revolt, and was briefly imprisoned in the Tower of London before being kept in protective custody for a year in Woodstock. Elizabeth spent the remainder of Mary's reign in the background of affairs, while at the end of her reign Mary grudgingly acknowledged Elizabeth's right to succeed.

Elizabeth became queen at age twenty-five on November 17, 1558, following Mary's death, an anniversary that later became a national holiday. From the first, she was determined to rule unaided by a male consort, fulfilling the role of king and queen simultaneously as her sister had done in the first year of her reign. Surrounded by a coterie of essentially Edwardian advisors headed by William Cecil, Elizabeth swiftly established her authority. When Spanish Ambassador Count Feria suggested she owed her throne to her former brother-in-law Philip II, Elizabeth scoffed at the notion, telling him she owed her throne to her people.[52] She had a host of problems to deal with, most importantly creating a religious settlement that would be acceptable to most of her subjects, resulting in the creation of an established Protestant Anglican Church, Elizabeth's most durable achievement. Another dilemma was the Tudor succession. Elizabeth was the last of the Tudors. For the duration of her reign Elizabeth failed to marry or name an heir, eschewing what most queens considered to be their most important function, despite numerous offers and courtships with various continental Protestant and Catholic princes. Because of this, her closest hereditary heir was her Catholic cousin Mary Queen of Scots.

Mary Queen of Scots' English captivity symbolized Europe's religious polarization between Catholic states such as France and Spain and Protestant ones such as Scotland and the Netherlands, which launched a rebellion in 1568 against their Catholic feudal overlord, Philip II of Spain. Despite the efforts of a series of pan-Protestant hawks from Robert Dudley, Earl of Leicester to Robert Devereux, Earl of Essex, Elizabeth remained a reluctant and indecisive warrior queen, offering only half-hearted aid to Protestant Huguenots at Le Havre in 1562–1563 and La Rochelle in 1572–1573, and only agreeing to aid the Dutch in the mid-1580s when it became clear that England's national interest depended upon it. These actions, along with the execution of Mary Queen of Scots, resulted in the 1588 invasion of the Spanish Armada, which was stymied by a combination of adverse weather conditions and superior English seamanship. The Armada victory also coincided with the achievements of the Elizabethan golden age of literature and theatre, in the works of Christopher Marlowe, William Shakespeare, and Edmund Spenser. Nevertheless, late Elizabethan England was plagued by runaway inflation, political corruption, a series of bad harvests, and war with Spain and a prolonged Irish rebellion, both of which continued after Elizabeth's death in 1603.

By nature, Elizabeth was a conservative monarch, carefully guarding her prerogative from the men who served her in council and in parliament.

Elizabeth usually took swift action with men who challenged her authority, jailing the Puritan MP Peter Wentworth in 1576 for a speech critical of her influence upon parliamentary business, and in the following year suspending from office her Archbishop of Canterbury, Edmund Grindal, for his refusal to silence puritan evangelists known as "prophesiers." She preferred to take counsel with ministers individually, rather than face the collective cabal of her privy council. Elizabeth had a good eye for talent and was notoriously loyal to her servants such as William Cecil, Lord Burghley and Sir Francis Walsingham, who both died in office elderly and in ill health. Her mercurial personality kept both counselors and subjects on their toes, as her godson Sir John Harington once explained:

> When she smiled, it was a pure sunshine that everyone did choose to bask in if they could; but anon came a storm from a sudden gathering of clouds, and the thunder fell in wondrous manner on all alike.[53]

As a rule, Elizabeth preferred to move slowly in her decision-making process and often drove her ministers to distraction by her indecisiveness. Another frequent criticism of Elizabeth during her own lifetime was her willingness to dissemble; as Elizabeth became a master at creating forms of plausible deniability for a host of endeavors such as "winking" at the actions of privateers and pirates disrupting and seizing Spanish new world trade, while essentially "privatizing" English military support for the Dutch war of independence. She also tried to deny her complicity in the execution of Mary Queen of Scots.

Elizabeth's innate conservatism also drove her fiscal policy. Due to the runaway inflation that gripped England and Europe over the second half of the sixteenth century, a stagnant crown income did not adequately cover the costs of her government. But if Elizabeth wished to tackle fiscal reform, she needed to call parliaments, which she was reluctant to do, because her parliaments pressured her to marry, name a successor, and make further changes to her religious settlement. Over the course of forty-four regnal years, Elizabeth called parliament sparingly, with thirteen sessions that sat for a total of forty-seven months. Because of these factors, Elizabeth never made any meaningful attempt to reform England's feudal tax structure as Isabella had done in Castile. She also avoided costly wars and foreign interventions as much as she could, considering a sound currency and a balanced budget more important than an expansive foreign policy or the acquisition of new-world colonies. Without adequate resources to reward her ministers and servants, Elizabeth condoned corruption at the highest levels of government, handing out monopolies as a form of patronage at the end of her reign. Nevertheless, she had played the role of queen quite well given her limited resources, controlling her policy more than any other Tudor.[54]

Elizabeth also strove to create perceptions about herself for international consumption, in the letters she wrote to foreign potentates from Sultan Mulay Ahmad Al-Ansur of Morocco to Tsar Ivan IV "the Terrible" of Russia and the portraits that accompanied them, placing Elizabeth's image in all the major courts of Europe.[55] But Elizabeth herself never left England; she was an entirely domestic monarch, "mere English' as she liked to say, drawing upon reserves of native goodwill enjoyed by her grandmother Elizabeth of York and her sister Mary in the first year of her reign.[56] She was also a true populist monarch, impressing upon her contemporaries the belief that she sincerely loved her subjects and was concerned about their welfare. Her long reign produced the first feelings of English national identity, wrapped up in the idea that being a good Englishman was being a loyal subject to a Protestant queen favored by God. If her reign failed to end on a high note, her historical reputation has done quite well in the half millennium since her death.

So how does Elizabeth measure up in the principal categories of queenly achievement? Creating a successful marriage and providing for the succession is at the top of that list, yet Elizabeth ultimately chose not to marry. It is instructive to note that from the moment Elizabeth became queen, there was no individual in England who could compel her to marry. The ability to remain unmarried was perhaps the most precious commodity of regnant queenship. Among the early modern female rulers who followed Elizabeth in Europe – Anne of England, Christina of Sweden, Maria Theresa of Austria, Maria of Portugal, and four eighteenth-century Russian empresses – only Anne, Maria, and Maria Theresa married, marriages which took place before they came to their thrones when they were wards of their fathers. In contrast, when women came to their thrones unmarried, as did Elizabeth, Christina of Sweden, and Russia's ruling empresses, remaining unmarried was a viable option, as none of them had any interest in sharing their prerogative with a husband, and, with the exception of Catherine II of Russia, all provided for the succession through collateral male heirs.

But whether Elizabeth was always determined to remain unmarried, or the right candidate simply never surfaced, she made the most of her marriage negotiations for over two decades, playing the marriage card in a variety of negotiations with both Habsburg archdukes and French Valois princes. Elizabeth served as her own marriage broker, the exclusive right of regnant queens, declining to follow Mary's example of creating the perception that her realm would decide her marriage for her. Elizabeth's requirements made the choice of a male consort difficult. She was not interested in a long-distance husband, telling Erik XIV of Sweden, one of her early foreign suitors, that she was "not to marry an absent husband."[57] She also did not wish to marry a man she had not met, echoing the marital predilections of her father, Henry VIII, although she refused to allow Erik to visit England.

But if Elizabeth preferred a full-time husband resident in England, she was also worried about the relationship between a husband and her royal prerogative; drafts of marriage treaties with various European princes were basically the kind of pre-nuptial agreements that both Ferdinand of Aragon and his grandson Philip II of Spain agreed to in their marriages to regnant queens which precluded them from appropriating their wives' regal power. But just as complicated as the power-sharing problems was the issue of religion. Susan Doran has argued that Elizabeth was sincere in her marriage negotiations with Archduke Charles and Francis, Duke of Anjou, which ultimately failed because she correctly perceived that her subjects would not accept a consort who insisted upon practicing Catholicism while married to the queen.[58] Especially in the case of Anjou, public tributes to the Virgin in 1578 were coded public reactions to the prospect of a Catholic marriage that Elizabeth, as an entirely populist monarch, listened to.

But Elizabeth not only declined to marry, she refused to name a successor. Elizabeth was particularly pressed by the parliaments of 1563 and 1566 on the issue of marriage and the succession, which she continually deflected, sometimes forcefully, in defense of her queenly prerogative. While other early modern queens found it useful to designate collateral male heirs during their reigns, Elizabeth was dead set against this; having been first in line to her sister's throne, Elizabeth insisted that she would not put another individual through that experience. She also had no desire to compete with the "rising sun" of a designated successor. At the same time, in her final years, she threw no barriers in the way of the eventual succession of James VI of Scotland, the son and successor of Mary Queen of Scots.

But Elizabeth made up for a lack of direct heirs of her body by casting herself as a metaphorical mother to her people, appropriating the maternal side of queenship in her speeches and public utterances without the complication of an actual husband and children. She did this in 1563, after parliament called upon her to do her "motherly" duty of marrying and bearing children, replying that "I assure you all that though after my death you may have many stepdames, yet you shall never have any a more mother, than I mean to be unto you all." Nearly forty years later, Elizabeth reiterated this sentiment during her 1601 Golden Speech to her final parliament: "and though you have had, and may have, many princes more mighty and wise sitting in this seat, yet you never had nor shall have, any that will be more careful and loving."[59]

Elizabeth also took seriously the obligations of being a godmother to dozens of children, both English and foreign born, which surely justified the "motherly" tone Elizabeth took in her letters to James VI of Scotland.[60]

The marital intimacy that Elizabeth deprived herself of she sought in other ways. At the beginning of her reign Elizabeth's intimate behavior with her married Master of the Horse, Robert Dudley, was scandalous. After the suspicious death of Dudley's wife, Amy Robsart, found dead with her neck broken at the bottom of some stairs, Elizabeth ultimately decided she could not risk marrying one of her own subjects, despite her obvious affection for him. Although they never married, Elizabeth remained emotionally attached to Dudley, whom she created Earl of Leicester, for the rest of his life, which fed the rumor mill of their alleged sexual relationship, which included accusations of secret bastard children.[61] But Elizabeth also enjoyed the company of other handsome men who populated her court, such as Christopher Hatton, whose talents as a courtier catapulted him into Elizabeth's affection and her Privy Council, the Renaissance swashbuckler Walter Raleigh, and the youthful and impetuous Earl of Essex, her final royal favorite. If Elizabeth took sexual lovers, she did a superlative job of keeping it secret, despite rumors to the contrary which had at their basis the belief that youthful unmarried women were unable to control their sexual impulses.[62]

Elizabeth's ability to deflect pressures on her to marry and order her succession was indicative of her skill at creating perceptions and representations of her queenship. Her court was famous for the forms of political culture that emerged during her reign, such as the discourse of courtly love which emerged as a mode of communication with the Queen. While medieval queens were also the object of such discourses, their unavailability was because of their married state. In the case of Elizabeth it was centered on her virginity, a trope both classical and biblical. Elizabeth was equated with Astraea, the virgin goddess of purity and innocence, Minerva, the Roman goddess of wisdom, and Belphoebe, the virgin goddess of hunting, in works of poetry such as Edmund Spenser's the *Fairie Queene* (1590), which also identified her with Gloriana, a figure employed as a propaganda device in Elizabeth's final decades which idealized the Queen as a providentially provided virgin goddess who was both wise and virtuous.[63]

Courtiers like Walter Raleigh and Christopher Hatton wrote poetry in the style of courtly love directly to the Queen, who frequently wrote back in the same type of allegoric terms, both cryptic and untouchable. But an even larger public also engaged in this discourse, as subjects dedicated panegyrics which were presented to the Queen when she visited towns and cities, and presented allegorical plays which extoled her virtues while offering cryptic advice on policies she should pursue, such as during her visit to the port town of Bristol in 1574, whose three-day mock battle called upon the queen to play the role of peacemaker, a role important to a town whose livelihood was based on trade.[64]

These forms of discourse complimented Elizabeth's legendary vanity, which encouraged the idea that Elizabeth never got old, but was always beautiful, pure, untamed, and unattainable, as Essex lamented in Elizabeth's final years, "I loved her whom all the world admired, I was refused of her that can love none."[65] Elizabeth's image as a Petrarchan goddess of courtly love co-existed with that of the Virgin queen, an identification that co-opted the imagery of the Virgin Mary. But allegories of Elizabeth's virginity were just as much mythological as they were Christian, especially in her final years, as she increasingly became identified with the moon goddess Diana, an example of how subjects and courtiers alike used Renaissance imagery to shape understandings of Elizabeth. This mode of communication reached its apotheosis in 1575 when Leicester royally entertained Elizabeth at Kenilworth Castle for nineteen days. The carefully staged masques and dialogues commented upon Elizabeth's virginity in a variety of ways, some of which required a royal reply, as Leicester made one last-ditch effort to convince Elizabeth to marry him. Elizabeth "honored" other wealthy and influential subjects by visiting them at their country homes during her summer progresses. These visits in turn generated architectural improvements to many noble houses and literary descriptions, such as Thomas Churchyard's 1574 description of Elizabeth's visit to Bristol, and George Gascoigne's *The Princely Pleasures at the Court of Kenilworth* (1576), which allowed Elizabeth's literate subjects not able to see her in person to read of the celebrations and the Queen's reactions to the entertainments performed for her during these visits.[66]

Elizabeth's visit to Kenilworth was a facet of a larger Elizabethan project, which was to show herself to her people and listen to what they had to say, creating a sense of community with her subjects and the perception that she cared about her people. Elizabeth's five-day visit to Norwich in 1578 was a classic example.[67] As described by contemporaries Thomas Churchyard and Bernard Garter, Elizabeth listened patiently and graciously to several religiously and politically charged pageants, including one delivered by Protestant refugees from France.[68] While Elizabeth never ventured further than the Thames Valley, East Anglia, and the southern and western shires on her summer progresses, she made sure her subjects saw her, often taking along foreign ambassadors, so they could see firsthand the reciprocal relationship of affection between the Queen and her people. In August 1588, in the face of the Armada invasion, Elizabeth left her bodyguards behind to address her troops at Tilbury, which produced what is her most famous quote, "I know

I have the body of a weak, feeble woman; but I have the heart and stomach of a king," creating an aura of maternal care encased by martial valor.[69] After her death, Sir Walter Raleigh told King James I that one of the reasons Queen Elizabeth had been so popular was because she was perceived as a queen who had concern for the poor, earning during her lifetime the enduring sobriquet "Good Queen Bess."

Elizabeth's ability to communicate was the cornerstone of her legacy as queen. As a superbly educated Renaissance prince, Elizabeth was keenly aware of the power of language, both in speech and in printed form, to shape perceptions of her queenship. Elizabeth wrote her own speeches to parliament and delivered them in person, sometimes to rapturous reception, as in her 1601 Golden Speech, in which she completely turned around a potentially ugly parliamentary session, furious about the granting of monopolies, with a rhetorical flourish of maternal love and care that left many members in tears. But she could also be blunt, admonishing her 1566 parliament for its temerity in calling for her to settle the succession.

Elizabeth was also a prodigious letter writer, conducting foreign policy and negotiating trade relationships with nations as diverse as Morocco, the Ottoman Empire, and Tsarist Russia. She also wrote poetry, such as her famous 1581 lament "On Monsieur's Departure," as well as poetic answers to poems addressed to her with the parameters of the dialogue of courtly love. Elizabeth also embodied the role of religious queen in the prayers she wrote, in a variety of languages, which also provided rhetorical devises for Elizabeth to justify her ability to overcome the perceived handicaps of her gender.[70]

As a Renaissance queen, Elizabeth remained a dutiful scholar of letters and languages. In 1593, in her leisure time, she translated Boethius' *The Consolation of Philosophy* into English. Her blistering ex tempore Latin rebuttal to a Polish ambassador's insulting address in that same year remains an episode unparalleled in the diplomatic annals of Early Modern Europe.[71] Elizabeth's vivacious personality, coupled with her linguistic ability, rendered her a superb diplomat, a talent all Elizabethan historians can attest to. In comparison to the rest of the queens of Early Modern Europe, Elizabeth's level of education and her continued interest in improving her intellect place her in the top strata of educated early modern queens.

Another major facet of Elizabeth's legacy was the construction of visual representations of herself as queen. Elizabeth created perceptions about her queenship with her wardrobe, hairstyles, jewels, and the material culture she surrounded herself with.[72] As queen, Elizabeth was dedicated to her public duties and her private studies and leisure activities, which included music and dancing, but she always made time for her personal adornment for the public consumption of her royal court.[73] Contemporaries noted Elizabeth's vanity, but the attention paid to royal deportment was another standard feature of early modern queenship. As a virgin queen, Elizabeth was able to avoid transitioning into older age. Instead, Elizabeth remained officially ageless, a form of courtly cultural reference unique among the royal courts of Early Modern Europe. Within this context, Elizabeth charmed and flirted with men her entire life, for both political and personal reasons. This was also an integral facet of her mode of diplomacy, often venturing beyond the parameters of the more matronly and austere diplomatic styles of Catholic queens such as Catherine de Medici of France. Elizabeth's portraits and coinage also conveyed myriad images to convey Elizabeth's authority, to celebrate her virginity, and to recognize her providential success in fulfilling the goals of her queenship.

Quite unlike her father, Elizabeth was not a builder, nor did she commission a tomb. While her reign saw an explosion in noble and gentry home building in the English Renaissance style, Elizabeth did not build any palaces herself, another aspect of her innate fiscal conservatism. Despite the opulence displayed by her royal person, Elizabeth's was in fact a no-frills queenship, one of the most fiscally responsible in English history. Rather than spending resources she did not possess for grandiose monuments in marble and fresco, Elizabeth trusted in the benefice of her rule to be her legacy, as expounded by generations of learned scholars, who, once Elizabeth was in her grave, began the erection of her reputation as a singular queen.[74] While modern historians may point out her deficiencies and speculate on the true motivations behind her most controversial policies, they will never deprive Elizabeth of the coveted place she occupies in the history of British queenship; all of Britain's early modern queens pale in her formidable shadow. But she is hardly the archetype British queen in terms of her approach to marriage, family, and dynasty. However, Elizabeth's style of ruling was instructive to later generations of regnant queens such as Christina of Sweden, Anne of Great Britain, and all of Russia's eighteenth-century ruling empresses (see Chapters 5 and 6 below).

SIXTEENTH-CENTURY SCOTTISH QUEENSHIP

While the medieval kingdoms of England and Scotland shared the physical space of the island of Britain, queenship in both developed different trajectories reflective of both the internal and the foreign imperatives of each state. Since the Norman Conquest of 1066, England only had one Scottish-born queen, Edith/Matilda, the consort of the Norman King Henry I (r. 1100–1135), but numerous French consorts, from Eleanor of Aquitaine to Margaret of Anjou, as well as Flemish, Bohemian, and Iberian queens, all reflective of wider European commercial, dynastic, and strategic interests. In contrast, later medieval Scotland had several English-born queen consorts, reflective of Scotland's position as the lesser of the two British kingdoms, as well as Flemish and Scandinavian queens, equally reflective of Scotland's North Sea mercantile interests.[75]

At the beginning of the sixteenth century, Henry VII of England negotiated a marriage alliance between James IV of Scotland and his elder daughter Margaret.[76] Although Scotland at the dawn of the sixteenth century was poorer, less cultured, and much more decentralized politically, with clans holding sway over the rugged and mountainous highlands and isles, James IV was a refined and highly educated Renaissance prince, who possessed a great facility for languages, including highland Gaelic.[77] In a more traditional Scottish vein, James had also sired a pack of illegitimate children with a variety of Scottish noblewomen, as was common for Scottish monarchs, who made their way into the ranks of the Scottish nobility.

His bride was well trained for her future role as a consort, having studied music, dancing, Latin, and French, as well as hunting and archery. Scotland welcomed her with open arms, with pageants, poems, and a spectacular wedding in Edinburgh. In March 1504, Margaret was crowned Queen of the Scots, three years before she gave birth to her first child. Once the marriage was consummated, Margaret was pregnant for much of the duration of James IV's reign. Like her sister-in-law Catherine of Aragon, however, Margaret had difficulty producing children who could survive infancy. Out of seven pregnancies while married to James IV, only one son, the future James V, survived (b. 1512).

Margaret's loyalties were sorely tested after her father's death (April 1509) and the accession of her younger brother Henry VIII, who was eager to renew the Hundred Years War with France and regain the French territories of his Angevin ancestors. James IV had reconfirmed the peace with England upon Henry VIII's accession, but Henry's 1513 French invasion compelled him to choose between England and the traditional French alliance. Ultimately James chose the latter. While Henry VIII laid siege to the French city of Therouanne, James IV invaded the north of England. At the Battle of Flodden Field, between 9,000 and 10,000 Scots were slaughtered, including the king and most of the Scottish nobility.

As a widowed dowager queen in possession of the infant king, Margaret was in a powerful negotiating position. Not quite twenty-four years old and three months pregnant, Margaret swiftly moved to the safety of Stirling Castle, her dower castle, as her future daughter-in-law Mary of Guise would do thirty years later, where James V was crowned. Soon after, a truncated assembly of Scottish peers, aware of both her physical possession of the king and her status as heiress presumptive in England, approved Margaret as regent, despite their claims that it was against Scottish law to have a female ruler.[78]

At this critical juncture Margaret remarried. Often, early modern dowager queens remained unmarried if they wished to lay claim to regal power, which ultimately derived not only from their blood relationship to the minor king but also from their conjugal relationship with their dead husband. Mary of Guise, and the French dowager queens Catherine de Medici and Anne of Austria all followed this model. But the reasons Margaret Tudor remarried had a significant sexual and emotional component; she later admitted as much in a letter to her brother Henry VIII as well as on her deathbed. But she may well have wanted a powerful Scottish nobleman by her side; the year following the disaster at Flodden had been especially stressful, and the pressures coming from the Anglophiles and the Francophiles at the Scottish court coupled with her own physical needs resulted in her marriage in August 1514 to Archibald Douglas, Earl of Angus.

As regent, and as a sovereign woman and the mother of an underage king, Margaret considered herself free to exercise her prerogative and remarry. Margaret invariably saw her future tied to Scotland and the kingship of her son, making a foreign marriage for her undesirable. But marriage to a subject also had its drawbacks; admittedly, the Scottish nobility lacked homogeneity, but the Douglas clan, though powerful and influential, were enemies with most of the other noble clans, ultimately resulting in victory for the Francophiles, who sacked Margaret from the regency and took possession of the king, while Margaret and Angus fled to England, where she gave birth to her daughter Margaret Douglas.[79]

After returning to Scotland, Margaret labored to maintain cordial relations with her maturing son, as well as a measure of queenly influence, negotiating a rapprochement between James V and Henry VIII in 1534 and a proposed meeting in 1536 that never materialized. While she did her best to orient her son into the English orbit, James preferred the "auld alliance" with France as did his father. James thus sailed to France in 1537 to marry Madeleine, a daughter of Francis I of France, leaving Margaret in the role of regent, a testament to the motherly bond that had survived amid a plethora of crises. After Madeleine died shortly after arriving in Scotland, James took another bride, Mary of Guise, who arrived in 1538.

Mary of Guise's consortship was relatively brief, four years, but she was as well trained as any sixteenth-century queen; her performance as both a consort and a dowager earned for her a mostly positive press; most contemporaries agree she was wise, prudent, and courageous in the face of adversity, although her detractors, particularly John Knox, had powerful religious and misogynistic motivations for their less than flattering characterizations of her, which included accusations of promiscuity, a conventional means of besmirching a queenly reputation.[80]

At age eighteen Mary took up residence in the court of Francis I, where she married Henri d'Orleans, duc de Longueville, to whom she bore two sons, only one of whom survived infancy, and attended the wedding of James V of Scotland and Princess Madeleine in 1537, the same year her husband died. After Madeleine's death, Mary was prevailed upon to become her successor, which meant leaving her young son in France, while a rather generous dowry was arranged for her marriage to the widowed Scottish king, and she arrived at Fife in 1538, only months after losing her first husband, whose final letter to her she kept until her death.

Whatever reservations Mary may have brought to her marriage and journey to a distant kingdom, she immediately set to work to create her own queenly reputation, lavishing favor upon dowager queen Margaret Tudor and creating a model of royal domestic tranquility. In turn James considered himself as much a Renaissance prince as his uncle Henry VIII, filling his court with continental craftsmen, scholars, and musicians, and providing Mary with a lavish coronation, as was the custom for Scottish queen consorts, and finishing the renovations of Falkland Castle in the French architectural style.[81]

As James V did his best to create the conditions for Mary to adjust to her new life in Scotland, she responded in the best way possible, bearing a son, James, in May 1540, and another one nearly one year later, but both infants died on the same day in April 1541. In the spring of 1542, Mary conceived again, giving birth to a daughter, Mary (Queen of Scots) in December. By this time dowager queen Margaret had died, removing the last advocate around the king for a continued alliance with England. After James spurned a proposed meeting at York with Henry VIII in 1541, Henry retaliated with a cross-border invasion. James responded with a counterattack, resulting in a stunning Scottish defeat at Solway Moss (November 24, 1542). This defeat, coupled with the news of the birth of a daughter, hastened James's death at the age of thirty.

Widowed once again at age twenty-seven, Mary of Guise never looked back, spending the rest of her life defending her daughter's throne and the French alliance that she was convinced was necessary for the survival of an independent Scotland.[82] Much like her mother-in-law Margaret, Mary was compelled to negotiate a difficult path between coexistence with England, Scotland's closest neighbor, and the traditional alliance with France. In control of the person of her daughter, and claiming a place on her regency council, Mary joined the Scottish Parliament in rejecting a proposed marriage between Mary Queen of Scots and the future Edward VI, resulting in the English "rough wooing" invasions. By 1548, Mary had succeeded in convincing the Scottish parliament that her daughter's safety could only be assured in France, as English bellicosity considerably eased the selling of what was a centuries-old direction in Scottish foreign policy.

At this juncture, Mary could have easily returned with her daughter to France, where her son Francis also lived, to enjoy a relaxing widowhood or perhaps another marriage. Despite her relative youth, however, Mary of Guise remained in Scotland until 1550, when peace was achieved between England, France, and Scotland. Mary then returned to France, to arrange her daughter's marriage alliance and gain support for her bid to become a formal regent in Scotland. Mary's year-long sojourn ended with her return through England, where she was lavishly entertained by fourteen-year-old Edward VI, who gave her a diamond ring and introduced her to his seventeen-year-old sister, the future Elizabeth I.

By 1554, Mary assumed the regency of Scotland. With vigor and determination, Mary imposed a king-like authority upon her daughter's kingdom, enforcing the laws, going on progress, and financing her government through the profits of her industrial enterprises. At the same time, Mary governed, as her Guise relatives had advised, with "conciliation, gentleness, and moderation," much in the manner of her neighbor, Mary I of England, who, as we have seen, also brought a queenly approach to her female kingship. But despite Mary's political skill and acumen, the outbreak of the Scottish Reformation, a more grassroots movement than that which emerged in England, stymied her ability to create political consensus. While the first three years of Mary's formal regency witnessed a stabilization of royal control, the events of 1558–1560 spiraled out of control, necessitating her continued presence in Scotland, at the expense of missing her daughter's wedding to the dauphin in France. Even before this, in 1557, Mary induced the Scottish parliament to enter the Habsburg-Valois war of 1557, in which England had entered on the side of Spain, resulting in a series of border skirmishes. But it was a pyrrhic victory; Mary I of England died in November 1558 and was succeeded by her half-sister Elizabeth, whom the Lords of the Congregation swiftly viewed as their natural ally.

Mary was initially successful in military operations against the Protestants as English troops were repulsed, but the promised French convoy from Calais never arrived after an English fleet showed up in the straits of Fife. Mary's health slowly deteriorated, with the kind of swelling in her legs and resulting lameness that her daughter would also suffer from. In the spring of 1560, Mary met with the Lords of the Congregation, desirous of peace, and begged them to maintain the French alliance as well as her daughter's queenship. She died in June, fearful for the future of her daughter's crown in a Protestant Scotland.

Within the larger context of Early Modern European queenship, Mary of Guise set a standard for queenly achievement. She had married James V swiftly after the death of her first husband, leaving her young son in France to become Scotland's queen, quickly bearing a series of children for her husband before his untimely demise, four years into her queenship. As a still youthful and eligible widow, Mary put her daughter's interests before her own, remaining unmarried and in Scotland, securing a future king for her daughter while negotiating as best she could the dynamic vagaries of the Scottish Reformation with skill, confidence, and determination. Mary of Guise's dowager queenship was a powerful model for Catherine de Medici, who in 1560 began her own tumultuous career as both regent and powerful player in French politics.

Mary of Guise's successor as queen consort was Anne (or Anna) of Denmark (1574–1619), the queen of her grandson James VI of Scotland (1566–1625).[83] As Margaret Tudor and Mary of Guise brought English and French conceptions of queenship to Scotland, Anne of Denmark brought a Danish version of queenship to her adopted homeland, having enjoyed a close relationship with her parents, Frederick II and Sophie of Mecklenberg-Gustrow, quite unlike James, who never knew his parents. Anne was particularly close with her mother, Queen Sophie, who supervised her children's education and later brokered Anne's marriage with James VI, providing her daughter with a generous £150,000 dowry, as well the example of a powerful and engaged hands-on queenship (see Chapter 5).[84]

As was typical in such negotiations, the prospective bride and groom had exchanged portraits, purportedly to stimulate the love expected to grow between them once they were married. Both James and Anne played this role to the hilt during their long-distance courtship. Anne had reportedly fallen in love with the portrait James had sent her, while James also had convinced himself of his love for his bride-to-be, a common form of official devotion that was a standard feature of the dynastic conventions surrounding royal marriages. In reality, James and Anne were ill-matched, both emotionally and intellectually, a frequent circumstance of dynastic marriages. Like most of her predecessors as queens of Scotland, Anne bore the legitimate heirs while her king looked for love elsewhere, a common enough situation in Early Modern European royal marriages. Due to the dynastic nature of most European polities, queenly sexuality was closely watched and guarded; the easiest way to besmirch a queen's reputation was to accuse her of sexual infidelity.

In contrast, infidelity was an accepted part of Early Modern European king-ship provided the king fulfilled the dynastic obligation of perpetuating the dynasty with his lawfully wedded queen.

Scottish kings had a propensity for sexual relationships outside the bounds of marriage, resulting in children who were acknowledged and ushered into the Scottish and British nobility. Stuart kings usually found suitable hus-bands for their royal mistresses while simultaneously paying their queens all due honor and respect. In turn, Scottish queens learned to accept, in varying degrees, this inescapable facet of Scottish kingship. This was the experience of Margaret Tudor and Mary of Guise as it would be for Catherine of Braganza and Mary of Modena in the seventeenth century. James VI only deviated from this model in his choice of intimate partners. Historians in general have long been reluctant to discuss James VI's sexuality, and neither James nor a string of royal male favorites from Esme Stuart to George Villiers left a description of what went on in the royal bedchamber. But where there is smoke there usu-ally is fire; James's letters, coupled with observed commentary of his behav-ior, identify a king who preferred love and intimacy with other men. Further, James did not have any observable sexual relationships with any other women besides his queen. Although male favorites did not produce children, James nearly always provided advantageous marriages for them while lavishing patronage upon their children, in the tradition of his Scottish predecessors.

This was the bitter pill Anne had to swallow soon after the celebrations of her arrival in Scotland had subsided. If Anne had hoped for a more companionate and intimate marriage and family life such as her parents had enjoyed, James cushioned the blow somewhat by according his queen all due rank and honor befitting her position. The one area where they did work together productively was propagating the dynasty. The first pregnancy took three years to arrive; James's initial reluctance in the royal bedchamber may have been spurred by contemporary murmurings about his appetite for male favorites, and it may have been a combination of defending his masculine kingly honor as well as the dynastic need to propagate the dynasty that finally resulted in a string of pregnancies over a thirteen-year period, with three children, Henry (b. 1594), Elizabeth (b. 1596), and the future Charles I (b. 1600), surviving childhood.

Child raising emerged as a divisive issue between James and Anne, who had been raised directly by her mother, Queen Sophie, whose powerful maternal instincts carried considerable political repercussions, especially after the death of her husband and during the regency of her underage son. Like her mother, Anne expected to have a direct hand in the raising of her eldest son, Henry. But James had a completely different idea concerning the role his queen should play in the tutelage of his heir. Scottish heirs to the throne endured a particularly violent and unstable history over the course of the fifteenth and sixteenth centuries, as royal minorities created the conditions where youthful Scottish monarchs had to be physically protected from their own subjects, as evident in the histories of the minorities of James V, Mary Queen of Scots, and James VI himself. Determined to safeguard the person of his heir, James refused Anne guardianship of her son, placing him under the guardianship of John Erskine, Earl of Mar, behind the safety of the walls of Stirling Castle, as he, his mother, and his grandfather also had been.

This was a major bone of contention between James and Anne. Historians have generally dismissed Anne's intervention in factional politics as personal in nature, but the conflict was in fact a clash between competing conceptions of queenship. James had never known another queen, while his own kingship was a hard-fought battle for control waged over the course of his entire minority reign. Invariably, he was resistant to the type of vibrant and autonomous queenship Anne strove to create for herself, which to her included control over the upbringing and marriages of her children. Anne's tenacity paid off following the death of Elizabeth I in March 1603, when Anne finally secured access to her eldest son. Like Anne Boleyn, Anne was not afraid to cross her husband in the public spaces of the royal court; more than once he publicly betrayed his impatience with his consort's petulance, which he attributed to her being a king's daughter. In 1600, in fact, after James narrowly escaped an assassination attempt in the so-called Gowrie Conspiracy, he requested Anne to dismiss the Ruthven sisters of the conspirators. Anne refused to dismiss Beatrix Ruthven from her service, which resulted in a series of very public rows.

While James and Anne failed to create a companionate marriage, Anne pursued a separate life for herself as a queen dedicated to promoting the visual arts. Like her husband, Anne was extravagant, living beyond the means of her income. But she spent tastefully, designing her residence at Dumfermline and its gardens and avidly collecting paintings of all kinds as well as jewelry, which adorned her person. Anne also dressed sumptuously, creating a visual sense of a royal queenly style not seen in Scotland since the days of the youthful Mary Queen of Scots.[85]

THE CATHOLIC QUEENS OF SEVENTEENTH-CENTURY BRITAIN

Like her husband, Anne of Denmark spent her reign as Scottish queen patiently waiting for the death of Elizabeth I of England, when she would become queen of both British kingdoms. As the English warmly welcomed the accession of a king after half a century of female rule, a coterie of English noblewomen, led by the countesses of Worcester and Pembroke and ladies Rich and Kildare, rushed north to usher a pregnant Anne, newly reunited with her son Henry, down to Windsor. This royal progress helped lay the representational groundwork for her British consortship in the richness and splendor of her traveling retinue, replete with the latest in coach technology, as nobles along their path outdid each other in entertaining Anne and her companions before James himself joined his queen.[86] While Anne had little in common with her sixteenth-century Scottish forbears in terms of temperament and queenly outlook, she established several trends that characterized seventeenth century British-queenship.

The first was her continued patronage of the visual arts. Anne's spending, although it incurred contemporary criticism for a king and queen sorely lacking in fiscal restraint, provided long-standing evidence of an engaged and autonomous British queenship devoted to style and taste. While James spent much of his time out of the capital in the countryside hunting, to the dismay of his councilors, or huddled with his male favorites within the confines of his homosocial bedchamber, Anne established her own separate household in the center of London, with Somerset House as her principal residence. Most importantly, Anne created a salon-like space within this household that attracted playwrights, artists, musicians, and leading members of Jacobean political society.[87] Anne was also a devoted patron of plays and masques, utilizing such luminaries as Ben Jonson and staging masques filled with breathtaking spectacle, which she herself occasionally performed in, to the consternation of the English Puritans, who condemned the appearance of women on the stage. On those occasions when James accompanied his queen to a play, he frequently fell asleep.[88]

Anne was also a builder, employing the protean talents of Inigo Jones not only for his designs for her masques, but also for his architectural genius, building the Queen's House at Greenwich, a classic example of Palladian architecture, whose gardens Anne designed herself. Anne's interest in painting reached new heights in England. She patronized such influential artists as Isaac Oliver, Daniel Mytens, and Paul van Somer, who painted the queen in her final years, resplendent in her hunting gear and plumed hat, leading her steed and surrounded by her dogs with a look of confidence and contentment, the final image of a queen whose official portraits reveal a stylish and elegant, if not sexually suggestive queen who ushered in the arrival of the bosom in royal portraiture. Anne also bequeathed many still lifes and pastoral works to the royal collection, which was greatly expanded by her son Charles I. As James's biographer Alan Stewart has remarked, a good measure of the culture that is labelled Jacobean received its encouragement and patronage from Anne of Denmark, who played a central role in the making of the visual manifestations of her queenship.[89]

But Anne's queenship was also indicative of other trends, some of which contributed to the later instability of the Stuart dynasty. During the sixteenth century both England and Scotland had become Protestant nations. James VI and I had been raised Protestant and recognized the utility of maintaining England's episcopal Anglican hierarchy. Nevertheless, by 1600 Anne had converted to Catholicism. Why this occurred is impossible to determine; she had to have been aware that most of her subjects in England and Scotland were Protestants. It certainly would have made political sense to remain Protestant if she aspired to the kind of populist popularity that Elizabeth I and previous English consorts such as Elizabeth of York had enjoyed from their subjects.

But Elizabeth I's pragmatism towards religion was exceptional; Anne was very much a woman of her times within a culture that still was providential in its world view. In all probability, Anne experienced a sincere religious conversion. Anne noticeably declined to take the Anglican communion at her coronation, but she invariably recognized, or James compelled her to recognize, the political economy of keeping both her conversion and her religious observances quiet. Even so, the Scottish Kirk, the Anglican hierarchy, and the English Puritans all took exception to the religiosity of a Catholic queen. It is not at all clear whether this concerned Anne. Literacy and the proliferation of forms of mass communication increased exponentially over the course of the seventeenth century, spurring the rise of an increasingly informed and politically motivated civil society, which scrutinized the religious practices and the extravagance of British queens for the remainder of the Stuart era, as Anne's successors would learn to their cost.[90] As Michelle White has suggested in her work on Henrietta Maria, what their subjects said about Catholic Stuart queens may not have been true, but, for the most part, these queens failed to shape the narratives constructed about them by their contemporaries within literate political society.[91]

The queenship of Henrietta Maria, the wife of Charles I, who succeeded his father in 1625, also endured a plethora of adverse public opinion.[92] A daughter of Henri IV of France, a former Protestant who famously converted to Catholicism to gain his throne, Henrietta Maria brought a dogmatic attitude to religion with her to England, maintaining and promoting her Catholicism in marked contrast to the religion of her husband and most of his subjects.[93] Trained in the usual aristocratic pursuits of music and dancing, her formal education was rudimentary at best, and she lacked intellectual pursuits although she possessed a refined artistic aesthetic. Only fifteen when she married the twenty-five-year-old Charles I in 1625, her marriage contract assured her of her right to worship Catholic in her own chapel with twenty-eight Catholic priests.

She arrived in England with a sizeable French entourage, and declined to be crowned with Charles, the highest honor an English queen can receive at the onset of her reign, because she would not take Anglican communion, a stipulation that Anne of Denmark had been able to bypass in 1603. The marriage itself got off to a rocky start, but after Charles dismissed most of her French entourage and royal favorite the Duke of Buckingham was assassinated (August 23, 1628), Charles and Henrietta Maria grew much closer, bringing a tone of austere domesticity to their royal court, in marked contrast to the relative licentiousness of the later Jacobean court. The heirs duly followed; Henrietta bore six children who survived to adulthood, including two British kings.

As a princess of one of the most prestigious kingdoms in Europe, Henrietta Maria used her income to keep up with the latest French styles and artistic trends. Continuing the trends of Elizabeth I and Anne of Denmark, Henrietta Maria subscribed to the belief that a queen should be the best dressed and coiffed woman in her kingdom, and she did her best to maintain this status. Henrietta was just as enamored with staging masques as her predecessor, keeping Inigo Jones on the royal payroll for his spectacular stagings that also featured the queen performing. Many of the masques Henrietta Maria commissioned contained pro-Catholic themes and allegories, which the Puritans particularly found offensive. Henrietta, along with Charles, also spent lavishly on paintings and patronized artists such as Anthony van Dyke and Orazio Gentilschi, while greatly enlarging the royal collection in the process.[94]

Much like her predecessor Anne of Denmark, Henrietta felt no compulsion to emulate the queenly strategies of Elizabeth of York, Catherine of Aragon, or Elizabeth I in the construction of their queenships, in terms of their efforts to become popular queens in contemporary popular consciousness. Neither made a reputation for charity or concern for the poor; the sincerity of their religious beliefs, normally a positive category of queenly prestige, worked against both in their Protestant kingdoms; and neither was inclined to go on progress to show themselves to their subjects as Elizabeth I had routinely done. Instead, the queenships of Anne of Denmark and Henrietta Maria played to the upper echelons of the British aristocracy who populated the royal court, rather than the burghers and gentry who filled the seats of the House of Commons, which possessed the right to approve all taxes within a still essentially feudal fiscal structure that expected their monarchs to pay for the costs of their government and household establishment out of the crown's income.

The first two Stuart kings experienced difficult relationships with their parliaments, but Charles I (r. 1625–49) dispensed with calling parliaments altogether for eleven years after the disaster of his 1629 meeting, which attempted to saddle him with the Petition of Right, the most overt limitation on the king's prerogative since Magna Carta, without granting him the taxation which had been the reason for the parliamentary meeting. Charles's subsequent sources of extra-parliamentary income, most notoriously "ship money," an antiquated feudal levy on coastal communities that Charles extended to the rest of his kingdom without parliamentary approval, also contributed to his growing unpopularity during the 1630s. Henrietta Maria did not appear to be concerned or aware of any of these developments, at least until they challenged her husband's prerogatives and his throne.

Henrietta's queenly myopia was the result of her conception and approach to queenship. As a princess of a wealthy, powerful, and influential European kingdom, Henrietta never made a serious effort to identify with her adoptive kingdom. In contrast, her mission as a British queen was to make the royal court more *French* as well as more *Catholic*; she never mastered the English language and attempted to sway her children religiously in the direction of Catholicism, even though they were the heirs of a Protestant kingdom.[95] Henrietta's queenship was also much more domesticated than that of Anne of Denmark, who spent much of her English reign creating a queenly space for herself separate from her husband. More devoted to each other than James I and Anne of Denmark, Charles I and Henrietta Maria spent much of their time together, requiring much more privacy for the family life they cherished, as Henrietta's queenship was bound up in raising her children within the bubble of a royal establishment.

With the outbreak of Civil War in August 1642, when Charles I raised his standard at Nottingham against the parliamentary forces, Henrietta Maria emerged as a liability for the royalist cause. Her image in the popular press was that of a subversive, extravagant, and foreign Catholic queen who cared nothing for her adoptive kingdom. The outbreak of war compelled Henrietta Maria to pay attention to her kingdom's affairs, as well as broaden the scope of her queenship, urging Charles to take a hard line with parliamentary agitators such as John Pym, whose demands sought to dismantle much of the king's traditional prerogative. Perhaps the most salutary feature of Henrietta Maria's queenship was her devotion to her husband, rejoining him in Oxford in 1643 after landing in Yorkshire and conferring with various royalist allies, and rejecting pleas from the parliamentary leaders to intercede with her husband for peace. In these actions she rejected the traditional queenly role of peacemaker to play an active and engaged role in the royalist cause, although as the war dragged on, she urged Charles to negotiate with Parliament, now dominated by hardline Puritans such as Oliver Cromwell. By this time, she was living as an exile in Paris, just as the tumults of the Fronde were shaking France during the minority of her nephew Louis XIV.

On January 31, 1649, after a brief trial, Charles I was beheaded in London, inaugurating a Republican experiment in Britain that lasted until Henrietta Maria's eldest son was restored as Charles II in October 1660. In the meantime, Henrietta Maria settled down to a life as a widowed and exiled dowager queen, founding a convent at Chaillot where she lived for much of the 1650s. When she returned to England in 1660 for the accession of her eldest son, Charles II, she was nearly forgotten in the restoration celebrations. Diarist Samuel Pepys described her a "very plain old woman" in her widow's weeds. In all likelihood, she was unconcerned by this lack of attention, given that connecting with the mass of her English subjects had never been a priority of her queenship.

In the face of continued animosity towards Catholicism in Restoration England and Scotland, Britain's next two queen consorts, Catherine of Braganza and Mary of Modena, both devout Catholics, developed their queenships under particularly adverse circumstances. The institution of monarchy itself entered a period of crisis and redefinition, which culminated in the Glorious Revolution of 1688–1689. Among the many results of this process was the dictum that the monarch must be Protestant, a development no doubt influenced by a succession of four Catholic queen consorts over the course of seventeenth-century Britain.

For Charles II, Catherine of Braganza's sizeable dowry trumped the complication of her Catholicism, which included lucrative trading concessions in the Mediterranean and India.[96] She had led a rather cloistered life in Portugal before her arrival in England in 1662. The licentiousness of Charles II's court must have come as something of a shock, which was itself a reaction to the austere regime of the Puritans during the interregnum after Charles I's death. Guaranteed her right to worship Catholic, her choice of religion did not make her initially popular with the English people, although whether this mattered to her at all is not clear from the historical record. Her Catholicism also deprived her of the opportunity for an English coronation, which represented a significant form of bonding to her adopted kingdom. She had not studied English before her arrival, which made her integration into court life more difficult. Finally, Charles expected her to have his current mistress, Barbara Palmer, later Duchess of Cleveland, installed as a bedchamber attendant, which initially caused her extreme emotional distress.

Such difficulties could be overcome by the birth of an heir, but after several miscarriages over the course of the 1660s she no longer conceived; her intense desire for a child was revealed in an episode when she was dreadfully ill and imagined she had children. Because of these factors, historians have traditionally considered her a neglected and marginalized queen. More recent assessments have suggested that Catherine made a more imaginative and nuanced use of her queenly prerogatives, making the best of what was available in the construction of her queenship. Lacking the focus of a royal nursery as a parade of fecund Protestant royal mistresses stole the royal spotlight from her, Catherine marshalled her resources to create areas of influence and power underneath the radar of Restoration society.[97]

What all the Catholic Stuart queens of the seventeenth century had in common was the scope of their artistic patronage. Catherine employed Italian musicians in her chapel and lavished patronage on painters like Benedetto Gennari.[98] Catherine also remained devoted to the Catholic religion in England, quietly bestowing patronage upon Catholic establishments without exciting the kind of furor that later surrounded her during the anti-Catholic hysteria whipped up by the Popish Plot of 1678. Her exoneration was a testament to the broad-based affection she had been able to create within Stuart society despite her childlessness and her Catholicism. Catherine's use of her queenly influence was subtle and focused; she came to terms with Charles II's serial promiscuity although it offended her sense of morality, even taking a page from Anne of Denmark's playbook, neutralizing Barbara Palmer by promoting other women as Charles's mistresses, as Anne of Denmark had helped dispose of the worthless and obnoxious Robert Carr, Earl of Somerset, by promoting George Villiers as her husband's new royal favorite. None of this gave her any pleasure, but she largely maintained her dignity, composure, and good nature despite the obvious disappointments for the twenty-two years of her queenship. Perhaps the final testament to her character was the devotion of Charles II, who refused calls to divorce her and rallied to her defense during the Popish plot, fulfilling one of the long-established precedents of Stuart kingship by honoring his queen in the public spaces of the royal court.

Following the death of Charles II in 1585, James II and his second wife, Mary of Modena, ascended the English and Scottish thrones as Catholics. This was a volatile issue, one that had first erupted during the Exclusion Crisis of the later years of Charles II, which attempted to bar Catholics from the throne by parliamentary statute, giving rise to party politics, with Tories favoring an indefeasible hereditary right, while Whigs, employing an emergent contract theory of governance, insisted that Parliament had the right to alter the succession.

Caught in the middle of this debate was England's only Italian queen consort, Mary, a daughter of the Duke of Modena.[99] Her portraits reveal a slender, captivating woman, known for her charm, warmth, and devotion to family. She had been well trained for her future role; she was superbly educated in letters, music, and art, and she was fluent in several languages, proficient in Latin, and later mastered English as Henrietta Maria and Catherine of Braganza had never done, making her the best-educated British queen since Elizabeth I. All these qualities should have boded well for a successful run as a future queen consort of England.[100]

As a queen in waiting, the production of heirs was for Mary of paramount importance. In the first twelve years of her marriage she conceived eight times, with four live births, but none of her children had survived by the time she became queen in 1685. The death in 1681 of her four-year-old daughter Isabella, her only child to survive infancy, took a severe toll on her physical and mental well-being, and she had just one more pregnancy after this in 1682, resulting in another daughter who lived only a few months. After this, there were no more pregnancies for five years. In the face of her husband's constant infidelities and her reproductive disappointments, Mary set out to make her reputation in the time-honored fashion of seventeenth-century Stuart queenship, by lavishing artistic patronage and promoting the Catholic religion in England. Like Catherine of Braganza, Mary possessed highly refined, Italianate tastes in art, music, and architecture, reflective of the continental connections between queenship and the patronage of baroque art. Nevertheless, her erudition, her personality, her exquisite taste, and her personal piety were no guarantee for popularity in an age when international Catholicism was considered the greatest threat to British security. On many occasions her carriage was pelted with stones and garbage simply because she was Catholic.

But James II's reign initially began in a spirit of conciliation and compromise. Seeking to be recognized as a legitimate monarch despite his Catholicism, James spared no expense for his and Mary's crowning, the grandest double coronation since that of Henry VIII and Catherine of Aragon in 1509, although both underwent a private anointing by a Catholic priest before they submitted to the full Anglican rights of the coronation ceremony in Westminster Abbey. The ceremony was a tribute to a still childless Mary of Modena, who sat on her throne as graciously as she could in the three years of her consortship, one of the shortest in early modern history, continuing to endure James's infidelities until late 1686, when she demanded he put away his mistress Catherine Sedley. Soon after taking the waters at Bath, Mary conceived again, to the joy of Catholic Europe and the consternation of English Protestants, who expected James's eldest daughter Mary, married to William, Prince of Orange, to succeed him.

In June 1688, Mary gave birth to a son, perhaps the most documented royal birth in British history. The birth of an heir who would be raised Catholic coincided with James's efforts to create religious toleration, which included suspending the laws and attempting to influence parliamentary elections to push through his legislative agenda. In response, leading Protestants urged William of James to invade England and reform the king, who landed a sizeable armed force at Torbay in October 1688. As support for the king crumbled, James sent Mary and their infant son James to France, where he soon followed, effectively deserting his crown. In England, a convention of estates effectively disbarred the infant Prince of Wales and offered the crown jointly to the Prince and Princess of Orange, after they agreed to several limitations upon the royal prerogative, including the dictum that the monarch, and by implication, his queen, must be Protestant.

In histories discussing her husband's deposition and the subsequent Glorious Revolution, Mary of Modena is barely mentioned. Not surprisingly, she stood by her king as she transformed into an exiled *de facto* dowager queen. Paradoxically, her life as an exiled queen may have been more satisfying than her three years as Britain's reigning consort, when all her queenly talents, her intelligence and education, her mothering skills, and her wit and gaiety had been buried under her public perception as a Catholic queen. In France, living off Louis XIV's charity at Chateau de St. Germain-en-Laye, Mary rolled up her sleeves to do what she could to help recover a crown that in the Catholic world view she and her husband could not be deprived of, selling her jewels to help support James's unsuccessful invasion of Ireland in 1690, as her mother-in-law had done fifty years previously. She also had a particular care for her husband's Jacobite supporters, dispensing what charity she had to their families in a salutary if conventional queenly tradition. As James aged, the still relatively youthful Mary gradually carved an independent life for herself, becoming a mainstay at Versailles, where she enjoyed both Louis XIV's favor and her status as a queen. At the same time, she remained a devoted mother, giving birth to a daughter in 1692 and later assuming the regency for her son following James II's death in 1701. As Mary of Guise had for her daughter a century and a half previously, Mary of Modena remained unmarried and dressed in widow's weeds for the remainder of her life. Despite her continuing efforts on behalf of the Jacobite cause, which sought to place her son James, known as the "Old Pretender," on the British throne, she refused to allow him to be sent to Scotland to be raised a Protestant as a child, which could have considerably boosted his chances of succeeding William III or Anne as a legitimate hereditary candidate.

As historian Andrew Barclay has remarked, Mary of Modena possessed nearly all the qualities that in an earlier age would have made her a successful and popular queen; she was intelligent, loyal, attractive, artistically motivated, conventionally pious, and a good wife and mother, but by the late seventeenth century the confessional divide was too much of a hurdle for her to either stabilize her queenship or create any form of lasting legacy in England. After her son came of age, she lived out her final years at the same French convent that Henrietta Maria had founded, completing a sort of exiled Catholic queenly tradition that exalted marriage and motherhood as the defining qualities of their queenships. But what was also a defining feature of all the seventeenth-century Stuart consorts was their collective inability to recognize, engage, or combat the wide-ranging political implications that their religious beliefs imposed upon their queenships, as Protestantism emerged as a major feature of emergent British national identity for the remainder of the early modern era. This facet of seventeenth-century British queenship has served to obscure the achievements of these queens as substantial cultural pollinators as well as patrons of domestic arts and architecture.[101]

QUEENSHIP UNDER MARY II AND ANNE

Like the sixteenth-century Tudor dynasty, the Stuart line came to its end with a pair of regnant queens, neither of whom were able to perpetuate the Stuart dynasty. Despite this similarity, there were important differences between these two groups of queens. Both Mary I and Elizabeth I came to their thrones as unmarried women, who succeeded by both statutory and widely recognized hereditary rights. Both also had received superlative Renaissance humanist educations, and functioned as independent female magnates prior to their accessions, while exercising total control over their respective options towards marriage. In contrast, both Mary II and Anne served as diplomatic pawns in their dynastic marriages prior to their accessions, with completely different outcomes for their respective husbands. Neither received the kind of education requisite for their respective places in the Stuart dynasty, although they received the usual aristocratic training in such domestic arts and pastimes that were more preparations for marriage and a possible consortship than as ruling queens. Not surprisingly, the queenship of Mary II (r. 1689–1694) more closely resembled those of Elizabeth of York and Catherine of Aragon rather than either Mary I or Elizabeth I, while Anne co-opted the successful strategies of regnant queenship in the formulation of her much more autonomous queenship.

By the time she was ten, when it was clear that Catherine of Braganza would not be bearing heirs for Charles II, Mary Stuart, the eldest daughter of James, Duke of York, stood second in line for the English and Scottish thrones. Like her great-great-grandmother Mary Queen of Scots, for whom she was named, Mary was tall, graceful, and physically attractive. She was trained to be a consort, with the emphasis on music, dancing, and the other graceful arts rather than the scholarly regimen of Mary I, Elizabeth I, or even her stepmother Mary of Modena.[102] Despite his Catholic sympathies, Charles II recognized the political economy behind having his nieces raised as Anglicans. Their tutelage, by Henry Compton, bishop of London, stuck; despite the influences of their father and stepmother, both Mary and Anne embraced the Church of England not only as a means of spiritual comfort but also as a manifestation of British national identity.

Charles II also arranged to have his nieces marry Protestant husbands. For Mary this was her first cousin William, Prince of Orange, a Dutch stadtholder as well as a grandson of Charles I. Married at age fifteen, she cried as she walked down the aisle at St. James's Palace. But once in Holland, contemporaries tend to agree that she became devoted to William, despite his lack of social graces, whose mission in life was to thwart the expansionist policies of the Catholic Louis XIV of France. William's long-standing desire to inherit the English and Scottish thrones was based mainly on the resources these kingdoms could provide in a series of conflicts that did not come to an end until the Peace of Utrecht in 1713.

Mary had no independent dynastic ambitions, considering that her place in the succession could be put at William's disposal, who apparently anticipated a sort of crown matrimonial when she eventually succeeded her father. Like her grandmother Henrietta Maria and her stepmother Mary of Modena, Mary embodied conventional gendered expectations for royal women. She was pious, gracious, and supportive of her husband's ambitions, achieving a large measure of popularity in Holland for these efforts, although she was unable to bear children, which was a profound disappointment for her. In these actions and attitudes, she closely resembled the outlook of her stepmother Mary of Modena, with whom she enjoyed a warm and affectionate relationship prior to her marriage, unlike her sister Anne, who viewed her stepmother with apprehension.

As a family-oriented woman, Mary was torn by the conflicting loyalties of family and politics that the Glorious Revolution imposed upon her, which made it impossible for her to be a good daughter and a good wife at the same time. After James II left England in December 1688, effectively vacating his throne, Mary arrived in England from Holland at the beginning of 1689 just as the debates between William and the convention of estates concerning the British succession were concluded. But Mary found it difficult to appear joyous on the eve of her accession, and she took very hard the criticism of her as an ungrateful and traitorous daughter. Nevertheless, Mary possessed the kind of nativist political capital enjoyed by Elizabeth of York as an English-born princess, which she deployed to ensure that William would be king, making it clear to the Convention Parliament that she would not accept anything less. In the Declaration of Right, later enacted into statute as the Bill of Rights, William and Mary were offered the crown jointly, a constitutional anomaly never repeated.[103]

Tudor queenship loomed large in the deliberations concerning the succession. William's known desire to possess a full-fledged kingship needed to be made compatible with the Tudor-era precedents regarding female rule, which recognized a woman's ability to inherit and wield the kingly office even if they were married.[104] Thus, Mary's was a hybrid queenship, one formulated to satisfy immediate political concerns. To Tories able to stomach the disbarment of the infant Prince of Wales, Mary was unquestionably the hereditary claimant as the Convention claimed the right to confer upon William a form of crown matrimonial, granting to him alone the powers and prerogatives of kingship which had accrued to Mary by hereditary right. To Whigs, however, William and Mary and their heir Anne were unquestionably parliamentary monarchs, whose legitimacy derived primarily from the succession provisions of the Bill of Rights. But to the nation at large, William III and Mary II were a pair of unquestionably *Protestant* monarchs, the first occasion when both the king and queen of England and Scotland were both Protestants since the advent of the Reformation.

Despite the "jointness" of their reign, William III and Mary II separately presented different conceptions of monarchy to their subjects. Although unimpressive physically, William was primarily a warrior king, bringing England into the European coalition fighting Louis XIV of France during the Nine Years War. While William appreciated the resources England brought to bear, he had little patience for either party politics or the processes of parliament, with little desire to socialize with his subjects, and he lacked the kind of personality conducive to courting popularity. After defeating James II in Ireland in 1690, William spent most summers for the remainder of his reign fighting the Nine Years War against Louis XIV on the continent.

This left Mary with considerable latitude to create the public face of their joint reign. The religion of the monarch was just one of many issues decided during the Glorious Revolution, which reinstated queenly religiosity as a means to enhance rather than detract from the creation of a queenly reputation. Publicly, Mary embodied the role of consort, making clear her distaste for politics, and practicing an ostentatious piety that positively resonated with large segments of the British public, while creating a model of marital domesticity and moral probity not seen since the days of Charles I and Henrietta Maria. At the same time, Mary followed in the Stuart queenly tradition in the attention she paid to royal adornment. As Rachel Weil has argued, not since Elizabeth I had a queen found the balance between representing herself as an object of courtly love and a semi-deified paragon of virtue with such precision.[105]

Mary's grasp of her unique role within her and William's joint reign also allowed her to negotiate the constitutional ambiguities of a queen regnant who reigned but did not rule both seamlessly and flawlessly.[106] The issue first arose in 1690, when parliament passed a regency bill that vested Mary with full regal power in conjunction with a nine-man council when William was out of the country. In doing so, Parliament was simply codifying long-established precedent reaching back to Matilda of Flanders, Catherine of Aragon, and Katherine Parr, experienced queens capable of handling the reins of the kingly office when necessary. As she exercised regal authority, Mary II's approach was reflective of that of Mary I. Mary II squared her exercise of regal power with conventional notions of womanhood, which required wives to be subservient to their husbands, while behind closed doors exercising a decisive influence when William was out of the country, issuing proclamations combatting vice and licentiousness, and on one occasion arresting her own cousin, the Earl of Clarendon, for treason.

There does seem to be some disconnect between Mary's advertised wifely distaste for politics and the performance of her duties as regent. Contemporaries considered that Mary exercised these powers quite effectively, but also noted how quickly she ceded the spotlight back to William when he returned from campaigning, when she returned effortlessly to the role of a gracious and deferential consort, performing fancy needlework with her ladies in a time-honored queenly fashion. In terms of her queenship, if we consider Mary to have been a consort possessed with a regnal title, she was the most powerful female consort since the eleventh-century Matilda of Flanders, in terms of the political power she exercised on behalf of her husband.

The only chink in her queenly armor derived from her publicly tempestuous relationship with her sister Anne, who reluctantly accepted her place in the succession after William. In 1692, when Anne's chief lieutenant and advisor, John Churchill, was accused of corruption, and Anne refused to dismiss his wife Sarah from her service, a rupture occurred in the sisters' relationship. It remained unresolved when Mary died suddenly of smallpox in December 1694 at the age of thirty-two. She was the most eulogized Stuart queen of the seventeenth century, who created a queenship much more in sync with the national sentiment than any of her recent predecessors. This was in fact the most enduring aspect of her legacy, as her successors for the remainder of the early modern era in Britain recognized the primacy of the Protestant religion, the force of public opinion, and the utility of cultivating such queenly attributes as being good wives and mothers who led exemplary lives filled with piety and moral probity.

This was most evident in the reign of Anne, the last of the Stuarts, who succeeded William III as a *bona fide* queen regnant in 1702. Only recently has Anne been considered to be more than just a competent queen; her historical reputation has been in a process of constant refinement since the publication of Sarah Churchill's 1742 memoir, *An Account of the Conduct of the Dowager Duchess of Marlborough*, a damning, self-serving account of Anne's allegedly grave social and political deficiencies, published nearly thirty years after her death, which characterized her as lacking intelligence and confidence coupled with an inordinate need to rely on others.[107] Subsequent Whig historians, who suspected her of harboring Jacobite sympathies, gave Anne very little credit for the accomplishments of her reign, which witnessed a flowering of English arts, letters, and science coupled with a quantum leap in British imperial might and wealth.[108]

By the later twentieth century, Anne's performance as queen began to be viewed in a much more favorable light, but she has never attracted much sympathy as a biographical subject.[109] While her sister Mary was gay and vivacious, and considered a great beauty, Anne was much more reserved and less outgoing. Perhaps more than any other British queen, Anne suffered formidable physical challenges, including an eye condition that gave her a weepy, myopic look. She also inherited the propensity for gout and lameness that had plagued both Mary of Guise and Mary Queen of Scots, as well as obesity, no doubt aggravated by a nearly continuous series of pregnancies over a seventeen-year period, following her marriage to Prince George of Denmark in 1683 at the age of eighteen.

But Anne never let her physical challenges get in the way of pursuing her queenly objectives, bringing an entirely different attitude to her dynastic prospects than her sister Mary, whose approach to queenship mirrored her position as a dutiful and obedient wife. In contrast, Anne was the dominant partner in her marriage to Prince George, who was amiable but shy and lacked any political ambitions, making him the ideal consort in waiting as Anne looked forward to her own "sunshine day" when she would be a queen regnant.[110] When it became clear that William and Mary would not produce children, Anne and George stepped in to provide for a Protestant succession, ultimately with tragic results, with only one child, William, Duke of Gloucester, born 1689, surviving infancy. Even more so than William and Mary, Anne and George presented the image of a loving, companionate, and monogamous marriage, a conventional means for achieving prestige and popularity for a queen in waiting.

While presenting the public image of a virtuous and devoted wife, Anne remained focused on her dynastic prospects, refusing to attend the birth of the Prince of Wales in June 1688 and then suggesting to her sister Mary that the baby was an imposter, smuggled into the birthing chamber in a warming pan, a patent falsehood that flew in the face of conclusive evidence to the contrary. Abandoning her father apparently caused Anne much less grief than it did her sister, and she gave her full support to the Convention Parliament that recognized her as William and Mary's successor. But relations between William and Mary and Anne quickly deteriorated, as Anne cultivated her own political following, with John Churchill as her chief lieutenant, obtaining a measure of financial independence from Parliament as William blackballed Prince George from participating in military affairs in retaliation. William and Anne formally reconciled after Mary's death in 1694, but Anne remained very much on the outside of his administration, although she functioned as a hostess for various court occasions, playing the role of a quasi-consort.

Quite unlike her sister Mary II, who embodied wifely subservience within her queenship, Anne was intent on wielding a queenly prerogative like that of Elizabeth I within the context of her companionate marriage. Prior to her accession, George of Denmark had been useful as a political proxy, enjoying honorific positions such as being created a Garter knight by Charles II and taking a seat in the House of Lords as Duke of Cumberland, while Anne embodied her wifely virtues as Princess of Denmark. But following William's death in 1702, Anne was freed from the shackles of female coverture, creating a bold new precedent by denying her husband royal status as a king, as the wives of kings assumed when they were crowned alongside their husbands as queens. Instead, Prince George remained simply the Duke of Cumberland, standing on the sidelines as Anne was crowned Queen. It is not perfectly clear why this occurred; Anne possessed ample prerogative to make her husband a king if she had wanted to, yet George's personality, his lack of ambition, and his declining health may have been the factors that led Anne to deny her husband the kind of king consortship that Philip of Spain had enjoyed during his marriage to Mary I.[111] But Anne ameliorated the potential social fallout from the obvious disparity in status between herself and her husband by playing up her role as a devoted wife, lobbying to have George named commander in chief of the European coalition forces fighting Louis XIV. Denied this, Anne made her husband Lord High Admiral and generalissimo of all English land forces and pushed a bill through parliament granting George an astounding £100,000 annuity in case he outlived her. For his part, George of Denmark played his role nicely, smiling and deferential, as a form of unofficial male version of a queen consort until his death in 1708.

In this sense, Anne had it all, a ruling queen like Elizabeth I, with a supportive and loving spouse by her side, the exact opposite of the William and Mary marital dynamic. Like all successful female rulers, Anne's recognized that queenly success depended on embodying positive womanly virtues. In his coronation sermon, Archbishop of York John Sharpe described Anne as a nursing mother to her kingdom, reminiscent of both Mary I and Elizabeth I's identifications as symbolic mothers to their people. Although she was a childless queen, Anne looked the part of a maternal figure, as Victoria would later do in the nineteenth century, exuding a decidedly matronly vision of queenship. Anne was a strict "mother" to her people; moral probity and sobriety were perennial themes echoed in her proclamations, while Anne also participated in many of the ritualistic features of queenship, making pilgrimages, declaring fasts, presiding over thanksgivings, such as the one to commemorate the Act of Union in 1707, as well as opening parliaments and leading public processions commemorating English victories in the War of the Spanish Succession.

Anne also took her religious duties as queen seriously, making the defense of the established church a significant aspect of her queenship. Indeed, no monarch after her played such as a hands-on role in their capacity as supreme governor of the established church. Anne's zeal for the established church prevented her from having any sympathy for her younger half-brother James, the "Old Pretender," who refused to convert to Protestantism. Anne also revived, for the last time, touching for scrofula, the "king's evil," tapping into the mystical elements of regnant queenship appropriated by her Tudor predecessors Mary I and Elizabeth I. Anne participated in these acts of royal theatre despite her physical challenges, demonstrating her flair for encasing her kingly prerogative within the public face of her queenship and making this otherwise physically challenged woman into a popular and esteemed monarch; few saw her, as Sir John Penecuik did in 1706, immobile and writhing in agony with an attack of gout. As Robert O. Bucholz has argued, Anne's womanly virtues contributed to her popularity, which may have simultaneously obscured her agency in the major accomplishments of her reign.[112]

Anne only failure as queen was the inability to further the Stuart dynasty through the female line. Her seventeen pregnancies only produced one child to survive infancy, the duke of Gloucester, who died at age eleven in 1701. In response Parliament passed the Act of Settlement, which settled the succession on the House of Hanover, Protestant descendants of James I. Anne may have been the last of the Stuarts, but her performance as queen anticipated the future in terms of the relationship between monarch, parliament, and party politics that characterized the reigns of her successors George I and II. In terms of foreign affairs, Anne remained focused on Britain's position within a globalized European balance of power, championing Britain's own far-flung economic and strategic imperatives, making her the most bellicose of British ruling queens, authorizing and sustaining a supreme war effort in the midst of virulent party politics. Yet no one ever accused her of being a virago, a final testament to her ability to cloak her kingly prerogative in the trappings of decidedly maternal yet effective queenship, which was perhaps the most successful of the Stuart dynasty in Britain.

GERMANIC QUEENSHIP UNDER CAROLINE OF ANSBACH AND CHARLOTTE OF MECKLENBURG STRELITZ

When he became king in 1714, George I arrived in Britain accompanied by his long-time female companions, Madame Kielmansegge, and Madame Schulenburg, later created Duchess of Kendal, who had borne him three illegitimate children. George I was not concerned with making his royal court an example of royal virtue as Anne had, or as a strategy to create and deploy royal influence within a parliamentary-dominated political culture. He was thoroughly Germanic in his tastes, decidedly anti-intellectual, and lacking artistic refinements. George I remained focused on his role in the politics of the Holy Roman Empire as Elector of Hanover while acquiescing to what became known as the Whig Oligarchy, which controlled parliament until the accession of George III in 1760, making the Tories both a form of permanent party in opposition, as well as the natural political allies for disgruntled members of the Hanoverian royal family. This left his eldest son and heir, George Augustus, and his wife, Caroline of Ansbach, created Prince and Princess of Wales soon after their arrival in Britain, with the task of winning over the British people to the Hanoverian dynasty.[113] Their success in this regard was largely due to the multifaceted efforts of the ambitious, creative, and charismatic Caroline, who created the most powerful queenship of any early modern British consort.[114]

Caroline came to her marriage through the nexus of Germanic dynastic politics. She was the daughter of Frederick William, Margrave of Brandenburg-Ansbach, a cadet branch of the Hohenzollern royal family. The

Hohenzollern's relationship to the Prussian royal court in Berlin provided the context for Caroline to be considered as a potential bride for George Augustus; he was impressed with the lively, witty, and attractive young woman, who, from the time of her marriage in 1705, had plenty of time to plan for her eventual accession as queen of Great Britain. Like the marriages of Charles I and Henrietta Maria and later George III and Charlotte of Mecklenburg-Strelitz, George Augustus and Caroline's marriage was a thoroughly companionate one, as the business of their royal relationship mixed with the obvious pleasure they took in each other's company. Most importantly, Caroline fulfilled her dynastic responsibilities; she had ten recorded pregnancies, with seven children, two sons and five daughters, living to adulthood.

While they were propagating their dynasty, George Augustus and Caroline received a constant stream of British political, intellectual, and artistic visitors in the final years of Anne's reign, such as the Duke of Marlborough, The Earl of Clarendon, and his secretary, poet John Gay, who offered Caroline tutorials on the London social scene. In this way, Caroline began the process of creating relationships within and acculturating herself to British society, including a crash course in conversational English.[115] By the time she arrived in London in 1714, Caroline seamlessly stepped into the role of Princess of Wales, the first woman to do so since Catherine of Aragon more than two centuries earlier, using the role as an apprenticeship for her later queenship.[116]

If Caroline appeared to be more conscious of what it took to be a popular and influential queen than earlier Tudor or Stuart queen consorts, she also lived in a world in which much larger segments of the British public were aware of the monarchy and its workings, as expanding forms of literacy gave way to ever evolving forms of print media. Pamphlets, scandal sheets, periodical literature, and novels created a wide variety of impressions and characterizations of the Hanoverian monarchy, for better and for worse. For her part, Caroline quite obviously put much thought into devising a strategy that would make her queenship successful and powerful. Her tutelage under both Queen Sophia Charlotte of Prussia and her husband's grandmother the Electress Sophia instilled in her a conception of queenship that went far beyond the social or the ornamental. While Caroline was very much a woman of her times, keeping abreast of the latest intellectual, artistic, and scientific developments, the basic categories to measure queenly success had remained roughly the same over the course of the early modern era: to adopt the language and culture of their kingdom, to bear heirs to continue the dynasty, and to be supportive of the king and create a sense of domestic harmony.[117] A successful queen also possessed an impeccable character, dispensing charity, guarding her chastity and moral behavior, setting an example of queenly yet

Protestant piety, serving as intercessor between king and subjects, patronizing artists and scholars, and serving as the arbitress of fashion and taste at the royal court. More than any other early modern British consort, Caroline accomplished all these queenly goals.

At the same time, Caroline was a shrewd political animal who grasped that the lack of continental-style regal authority could be compensated for by royal influence and patronage directed towards the ruling and propertied classes represented in the House of Commons, which provided the funding for the maintenance of the monarchy through the medium of the Civil List. While still Princess of Wales, Carolina had already forged a working relationship with Robert Walpole, the most successful parliamentary manager of the eighteenth century, usually called Britain's first prime minister, who was a dominant figure in parliamentary politics until his death in 1745. The Prince and Princess of Wales's court was informal and vibrant, centered in Leicester House in London and Richmond Lodge in Kew, as Caroline formed relationships with artists, scholars, inventors, and the women of the political elite, who took positive impressions of Caroline home with them to their husbands.[118]

Once on the throne in 1727, Caroline's queenly agenda was ambitious, influencing parliamentary politics, patronizing artists and scholars, encouraging industrial and commercial enterprises, and serving as the arbitress of the London social scene. A number of contemporaries believed that Caroline was the true power and brains behind the throne, as a contemporary satire maintained; "You may strut, dapper George, but 'twill all be in vain, We all know 'tis Queen Caroline, not you, that reign."[119] What is much more certain is that Caroline enjoyed her husband's trust, affection, and confidence for the duration of their marriage. She did this by being a companionate wife and a good mother and by accommodating her husband's sexual predilections as no consort had quite done before.

It was the rare queen in Early Modern Europe who did not have to deal with kingly infidelity. British queens from Catherine of Aragon to Mary of Modena occasionally betrayed their anger towards kingly infidelity, but Caroline remained on amicable terms with women such as Henriette Howard, George II's long-time mistress. This was an entirely pragmatic approach to the most endemic of situations straining the relationships of early modern kings and queens, although Caroline kept her husband's mistresses on a short leash within the royal court. It appears that Caroline recognized the distinction between the sex her husband desired with other women, and their marital partnership, which included a physical component but encompassed so much more, including political counsel and influence, delivered and exercised in the queen's bedchamber. Only in the last year of her life did she object to her husband's final mistress, Amalie von Wallmoden, yet upon her deathbed, when she suggested George should marry again, he refused to consider the notion and remained true to his word for the rest of his life.

As Caroline of Ansbach anglicized the Hanoverian monarchy, her successor, Charlotte of Mecklenburg-Strelitz, reinvested it with its Germanic roots. When George III succeeded his long-widowed grandfather George II in 1760 at the age of twenty-two, the search for a consort began immediately. George III embraced the bride chosen for him, Charlotte of Mecklenburg-Strelitz, a seventeen-year-old daughter of a minor northern German princeling, selected because she would have no experience with politics or party intrigue, a decision perhaps taken in reaction to Caroline of Ansbach's highly politicized queenship. She had not been well educated either, perhaps yet another reason why she was chosen as consort, and she willingly obliged her husband's request to not meddle in politics.[120]

The success of George and Charlotte's marriage, at least for the first twenty-six years, was a testament to their mutual devotion to duty; they first met on the day of their marriage and were crowned together two weeks later in September 1762. As often happens in marriages of this kind, devotion to duty turned into devotion to each other; the marriage was entirely companionate, resulting in a record-breaking thirteen children surviving to adulthood. In marked contrast to his Stuart and Hanoverian forbears, George III remained sexually faithful to Charlotte, a testament to the moral characters of both. Charlotte in turn cultivated the image of a devoted mother, a perennial means of creating queenly prestige, with pastoral-like scenes with her children comprising the dominant theme of her portraiture.

In the scholarly tradition of her illustrious predecessor, Charlotte continued her education after becoming queen, with a particular interest in science, endeavoring to become an enlightened queen by participating in what Clarissa Campbell Orr has termed a northern republic of letters, fusing her dynastic connections with the royal houses of Germany and Denmark with an intellectual exchange of philosophical and scientific learning and Christian piety conducted within a culture of rational domesticity.[121] Within this context, Charlotte put her enlightened rational piety to work in her acts of charity, particularly in her penchant for establishing orphanages. While her motives were undoubtedly sincere, this was a perennial means to earn queenly prestige; at the end of her life she established a hospital in London for expectant mothers, still operating today as Queen Charlotte's and Chelsea Hospital.

But Charlotte's insular and domesticated queenship was thrust into the open glare of public opinion when George III began to suffer from what is

believed to be the effects of porphyria in 1788, which incapacitated him, forcing a regency crisis that exposed the fissures within the royal family, whose
public image had been crafted as a model of familial harmony. George and
Charlotte set a high bar for moral probity for their children, keeping their six
daughters at court under their watchful eyes long past marriageable age, while
the sons by and large failed to live up to their standards. The Prince of Wales
was the worst offender, racking up gambling debts and taking a common-
law wife. The prince emerged as an oppositional figure in the regency crisis
of 1788, which pitted Charlotte's queenship between radical Whig politician
Charles James Fox, who argued that the prince should assume full regal
power, and William Pitt the Younger, determined to set parliamentary limits
upon any proposed regency. It was revealing of Charlotte's thoroughly domesticated conception of her queenship that she refused to consider herself as a
candidate for a regency, as many of her predecessors had been, most recently
Caroline of Ansbach, whom George II had left in power during his absences
on the continent in place of his eldest son the Prince of Wales. Instead, in
the compromise worked out in parliament in 1789, Charlotte retained control over her household and the person of the king, the only forms of power
Charlotte desired. But before the bill could take effect, George III recovered, at
least temporarily, effectively tabling the issue of a regency for another twenty
years.

But Charlotte's queenship did not recover. As the French Revolution and
the Napoleonic wars that followed shattered queenships all over Europe,
Charlotte eventually becoming unable to handle George III's increasingly
erratic behavior. He suffered relapses for the remainder of his life until he
became completely incapacitated in 1811, necessitating a formal regency
assumed by the Prince of Wales, although Charlotte remained his legal guardian until her death in 1818, which earned her the distinction as the longest-
reigning queen consort in English and British history at fifty-six years. Yet
her fame as a queen never matched the duration of her queenship. This was
a testament perhaps to her desire to eschew the type of political dimension
many previous queen consorts had sought as she delineated the distinctions
between the public and private functions of her queenship, attitudes presag-
ing the modern era that had already begun by the time of her death. But her
legacy lives on, in the gardens and decorations of Frogmore House at Windsor,
in the botanical gardens at Kew, in the names of numerous towns, cities, and
islands around the globe, and in the paintings that depict a contented and
devoted wife, which created a public image of domestic harmony and moral
probity that Queen Victoria and all the subsequent Windsor queens of the
twentieth century have sought to emulate.

CONCLUSION

Over the course of the early modern period, British queenship went through several distinct phases. In the sixteenth century, Tudor queenship was primarily a domestic affair. Out of nine queens, seven were queens consort, and two were queens regnant, with only two foreign-born queens. Of the seven native-born queens, three were the daughters of kings, while the remaining four derived from the aristocracy and gentry classes, making Tudor consortship relatively free of foreign influences, although Catherine of Aragon and Anne Boleyn brought continental understandings to their queenships. This type of domesticated queenship continued under Mary I, whose reign broadened the meaning of English queenship, as she and her successor Elizabeth I were considered within Tudor political theory to have combined the body politic of kingship with the body natural of a woman. Both women were also queens, performing a broad array of queenly functions, surrounded by women in their privy chambers. Nevertheless, they diverged on the question of marriage; while Mary chose her own husband, Elizabeth I effectively ruled simultaneously as king and queen, avoiding both marriage and naming a successor while presiding over "the Elizabethan Age," as England experienced the full flowering of the European Renaissance. Elizabeth's decision to remain unmarried was quite influential on later unmarried European queens regnant.

In contrast, sixteenth-century Scottish queenship was entirely a foreign affair, as was common on the European continent, with Margaret Tudor of England and Mary of Guise of France bringing English and French understandings of queenship to Scotland. Both were widowed as mothers of infant monarchs, but while Margaret chose to remarry, which destabilized her regency, Mary of Guise remained unmarried and entirely fixated on preserving her daughter's Scottish throne. Mary Queen of Scots went through several phases of queenship, as a minority queen regnant, queen consort of France, and ruling queen of Scotland. Mary's queenships were as wide ranging as European queenship could get, playing the role of minority queen, consort of France, queen regnant, and later dowager of Scotland. Anne of Denmark brought a particularly Danish approach to queenship that put her at odds with her husband, James VI, particularly over the raising of their children. Nevertheless, in the face of James's relationships with his male favorites, Anne carved out an autonomous queenship for herself in the breadth of her patronage of the visual arts and architecture. Anne also converted to Catholicism, creating a pattern for her seventeenth-century successors as British queens consort, Henrietta Maria, Catherine of Braganza, and Mary of Modena, all of whom reigned as the Catholic queens of two Protestant kingdoms. Nevertheless, all of Britain's seventeenth-century Catholic queen consorts were champions in creating forms of material culture and patrons of the visual and musical arts, adding cultural pollinator to the resumé of British queenship.[122]

Like the Tudor dynasty, the Stuart dynasty came to an end with two queens regnant. In many respects, Mary II was a quasi-consort, in that full regal power was reserved to her husband William III in the Glorious Revolution settlement. Mary, however, created the public face of their joint reign, enjoying the most popular British queenship since Elizabeth I. Anne's succeeding queenship was also popular, as she strove to create an autonomous regnant queenship while enjoying a thoroughly companionate marriage. With her death in 1714, British queenship made a turn for the Germanic with the succession of the House of Hanover. While Caroline of Ansbach and Charlotte of Mecklenburg-Strelitz both enjoyed companionate marriages with George II and George III, they offered contrasting versions of queenship. Caroline was educated and outgoing, working hard to become Anglicized before her arrival in England. She was also a politically minded queen, who succeeded in all the categories of queenly achievement, making her the most powerful and influential of early modern British consorts. Charlotte's queenship was also successful, but in a much more traditional vein. In fact, the areas where Charlotte succeeded, in creating a companionate marriage, bearing the royal heirs, and demonstrating piety and a charitable concern for her subjects, sound remarkably like the pattern for success followed by Elizabeth of York nearly three centuries earlier.

3 Anne of Austria and Franco-Iberian Queenship

On June 9, 1660, Anne of Austria attended the marriage of her son, twenty-one-year-old King Louis XIV of France, to her niece, the Spanish *Infanta* Maria Theresa, the daughter of her brother, King Philip IV of Spain. Anne herself had helped broker the marriage, which sealed a peace between France and Spain she had long sought to bring about.[1] Two days previously, Anne had met her niece at the Franco-Iberian border, on the same bridge she herself had crossed over to France from forty-five years previously, offering her affection and keeping her close at hand, in the bosom of her family, until the nuptials were celebrated at Saint Jean de Luz. With these activities concluded, Anne relinquished the queenly spotlight to her daughter-in-law as the marriage celebrations continued in Bordeaux and then in Paris.[2] Nevertheless, in her final years, Anne enjoyed a level of popularity across France that had eluded her for most of her queenship, a testament to both her patience and her tenacity.

THE QUEENSHIP OF ANNE OF AUSTRIA

Like Mary Queen of Scots and many other early modern queens, Anne of Austria's queenship went through several distinct phases.[3] Born a Spanish *infanta* in 1601, her mother Margaret was a Habsburg Austrian Archduchess, whose marriage to Philip III of Spain (r. 1598–1621) was characteristic of the perennial inter-breeding between the Spanish and Austrian royal families. Both of her parents were intensely religious, reflective of the ideals of the Counter-Reformation, and Anne's education was focused on developing her personal piety, a quality that occupied a large share of her queenly persona, which was a conventional means to earn queenly prestige.[4]

When Habsburg Spanish monarchs fought their Valois and Bourbon counterparts, their queens often played the roles of conciliators and peacemakers, as ties of blood competed with national loyalties for the hearts and minds of French and Spanish queens. The experience of Anne of Austria is a prime example of this particular conundrum of queenship. Her marriage had been negotiated when she was eleven, part of a double arrangement that saw Louis XIII's sister Elisabeth married to Anne's brother the future Philip IV of Spain.[5] As daughters of the two premier royal houses of Europe, both Anne and Elisabeth were taught from an early age to be proud of their lineage, which complicated their training as future queens; Spanish and French princesses were routinely expected to use their influence as queens to promote the interests of their natal countries with their husband as well as their children.

The marriage was reportedly consummated the evening following the wedding, but afterwards Louis chose not to cohabitate with Anne for several years, delaying the process of propagating the dynasty. Although their youth and respective physical developments may have called for patience, the emotional bonds characteristic of so many royal marriages never seemed to develop between the king and queen. Their efforts to procreate were sporadic over the duration of their marriage, with a series of miscarriages in the early years of their marriage. At the same time, steps taken to create conjugal understanding were complicated by Anne's devotion to her family and their interests, which was at odds with chief minister Cardinal Armand Jean du Plessis Richelieu's foreign policy.[6]

Under these conditions, Anne withered on the sidelines, comforted by the Spanish members of her household, without making any significant efforts to adapt to her new home. Her husband was inclined to be dominated by royal favorites, first by Charles d'Albert, Duke of Luynes, and then Cardinal Richelieu, who got his start in royal service as a protégé of Anne's mother-in-law, dowager queen Marie de Medici, as well as serving as Anne's first almoner, an irony not lost on either woman. Saddled with a moody and petulant husband, Anne's inability to create a companionate marriage contributed to her public persona as a marginalized, foreign queen.[7] Denied access to patronage, all she could do as queen was to create a reputation for queenly religiosity. But her persistence in communicating with the Spanish and Imperial royal families, under Richelieu's unceasing gaze, contributed to the continued friction between the royal couple.

Despite all this friction, there were still attempts at propagating the dynasty. At the end of 1637, Anne conceived again and in September 1638 gave birth to a son, the future Louis XIV. Two years later she delivered another, Philippe, later Duke of Orleans. The births of her sons ensured her future in France, but they failed to create any form of emotional intimacy with Louis, perennially incensed with Anne's continued efforts to correspond with the Spanish court. By 1643, as Louis entered his final illness, the king was convinced Anne would revert to a pro-Spanish policy once he was dead, and he labored to make her projected regency as powerless as possible, despite precedents in France, reaching back to the thirteenth century, for a queen mother to wield regal authority during the minority of her son.

But despite a lack of administrative or executive experience, upon Louis XIII's death (May 14, 1643) Anne traded the sumptuous queenly attire of her consortship for the widow's weeds of her dowager queenship, which broadcast to the kingdom the kinship ties to both the dead and the underage king. But she gave herself little time to grieve, passing on the customary forty days of secluded mourning to overthrow the limited regency devised by Louis, replaced by a much more powerful one, which had the official backing of the 4 ½-year-old Louis XIV. In a *lit de justice* held on May 18, 1643, Anne was invested as regent for the underage Louis XIV.

As we have seen in sixteenth-century Scotland, there were two options for a dowager queen wishing to exercise power during her son's royal minority; to remarry to a powerful male ally or remain a widow. Anne chose a third option, remaining unmarried and emphasizing her role as a dutiful widowed mother, yet choosing a male favorite to help her rule, a particularly Spanish approach to rule, as the role of the male favorite, or *valido*, became well entrenched in the seventeenth-century Spanish monarchy. Those expecting a wholesale purge of Richelieu's former cronies were shocked when Anne announced Jules Raymond Mazarin, a former Italian papal envoy who had become Richelieu's protégé, would remain in her newly constituted regency council. Like Mary of Guise in Scotland, Anne sought a middle ground, endeavoring to rise above the fierce rivalries that always accompany royal minorities, rewarding her own friends yet not seeking retribution against Richelieu's family and clients.[8]

Created a cardinal in 1639, Mazarin obviously played a major role in these critical decisions. Anne and Mazarin certainly worked well together, quite unlike the experience of Louis XIII and Richelieu, who often treated the King with undisguised contempt.[9] In contrast, Mazarin was pleasant and deferential to the Queen, patiently serving as her political tutor, and guiding her through the events that brought her full regal power. In turn, Anne handed over control of Louis's education to Mazarin, who grounded the young king in the realities of European politics and the expansiveness of his own royal position. If the key to running a successful minority regime is to enjoy the confidence of the maturing king, Anne and Mazarin's regency can be considered a success.

If anything, it was perhaps too successful; later, during the series of revolts known as the Fronde (1648–1653), a number of the *mazarinades*, a series of pamphlets attacking the regency, accused the pair of being lovers, or even being secretly married.[10] These printed broadsides were often written in pornographic and scatological terms, an almost textbook means of besmirching the reputation of a widowed queen, whose exemplary and undoubtedly sincere religiosity makes it unlikely that anything more than a successful political partnership existed between Anne and Mazarin.[11] Rumors of a secret morganatic marriage between them were reflective of contemporary notions that a still relatively youthful widowed queen would not be able to control her sexual urges.

Unfortunately, despite his administrative talent, Mazarin, like so many other brilliant royal servants, was rapacious, depicted in the press as an Italian carpetbagger, who enriched his own Italian kinsmen at the expense of the French. This was aggravated by the crushing demand for further taxation for the war effort; even after the Peace of Westphalia (1648) which ended the Thirty Years War, the war with Spain continued.[12] Yet Anne and Mazarin pressed ahead despite the negative press; apparently Mazarin was able to convince Anne that continuing the policies of Louis XIII and Richelieu, including the war with Spain, was in the best interests of her son's kingship. With the conclusion of peace with Spain in 1659, Anne achieved what she could not while Louis XIII lived, to once again enjoy cordial relations with her natal family. Following Mazarin's death in 1661 she retreated to her beloved Val-de-Grace, the church she had built on a Benedictine monastery, where she died five years later of breast cancer. She was interred next to her husband in the royal vault at St. Denis, outside of Paris, fully his equal in death as a ruler of France.

SIXTEENTH-CENTURY HABSBURG/VALOIS RIVALRY

Anne of Austria's role as a peacemaker was typical of the early modern queens of Spain and France, which, during the sixteenth and seventeenth centuries, were the most powerful kingdoms in Western Europe. It is a paradox of the history of queenship that nations which frequently fought each other also engaged in a large measure of dynastic intermarriage; during the Middle Ages as England and France fought the Hundred Years Wars, English kings frequently took French princesses for brides, while among the Iberian kingdoms of Castile, Portugal, Aragon, and Navarre there was such frequent dynastic intermarriage that it practically bordered on the incestuous, policies that continued under the Spanish and Austrian Habsburgs.

By the beginning of the early modern era, both Spain and France had experienced large measures of dynastic consolidation. Medieval France was characterized by largely autonomous feudatories, but following the mid-fifteenth-century victory over England in the Hundred Years War, only

Brittany and Burgundy were left as independent duchies. The Valois kings Louis XI (r. 1461–1483), Charles VIII (r. 1483–1498), and Louis XII (r. 1498–1515) all labored to consolidate their control over these regions. Louis XI did his best to obtain Duchess Mary of Burgundy (1457–1482) as the wife for his heir Charles. But Mary selected Maximilian, a Habsburg Austrian Archduke, a marriage with fateful consequences for both France and Spain. Maximilian later became Holy Roman Emperor in 1486, but by this time Mary was dead, after bearing a son, Philip, and a daughter, Margaret.

Maximilian later sought the hand of Anne of Brittany (1477–1514), the daughter and heir of Duke Francis II, the other of France's independent feudatories, while his daughter Margaret of Austria was affianced to Charles VIII of France, who succeeded as a minor in 1483.[13] Following the death of Francis II of Brittany in 1488 and Anne's accession as duchess, Anne de Beaujeu, *de facto* regent of France, became alarmed when Anne became betrothed to Maximilian, whom she married by proxy in 1490. The next year, however, Charles VIII invaded Brittany and swiftly married fourteen-year-old Anne before Pope Innocent VIII could annul Anne's previous proxy marriage to Maximilian and his own betrothal to Maximilian's daughter Margaret, who left the French court in tears after spending much of her childhood there. After being required to present herself naked before Charles's representatives, who assessed her potential for childbearing, Anne brought her own bed to the wedding in protest.

Anne went through several phases of queenship. Like his father, Louis XI, Charles VIII had little use for his queen other than her childbearing duties. These were ultimately unsuccessful, with no living children by the time of Charles's death in 1498, despite seven pregnancies. While Anne mourned her husband, she swiftly moved to recover control over Brittany, where she was welcomed as duchess, convening the estates as their sovereign ruler. At the same time, she entered into negotiations with Charles's successor, Louis XII, to become queen of France for the second time, as stipulated in the terms of her first marriage contract. This time, as a rather seasoned twenty-one-year-old widow, she was a party to the negotiations, which allowed her to remain in control of Brittany, including stipulations regarding the Breton succession. Schooled in the harsh realities of Franco-Breton politics from an early age, Anne realized that her position as Queen of France offered her the best opportunity to retain control over her duchy. For his part, Louis XII treated Anne with much more consideration than his predecessor. Both were able to create the perception that they had affection for one another, although Louis had to negotiate a rather sordid annulment from his first wife, Jeanne, the daughter of Louis XI and Anne's former sister-in-law. The magnificence of her funeral was a testament to Louis XII's abiding affection for his queen as well as an indicator of the prestige and influence of her queenship.[14]

Like her contemporaries Isabella of Castile and Elizabeth of York, Anne set a standard for queenly achievement. She was a Renaissance queen; her ducal and royal courts were filled with Italian humanists and artists, and as queen she was sought after as a patron of both scholarship and the arts, personally decorating the chateaux at Blois and Amboise with Renaissance magnificence.[15] As Cynthia Brown has argued, Anne's library, filled with books she had commissioned and books that were dedicated to her, was an effective form of image and legacy making.[16] Her religiosity was also part of this process; knowing full well the power of queenly chastity and moral probity, she exerted a powerful, if heavy-handed, control over the young noble women who were educated in her royal household. Her cultivation of the image of Saint Anne, the mother of the Virgin Mary, was reflective of the conventional means to earn queenly prestige, while literary and visual representations of biblical figures such as Esther, whose mercy tempered the rigor of King Ahasuerus, also were used to bolster Anne's authority as queen.[17]

Despite her wide ranging queenly and ducal duties and interests, Anne took her childbearing duties seriously, with a total of sixteen pregnancies over the course of her two marriages, with only two daughters from her second marriage, Claude and Renee, surviving to adulthood. Because of the Salic law, neither could succeed to the French throne. They were, however, able to succeed to the ducal throne of Brittany. Wishing to preserve Breton autonomy, Anne betrothed Claude to Charles of Castile, the future Emperor Charles V, meeting with his parents, Philip and Juana of Castile, in Lyon in 1503. But Louis XII broke the engagement and eventually married Claude to Francis of Angouleme, her father's successor, which finally bound Brittany to the French crown. Following Anne's death in 1514, Louis XII married the eighteen-year-old English princess Mary Tudor, in the vain hope of gaining a male heir. But after less than three months of festivities following his marriage, Louis XII died in January 1515. But despite their differences over the marriage of their daughter Claude, Anne and Louis, as Kathleen Wellman has noted, were the last pre-revolutionary king and queen to forge both a personal and a political partnership within their marriage

The Iberian kingdoms – Castile, Aragon, Navarre, and Portugal – also went through a late medieval process of dynastic consolidation. For centuries these kingdoms had blended rather intense forms of intermarriage, including uncle-niece unions, with marriages within the wider pan-European royal kinship network. By the beginning of the sixteenth century, the Portuguese House of Aziz was deeply intertwined dynastically with the offspring of

Isabella and Ferdinand, while Navarre saw its lands south of the Pyrenees confiscated by Aragon as its ruling house later acquired the French crown in 1589. The Habsburgs also infiltrated the inter-Iberian kinship with the marriage of Juana of Castile to Archduke Philip the Handsome, the son of Mary of Burgundy and the Emperor Maximilian in 1496.[18] Similar to Anne of Austria's 1614 marriage to Louis XIII, Juana's was actually a double marriage, with Margaret, the spurned fiancé of Charles VIII of France, marrying Juana's brother Juan, the heir to the Castilian and Aragonese thrones. The evidence of her earlier life suggests a rigorous training in queenship, as Juana emerged as a formidable scholar, especially in languages. She was also known for her intellectual precocity, one that led her to question some the basic tenets of the Catholic Church, which her militantly orthodox mother found disturbing. As we have seen in Chapter 1, a series of tragic deaths within the Spanish royal family left Juana as the heir to Castile by 1502, when she was named Princess of Asturias, a title usually given to male heirs to the throne, a position analogous to Prince of Wales in England, and Dauphin in France.

Following her marriage, Juana began to display signs of mental instability, which Isabella's own mother also suffered from. Such traits were undoubtedly exacerbated by the condition of her marriage. Despite his wife's pedigree and her alleged beauty, Philip declined to publicly honor her, effectively marginalizing her in his ducal court while lavishing attention upon his mistresses. But marital discord did not prevent the production of heirs; Juana was exceptionally fecund, producing six children who survived infancy, including future queens of France, Denmark, and Portugal and two Holy Roman Emperors. Nevertheless, the marriage was far from companionate, as Philip placed severe restraints upon Juana's freedom of movement during their residency in Flanders, which prevented her from building an autonomous base of power in Castile as heiress presumptive.[19]

In 1502, Juana and Philip took a grand tour of Spain, to receive the fealty of the Castilian Cortes as heir to the throne. Following Isabella's death in 1504, Juana inherited the Castilian throne. But whether she was unstable, or even insane, Juana was the victim of both her husband's and her father's ambitions, policies furthered by her eldest son Charles after he came of age. Ferdinand's reluctance to give up power in Castile, and his remarriage to Germaine of Foix, arranged by Anne of Brittany, in the hopes of producing a male heir for Aragon, swayed the Castilians into supporting Philip, who recognized him and Juana as monarchs after landing in Spain in July 1506. Ferdinand quickly conceded, although he and Philip were agreed that Juana's alleged mental instability, which earned her for the enduring soubriquet "La Loca," should bar her from the exercise of regal power.[20]

But Philip's actual reign was short-lived; he died in September 1506, and the government of Castile once more was thrown into confusion. Juana had apparently tried to rule alone, but the government fell into disarray, while a shadow regency led by Archbishop Cisneros also failed to stabilize the kingdom. Once again, Ferdinand stepped into the breach, steamrolling his daughter into a regency arrangement that effectively left her in a form of protective custody in the nunnery of Santa Clara at Tordesillas that would last until the end of her life, at age seventy-five. Her son Charles, who succeeded Ferdinand as king of Aragon in 1516, perpetuated this situation, with his mother as his nominal co-ruler in Castile, ruling the Spanish kingdoms until his abdication in 1556, a year after Juana's own death. The story of Juana's treatment at the hands of her father, her husband, and her eldest son presents a tragic counterpoint to her mother's reign, emphasizing the role that personal will and presence of mind played in a regnant queen's ability to maintain her access to power within the institution of marriage.

Dynastic consolidation was also behind the marriage of Claude of France, the daughter of Anne of Brittany and Louis XII, who also suffered miserably at the hands of her male relatives. Claude married her father's heir, Francis of Angouleme, in May 1514. Eight months later Claude's father died and her husband succeeded him, as Francis I. The contemporary of Henry VIII of England, Francis was a Renaissance prince, ushering all its facets into his magnificent royal court. But Claude was not a Renaissance queen on the level of her mother, or Isabella of Castile or Elizabeth of York. Instead, much like the dichotomy between Isabella and Juana in Castile, Claude relinquished the authority over the duchy exercised by her mother in April 1515, soon after Francis became king, later willing the duchy to her eldest son, the dauphin Francis. Like Juana, she was overshadowed by other women: her mother-in-law, Louise of Savoy; Francis's sister, Marguerite of Angouleme; and Francis's first official mistress, Francoise de Foix. Together this trio of women ransacked Claude's queenship for its component parts. Louise of Savoy milked her position as Francis's mother for all it was worth, operating as a quasi-queen in a fashion like Margaret Beaufort in England.[21] She was educated, opinionated, and experienced, remaining a part of her son's inner circle until she died. Marguerite of Angouleme was well educated in the latest humanist thinking from both Italy and within France, attracting scholars and artists alike. Francoise de Foix was reputedly beautiful and cultured, joining Francis's court in 1516 along with her husband, Jean de Laval, Count of Chateaubriant.

What was left for Claude was the role of royal baby-maker. Despite her marginalization at court by Francis's mother, sister, and mistress, Claude played the role of an obedient and pious queen who took her dynastic responsibilities seriously. Like her mother, she is best remembered for being perennially pregnant. She was far from healthy, small of stature, suffering from scoliosis which hunched her back, but this did not stop Francis I from routinely bedding her from age fourteen, producing seven children in ten years, several of whom grew to adulthood, including the future Henri II. Her health and constant pregnancies eventually limited her mobility. In her final years she was a virtual invalid, plagued with obesity, a hip deformity, and, as Francis's biographer R.J. Knecht has alleged, syphilis, the by-product of her husband's prodigious sexuality. She died in 1524 at Blois, worn out from a series of pregnancies that would have tried the health of the most robust of queens.

If Claude was the unloved baby-maker, her successor, Eleanor of Austria (1498–1558), was the shopworn dynastic pawn. The eldest daughter of Juana of Castile and Philip of Burgundy, and the sister of Emperor Charles V, Eleanor already had plenty of experience being a queen by the time she married Francis I in 1530. She was from birth a hot commodity on the marriage market; her potential bridegrooms included the future Henry VIII, who later married her aunt Catherine; Louis XII of France; Antoine, duke of Lorraine; and King Sigismund the Old of Poland. Her first marriage was indicative of the politics of dynastic consolidation, which was a noted feature of the Spanish Habsburg dynasty. As the marriage of Isabella and Ferdinand united Aragon and Castile dynastically, intermarriage with the royal house of Portugal was also a priority. Eleanor's brother Charles V continued this tradition, marrying Eleanor in 1518 to her uncle by marriage, Manuel I of Portugal, twenty-eight years her senior, who had previously been married to two of her mother Juana's sisters, Isabella and Maria. Manuel died in 1521, leaving her a widow with two small children: the infante Charles, who lived only a year, and a daughter Maria, later Duchess of Viseu.

Following her husband's death, Eleanor returned to Castile for further dynastic duty, forced to leave in Portugal her daughter Maria, whom she would not see again until shortly before her death in 1558. This time it was as a peacemaker. Francis I of France continued the tradition of his Valois predecessors in the quest for Milan and other territories in Italy. But in 1525, as Francis laid siege to Pavia, the imperial army defeated his forces and captured the king, who was eventually moved to Spain as a prisoner. In 1529, Louise of Savoy, and Margaret of Austria, Duchess of Savoy, the former fiancé of Charles VIII of France, negotiated the peace of Cambrai between Francis and Charles, which included the marriage between Francis and Eleanor.[22]

The Treaty of Cambrai was indicative of the peacemaking roles the royal women of France and Spain were called upon to play in the continued wars between the two kingdoms. As Queen of France, peacemaker was the only option left open to Eleanor during her sixteen-year marriage to Francis. On the one hand, Francis and Eleanor were evenly matched in the status, a factor extremely important to the politics of Renaissance monarchy; marriage to the daughter of a queen who was a queen herself as well as sister to a Holy Roman Emperor reinforced Francis's position as one of the most preeminent monarchs on the continent of Europe.

But the marriage was not companionate. No children resulted from the marriage as the King already had a trio of sons to succeed him and two daughters to marry into the royal houses of Europe. As we have seen, Francis married dynastically but sought love elsewhere. Like Claude before her, Eleanor was forced to take a backseat at court to Francis's second official mistress, Madame d'Etampes. Francis I in fact instituted an enduring tradition in early modern France that essentially compartmentalized the role of queen, in which the informal aspects of the queenly role were parceled out to royal mistresses and royal favorites; in varying degrees, *all* of France's early modern queens from Claude to Marie Leszczyńska suffered this fate.[23]

This left Eleanor to pursue motherhood and the role of peacemaker as alternatives to making her name as queen. Because no children resulted from the marriage, Eleanor did her best to fill the role of stepmother. Eleanor apparently got on well with the Dauphin Francis, but he died in 1536 at the age of eighteen. The new heir, the future Henri II, was decidedly anti-Habsburg, no doubt caused by the rigors of his incarceration in Spain as a hostage for his father. Ironically, Eleanor did find a short-term ally in Diane de Poitiers, a member of her household who later became Henri's mistress, because of her devotion to the Catholic religion, while she also encouraged a marriage between Francis I's younger son Charles and a Habsburg princess, resulting in the Treaty of Crepy in 1544. Ironically again, she was assisted here by Francis's mistress the Duchess d'Etampes, as the dauphin Henri was entirely opposed to such an alliance.[24] But Charles died the next year. Eleanor appears to have enjoyed cordial relations with Francis's daughters, participating in the marriages of Catherine de Medici to the second son Henri in 1534 and Madeleine to James V of Scotland in 1537, although she failed to pull off a marriage between her stepdaughter Marguerite and Charles V's son Philip in 1538. But the formalized, ritualized spaces surrounding royal marriages and other social functions, such as the baptism of the future Francis II in 1544 and the various royal marriages, were the one area of her queenship in which Eleanor's role as queen could not be denied to her.

Eleanor's Spanish counterpart was her cousin, Charles V's consort, Isabel of Portugal. This marriage, celebrated in 1526, epitomizes the quest for dynastic consolidation that was at the heart of Habsburg policy. As the successors in Spain of Isabella and Ferdinand, the Habsburgs, who combined Austrian, German, Italian, and Burgundian territories through their marriage alliances, continued the quest to intermarry into the Portuguese royal house of Aviz. This process had begun when Isabella of Castile married her namesake eldest daughter to Prince Afonso of Portugal in 1490 and later to his uncle and successor Manuel in 1496, who later married Isabella's third daughter Maria, the mother of Isabel of Portugal. Eleanor's sister Catherine in turn later married Manuel and Maria's son Jao III, the culmination of a series of intermarriages that later made possible a Habsburg claim to the Portuguese throne in 1580.

Over the course of her thirteen-year reign as Holy Roman Empress and queen of the Spanish kingdoms, Isabel of Portugal comes down to us as a distant but dignified queen whose recorded historical legacy was literally without flaw, as suggested in the Titian portrait painted nine years after her death in 1539, which displays an aloof woman with delicate features looking off into the distance as clouds gather in the landscape behind her. Indeed, what we know about her role as queen would make a perfect advice manual for successful queenship, as she was known primarily as a dutiful and loving wife, a hands on mother, and a competent helpmate to her husband. How much of this is part of a carefully constructed and filtered legacy is difficult to determine.[25] But if we take what we know about her at face value, she presents us with a straightforward story of queenly success, the true inheritor of the queenship of her grandmother Isabella of Castile.

Although King of Castile and Aragon since the death of his grandfather Ferdinand in 1516, Isabel's cousin Charles V had been raised in the Netherlands and spoke no Spanish while inserting numerous Burgundian and Austrian administrators in the government of his Spanish kingdoms, resulting in a series of *Communero* rebellions in 1520 and 1521, which had risen up against Charles's foreign advisors and administrators. Thus an Iberian consort who could serve as regent while Charles was in Flanders and elsewhere in Europe could help soften his perception as a foreign king; the Cortes of both Castile and Aragon had advocated the match. What Isabel also had going for her was a place in the Portuguese succession, and a one million ducat dowry, especially appreciated by the perennially cash-starved Charles.

The marriage took place in March 1526 in Seville. Both considered the sacrament of marriage a duty, and both came to the marriage with a determination to make it a companionate one. This attitude became an enduring feature of early modern Spanish queenship. Whether genuine or calculated, the pair immediately created the perception of a loving couple, reportedly not noticing anyone but themselves during their honeymoon. They immediately got down to work in the family business, with son Philip, later Philip II, being born in 1527, and two daughters, Maria and Joanna, following in 1528 and 1535.

Isabel's queenship also had a political dimension, as she experienced on-the-job training in the early years of her queenship to prepare her to be a regent in Spain while the emperor tended to his far-flung dominions in the rest of Europe, fighting German Protestants, the French in Italy, and the Turks on land in Central Europe and in the Mediterranean Sea. Even though she was Duchess of Burgundy, Holy Roman Empress, and Archduchess of Austria, she never had the opportunity to visit these lands but remained in the Iberian Peninsula with her children, who were raised Spanish. In 1529 Charles left Spain, leaving his wife as regent to be assisted by a royal council. In this dimension of her queenship, she was the true inheritor of Isabella of Castile.

Charles's decision not to keep his wife close by his side, but with their children in Spain, worked wonders in shoring up support for the Habsburg dynasty in Spain because Isabel was also a granddaughter of Isabella and Ferdinand. Ultimately, the path to queenly success for Isabel was perform-ing the roles of wife and mother with consummate skill, keeping within the bounds of appropriate gender roles. The first three years of her marriage were formative, her children were born, and she got to know her husband by the time of his departure to Italy and elsewhere on the continent. Once Charles was gone, she created a close-knit family unit, participating in her children's education, personally disciplining them, and imparting to them a love for the land and cultures of the Iberian Peninsula. In the tradition of her grandmother Isabella of Castile, Isabel presided over an opulent royal court, while her house-hold accounts reveal a queen who invested heavily in rich fabrics and jewels.[26]

For all intents and purposes, Isabel's marriage was a long-distance rela-tionship. Politically, it served Charles's purposes; with a picture perfect, flesh and blood Iberian royal family in Madrid, he was much freer to continue his peripatetic existence. Isabel only saw Charles a few more times after this, from 1532 to 1535 and then in 1538, when she conceived her final child, whose birth killed her in May 1539. Although he possessed just one son and two daughters and was only thirty-nine, Charles did not remarry, a remarkable testament of devotion from an otherwise dynastically motivated monarch.

THE MEDICI QUEENS OF FRANCE

Like Anne of Austria, both Catherine de Medici (1519–1589), consort of Henri II of France (r. 1547–1559), and Marie de Medici (1575–1642), the consort of Henri IV (r. 1589–1610), went through several stages of queenship, achieving the height of their influence and power as dowager queens and regents. Quite unlike her immediate predecessors as consort, Claude and Eleanor of Austria, Catherine could not boast of illustrious lineage, although on her mother's side she was descended from the prestigious French house of La Tour d'Auvergne.[27] But on her father's side she was descended from the Medici family, a family of merchants and bankers who had ruled Florence for much of the fifteenth and early sixteenth century; she never entirely shook the image of the Italian queen and the shopkeeper's daughter in French aristocratic circles.

While members of the noble classes enriched themselves by marrying daughters of wealthy merchants, few of these women broke through the glass ceiling of queenship. In 1533, however, a cash hungry Francis I sought an alliance with Medici Pope Clement VII against Charles V, and approved Catherine's marriage to his second son Henri, duke of Orleans, which was celebrated in Marseilles with the consummation reportedly witnessed by the French king. Francis was impressed with his new daughter-in-law; Catherine possessed an engaging personality, a well-developed artistic aesthetic, and a taste for sumptuous clothing and jewelry. Unfortunately, her charms were lost on a husband who showed little interest in her, preferring his mistresses to Catherine's bedchamber. But Catherine never acknowledged this plain and massive fact within the spaces of the French court. Undaunted, she cultivated the various noble ladies who populated the spaces of the royal court. Catherine also cultivated Francis I himself, who appreciated feminine wit. But the death of Clement VII in 1534 ended the papal alliance, while in 1536, the king's eldest son, Francis, died, making Catherine's husband the Dauphin.[28]

For the first decade of her marriage, Catherine failed to conceive. In the meantime, Henri conceived an illegitimate daughter and in 1538 he took a permanent mistress, Diane de Poitiers, a widow twenty years his senior who became the third party of the ménage à trois of her marriage. Under enormous pressure to conceive, Catherine subscribed to all manner of fertility treatments, including placing cow dung on her private parts and drinking mule's urine. More effective was the treatment offered by Jen Fernel, a physician who helped the pair overcome some physical impediments to conception. Diane de Poitiers also encouraged Henri to sleep with his wife. It took ten long years, but first son Francis was born in 1544, followed in the next twelve years by ten more children, seven of whom lived to adulthood.

By the time Francis I died in early 1547, Catherine had experienced a thorough tutelage in French politics. As queen consort, she did her best to reassemble the fractured queenships of Claude and Eleanor of Austria into something more meaningful and powerful. She did not wholly succeed; Diane de Poitiers also ascended the throne of official mistress, and Catherine had

little choice but to tolerate her within the spaces of the royal court, even sharing control over her children's education with her. Henri allowed her little
political influence, as he did with Diane, and she played no role in the matrimonial negotiations for her children: the Dauphin Francis, who married the
youthful Mary Queen of Scots in April 1558, and her daughter Claude, who
married Charles Duke of Lorraine in January 1559.

It is curious that Catherine made no real claim to be a particularly pious
queen, as most medieval and early modern French and Iberian queens had,
although she was orthodox in her religious observances. Like Claude before
her, Catherine spent most of her consortship pregnant, while playing the
role of devoted and dutiful wife. She also continued to dress spectacularly,
and had herself painted as such, while engaging in the leisure activities of the
court, including hunting, which allowed her to have time with her husband
without the presence of Diane de Poitiers. Court chronicler Brantome called
her a superb horsewoman. At the same time, Catherine began to make her
reputation as a patroness of Renaissance arts. As queen consort, she collected
paintings, tapestries, and sculptures, knowing full well the power of displays
of Renaissance majesty within the royal court.

During the celebrations surrounding the marriage of her daughter
Elisabeth to Philip II of Spain in July 1559, Henri II was killed in a jousting
accident. This inaugurated a whole new phase of queenship for Catherine, one
for which she is most remembered, as the grieving widow and the determined
mother. Gone for good was the extravagant adornment of her consortship,
as Catherine immediately adopted the widow's weeds that she wore until she
died. Breaking tradition, Catherine went with the color black instead of white,
which was customary in France, and went far beyond all the necessary protocols for mourning in the ostentation of her grieving process. As Katherine
Crawford has noted, Catherine realized the power of iconography in the
creation of her representations. While many of the portraits painted of her as
consort display her as a proud and majestic queen, draped in royal splendor,
as a widow she was painted with her four sons as children, looking decidedly
matronly.

For Catherine, motherhood was her ticket to political prominence.[29]
The accession of fifteen-year-old Francis II, whose consort was Mary Queen
of Scots, was a *de facto* minority reign; the king was not prepared to rule,
with Mary's ultra-Catholic Guise relatives, duke Francis and the Cardinal
of Lorraine, vying for control of the regime with the Protestant House of
Bourbon, the first princes of the blood. Into this mix Catherine inserted
herself politically for the first time. Like her contemporary Elizabeth I of
England, Catherine was a hard-boiled realist, seeking a middle path between

religious extremism, as relations between the Catholic Guise and Protestant Bourbon camps grew increasingly violent during Francis II's brief reign.

Following Francis II's death (December 1560), and the accession of nine-year-old Charles IX, Catherine succeeded in gaining both the custody of the underage king and control of the government of the kingdom. The onset of a royal minority is always the acid test for the mettle of a dowager queen. Despite the Salic law, which forbade a female succession, royal mothers throughout French medieval and early modern history claimed regencies on behalf of their underage sons, going back to the eleventh century Anne of Kiev, who served as co-regent with Baldwin V of Flanders for her son Philip I. Over the course of the middle ages, Blanche of Castile, Isabeau of Bavaria, and Anne de Beaujeu had served as regents for sons and husbands, as had Louise of Savoy for her son Francis I. Catherine herself had served as a nominal regent for Henri II, without any real power.

But on the death of her husband, Catherine, with four young sons, made up her mind that she would be a political force during their reigns, motivated by her desire, as she wrote to her daughter Elisabeth, Queen of Spain, to preserve the French throne and kingdom for her Valois sons.[30] Having had a taste of the religiously motivated partisan divide during her eldest son's reign, Catherine was determined to control the minority regime of her second son. The widowed Mary Queen of Scots elected to return to Scotland as Catherine elbowed out the Guises and compromised with Antoine de Bourbon to gain the governorship of king and kingdom in exchange for the lord lieutenancy of the kingdom. In these actions, Catherine welded the familial role of mother as protector of her children to her political role as regent.

Like Anne of Austria in the next century, Catherine enjoyed a much wider ranging and full-fledged queenship as a dowager than as a consort, which tended to obscure the queenships of the wives of her three eldest sons. With access to royal income and patronage, she greatly expanded her career as an art patron, collecting paintings and commissioning painters such as Jean Cousin the Younger and Antoine Caron. Catherine deployed art and iconography as a means to create royal representations to create positive images of her regency, commissioning numerous paintings of herself in widow's weeds and surrounded by her children, creating the image of a harmonious family unit that was somewhat removed from their lived reality. But if Catherine abstained from gorgeous apparel herself, she could still be surrounded by beautiful objects, like tapestries and pottery, favoring classical and mythological illusions in her commissioned pieces, rather than the biblical allusions favored by most medieval and early modern French and Iberian queens. She also loved music and theatrics, making sure the Valois court was festive and entertaining on a grandiose scale. She also kept on hand a bevy of beautiful court ladies, "the flying squadron," to use their allurements upon the noblemen of the Valois court, to promote Catherine's political objectives.[31] Catherine also built two palaces, the Tuileries and the Hotel de la Reine, as well as renovating a number of chateaux in and around Paris, the hallmark of any powerful queen. She also built a tomb for herself and her husband at St. Denis, a miniature classical temple surrounded by Renaissance sculptures that housed their marble effigies.

During her regency under Charles IX (1560–74) Catherine attempted to play the role of peacemaker between Catholics and Protestants. Ultimately, this was a feat that could not be achieved, but Catherine tried her hardest. In 1561 Catherine called together the Colloquy of Poissons, in an attempt to wrest an accord from the Protestant and Catholic camps. After the meeting broke up in disarray, the duke of Guise massacred several dozen Protestants at Vassy, while Protestants, led by Louis de Bourbon, Prince of Condé, and Admiral Gaspard de Coligny, raised an army and seized La Havre with English assistance. Catherine came to Guise's aid and was present at the siege of Protestant-held Rouen in November 1562. But with Guise's murder in early 1563, Catherine was able to patch together a peace deal with the Protestants, and she issued the Edict of Amboise, which promised limited tolerance for Protestants. In these actions, Catherine strongly mirrored the actions of the Scottish dowager queen Mary of Guise, who in the previous decade also sought to find middle ground between Catholics and Protestants.

Catherine also played the role of dynast. With the death of her daughter Elisabeth the Spanish queen in 1568, Catherine sought another marriage alliance with the Habsburgs, which now had twin dynasties ruling Spain and the Holy Roman Empire, arranging for Charles IX's marriage to Elisabeth of Austria, which was celebrated in 1570. Elisabeth was the daughter of Maximilian II and Maria of Spain, the sister of Philip II, who married Elisabeth's sister Anna, who was also his niece. Elisabeth was the archetype Habsburg princess. She was well educated, a linguist, intensely religious, but uninterested in politics, having been brought up in a sheltered existence in Vienna. Following the marriage, she briefly caught her husband's fancy before he returned to his mistress, Marie Touchet, who reportedly murmured, "The German girl does not scare me." Elisabeth could not bring herself to formally greet any Huguenot nobles, and Catherine did her best to shield her from the licentiousness of the Valois court. Although she did bear a daughter, Marie Elisabeth, she could hardly hold her head up in the storm of the Wars of Religion or compete with the queenly influence of her mother-in-law; Elisabeth's also was a fractured French consortship. When she was first told of the St. Bartholomew's Day Massacre of 1572, and her husband's role in it, the only thing she could do was cry and then pray for the soul of her husband. After Charles IX's death, she returned as childless dowager queen to Vienna, where she later founded a convent and lived as a nun until her death.

Catherine also brokered the marriage of her youngest daughter, Marguerite, to the Protestant Henri of Navarre, who was first prince of the blood following her sons. The wedding was celebrated on August 18, 1572, bringing all the leading French Protestants to Paris for the ceremony. There is no clear explanation for why this final act of religious compromise was followed by the St. Bartholomew's Day Massacre. Charles IX had in fact grown close to Admiral Coligny, the Protestant leader, but five days after the marriage an assassination attempt was made on Coligny, perhaps on Catherine's instigation. Fearing Protestant reprisals, Charles IX apparently agreed to a Protestant massacre in Paris, which spread to the rest of France and lasted for several weeks, eventually killing tens of thousands of Huguenots.

How much blame can be assigned to Catherine cannot be established with any certainty, but even her apologists admit her complicity.[32] What is much more clear is that the massacre ended Catherine's ascendancy as a peacemaker between Catholic and Protestant factions, ushering in the legend of the "Black Queen," the patron of Nostradamus, who allegedly delved into the black arts to save the Valois dynasty, such as by poisoning Henri of Navarre's mother Jeanne as soon as she arrived in Paris for the wedding.[33] Much of the subsequent diatribe against her can be attributed to a vengeful Protestant press, but even her detractors admit she was as tough as her male adversaries, fearlessly inspecting the front lines at the siege of Rouen in 1562 in the face of enemy fire.

Two years after the massacre, the sickly Charles IX died, age twenty-three. He was succeeded by Henri III, Catherine's favorite son. Henri was a controversial king, intensely religious yet surrounded by effeminate men known as the "mignons." Henri dashed Catherine's hopes for another Habsburg match by marrying Louise of Lorraine, who had enchanted him while he was on his way to Poland after his election to the Polish crown, which he gave up immediately after Charles IX's death. Chosen for her looks, Louise was an enchanting young queen, apparently devoted to her husband despite his other predilections, but the union produced no issue; contemporaries seemed agreed that Henri's health precluded the likeliness of him producing an heir. Like Elisabeth of Austria before her, Louise counts among the most obscure of French queen consorts.

As she had with Charles IX, Catherine remained the *de facto* head of government, laboring to keep the peace as her youngest son Francis, Duke of

Anjou, championed the Protestant cause in both France and the Netherlands. In 1578, she made one last attempt, which ended in failure, to marry Anjou to Elizabeth I of England. But Anjou's death in 1584 precipitated a succession crisis, as Henri III's heir was now the Protestant Henri of Navarre. These events ushered in the final phase of the Wars of Religion, as Henri, duke of Guise, organized the Catholic League to prevent Navarre from inheriting the throne, later allying with the equally orthodox Philip II of Spain in the Treaty of Joinville. Henri III vacillated between support for Navarre and the Catholic League, in what became known as the War of the Three Henris, as Catherine looked on helplessly. She died in January 1589 after learning that her son had ordered Guise's assassination. She ranks among the most capable of female rulers in sixteenth-century Europe. Her claims to regal power were based on familial models that reached back to the middle ages, but in her case they were applied to an increasingly modern and bureaucratic state. That she managed to keep this machinery working during a particularly violent and unstable age is perhaps the greatest testament to her queenship. Her ability to do so created the powerful model that her successors Marie de Medici and Anne of Austria built upon.

With Henri III's death, France's titular queen was now Catherine's youngest daughter, Marguerite, the wife of Henri IV.[34] At the time that her husband became king, however, she was in exile at the Castle of Usson in the Auvergne, where her brother Henri III had imprisoned her in 1586. Described by contemporaries as beautiful, intelligent, and sensuous, Marguerite defied the gender norms of queenship, taking a series of lovers, before and after her marriage, the frequent pastime of French kings; this she had in common with her husband. But within monarchical systems that placed a premium upon a hereditary succession, Marguerite's failure to guard her female chastity damaged her relationships with her brothers Charles IX and Henri III as well as her mother, who eventually cut her out of her will entirely. During her periods of incarceration she wrote her memoirs, a rarity for any early modern queen, writing candidly about her relationships with her mother, brothers, and husband.[35]

By the time Henri had become king in 1589 Marguerite was thirty-six, not necessarily past childbearing age, but there was no attempt at a reconciliation; by her own admission, despite their mutual sexual appetites, Marguerite had stopped sleeping with Henri by the early 1580s. Over the course of the 1590s, as Henri brought stability to France, he began efforts to secure an annulment so he could remarry, as Henry VIII had done with Anne Boleyn. Henri encountered much less interference, thanks in part to Marguerite's cooperation; she received a generous severance package, which included retaining the title of Queen.

But while Marguerite was queen of France and Navarre, she did not fulfill any of its functions. In her own words she was a "queen without a throne." With the role of queen temporarily in abeyance, Henri's mistress Gabrielle d'Estrées appropriated some of its functions, as did the mistresses of Francis I and Henri II, using her contacts with the wives of Catholic League members for diplomatic purposes, which earned her a chair at Henri IV's council. Gabrielle also bore Henri several children, whom he not only acknowledged but legitimized. Nevertheless, Henri was prevailed upon to remarry and provide legitimate heirs for the Bourbon dynasty. In his choice, a sizeable dowry trumped dynastic prestige. Marie de Medici was the daughter of Francesco I de' Medici, Grand Duke of Tuscany, and Archduchess Joanna of Austria, the daughter of Holy Roman Emperor Ferdinand I, which made her as much Habsburg as Medici.[36] Henri swiftly went to work to propagate the dynasty; Marie was already pregnant with the future Louis XIII when she arrived in Paris, when her husband introduced her to his current mistress Henrietta d'Entragues, who was also heavily pregnant.

But Marie was no Claude, Eleanor of Castile, or Catherine de Medici, patiently enduring her husband's infidelities. She possessed a fiery temper and gave her husband a number of public tongue-lashings for his lack of respect for her position. She also had heated confrontations with Henri's mistresses but had little choice but to put up with them, as they continued to bear the king bastard children. But Marie kept pace with her nemeses, fulfilling the primary duty of queenship, bearing five children who lived to adulthood, including future queens of Spain and England. But the marriage was hardly companionate; Henri IV denied Marie the political role he had accorded Gabrielle d'Estrées, his first official mistress, telling her to mind her own business when she pressed him to accept the dictates of the Council of Trent, which had defined the orthodoxy of the Counter-Reformation. Although Henri had converted to Catholicism to stabilize his claim to the throne, in 1598 he issued the Edict of Nantes, which granted tolerance to Protestants, effectively ending the French Wars of Religion.

Denied a political role, motherhood became the defining facet of Marie's consortship, as it had been for Catherine de Medici before her. Marie raised her children as though they were prize horses, to maximize their dynastic value. She was a strict disciplinarian and somewhat overbearing in the raising of her children. Her eldest son especially endured a rough tutelage as a future king, which hardly endeared his mother to him. But despite his serial womanizing, Henri IV acknowledged his queen's contributions to the future of his dynasty; despite the public rows, he occasionally wrote affectionate letters to Marie, and in public he usually treated her with the respect due to a queen of

France. Marie also received a tutelage in French queenship from Marguerite of Valois, whom Henri had allowed to return to Paris in 1605. The two women eventually became fast friends, as Marguerite doted upon the royal children and tutored Marie in the intricacies of French royal etiquette.

But when Henri IV was assassinated in 1610 on the day after Marie's coronation, Marie moved swiftly to fill the void, wasting no time in getting herself recognized as regent for her nine-year-old son Louis XIII. As we have seen, there was a strong precedent for female regencies, which Marie was able to build upon. But unlike Catherine de Medici, who did her best to find the political middle ground during the Wars of Religion to stabilize the throne for her sons, Marie unabashedly sought power for her own sake. As Katherine Crawford has argued, her regency was the last gasp of a form of political theory grounded in the notion of the state as a family writ large, utilizing her position as mother to the king as the legitimizing force of her claim to regency, recognizing the nine-year-old king's capacity to choose his own regent, and trumping the claims of the first princes of the blood, including the Bourbon Prince of Conde, her main challenger, who was second in line to the throne after Marie's younger son Gaston, Duke of Orleans. Only then did she undergo forty-six days of mourning highly reminiscent of Catherine de Medici's in the ostentation of her rites, which emphasized her familial connection to her dead husband, whose memory she wished to serve as regent.

But Marie's ability to claim the regency was not matched by her subsequent performance, as she reversed several of her husband's policies. First to go was Maximilien de Béthune, Duke of Sully, the mastermind of Henri IV's fiscal resurgence, whose centralizing policies and fiscal conservatism were at odds with a queen who loved to spend money. She also pursued a pro-Habsburg policy, negotiating marriages for Louis XIII with Anne of Austria and for her daughter Elisabeth with Anne's brother, the future Philip IV of Spain. She also depended heavily on advice from a pair of Italians, Leonora Dori Galigaï, who later married Concino Concini, who was created Marquis d'Ancre and a Marshal of France, despite a total lack of military experience. The pushback from the nobility resulted in the calling of the Estates General, the French representative assembly, which met in 1614 and 1615. In the meantime, Marie bought off Conde, in the Treaty of Sainte-Menehould, and successfully sailed through the meeting of the Estates with her authority still intact. As Charles IX had done in 1563, Louis XIII held a *lit de justice* to end his minority in 1614, prior to the meeting of the Estates, in which he reasserted his mother's centrality to his administration. In 1615, the Habsburg marriages of her children were celebrated.

But Marie was not content to relinquish power to her son as he progressed through his teenage years. Recognizing the talent of the future Cardinal Richelieu, who made an impressive performance in the meetings of the Estates and became Concini's right-hand man, Marie began to pursue a series of highly unpopular policies, including a wholesale sacking of the royal council, replaced by Concini's clients. These moves coincided with the rise as Louis XIII's royal favorite of Charles d'Albert Luynes, who in 1617 arranged the murder of Concini, the recall of his royal council, and Marie's arrest and imprisonment at Blois.

While Marie was later rehabilitated, as the Thirty Years' War raged in Europe, Richelieu urged the king to abandon his mother's pro-Habsburg policy to engage in war to contain the threat of Hispano-Austrian hegemony, making league with European Protestant powers such as Sweden and the Dutch Republic in the process. Marie seemingly secured Richelieu's dismissal in November 1630 after a heated confrontation with the king and his minister in what was known as the Day of Dupes. But Richelieu prevailed while Marie was exiled to Compiegne. She later escaped to Brussels, and then in 1638 to Amsterdam, where she was received quite royally. But Marie was perennially strapped for cash, visiting Protestant England in 1538 where her youngest daughter Henrietta Maria was Queen. Marie was hardly popular in a Protestant kingdom on the verge of a Puritan revolution, and she was packed off with a £10,000 bribe to leave the country. She ended up in Cologne, where she died in July 1542, still unreconciled with Louis XIII.[37]

Despite the political failures of her regency, Marie recognized the power of royal iconography, which remains her greatest legacy. At the start of her regency, she commissioned numerous paintings to illustrate her relationship to her underage son, which depicted her as her son's protector and natural councilor. In 1615, she began work on the Luxembourg Palace, her greatest architectural legacy, commissioning Peter Paul Rubens to paint the Medici Cycle, a series of twenty-four paintings depicting the major events of her life, which hang in the Louvre today.[38] But their self-glorification ironically illustrated the failures of her dowager queenship, as their depictions of her transcended her position as wife and mother to foreground herself, in monumental, gender-bending terms, and in this process transgressing proper female deference as both a consort and a dowager.[39] Her ardent desire for political primacy, well into the adult reign of Louis XIII, provided an instructive model for her daughter-in-law Anne of Austria to consider as she constructed her own regency during the minority of Louis XIV.

SPANISH QUEENSHIP UNDER PHILIP II OF SPAIN

Philip II of Spain (1527–1598), the contemporary of Elizabeth I of England, Mary Queen of Scots, and Catherine de Medici, ruled a polyglot empire that included the Iberian kingdoms (Castile, Aragon, Navarre, and later Portugal), Naples, Milan, Franche-Comte, the Netherlands, and a large New World empire in Mexico, the Caribbean, and South America. He was married four times, with each marriage pursuing different aspects of his and his father's dynastic policies. Unlike his father, Charles, who had been raised in the Netherlands, Philip was raised in Spain by his mother Isabel of Portugal and self-identified as an Iberian monarch.

His first marriage was to his double first cousin Maria Manuela, Princess of Portugal, celebrated at Salamanca in 1543 when she and Philip were both sixteen. Maria herself was the product of intense Iberian inbreeding; their son Don Carlos was delicate, deformed, and mentally unstable, and Maria herself died shortly after his birth in 1545. Philip remained unmarried until nine years after her death, when his father enlisted him as the husband of Queen Mary I of England (see Chapter 2). Mary also was Philip's cousin and was eleven years his senior. Despite his reluctance, Philip went through with the marriage, which sought to resuscitate the old Anglo-Burgundian and Spanish alliances and enlist England as an ally in the final stages of the Habsburg/Valois conflict that had gone on for most of the first half of the sixteenth century. Philip was invested as King of Naples in 1554 and in 1556 as King of the Spanish kingdoms, which made Mary the only absentee queen of Spain during the early modern era. But Mary died childless in England in 1558, and a year later, following the Treaty of Cateau-Cambresis, which finally ended the hostilities between France and Spain, a now thirty-two-year-old Philip married fourteen-year-old Elisabeth of Valois, eldest daughter of Henri II and Catherine de Medici.

Timing is everything in the selection of a royal bride. Philip was barely back on the market when the peace was concluded. But quite unlike his second marriage, Philip's marriage to Elisabeth (known as Isabel in Spain) blossomed into a warm and companionate marriage. The years of this marriage represented a period of relative cooperation between France and Spain, as Elisabeth threaded the needle of representing the interests of her natal family and creating a positive reputation as a Spanish queen. Elisabeth in fact provided a unique conduit of information between her mother and her husband in the flow of letters between them, without losing the respect and affection of either, especially as Catherine while regent pursued policies granting tolerance to Protestant Huguenots, which Philip, an ardent and dogmatic Catholic, was entirely opposed to doing. Despite her relentless efforts to influence her daughter politically and use her to gather intelligence from Spain, Catherine had a soft spot for Elisabeth as her letters attest. In turn, Philip gave up a life of casual mistresses to settle down to family life with Elisabeth, creating a powerful model of marital domesticity.

Quite unlike her mother, Elisabeth harbored no ambitions for a wider political role. She presided over Philip's court with dignity and grace, and her good nature even earned her the affection of Philip's unstable and sometimes violent son Don Carlos; she cried for days when Philip finally had to lock up Don Carlos. Nevertheless, Elisabeth met with her mother and her brother Charles IX in the south of France during his royal progress of 1564, performing a diplomatic role on behalf of her husband that accentuated her ability to be perceived as loyal to both her natal and her adopted countries, a significant achievement for any early modern queen.[40] She was also an amateur painter, having studied with the painter Sofonisba Anguissola at her husband's court. Less successful were her efforts to propagate the dynasty. Five years after the marriage, she miscarried twins, but gave birth to a daughter, Isabella Clara Eugenia, in 1566, and another daughter, Catherine Michelle, in 1567. She died the next year at age twenty-three, after giving birth to a stillborn daughter. Her death ended the closest relationship Valois France ever had with Habsburg Spain.

For his fourth wife, Philip married his niece, Anne of Austria (1549–1580), the eldest daughter of Emperor Maximilian II, who was also Philip's first cousin, and Maria of Spain, Philip's sister, continuing the policy of dynastic interbreeding between the Spanish and Austrian Habsburg families. Anne quickly picked up where Elisabeth of Valois had left off, endearing herself to her stepdaughters, who remained devoted to her for the rest of their lives. But she was also under intense dynastic pressure, because with the death of Don Carlos in 1568 Philip did not have a male heir. She did not disappoint, with five pregnancies in ten years of marriage. She was an entirely domesticated queen, which entirely served the purposes of Philip, who was as devoted to her as he was to Elisabeth of Valois. Yet tragedy struck once again, when Anne died of heart failure following her final pregnancy in 1580. Of her five children, only the fourth, later Philip III, lived to adulthood to succeed his father as king.

SEVENTEENTH-CENTURY SPANISH QUEENSHIP

Of the five seventeenth-century queens of Spain, two were French Bourbon princesses, while the other three had strong dynastic ties to the Austrian Habsburgs. These women were queens of many states united dynastically by the wearer of their crowns. But all of Charles V's descendants as kings of Spain followed his model of keeping their queens in Iberia during their reigns; no early modern Spanish queen visited the American colonies, or the Netherlands, or Italy. Like the sixteenth-century Empress Isabel of Portugal, these queens stayed in Spain, principally in Castile, as Madrid remained the primary seat of the Spanish royal court.

The royal women of seventeenth-century Spain exerted a powerful influence upon the history of the Spanish monarchy.[41] This was a tradition that reached back to medieval queens of Castile and Aragon, many of whom exercised formalized political power as consorts and regents. It would be the same under Philip III, who succeeded his father as king in 1597 at the age of eighteen. An undistinguished king, he was already under the influence of a *valido*, or official male favorite, Francisco Gómez de Sandoval, later created Duke of Lerma, by the time of his accession. It was Lerma in fact who negotiated Philip's marriage to Margaret of Austria (1584–1611), his first cousin once removed. Lerma's options were limited. The prestige of the Spanish monarchy required that queen consorts be of impeccable royal lineage as well as demonstrably Catholic in their religious belief. This limited Spanish options to daughters of French kings and Austrian Habsburg imperial archduchesses. There were no available Bourbon heiresses at the time, so the Austrian Habsburgs were literally the only options.

By the time Margaret became Queen of Spain in 1599 there had been three generations of interbreeding between the Spanish and Austrian Habsburgs, which included forms of cultural pollination between the royal courts of Vienna and Madrid; Margaret's approach to her role as queen was quite compatible with Spanish models. Philip III and Margaret were scrupulous in their pious monogamy, perpetuating the model of domestic harmony and compatibility laid down by their joint ancestors Isabella and Ferdinand. This narrative of pious domestic harmony was embedded in the baroque art that became the means to broadcast approved forms of royal representations, in terms of family portraits that featured their five children, sons Philip, Charles, and Ferdinand, and daughters Anne and Maria Anna, as the living symbols of Spain's dynastic continuity as a Habsburg kingdom.

Both Philip and Margaret underwent a strict upbringing in post-Tridentine Catholic teachings; both considered their religious piety and the purity of their religious beliefs to be among the most important tasks of monarchy, and they took these duties very seriously. For both, confessors were an integral part of their circle of intimates, as were the dowager empress Maria, the sister of Philip II, and her daughter, Margaret of the Cross, a Franciscan nun.[42] Within the relatively cloistered atmosphere of the royal court, these women went to work raising the children and promoting a pro-Austrian foreign policy that was at odds with that of the Duke of Lerma.

Philip was fond of his wife, whose fecundity only served to bind them more closely, especially after the birth of a male heir, the future Philip IV, in 1605. Both parents supervised their children's education, which went beyond letters, training in outdoor sports for the boys, and the domestic and musical arts for the girls, to how to behave in the highly ritualized spaces of the royal court. We can see how well these children learned these behaviors in the portraits painted of them at very early ages, looking like sober miniatures of adult men and women. The children were also taught the concepts of charity and compassion for the poor and were brought along to visit hospitals and orphanages, much as modern-day royals do today. But behind closed doors there was familiarity and accessibility that bound together the Spanish royal family, who frequently visited convents together to pray as well as to meet with nuns.

But outside of this familial unit, Lerma remained supreme over policy during Queen Margaret's lifetime. One of the few occasions when Margaret and Lerma were agreed was on the negotiations for the dual marriage of Margaret's oldest daughter Anne to the future Louis XIII of France and of Louis's sister Elisabeth to the future Philip IV, which crystalized following the assassination of Henri IV in May 1610, when the queen-regent Marie de Medici was more amenable to a marriage alliance with the Spanish Habsburgs. By the time the contracts were finalized, Margaret had died, following her eighth pregnancy in October 1611. If she was frustrated in her war of wills with Lerma, she left a queenly legacy very much in keeping with the queenships of Isabella of Castile and Isabel of Portugal in the companionate nature of their marriages and their ability to produce and raise their heirs, themes prominent in the baroque funeral pageants performed all over Spain following her death. Philip died ten years after his queen in 1521, when he was succeeded by his son Philip IV.

Even before he had become king, Philip IV had been married to Elisabeth of Bourbon (1602–1644), known as Isabel in Spain, who had been raised in the bustling royal household of St. Germain-en Laye with her brothers and sisters Louis XIII, Christina, Gaston, and Henrietta Maria, along with Henri IV's brood of bastard children. She was thirteen when she arrived in Spain in 1615 to marry Philip, who was two and a half years her junior, spending the rest of her teenage years in the bosom of the Spanish royal court with her husband's younger brothers Charles and Ferdinand and sister Maria Anna.

Elisabeth was a popular queen. Perhaps because she spent her first six years in Spain as princess of Asturias before becoming queen, she had absorbed the knowledge of what it took to be a successful Spanish queen.[43] Most importantly, she was fecund, spending much of her married life pregnant, although only two of her eleven pregnancies produced issue surviving childhood: the male heir Baltasar Charles, whose 1629 birth greatly increased Elisabeth's stature as queen, and daughter Maria Theresa, born ten years later, who later married her double-first cousin Louis XIV of France. Elisabeth adapted well to the formality and pageantry of the Habsburg court, was always an eager participant in balls and masques, and appeared to enjoy attending bull fights and wild-animal fights, as well as religious pageantry of all kinds. Philip and Elisabeth projected the image of a happy royal family, adding another precedent in a line of companionate Spanish royal marriages going back to Isabella of Castile and Ferdinand of Aragon.

For her part, having been raised with the children of her father's mistresses, Elisabeth internalized Philip's womanizing with much more fortitude and grace than her mother did as Queen of France. While Philip was perhaps the most philandering of Spanish Habsburg kings, he was also jealous of his beautiful and vivacious wife. An episode early in her reign dramatically illustrated the stark differences in sexual propriety between Spanish kings and queens, when Queen Elisabeth was physically rescued and carried away from a theatre fire by her gentleman-in-waiting, the poet Peralta, who was later murdered for crossing the line of physical engagement with the Queen. Elisabeth learned her lesson, following the example of her predecessors in maintaining an unimpeachable moral probity. Years later, while visiting the palace of Buen Retiro a wealthy *converso* merchant who had supplied funding for the palace spontaneously offered the Queen a bouquet of flowers. But the Queen promptly turned her back, instantly recognizing the breach in protocol, while the merchant was forever banned from the palace.

Such anecdotes are as substantial as accounts of Elisabeth get in the historical record, suggesting that she was a thoroughly domesticated queen without political and administrative aspirations. But by 1640, Spain's continued involvement in the Thirty Years' War was bleeding Castile dry of taxes and resources. When Elisabeth's brother Louis XIII invaded Catalonia, and Philip sent an army there in response, he appointed Elisabeth as regent. Elisabeth stepped up to the challenge, convincing various municipalities to provide taxes for the war effort and pawning her jewels in Zarazoga in order to buy supplies. This undoubtedly helped save her husband's crown, as the Spanish Grandees were at the point of rebellion. Yet her final queenly triumphs were cut short by her death in 1644 at age forty-one following a brief illness in which she was repeatedly bled. It was said that she had died of overwork, as Philip kept her working in his government long after her official regency had ended. If the measure of a queen's worth can be measured in the depth of a nation's mourning and pageantry of her funeral obsequities, then Elisabeth Bourbon ranks as one of Spain's more exemplary queens.[44]

Philip IV might have remained a widower as had his father, but two years after Elisabeth's death, sixteen-year-old Baltasar Charles died, leaving Philip IV without a male heir, as his two brothers Charles and Ferdinand had already died young. In 1649, forty-four-year-old Philip IV married again, this time to an Austrian Habsburg, his dead son's former fiancé fifteen-year-old Mariana, daughter of Holy Roman Emperor Ferdinand III and Anna Maria of Spain, Philip's sister.[45] Mariana's was a much more difficult queenship than Elisabeth's. Much younger than her husband, Mariana came across as light-hearted and informal to the Spanish court. She was far from charmed with her husband, who fully expected her to begin producing male heirs as quickly as possible while he continued to spend time with mistresses and courtesans. In 1651 she gave birth to a daughter, Margarita Theresa, immortalized as a girl by Velasquez, who later became a Holy Roman Empress. But the three children who followed, including two sons, had died by 1661, when she gave birth to son Charles.

Mariana was thirty years old when Philip IV died in 1665. Quite unlike France, which had a long tradition of royal minorities and powerful royal women running them, in the Spanish kingdoms there had not been a royal minority since the early fifteenth-century reign of Juan II of Castile, when his mother, the English princess Catherine of Lancaster, ruled for him as queen regent. Isabella of Castile's regnant queenship and Elisabeth of Bourbon's regency were precedent for Mariana to be immediately recognized as both regent for the kingdoms and custodian of the underage king.[46] Following a brief period of mourning when she only saw women, Mariana gave no thought to remarriage as she went beyond mere widow's weeds to adopt the habit of a nun for the rest of her life, which signaled a divine calling for her regency.

As much as she might have liked to have retired to a convent, Mariana dedicated the rest of her life to making sure her son, the last of the direct line of Spanish Habsburgs, was taken care of, keeping him on a short leash to prevent any factions at court from influencing him. Charles II was the product of severe inbreeding, inheriting seemingly all the regressive Habsburg traits, with a lower jaw so extended he could not chew his food and had to swallow it whole, which created chronic gastric discomfort. His tongue was too big for his mouth and he didn't begin walking until age ten. At the onset of the European Age of Reason, as Enlightenment thinking held up a mirror to all facets of human experience, the image of a disabled and impotent king trying to perpetuate a hereditary succession was patently absurd yet fervently desired and prayed for. But despite his disabilities, Charles continued to live, while the rest of Europe literally waited for him to die.

Culture and experience might have dictated that Mariana should be regent, by virtue of her position as wife of the last king and mother to the new one, which was reflective of the justifications for female rule that had been developing in Western European kingdoms. Quite unlike her predecessor Elisabeth of Bourbon, Mariana had no training whatsoever in administration or government, so she used the prevailing model of a *valido* to help her with her tasks along with the junta system of small councils favored by Philip IV's favorite, Olivares. *Validos* were always divisive figures, but Mariana compounded this by taking as her chief advisor a foreigner, her confessor Johann Eberhard Nithard, an Austrian Jesuit priest.

Although Mariana secured her authority in Spain, she was no match for the machinations of Louis XIV of France. Louis, who was aware of Charles II's deficiencies, went to war to claim the Spanish Netherlands (now Belgium), by right of his wife Maria Theresa, the daughter of Philip IV and Elisabeth of Bourbon, on the pretext that his queen's renunciation of her succession rights in Spain was void because her dowry had not been paid. What was known as the War of Devolution lasted three years, with Spain ultimately losing a portion of the Spanish Netherlands to France, while Spain suffered reverses in attempts to retake Portugal. Opposition to the foreign *valido* and the defeats of the war swept Don Juan of Austria (1629–1679), a bastard son of Philip IV, in as opposition leader to Mariana's regency.[47] Don Juan had been acknowledged as the king's son in 1642, and he served his father militarily in Naples, Sicily, Catalonia, and Portugal. Mariana was entirely opposed to him and tried to instill this into her son, but by 1669, after successfully leading risings in Aragon and Catalonia, Don Juan had forced Nithard into exile. Seven years later, the rise of another *valido*, Fernando de Valenzuela, 1st Marquis of Villasierra, who was rumored to be Mariana's lover, prompted another rising by Don Juan, who exiled Mariana to Toledo and Valenzuela to the Philippines.

Before he died in 1679, Don Juan had arranged Charles II's marriage to Marie Louise of Orléans (1662–1689), the daughter of Philippe, duke of Orleans, brother to Louis XIV, and Henriette, daughter of Charles I and Henrietta Maria of England. Marie Louise faced immense pressure to conceive a child, which never happened, although she claimed her share of false pregnancies. While Charles II was quite enthralled with his queen, and desired her sexually, there was some impediment to conception, as neither of Charles II's queens ever conceived. Chances are good that Marie Louise soon learned that she would not be able to deliver an heir to the Spanish throne. Despite Charles II's obvious physical deficiencies, which were skillfully concealed from the Spanish people, Marie Louise's inability to conceive made *her* unpopular. In time she became irritable, and gained considerable weight, and when she died in 1689, probably because of appendicitis, it was widely suspected that Mariana had her poisoned so Charles could remarry. Most scholars dismiss these rumors, but they do reveal the intense anxiety surrounding the Spanish succession.

Not surprisingly, Charles II was back on the marriage market, as if the Spanish court somehow believed that another queen would solve the succession dilemma. This time, as it had in the past, the pendulum swung back from Bourbon France to the Holy Roman Empire and the Austrian Habsburgs. Maria Anna of Neuberg was the daughter of Philip William, Elector Palatine, but her sister Eleanor was married to Holy Roman Emperor Leopold I and was the mother of the future Emperor Charles VI. Despite their pedigree, her family was poor, and she endured a much delayed journey to Spain, where she married Charles II on May 14, 1690.

Much like her predecessor Maria Louisa, Maria Anna was unable to perpetuate the Spanish succession. This created a bizarre situation in which the real culprit was the king, a fact no one could openly acknowledge, while the opprobrium for the lack of an heir was borne by the queen. Maria Anna was left with two options. First, she worked very hard to send all liquid assets, including jewels and works of art, back to her impoverished family in Germany. The second was to ensure the Spanish succession to her nephew the Archduke Charles.

In order to do this, she needed to control her husband, which put her in the crosshairs of dowager queen Mariana, who functioned as regent long past Charles's official majority began in 1675. Like her predecessor, Maria Anna also claimed to be pregnant on a number of occasions, which eventually turned such pronouncements into a theatre of the absurd. She also encouraged Charles to participate in exorcisms, in the hope that his afflictions could be cured and she would be able to bear a male heir. Mariana, however, wanted her great-grandson Joseph Ferdinand of Bavaria, born in 1692 and the grandson of her daughter Margarita, to succeed Charles. In the meantime, Louis XIV of France was intent on claiming the throne for his grandson, Philip, Duke of Anjou.

As the rest of Charles II's reign played out, an increasingly impoverished and unstable Spanish monarchy became the focus of Europe, as issues of balance of power between leading European states were in a state of uncertainty while Charles II continued to live. In 1696, Queen Mariana died, and in 1699, young Joseph Ferdinand followed her to the grave. Charles himself died on November 1, 1700, succeeded by his Bourbon cousin Philip, and the ensuing War of the Spanish Succession.

With the exception of the final three, the Habsburg queens of early modern Spain, from Isabel of Portugal to Elisabeth of Bourbon, created a model for active and engaged queenship, centered around religiosity, marriage and motherhood, and domestic harmony. In contrast, the queenships of Mariana, Marie Louise, and Maria Anna mirrored the slow deterioration and the sterility of the Spanish monarchy. Maria Anna lived the remainder of her long life in obscurity, first in Toledo, then a long exile in Bayonne France, returning to Spain only in 1739, one year before her death.

THE LATER BOURBON QUEENS OF FRANCE AND SPAIN

Maria Theresa, the only surviving issue of Philip IV of Spain and Elisabeth of Bourbon, married Louis XIV of France in 1660 according to the terms of the Treaty of the Pyrenees. The purpose of the marriage was one longstanding in Franco-Iberian history, to bring peace between the two nations. Ironically enough, the marriage created the pretext for later dynastic conflict with Spain. Maria Theresa experienced a classic Habsburg education within the cloistered atmosphere of the Spanish court, focused mainly on piety, etiquette, and social graces, and short on letters and culture. Although her mother died when she was six, she gained a companion in her father's second wife, Queen Mariana.

Maria Theresa was the second Habsburg queen of France in the seventeenth century, and her mother-in-law Anne of Austria treated her with kindness and affection until Anne's death in 1666. It was her fate, however, to be married to the self-proclaimed "Sun King," whose reign embodied the apotheosis of absolutist rule and whose interests and energies literally left Maria Theresa in the dust. Louis was duly devoted to her during the first year of the marriage, and her first child Louis, *Le Grand Dauphin*, was born in November 1661. Once he had his heir, Louis dutifully followed in the grand tradition of the Valois and Bourbon kings of France by enjoying a parade of official mistresses, starting with Louise de La Vallière, followed by Françoise-Athénaïs, Marquise de Montespan, both of whom bore the king several children, and concluding with Françoise d'Aubigné, Marquise de Maintenon, with whom Louis entered into a morganatic union after Maria Theresa's death and which endured for the remainder of Louis XIV's life.

Like Francis I, Henri II, and to a lesser extent, Henri IV, Louis XIV accorded his queen all due honor, dining and sleeping with her regularly, while she amused herself with card games, a troupe of buffoons, and a pack of lapdogs. His subjects admired her for her virtue and piety, as well as her male heir.

But the marriage was less than companionate. Like Francis I's queens, Maria Theresa lacked the intellectual and artistic sensibility to compete in the royal court situated at Versailles, the palace west of Paris where Louis XIV lived among his aristocracy according to a highly stratified social order of etiquette. Modest and religious in the tradition of Spanish Habsburg *infantas*, Maria Theresa ceded the court spotlight to Louis XIV's mistresses, whose beauty, wit, and ability to entertain allowed them to co-opt the informal functions of queenship. Although Madame de Montespan sometimes treated her rudely, there were no scenes like those of Marie de Medici, and Maria Theresa found welcome and sympathetic relief in Madame de Maintenon, who engineered a reconciliation between the king and queen in the final years of Maria Theresa's life. In this regard, she followed in the tradition of Claude, Eleanor, and Catherine de Medici, queens who maintained their dignity and composure in the face of their husband's serial infidelities. When Maria Theresa died in 1683, Louis remarked that her death was the only trouble she had ever caused him.

With the death of Maria Theresa, there would be no queens in France until 1723, although Madame de Maintenon functioned as an informal queen for the remainder of Louis XIV's reign, serving as the king's companion, but also as an *ex-officio* minister of state, exerting powerful influence over domestic, foreign, and ecclesiastical affairs, a feat not duplicated by *any* of the early modern queen consorts of France.[48] But in Spain, the death of Charles II sparked a Europe-wide scramble for the Spanish throne. In his will, Charles II had left his throne to sixteen-year-old Philip, duke of Anjou, the second son of Louis XIV's eldest son and heir, *Le Grand Dauphin*, who crossed the Spanish frontier on January 28, 1701, to become the first Bourbon king of Spain as Philip V.

For the remainder of the early modern era, the new dynasty, comprised of four kings and five queens consort, signaled a resurgence which halted Spain's long seventeenth-century decline. Most importantly, Spain became a unitary kingdom under the Bourbons, albeit a smaller kingdom, as a result of the War of Spanish Succession, in which Spain lost the Netherlands for good, while the Italian holdings were also severely diminished. This war occupied the first thirteen years of Philip V's reign. Fearing a possible union of the French and Spanish crowns, a "Grand Alliance" of Britain, Holland, and Austria went to war against France and Spain with their own candidate, the archduke Charles (later Emperor Charles VI). As the new king was only sixteen, Louis XIV went about arranging his grandson's foreign policy, which included arranging for his marriage with thirteen-year-old Maria Luisa, the daughter of duke Victor Amadeus II of Savoy, in an effort to keep the duchy on the Franco-Spanish side of the war.

Philip V's most notable achievement, at age forty-six, was serving as the longest reigning king in modern Spanish history. An unexceptional man, he was exceptionally pious, repelled by bullfights and other blood sports, and prone to depression and periodic bouts of insanity. But he took his responsibilities seriously, leading the Franco-Spanish troops as the war came to the Iberian Peninsula, efforts that endeared himself to the Castilian people. He was also easily controlled, with the two women who married him exerting significant political control over him. He was also apparently a highly sexualized king, but because of his piety, he would only sleep with his wife. Thus, even in her teenage years, Maria Luisa exercised a large measure of control over her husband.[49] Much of this influence was positive; the queen worked tenaciously against the king's indolence, getting him out of bed and into the council chamber and field of battle. She was pretty and spirited, as well as fecund, bearing four children, two of whom would reign as kings of Spain. But she herself was under the influence of her *Camarera mayor de Palacio* (First Lady of the Bedchamber), Marie Anne de La Trémoille, princesse des Ursins, who functioned as a form of female *valido*, exercising the same level of control over access to the queen and control of her person as the count-duke of Olivares had exercised over Philip IV.

Maria Luisa, however, never enjoyed good health, and died of tuberculosis in 1714 at the age of twenty-six. Although she left behind two sons, Luis and Ferdinand, Philip V was back on the marriage market. The choice was skillfully arranged by Giulio Alberoni, an Italian cleric whose travels to the Spanish court brought him to the attention of Philip V, who made him consular agent for the Duchy of Parma. With these connections, Alberoni convinced Ursins, eager to continue as *valido* to the next queen, that Elisabeth Farnese, the twenty-one-year-old niece and heiress of the duke of Parma, would be docile and easy to control.

But when she arrived in Spain, in December 1714, Elisabeth (known as Isabel in Spain) swiftly disposed of Ursins, who was sent packing back to France, replaced by her own *valido,* Alberoni. Elisabeth was a whirlwind of a queen, the most powerful Spanish consort of the early modern era. She had been quite well educated, without any particular intellectual pursuits, nor was she particularly interested in being a popular queen, remarking that, "the Spanish do not like me, but I fully detest them also." She was fully intent on regime change, however, purging the court of its French elements, and creating her own Italianate court circle, guided by Alberoni, who was made a cardinal in 1715, and her Italian nurse Laura Pescatori, who created a powerful clientage network for the queen.

Philip V's queens were entirely successful in importing their native cultures into the Spanish court, quite unlike their sixteenth- and seventeenth-century predecessors, all of whom embraced Spanish culture during their tenures as queens.[50] They also enjoyed complete control over the person of the king, quite unlike their predecessors. Philip V's refusal to be physically separated from his wives shifted the locus of royal power to the domestic strongholds of their bedchambers and private apartments. The duke of Saint-Simon, a French diarist, once observed Philip and Elisabeth in bed with food, the queen's embroidery, and state papers all spread out as they prepared to meet with their ministers. She had an earthy wit, could be very charming but also overbearing, was prone to obesity, but early on realized that she would have to learn the business of government quickly as Philip's lapses in lucidity became more pronounced through time. Elisabeth's overriding ambition was to provide land for her sons Charles and Philip in Italy. To gain the financing for what became several decades of war devoted to just this purpose, Alberoni instituted modernizing reforms on administration, moving Spain in the more centralizing direction of France, and instituting measures to increase economic prosperity, such as eliminating internal customs duties, to improve Spain's military capacity, including the navy.

Elisabeth's ambitions were briefly sidelined when Philip V abruptly decided to abdicate his throne in January 1724, undoubtedly because of his own physical and mental problems. He was succeeded by his eldest son by Maria Luisa, seventeen-year-old Luis I, who died of smallpox after a reign of only nine months. Luis's death signaled the return of Queen Elisabeth, who convinced Philip V to reassume his throne. According to the terms of his abdication the next heir was twelve-year-old Ferdinand, the only surviving son of Maria Luisa. Elisabeth had little chance of gaining the regency, so to continue to rule Spain, she needed her husband back on his throne. But Elisabeth's decision to force him to reassume the throne was not in his best interests; Philip V suffered from periodic depression, psychosis, and catatonic states for the rest of his life. He was brought out of his stupor only by foreign military entanglements, which Elisabeth kept coming as she pursued the conquest of duchies and kingdoms for her own sons Charles and Philip.

Elisabeth was mostly successful in achieving her foreign policy objectives. In the Treaty of Vienna of 1731, her eldest son Charles was recognized as duke of Parma and Piacenza. But following the War of the Polish Succession (1733–1738) and the War of the Austrian Succession (1740–1748), Charles obtained the thrones of Naples and Sicily while his brother Philip became duke of Parma. The Italian wars, however, were a drain on the Spanish economy; as the people of Spain wearied of their sick king, they wearied also of a queen who ruled through foreign favorites while living extravagantly. As the ideas of the age of enlightenment infiltrated the royal courts of Europe, Elisabeth

never saw her queenship as a responsibility to rule for the benefit of her subjects, viewing her role as wielding a kingly prerogative for an incompetent husband and securing crowns and dynastic marriages for her sons and daughters.

One of the luxuries of being a powerful queen who lived long enough was
the ability to play the role of marriage broker. Not since Isabella of Castile,
another queen who lived a long full life, was a queen of Spain such an active
agent in the marriages of all her children, securing dynastic matches with
the royal houses of France, Portugal, and Sardinia for her two sons and two
daughters. Both Maria Luisa and Elisabeth Farnese proved adept at wielding
political power and dealing with foreign affairs, operating at times as *de facto*
queens regnant, and on other occasions, as partners with their husbands in
the manner of Isabella and Ferdinand of Spain. Both of these queens accepted
and manipulated the reality that regal power must be wielded through the
person of the king.

With the death of Philip V in 1746, his only surviving son from his first
marriage, thirty-two-year-old Ferdinand VI, ascended the Spanish throne.
Ferdinand inherited many of his father's more unfortunate mental deficiencies, which were more than compensated for by his wife, Maria Barbara, a
Portuguese *infanta* who married Ferdinand in 1729, in a double arrangement
that saw Elisabeth Farnese's daughter Mariana Victoria, the spurned fiancé
of Louis XV of France, marry Barbara's brother Joseph, the future king of
Portugal. These arrangements signaled a return to more traditional forms
of Iberian marriage alliances, as the Spanish Bourbons picked up where
the sixteenth-century Habsburgs had left off, by intermarrying with the
Portuguese royal house.

Despite her intelligence, education, cultured wit, and sense of royal deportment, Barbara was considered unattractive; Ferdinand was visibly shocked by
her appearance when he first met her. But they soon developed a close bond,
and the pair became as inseparable as Philip V and Elisabeth Farnese. Like
Elisabeth of Bourbon before her, Barbara benefitted from a long apprenticeship
as princess of Asturias, which allowed her to come to terms with her husband's
limitations, as well as to observe the powerful queenship of her mother-in-law
Elisabeth, who despised her stepdaughter-in-law. Despite his mental health
issues, Ferdinand was well educated and cultured, sharing Barbara's love of
music. Together they became Spain's first enlightened monarchs.

Unfortunately, the couple were unsuccessful in propagating the dynasty,
and Barbara suffered from lifelong asthma and later obesity. Nevertheless, as
the ideals of the Enlightenment permeated their reign, Ferdinand and Barbara
were intent on improving Spain materially, relying on two ministers, the pro-
French Marquis of Ensenada and the pro-British José de Carvajal y Lancaster,

who instituted a variety of reforms that initiated a process of further political and economic modernization that had begun under Philip V. But like his father, Ferdinand was somewhat indolent as well as timid. So like her two predecessors, Barbara was the motivator as well as the mouthpiece. Inevitably, both Ensenada and Carvajal learned that to make their ministry work they needed the queen, who functioned as an active agent in the formulation of policy, especially in the drive to achieve peace with Portugal, whose alliance with Britain was a complication with Spain's friendship with Bourbon France. In these actions she did the bidding of her natal country without drawing criticism for favoring foreigners as did Elisabeth Farnese.

Although Barbara was the third consort to wield such sweeping queenly power, she did so in a much more conventional fashion. Like so many Spanish and Portuguese queens before her, Barbara was a fervently religious queen, who took her devotions, moral probity, charity, pilgrimages, and dedication to building convents and monasteries as her own means of creating a queenly legacy, especially because she was childless. This was a switch from the more secular-minded Elisabeth Farnese, who only discovered charity and devotions after she became a dowager queen, undoubtedly to bolster her rather sagging popularity. But Barbara was sincere in her religiosity, refusing to flaunt the power she wielded, and conducting herself with dignity, modesty, and grace, serving as the balance between the dueling ministers Ensenada and Carvajal. Quite unlike the wives of Charles II, Barbara escaped the opprobrium of being a childless queen.

Under their administration, Spain was slowly extricated from European wars, with Spain refusing to enter the Seven Years War (1756–1763), which allowed for a Spanish treasury surplus for the first time in the early modern era. But Barbara's health had never been good; she died on August 27, 1758, of blood disease and asthma. Her final wish was to be buried in the convent that she and Ferdinand had founded, Las Salsas Reales, which aligned Barbara with so many previous Iberian queens who identified their queenships with moral probity, devotion to the Catholic religion, and charity. In the remaining year of his life, Ferdinand went completely insane, plunging the government into chaos before he died of a convulsive fit in August 1759, to be succeeded by his half-brother Charles III, who had been king of Naples and Sicily for twenty-four years. During the time it took for Charles to return to Spain, after a thirty-year absence, Elisabeth Farnese returned as regent, for one more moment in the sun, as her own dynastic dreams reached fruition with the accession of her eldest son.

Charles III is generally considered the finest king of Spain of the early modern era, as well as the epitome of a benevolent, enlightened monarch. Level-headed, jovial, hard-working, Charles had been a popular king of

Naples. He also enjoyed a completely companionate marriage to Maria Amalia of Saxony in the tradition of the Bourbon Spanish kings. The marriage was arranged by his mother, ever the dynast, who was determined to find an Austrian Habsburg bride for her eldest son. The closest she could get was the daughter of King Augustus III of Poland, Elector of Saxony, whose mother, Maria Josepha, was the daughter of Holy Roman Emperor Joseph I (r. 1705–1711). She was a humorless woman with a fiery temper, but she was a dynastically productive queen of Naples, bearing thirteen children in seventeen years, with seven surviving to adulthood. In addition to her childbearing duties, she was an active political agent in her husband's royal government. Once her first son was born in 1747, she obtained a formal seat in the council chamber. Ministers who crossed her usually lived to regret it, but she retained her husband's confidence throughout her life. But like her husband, she was imbued with the ideals of the Enlightenment, considering her queenship a duty to help make Naples a better place for its people, doing her best to keep Naples out of the War of the Austrian Succession, and refusing to tow the Franco-Iberian line on foreign policy.

Maria Amalia extolled two other queenly attributes: religiosity and legacy building. As busy as she was bearing children, supervising their educations, and helping her husband govern Naples, Maria Amalia tended to her devotions at a level that eventually brought her criticism because they exceeded those of monks and nuns. She was also heavily involved in several large-scale building projects, including the palaces of Cacerta, Portici, and Capodimonte, as well as the Teatro di San Carlo. Maria Amalia was a great collector of porcelain; her palaces featured works of porcelain made at the Capodimonte Porcelain Manufactory, which began production in Naples in 1743 under royal sponsorship. She later sponsored the beginning of a Spanish porcelain industry as queen of Spain.

The eighteenth-century Bourbon queens of Spain collectively wielded a powerful queenly prerogative in conjunction with their husbands, a power none of their Habsburg predecessors came close to possessing, while in France the only women who came to wield such queenly power were the mistresses of Louis XIV and Louis XV, Madame de Maintenon and Madame du Pompadour, and Marie Antoinette, France's final early modern queen.

THE BRAGANZA QUEENS OF PORTUGAL

From 1580 to 1640, the kings of Spain ruled Portugal in a union of Iberian crowns after the direct male Aviz line died out in the late sixteenth century. Portugal's two Habsburg Queens, Margaret of Austria and Elisabeth of

Bourbon, were absentee queens like their Stuart contemporaries in England, Mary of Modena and Henrietta Maria, who never visited their Scottish kingdoms. Nevertheless, like Scotland, Portugal maintained its own legal and governmental system, as did Castile and Aragon under the sixteenth- and seventeenth-century Habsburgs until Philip V issued the Nueva Planta decrees of 1707–1716, which achieved a formal union of Castile and Aragon. While Portugal achieved its dynastic independence under the Braganza kings in 1640, Portugal still remained within the Habsburg orbit, with Portuguese queen consorts exhibiting many of the same behavioral patterns as their Spanish counterparts, particularly in the custom of uncle-niece marriages that was also a feature of Spanish and Austrian Habsburgs, but also in the intensity of their religiosity, which emerged as a perennial feature of Portuguese queenship. The Braganza Queens also made a point of acculturating to their adoptive country, learning the language and customs and creating the perception that they cared about their Portuguese subjects.

Spanish rule collapsed in Portugal during the height of the Thirty Years War (1617–1647). The Dukes of Braganza, a cadet branch of the Aviz dynasty, were strategically placed to act when Philip IV of Spain assaulted Portuguese autonomy by imposing taxes and appointing Spanish administrators, arousing the Portuguese nobility into rebellion. A major player in the conspiracy to overthrow the Habsburg regime, known as "the Plot of the Forty Conspirators," was Luisa de Guzman (1615–1666), Castilian by birth, a descendant of the noble house of Medina Sidonia, who was the wife of John, Duke of Braganza. Luisa's support was critical in the efforts to place her husband on the Portuguese throne. When she was told of the possible dangers she would face, she is said to have remarked, "better a queen for a day than duchess for life." After Braganza assumed the throne as John IV, Portugal spent the next twenty-eight years getting Spain to formally accept its independence, which included its colonial empire in Brazil and India. But long before this goal was achieved in 1668, members of the Braganza dynasty quickly insinuated themselves into the pan-European royal kinship network, with consorts coming from Spain, Savoy, and the Holy Roman Empire.

From the moment Luisa de Guzman left Castile she followed a "Portugal First" campaign of cultural immersion while she bore the heirs who would continue the Braganza line. Following her husband's death in 1656, she became regent for her disabled thirteen-year-old son, Afonso VI. During this time Portugal remained embroiled in the Portuguese War of Restoration with Spain; Luisa was largely responsible for maintaining and modernizing Portugal's armed forces during this conflict, in which Portugal ultimately proved triumphant. Luisa also negotiated an alliance with England that proved helpful in the final stages of Portugal's independence effort, offering Charles II of England an attractive dowry for her daughter Catherine of Braganza that included Tangier and Bombay. As we have seen in Chapter 2, Catherine was shocked by the licentiousness of the Restoration Court in England, as Luisa had raised her in a typically Iberian cloistered and sheltered existence, where piety and moral probity were always emphasized. Despite her abilities and her energy, Luisa was unable to broker the marriage of her eldest son Afonso, who banished her to a convent in 1662, after his royal favorite, Luís de Vasconcelos e Sousa, Count of Castelo Melhor, convinced him that his mother was plotting to exile him. Nevertheless, for six years she had ruled Portugal as regent with firmness and resolve without any significant challenge to her authority, laying down a powerful precedent for her successors as queens.[51]

Portugal's next queen proved a worthy successor to Luisa de Guzman. The physically and mentally impaired Afonso VI, under the guidance of Louis XIV of France, married Marie Françoise of Savoy (1646–1683) in 1666 to secure Portugal as an ally against Spain. Known as Maria Francisca in Portugal, she had the distinction of becoming Queen of Portugal twice, as Anne of Brittany had done in France, by marrying two successive kings of Portugal. Because of his physical and mental impairments, Afonso was impotent, as was his counterpart in Spain, Charles II. But their wives had completely different outcomes. As we have seen, both of Charles II's queens were blamed for the lack of heirs, with his second queen, Maria Anna of Neuburg, ending her life in obscurity. Maria, however, was not content to remain married to an impotent king, attaching herself to the king's younger brother and heir, Peter, Duke of Beja, and participating in the palace coup that led to the ousting of the Count of Castelo-Melhor and Beja's assumption of the regency for the now exiled Afonso. By this time Maria had obtained an annulment, and had married Beja, later bearing one daughter, Isabel Luisa, but no further issue ensued.[52]

Nevertheless, Beja remained devoted to her, and their daughter was recognized as heir. Upon Afonso's death in 1683, Maria Francisca became queen again but died that same year in December. The choice of her successor thrust Portugal into the dynastic politics of late seventeenth-century Europe. While Maria Francisca's first marriage had been arranged to bring Portugal in on the side of France against Spain, Peter, in keeping with Portugal's long-standing English alliance, sought out his second consort from the Holy Roman Empire, choosing Maria Sophia of Neuburg (1666–1699), whose sister Eleonore Magdalene was married to Holy Roman Emperor Leopold I. The marriage chagrined Louis XIV as it delighted James II of England, who sent a yacht to fetch her from Brill to Plymouth before she embarked for Portugal. Apparently, a major selling point for Maria Sophia was her family's reputation for producing highly fecund women. Maria Sophia did not disappoint, bearing four sons and one daughter, but she brought several other qualities to her role as queen. Like her two predecessors, Maria Sophia set out to be a Portuguese queen. Described as well-mannered and sweet tempered, she gained the affection of her husband and her stepdaughter, while creating a reputation for charity and piety, founding schools and offering free medical care to many of the citizens of Lisbon.

The imperial connection continued under the reign of Maria Sophia's son John V, who married his first cousin Maria Anna (1683–1754), daughter of Leopold I and Eleonore Magdalene. At this stage, the Braganza consorts appeared to be following a pattern for queenly conduct which prioritized cultural assimilation, companionate marriage, dedication to family, and religious and charitable works. Maria Anna took this process one step further by instituting a reform of her court based upon the traditional practices of the Portuguese queens, an effort she put much energy into.[53] At the same time she brought the flavor of the Imperial court in Vienna in the magnificence of her parties, which often lasted for days. The marriage was happy, always a priority for Austrian archduchesses (see Chapter 4), although Joseph fathered a brood of illegitimate children who were raised at court. But although they led somewhat separate lives, Maria Anna assumed the role of regent when Joseph suffered a stroke in 1742. However, quite unlike Elisabeth Farnese in Spain, who was reluctant to give up power, Maria Anna relinquished power to her eldest son Joseph I after her husband's death in 1750. Joseph I inherited her love of opera, which originated in Italy, but came to Portugal via Vienna and its Italian queens Eleonora Gonzaga the Elder and the Younger (see Chapter 4).

Joseph I's choice of consort represented a return to inter-Iberian dynastic politics with his marriage to Mariana Victoria (1718–1781), the eldest daughter of Philip V of Spain and Elisabeth Farnese. Mariana was in fact the spurned fiancé of Louis XV of France (see below), which freed her to become part of a double marriage package that included the marriage of Joseph's sister Maria Barbara to the future Ferdinand VI of Spain. Both marriages turned out to be harmonious unions, although Mariana had to deal with her husband's mistresses, for which she castigated her husband in the public spaces of the court. Otherwise, Mariana was the perfect Iberian consort, deeply religious yet a lover of music and culture; she shared her husband's love of Italian opera, which played its own role as the great cultural pollinator of European royal courts.[54] Mariana also proved to be quite fecund, with eight pregnancies and four children who survived infancy.

Her queenship was marred by her husband's dependence on royal favorite, Sebastião José de Carvalho e Melo, 1st Marquis of Pombal, who had been a favorite of Dowager Queen Maria Anna. Following the Lisbon Earthquake of 1755, which destroyed the city, Pombal made a name for himself directing the rebuilding effort, eventually assuming control over the government, instituting a form of benevolent despotism based upon enlightenment principles, which modernized and streamlined the government, while not tolerating any opposition and filling the prisons with political opponents. Like her two predecessors, Luisa de Guzman and Maria Anna, Mariana also assumed the role of regent for three months following Joseph I's stroke and later death (February 24, 1777).

Now dowager queen, Mariana found herself in a unique position, one experienced only by Mary of Guise of Scotland and Maria Eleonora of Sweden (see Chapter 4), as the mother of a regnant queen, Maria I (1734–1816), who assumed the throne at age forty-three.[55] Maria, like Isabel Luisa, the daughter of Maria Francisca, was limited in her marriage prospects by the law of the Cortes of Lamego (1143), which, according to tradition, stated that a female monarch had to marry a Portuguese nobleman or give up her right to the throne. There was no factual basis for this law, but the tradition was revived and made law in 1640, betraying contemporary fears of another hostile dynastic takeover by the Habsburgs, and reinforcing the predilection towards uncle-niece marriages. Portugal was unique among European kingdoms in that they had laws defining the contours of female rule. In nearly every other case, preparing for the eventuality of a female ruler, in England, Scotland, Sweden, Russia, and Austria, was an ad hoc process.

Mariana Victoria used her political capital wisely as a dowager, negotiating peace with her brother as Anne of Austria had been able to do as a dowager queen, and playing the role of marriage broker, marrying her youngest daughter Maria Francisca to her eldest grandson Joseph, Prince of Beira. Her eldest daughter, Maria I, also wed closely within the family, marrying her father's younger brother Peter, who was seventeen years her senior. Despite the age gap, and the closeness in blood, the marriage turned out to be harmonious, with seven pregnancies and three children surviving to adulthood. Peter was the perfect consort, as Prince George of Denmark had been for Queen Anne of England, with no independent political or military ambitions. Instead they shared their love of the arts and the intensity of their piety. However, Peter assumed the title of King Consort upon Maria's accession according to another Portuguese succession law, as he had provided for the succession. Otherwise, he would have simply been Prince Consort, as was Ferdinand of Saxe-Coburg and Gotha-Koháry, the consort of Maria II of

Portugal (1819–1853), who did not assume the title of king until the birth of his son in 1837.[56]

Maria I was reputed to have been a competent ruler in the early part of her reign. Her mother, Mariana Victoria, served as an advisor until her death in 1781. But Maria was not mentally equipped to handle the rigors of regnant queenship. She probably inherited her madness from her maternal grandfather, Philip V of France, although it has been postulated that she suffered from porphyria, the disease her contemporary George III of Great Britain suffered from.[57] Her extreme religiosity spurred on her madness, which was brought on by the successive deaths of her husband in 1786 and her eldest son and heir in 1788. By 1792, as the early modern era in Europe drew to a close while the French Revolution entered its most radical phase, Maria's mental incapacity became permanent, although she lived another twenty-four years, dying in Brazil (in exile from Napoleon), where she was known as Maria la Loca. She is the exception to the rule of Braganza queenship, which in all other cases was a bastion for power in the Portuguese kingdom with a succession of queens who enjoyed the perception that they loved their husbands and cared for their children, while serving as helpmates and regents when the situation required it. All enjoyed reputations as good queens, fully acclimating to Portuguese culture, yet also serving as the great pollinators of culture, particularly baroque art and architecture and Italian opera.

THE FINAL QUEENS OF THE *ANCIEN REGIME* FRANCE

When Louis XIV died in 1715, he was succeeded by his four-year-old great-grandson Louis XV. Although a sickly child, Louis survived to the ripe old age of 66. When he died, legend has it that he said, "after me, the deluge," predicting the French Revolution, which broke out fifteen years after his death in 1774. Louis possessed a myopic view of the dynamic changes happening within his kingdom, ideologically, economically, and politically, as the ideals of the European Enlightenment permeated an increasingly critical and informed French civil society that viewed the essentially feudal institutions of government and church as hopelessly out of touch, as Voltaire so mercilessly lampooned in his novel *Candide* (1759). Over the course of the eighteenth century, French civil society became increasingly aware of the disfunction of the French monarchy as it was described and lampooned in pamphlets, broadsheets, songs and ballads, and works of theater and fiction.

Given this situation, Marie Leszczyńska (1725–1768), the consort of Louis XV, enjoyed success by following a traditional queenly playbook. She was the most atypical of French queens. Going back to Anne of Brittany, French queens were usually chosen for their dynastic luster or their sizeable dowries. Marie brought neither to her marriage. Her selection as queen was in fact the final power play of Louis XV's minority, the compromise between the Duke of Bourbon, currently serving as Louis's *de facto* regent, and the King's tutor and confidante, Cardinal André-Hercule de Fleury, Bishop of Fréjus. Seven years Louis's senior, Marie was the daughter of the penniless and landless Stanislaw I, deposed King of Poland, who was living in Alsace. She was plain but virtuous, with pleasant manners, reasonably educated, and possessed of a dignified bearing. She was also devotedly Catholic in the manner of Spanish *infantas* and Austrian archduchess. The marriage was celebrated in August 1725, after Marie presumably passed a medical examination to determine her childbearing capabilities, much as Anne of Brittany had undergone 250 years previously. She bore twin daughters two years later, then another daughter, and in 1729, a dauphin. Six more children followed.

As the twenty-two-year-old bride of a highly sexualized teenaged king, Marie was well placed to establish a form of sexual dominance over her husband, as her counterparts in Spain had done with Philip V. But early into her marriage, in December 1725, Marie lent her hand to the Duke of Bourbon's ill-advised attempt to dislodge the king's former tutor and advisor Cardinal Fleury from his counsels. The plan backfired, and at this point Marie lost whatever confidence her husband had previously placed in her, if he had any at all. For the next four years, Cardinal Fleury, who enjoyed wide-ranging influence over the king, tried to have her replaced as queen until the birth of the Dauphin secured the succession. While they continued to procreate for the next twelve years with regularity, by 1733, six years into the marriage, the king began satisfying his sexual passions with a string of mistresses. Marie had little choice but to deal with these women who inhabited the royal court. Starting in 1737, when the Queen informed her husband that she would no longer share their marital bed, the pair live separate existences while continuing to perform the ceremonial aspects of their roles, much as Francis I and Eleanor of Castile had done 200 years previously.

After her ill-fated attempt to intervene in politics, Marie took counsel, deciding that she would cultivate the image of a pious and virtuous queen who abstained from politics.[58] She cultivated a relationship with Cardinal Fleury, who later became her conduit to the king when she wanted patronage for her friends and relatives. But despite changing her ways, Marie never regained the king's affection or confidence. While in Metz in 1744, when Louis was quite ill and thought he would die, he sent away his mistress Marie Anne de Mailly and sent for the queen. But when Marie arrived, the king had recovered and refused to see her, although the crowds cheered her on her journey, on account of her reputation as a good queen who supported religious foundations, dispensed large amounts of charity, and was a good mother to her children. The next year, Madame de Pompadour ascended the throne of official mistress, co-opting many of the functions of queenship in the grand tradition of Francoise de Foix, Diane du Poitiers, and the Marquise of Maintenon. In this sense Marie's queenship most resembled the consortship of Catherine de Medici, another low-born queen who, despite her ability to propagate the dynasty, was completely left out of her husband's counsels and affections.

This was most clear in Marie's inability to play marriage broker, the final cornerstone of a successful queenship. The Dauphin had been married to the Spanish *infanta* Maria Theresa, a daughter of Philip V and Elisabeth Farnese, who died in 1745 following the birth of a daughter. Her replacement was the Duchess Marie-Josèphe of Saxony, daughter of King Augustus III of Poland, her father's rival who had replaced him on the Polish throne. Dynastically, the marriage was an affront to her, but she accepted the marriage with as much grace as possible, and later became very close to her daughter-in-law.

Marie compensated for her lack of influence by embracing the strict protocols of etiquette at Versailles, where she remained the highest-ranking woman in the kingdom, and received the outward respect of her husband's subjects within the ceremonial functions of the royal court. Multilingual, Marie enjoyed playing the role of interpreter at Louis XV's court, as when Mozart paid a visit to Versailles in 1764, and she was always especially cordial to Swedish diplomats, because Sweden's king, Charles XII, had helped her father gain the Polish throne. She was also a great lover of music, the famed castrato Farinelli came to Versailles to sing for her, and she sponsored Polish choral performances. She also had Voltaire banished from Versailles, after he wrote a poem suggesting the sexual relationship between Louis XV and Madame de Pompadour. Marie put up with the licentiousness of her husband's court, but she drew the line at any official recognition of this state of affairs.

When her official duties were finished, Marie retreated to the confines of her royal household and her own intimate circle of friends, such as her grand almoner Cardinal de Luynes, Duke Charles de Luynes, the great-great grandson of Louis XIII's favorite, and his wife, Marie Brulart, and Francoise de Mailly, Duchess de Mazarin, creating a form of private inner court that her successor, Marie Antoinette, was later resented for. But she got away with it because she successfully projected the image of a good queen. Like her two predecessors, Anne of Austria and Maria Theresa, Marie was devoted to the Catholic religion, and well known for her charity and her piety, the textbook means of earning queenly prestige that was a constant throughout the early modern era. She was also depicted as a devoted mother, staying out of court politics and refusing to engage in the more licentious aspects of the royal court, although she enjoyed a card game called *cavagnole*, which, along with her charities, kept her perennially in debt, despite a 100,000 livre annual allowance.

Marie's queenship was both conventional and traditional, reminiscent of the queenships of Claude, Eleanor of Castile, Anne of Austria, and Maria Theresa, and was received favorably in the highly critical court of public opinion. In contrast, Louis XV, whose disdain for his queen was well-known, was unable to reap any of the positive benefits of having a popular queen. In this sense, as Jennifer G. Germann has argued, Marie provided a queenly dichotomy to the royal image of the Bourbon dynasty, lauded for her charity and her piety while Louis was increasingly lampooned for his un-Christian-like womanizing, his costly dynastic wars, and the frivolity of his court life, which was contrasted with the relative austerity of Marie's lifestyle.[59]

Not surprisingly, Marie was more popular with the French people than her husband. When she died in 1768 at the age of sixty-five, she had been the longest-serving queen consort in early modern French history. But like her near contemporary Charlotte of Mecklenburg-Strelitz, another long serving queen, she earned praise as a thoroughly domesticated queen, quite unlike her ambitious, hard-boiled contemporary Elisabeth Farnese of Spain. She well knew she had been an unlikely choice for queen. While her marriage was not companionate, she had provided for the succession, and she provided for her successor a sometimes infuriating example of a good queen, who behaved by a traditional playbook for gaining queenly prestige. She was largely immune to the ideals of the Enlightenment, quite unlike her contemporaries Caroline of Ansbach of Great Britain and Louisa Ulrika of Sweden.

Marie Antoinette certainly hated the comparisons with her predecessor.[60] Along with Catherine de Medici she is the most well-known of early modern French queens, forever saddled in popular culture with the apocryphal quip, "let them eat cake," which symbolized her supposed indifference to the plight of the French people as she lived a life of conspicuous royal consumption.[61] Her marriage was the fifth and last early modern dynastic alliance between the Habsburgs and the royal houses of France. Born in 1755, the youngest daughter of Holy Roman Empress Maria Theresa and her consort Francis Stephen, Marie was raised in Vienna, but was not particularly well educated. She did, however, have a flair for music, singing, and fashion, displaying a coquettish charm within the imperial court in Vienna. Her timing was also good; while Marie had numerous older sisters, all of whom married into the various royal houses of Europe in their enviable positions as Habsburg

Austrian Archduchesses, it was she who made the best marriage of her siblings. In 1770, when Maria Theresa and Louis XV of France decided to end their mutual animosities and become allies in their mutual loathing of Prussia and Great Britain, Marie was the available daughter for Louis's heir, his eldest grandson, the Dauphin Louis Auguste.

When she first arrived in 1770 she was treated as if she was a fairy princess. But once the official celebrations surrounding the wedding were over, the hard reality of life at Versailles set in. Marie had a difficult time adjusting to life as dauphine. While so many of her predecessors brought noble ladies and confessors with them from their native lands, Marie came to Versailles at the age of fourteen without any Austrian attendants, or any idea how to behave within the complicated system of royal etiquette that bound the French court. Her arrival came only two years after the death of Marie Leszczyńska, which meant that the French court had long been used to the concept of a queen as a morally upright and religious nonentity, while royal mistresses such as Madame de Pompadour and later Madame du Barry expropriated the queenly role as companions to the monarch, royal hostesses for the court, and political advisors.

Marie was certainly a breath of fresh air, much as Lady Diana Spencer was to the modern Windsor dynasty in Britain, bringing a youthful playfulness and an enviable sense of style to the French court at Versailles. But these qualities were not universally welcomed at court, especially by those who had not made their peace with the Austrian alliance and referred to her as "L'Autrichienne" (the Austrian bitch). In turn, Marie grew to loath the exhausting ritual of court etiquette, and the constant comparisons to the saintly Marie Leszczyńska. Then there were royal princesses and the other ladies of the court, who had advised her to snub Madame du Barry, and the incessant letters from her mother, insisting that she maintain the Austrian alliance by acknowledging du Barry![62]

Marie's first few years in France were highly reminiscent of the early years in France of Anne of Austria, as a foreign-born queen saddled with a husband who had no interest in her whatsoever. In contrast to his wife, Louis XVI has never been a particularly sympathetic historical figure. He was well educated, in a conventional sense, although the major works of the Enlightenment were not a part of his curriculum. He was also raised to be pious and religiously observant; he and Louis XIII were the only early modern French monarchs who remained faithful to their wives. In this, Louis XVI joined the ranks of Philip V of Spain and George III of Great Britain as kings who set a moral example for their subjects as models of marital fidelity. But he lacked kingly qualities; he was remote, indecisive, and later prone to depression, while devoting much of his time to hunting and practicing his skills as a locksmith.

Marie responded to these pressures and her husband's indifference by becoming a fashion icon and attempting to carve out a private space for her queenship. It never seemed to dawn on Marie that her coveted role, first as dauphine, and later as queen, entailed responsibilities as well as privilege, or that she needed to create a positive public image for herself within the spaces of the court. The usual routes to achieving this were religious observances, dispensing charity, and bearing children. Marie, however, spent exorbitant sums on fashion, feathers, and fantastic hairstyles called "poufs" that sometimes reached three feet high, making it hard for the ladies imitating her to enter doorways and carriages.[63] Her extravagance continued after Louis XVI's 1774 accession, when popular antagonism to the monarchy was transferred to Marie. With her ample bosom, pale white skin, and luminous blonde hair, she was an eroticized queen, the first in early modern French history.

But being a beautiful queen was a double-edged sword. If anything, beautiful queens have to work harder to maintain their moral probity, as Anne of Austria did in the previous century, a queen who enjoyed the attentions of handsome men while being scrupulous in her religious devotions and charity work. Marie also had her charities, but she also had male friends, such as Axel von Fersen, a Swedish diplomat and soldier, who was suspected of being her lover and the father of her daughter. This was a remarkable contrast from the pious and charitable Marie Leszczyńska. The perception of Marie as an eroticized queen made her an easy target for any number of libels. No one ever accused Marie Leszczyńska of looking for lovers to quench her lust after she and Louis XV had stopped sleeping together, but contemporaries found it much harder to believe that a young buxom beautiful queen not particularly noted for her religious devotions who cultivated friendships with noblemen could remain chaste within a marriage that remained unconsummated for several years. Indeed, the royal court was ill prepared to control the narrative of Marie's queenship within the dynamic structures of an increasingly critical civil society that viewed her as a sexually promiscuous foreign queen serving the interests of her natal country.

Initially Marie made no attempt to neutralize her negative public image, unaware that her actions would be subject to a robust and increasingly bellicose public opinion, as voices in salons, pamphlets, ribald sheets, and novels and plays subjected her lavish lifestyle and suspected sexual promiscuity to ridicule. For Marie, her audience was the court, which both followed and criticized her fashion trends, until she retreated behind the walls of Petit Trianon, a chateau on the property of Versailles that had formerly been the retreat of Louis XV's mistresses Madame de Pompadour and Madame du Barry. Here, Marie created a much more informal life with her favored ladies, Marie

Louise, princess de Lamballe, and Yolande de Polanstron, duchess of Polignac. In doing so, Marie excluded the rest of Versailles society, which aroused aristocratic consternation, as the monarchy had always performed publicly at Versailles, from the moment they woke up until the moment they retired to bed. Even the King had to ask permission to visit Petit Trianon. By 1775 it was being reported in the popular press that the walls were covered in gold and diamonds, exemplifying the disparity between France's economic problems and the opulent lifestyle of the royal court. Later, Louis XVI built Marie another private getaway, the Queen's Hamlet, a working agricultural village where Marie would walk about in the garb of a shepherdess with her children and milk cows in the dairy, and in 1784, amid growing public outrage, Louis purchased for her Chateau de Saint Cloud, which cost 6 million livres.

Marie's growing unpopularity might have been mitigated by the production of heirs. But apparently Louis and Marie made little attempt at procreation. Seven years into the marriage, it took a visit by Marie's brother Emperor Joseph II of Austria to convince the pair to consummate the marriage, resulting in the birth of a daughter, Marie Therese, in 1778. With the birth of a dauphin, Louis-Joseph, in 1781, Marie emerged as a stakeholder in her husband's kingship, accepting his limitations, his lack of leadership qualities, and his indecisiveness, which she, as the daughter of Maria Theresa, would make up for. As the daughter of the premier female ruler of eighteenth-century Europe, Marie had been tutored to be an active and engaged queen, inserting herself into politics by supporting French entry into the American War of Independence while pursuing a pro-Austrian foreign policy, all of which required enormous outlays of funds from an already bankrupt royal treasury.

In this capacity Marie was the most powerful French queen consort since Anne of Brittany. But despite the production of heirs, with a second son born in 1785, Marie was pilloried in the press over the diamond necklace scandal, which she herself had nothing to do with. Instead, a group of conspirators convinced Cardinal de Rohan, a prominent member of the court and a former ambassador to Vienna, to buy a 2 million livre diamond necklace originally commissioned by Louis XV for Madame du Barry as a means to gain favor with the Queen, using a prostitute as a double for the Queen. When the plot was exposed, the Queen had Rohan arrested, although he was subsequently acquitted by the Paris Parlement. Instead, Marie, who already endured a popular reputation for frivolity, extravagance, and sexual promiscuity, was blamed by the popular press for using the scandal as a pretext to bring down her enemy Cardinal Rohan. Scholars tend to agree that this was the tipping point for Marie's queenship, which never recovered by the time the French Revolution erupted in 1789.[64] She did try to temper her image, commissioning paintings depicting her surrounded by her children. But what worked for Queen Charlotte of Great Britain was no match for the public image of the queen's extravagance and depravity that literally took on a life of its own in the popular press, which by the late 1780s depicted her as an incestuous nymphomaniac, constantly cuckolding her ineffectual husband.[65]

The French Revolution, which erupted in 1789, is considered the end of the early modern period in Europe; Marie Antoinette's queenship did not survive it. The Revolution was the result of a multiplicity of factors. Most importantly, the ideas of the Age of Enlightenment questioned many of the supposed maxims of Early Modern European society, and proposed solutions to France's essentially feudal social structure. French society was well aware that such ideas had been put into practice in America, which fueled a desire for popular representation within the absolutist royal government. A series of bad harvests also increased popular discontent with the regime. But nobles' and clerics'refusal to part with their feudal privileges resulted in the calling of the Estates General for the first time since 1615, which allowed Enlightenment ideas such as popular sovereignty and the equality of man to catch on like fire among the delegates of the Third Estate, who on June 20, 1789, assembled in a tennis court and pledged to create a French constitution.

From the very first, Marie Antoinette was an implacable foe of the Revolution; her first reaction was to order the Swiss guards to disperse the revolutionaries. By this time, it was clear to her that the Revolution would not be good for her queenship. For the first fourteen years of her reign, the French people had no means to respond to the negative public image of the queen. But following the Fall of Bastille (July 14, 1789), the traditional anniversary of the French Revolution, the royal family were subjected to indignities and violence, beginning with the forced march (October 5, 1789) from Versailles to the Tuileries, where they lived as virtual prisoners under the guard of the Marquis de Layfayette, the French hero of the American Revolution. Marie was also subject to increasing media coverage, known as the *Libelles*. These tracts, which began to be published four years after Marie's arrival in France, were similar to the *Mazarinades* of Anne of Austria's regency. By the end of the 1780s, they had assumed pornographic proportions, in which she was accused of incest with her younger son among her other sexual crimes, such as lesbianism.

While Louis XVI made half-hearted efforts to compromise with the Constituent Assembly, which wrote a constitution for France making Louis a constitutional monarch as "King of the French," Marie kept the lines of communication open to her brothers Joseph and Leopold, and later Leopold's son Francis II, successive Holy Roman Emperors, for outside help to stem the course of the Revolution. By 1791 Marie, the real power behind the tottering Bourbon throne, decided on escape (as so many members of the nobility and clergy, including the king's brothers, had already), in the infamous flight to Varennes (June 21–25, 1791), where the royal family were intercepted and returned to Paris in disgrace.

During the year between the flight to Varennes and the abolition of the monarchy and the founding of the First Republic (September 21, 1792), Marie urged Austria to form a coalition against France and bring the Revolution to a halt. In response, Emperor Leopold II issued the Declaration of Pillnitz (August 27, 1791), which warned the Revolutionary government to restore the king his powers. Subsequent Austrian hostilities towards France resulted in a declaration of war against Austria in April 1792. In turn, Austria allied with Prussia, issuing the Brunswick Manifesto (July 25, 1792), which threatened the people of Paris should the royal family endure bodily harm. All of these developments put the spotlight on Marie's position as a "foreign queen," a perception she was never able to shake over the course of her eighteen-year consortship. At the same time, the threat of foreign invasion caused the Revolution to move in a more radical direction, with the rise of the Jacobins and their leader, Robespierre, who were determined to root out counterrevolutionaries.

Marie was the ultimate counterrevolutionary; what she was hated for most at the beginning of her queenship, for being a foreign queen in sympathy with her natal country, was what she was hated for most at its end. In June and July 1792, the royal family were threatened by armed mobs at the Tuileries Palace and only escaped being massacred by their flight to the legislative assembly. They were subsequently imprisoned in the Temple as the Revolution entered its most radical phase, with the abolition of the monarchy, which was replaced by the national convention, as well as creation of the revolutionary tribunal dominated by the Jacobins. The savage murder and dismembering of Marie's close friend Marie de Lamballe on September 3 presaged the final indignities inflicted upon the deposed queen and her family.

To the revolutionaries in control of France's government, Marie Antoinette and Louis XVI were traitors to the French state, a perception and world view that Marie could not understand; her world view was dynastic and not statist. To Marie, kingship in France was still a heritable estate. Regardless of what happened to her, including the loss of her own queenship, Marie was determined to preserve her family and the succession rights of her sole surviving son, the dauphin Louis-Charles. Her response was a traditional one, like that of Henrietta Maria of England, to preserve her husband and her children.[66] It is in this one facet of her queenship that Marie had the most in common with so many of her early modern predecessors.

But eighteen years of sustained bad publicity surrounding Marie's performance as queen consort undoubtedly helped bring down the House of Bourbon. For the remainder of 1792 the royal family endured a close imprisonment while the Convention prepared to try Louis XVI for treason. Convicted by just one vote, Louis XVI was guillotined on January 21, 1793. For the remainder of her life, Marie endured a tormented existence, the likes of which no other early modern queen was subjected to. By June 1793, the moderates had been purged from the national convention as Robespierre and the Jacobins inaugurated the "reign of terror" to rid France of counterrevolutionaries.

In this context, "Widow Capet" was public enemy number one. Forcibly separated from her children on July 3, 1793, Marie was imprisoned in the Concierge. The failed "Carnation Plot" to free Marie probably hastened her trial, in October, for treason, for which her own son was coached to accuse her of incest. This charge shook Marie to her core and she called on all the mothers present, who offered her a final taste of sympathy and solidarity.[67] Convicted on October 14, 1793, she was guillotined two days later. The great revolutionary artist Jacques-Louis David sketched her in her final moments, dressed in white, her shorn hair hidden under a cap and her hands tied behind her back, dignified and resigned to her fate, a final show of queenly worth that the revolutionary propaganda machine could not take from her.

At the dawn of the modern age in Europe which the French Revolution brought about, a queen could serve as a representative of a nation, as Queen Charlotte of Great Britain was quite able to do as a devoted wife and mother of her nation. Marie Antoinette was just as symbolic, but in other ways, as the symbol of the Ancien Regime's corruption and extravagance, as the archetype wicked foreign queen, and as the eroticized sexual predator, perceptions which crowded out all other aspects of her life as queen, especially her role as a wife and mother. The modern age confronted her brutally. She was never able to control perceptions about her queenship, which became the fodder for her complicated historical reputation.

CONCLUSION

The early modern history of France and Spain is the story of frequent warfare between the two kingdoms, while the peace that was routinely achieved frequently involved the dynastic interbreeding of French Valois and Bourbon and Spanish and Austrian Habsburg queen consorts. Over the course of the sixteenth and seventeenth centuries, France had three native-born queen consorts, three Spanish, two Italian, two Austrian, and one each from Lorraine and Poland. In Spain, the native-born queens Isabella and Juana of Castile were followed by four Austrian queen consorts, three French, two Portuguese, and one from Saxony-Poland. The patterns of consort recruitment suggest a concentric circle that swoops south from France through Iberia, then eastward to Italy, and north to Austria. But in the seventeenth and eighteenth centuries, an even stronger triangle developed between France, Spain, and the Habsburg dominions, which represented the three premier monarchies of the early modern period. The result of this was an intense form of cultural cross-pollination, as Austrian composers like Mozart performed at Versailles, which itself set the standard for the ostentatious baroque courts of Vienna and Madrid, while powerful French and Spanish consorts like Catherine de Medici and Elisabeth Farnese imported Italianate influences in art and music to their respective courts.

As Catholic-majority kingdoms, religious observance, piety, and devotion to charitable concerns were the nearly universal qualities of Franco-Iberian queenship. Both Isabella of Castile and Anne of Brittany set powerful examples for queenly piety that most of their successors sought to emulate. What all these queens had in common was their devotion to the Catholic faith, which was an important element of their queenly personas. Those who deviated from this model, such as Catherine de Medici, Elisabeth Farnese, and Marie Antoinette, suffered attacks upon their reputations. Many early modern French and Spanish queens also fulfilled the role of peacemaker. Eleanor of Castile, Elisabeth of Valois, Anne of Austria, Maria Theresa, and Marie Antoinette were all married to cement alliances between France and the Spanish and Austrian Habsburgs, while agreements such as the Treaty of Cambrai, known as "The Ladies Peace" (1529), and the Treaty of Cateau-Cambrésis (1559), which ended the Valois-Habsburg War, were indicative of the role royal women could play in the peacemaking process.[68]

But the regional differences between queenship in Spain and France were significant. In France, the role of queen was essentially fractured. Anne of Austria's consortship is emblematic of early modern French queenship; most French kings did not enjoy companionate marriages with their queens. Kings from Francis I to Louis XV kept official mistresses who assumed many of the informal roles of queenship while also serving as political advisors, effectively marginalizing queens from Claude to Marie Leszczyńska. Only three French queens, Marie de Medici, Anne of Austria, and Marie Antoinette, were ever accused of promoting the interests of their natal country over France, while the rest of France's queens were able to successfully adapt to French culture and language. A select few, Anne of Brittany, Claude, Maria Theresa, and

Marie Leszczyńska, were able to enjoy the contemporary reputation of a good queen. But while France had a history of marginalized consorts, it also had a history reaching back to the middle ages of powerful queen regents. Catherine de Medici, Marie de Medici, and Anne of Austria all left a much stronger imprint of their queenships as dowagers and regents than as consorts.

In Spain and Portugal, queenship was much more cohesive than it was in France. In addition to her successes as a female king, Isabella of Castile also laid down a powerful example of queenship for her successors as queens of Spain to follow, many of whom were her direct descendants, which emphasized companionate marriage, motherhood, piety and charity, and legacy building through the arrangement of dynastic marriages and the building of churches and monuments. If her daughter Juana was the exception to this model of queenship, Isabel of Portugal, the wives of Philip II, and Spain's seventeenth-century queens all strove to achieve these goals. The religiosity of Iberian queenship was especially pronounced, which complemented that of Spanish kingship; kings from Philip II to Philip IV enjoyed close relationships with their queens, and, with the notable exception of Philip IV, remained sexually faithful to them. This situation was repeated with the eighteenth-century Bourbon queens, who all enjoyed intimate relationships with their husbands, while serving as political helpmates to their husbands when necessary. The Braganza Queens of Portugal also followed a similar trajectory in the forms and functions of their queenships.

For those queens able to control their income and access patronage, legacy building was also an integral facet of Franco-Iberian queenship. The library of Anne of Brittany, the tomb of Henri II and Catherine de Medici, the Rubens Medici Cycle panels in Paris, and the church and monastery of Val-de-Grace are the still existing and visible models of the efforts of early modern French queens to create and establish their legacy, while Marie Antoinette left her own imprint upon the grounds of Versailles in the homes she created to escape from the stifling atmosphere of court life. The Medici queens of France recognized the power of iconography to shape perceptions about their queenship and bolster their queenly legacies. There is not quite the level of legacy building in Spanish queenship, partly because most Spanish queens after Isabella and Juana of Castile did not live to middle age, which prevented them from building tombs or engaging in marriage brokering. But in comparison to their French counterparts, most early modern Spanish queens were recognized by their subjects as good queens.

One of the more difficult aspects of queenly legacy building was the ability to control the narratives of their queenships, an impossible feat for most of Europe's early modern queens. At the beginning of the early modern era,

Isabella of Castile and Anne of Brittany were able to exert control over the narratives of their reigns, patronizing hagiographic writers to tell the story of their queenships. Isabel of Portugal also benefitted from positive descriptions of her queenship. But in France, Catherine de Medici suffered a blackening of her name during the French Wars of Religion while Anne of Austria proved an easy target for the onslaught of the *mazarinades*, which besmirched her sexual reputation during the series of Fronde rebellions that defined her regency. It appears that Spanish queens were much more insulated from the opinions of their subjects than their French counterparts, although Elisabeth Farnese of Spain well knew of her subject's distaste for her, which did not disturb her in the slightest.

But in France, public opinion was much more bellicose, as French civil society began to increasingly view the monarchy through the lens of Enlightenment thinking. As we have seen in Britain, queens such as Caroline of Ansbach responded well to the increased visibility of queenship by courting the popularity of the masses, while her Spanish contemporary Elisabeth Farnese made it clear she had no interest in gaining the approval of her subjects. Marie Leszczyńska also enjoyed a mostly sympathetic press for her traditional and benign queenship. But no queen of Early Modern Europe represents the crushing arrival of the modern world as does Marie Antoinette, who was pilloried during her own lifetime for her inability to recognize just how much the visibility of queenship had changed from her sixteenth- and seventeenth-century predecessors.

4 The Empress Maria Theresa and Queenship in the Holy Roman Empire

On June 25, 1541, Archduchess Maria Theresa of Austria (1717–1780), the daughter and heir of Holy Roman Emperor Charles VI (r. 1711–1740), was crowned *King* of Hungary in Pressburg (now Bratislava, Slovakia).[1] The success of this event was crucial to establishing Maria Theresa as her father's successor in the various principalities that made up the polyglot Habsburg dominions, and it was stage-managed down to the smallest detail. The support of Hungary was vital. The Habsburgs, Holy Roman Emperors since the later Middle Ages, had been kings of Hungary since 1526, but the Diet and the nobility enjoyed considerable autonomy; Maria Theresa could not pass laws or wield her prerogative until she was crowned. But the Hungarians only crowned kings and queen consorts. While Maria Theresa later demanded that both the Hungarians and Bohemians accept her husband Francis Stephen as her co-ruler, he was not crowned alongside her at either of her coronations, as the consorts of kings normally were. But if the traditional method of crowning a king and queen together had been followed, Maria Theresa would have been crowned a consort. So, the Hungarian nobility kept Francis Stephen in the background while she underwent the crowning of a king as a woman.

Nearly all sources agree that Maria Theresa's performance was flawless. After the primate of Hungary crowned her with the heavy crown of St. Stephen, she was invested with both the scepter and an apple before mounting a horse to be girded with the St. Stephen's sword. She then led a procession through the city, stopping to knight forty-five noblemen before taking her oath and scaling on horseback a manmade hill (comprised of soil from all parts of Hungary), where she sliced the air four times with her sword as she vowed to defend her kingdom and its subjects. Maria Theresa's coronation remains the most famous in Hungarian history, and historical reenactments of the ceremony were performed in Bratislava in 2011 and 2016.

THE QUEENSHIP OF MARIA THERESA

Maria Theresa is generally considered one of the more successful Habsburg rulers of the early modern era.[2] Like her male predecessors, she wore many crowns and coronets, as Holy Roman Empress, and sovereign prince of Austria, Hungary, Bohemia, Croatia, Transylvania, Galicia, the Austrian Netherlands (Belgium), and a host of other smaller Central European principalities and duchies, territories possessing their own customs, laws, and languages. Except for the electoral imperial crown, Maria Theresa inherited these lands as her father's eldest daughter and heir. She was the first female heir to the Habsburg dominions, whose direct male line ended with her father, Holy Roman Emperor Charles VI (r. 1711–1740), who, earlier in his career, was the Habsburg claimant to the Spanish throne during the War of the Spanish Succession.

Like all hereditary monarchs, Charles VI was eager for sons, but his dynastic marriage to Elisabeth Christine of Brunswick-Wolfenbüttel only produced two daughters to survive infancy.[3] Four years before Maria Theresa's birth in 1717, Charles VI promulgated what was known as the Pragmatic Sanction, which set aside the Salic law that had long governed Habsburg inheritance in order to keep the Habsburg estate together in the event of a female succession. Charles VI spent the rest of his reign getting his fellow European princes to accept it.

But despite his mania to guarantee a female succession, Charles VI was diffident about the prospect of female rule. Quite unlike his counterpart in Spain, Philip V, whose queens participated in exercising his royal prerogative, Charles VI kept Elisabeth Christine firmly within the domestic realm of her queenship. In this spirit, Maria Theresa and her younger sister, Maria Anna, were raised to be consorts, learning music (a mainstay of the Austrian Habsburgs), singing and dancing, the intricacies of court ritual, and outdoor recreational activities appropriate for the female gender. This was a myopia common to Early Modern European monarchies, in which kings with female heirs declined to adequately educate their daughters or give them practical experience in statecraft; long gone were the days when the superbly educated Habsburg archduchesses Margaret of Austria and Mary of Hungary performed a myriad of official duties on behalf of Holy Roman Emperor Charles V. Much like Henry VIII of England's succession statutes, Charles VI's Pragmatic Sanction was more focused on ensuring that his daughter inherited the estate of the Habsburg dominions, rather than preparing her to rule as a prince; Charles VI viewed Maria Theresa primarily as the conduit to male grandsons to further the Habsburg dynasty through the female line. Because of this, the choice of her husband was of immense importance to the future of the dynasty.

As the eldest daughter of a reigning Holy Roman Emperor, Maria Theresa's marriage carried with it the possibility of rearranging the power balance of Europe, a fundamental issue of European politics since the Peace of Westphalia (1648) that propelled nearly all the conflicts of the eighteenth century, from the War of the Spanish Succession (1701–1714) to the Seven Years War (1754–1763). It was in this spirit that in 1725 a coalition of European states quashed an attempt to marry Maria Theresa to the future Charles III of Spain, a dynastic move highly reminiscent of the dynastic alliances between Austria and Spain that had characterized much of the sixteenth and seventeenth centuries.

The House of Lorraine was chosen instead. The duchy had been long coveted by the kings of France, the perennial enemy of the Habsburgs since the sixteenth century, while the House of Lorraine had close dynastic connections with the Habsburgs and had served Charles VI admirably in his various wars. But the first candidate, Leopold Clement, died of smallpox before his first scheduled visit to Vienna in 1723. In his place came his younger brother, Francis Stephen, who arrived at the court in Vienna at the age of fifteen, when Maria Theresa was six. Later, when there was talk of marrying her to the future Charles III of Spain and the future Frederick II of Prussia, she made clear her objections to her father as well as her desire to marry Francis Stephen of Lorraine.

Some other queens, such as Mary I of England and later Queen Victoria of Great Britain, chose their husbands after their accessions, but Maria Theresa, like Isabella of Castile, chose hers while still a royal heiress. Maria Theresa lobbied hard for Francis Stephen, for whom she fell practically from first sight. For Francis Stephen, it was more complicated. Part of the price of Maria Theresa's hand was to surrender Lorraine to the father-in-law of Louis XV of France in exchange for the Grand Duchy of Tuscany, a deal which resolved the War of the Polish Succession (1733–1738). Once the surrender was accomplished, the marriage was celebrated, on February 12, 1736.

Charles VI made clear that he intended Francis Stephen to rule for his daughter after his death. Earlier in his reign he expressed doubts concerning the viability of a female ruler, saying "a realm cannot be trusted to a mere woman," but whether Charles VI recognized his son-in-law's limitations or had any inking of the qualities his daughter possessed is open to conjecture. But when he died, his heir was unquestionably his daughter. By her own admission, Maria Theresa was ill-prepared to inherit her father's dominions when

Charles VI suddenly died in October 1740 (according to Voltaire, after eating poison mushrooms).

> I found myself without money, without credit, without army,
>
> without experience and knowledge of my own, and finally,
>
> also without counsel because each one of them (her father's
>
> ministers) at first wanted to wait and see how things would develop.[4]

What did not happen was Francis Stephen taking charge of his wife's prerogatives, as William of Orange had done in England in 1689 and Frederick I in Sweden in 1720 (see Chapter 5). Instead, he stood aside as Maria Theresa faced the cabal of her father's ministers, many of whom were responsible for the deplorable state of Austrian affairs, which included a bankrupt treasury and a dilapidated army. Like Mary I, Elizabeth I and Anne of England, Isabella of Castile, and the regents Catherine de Medici and Anne of Austria, Maria Theresa began her reign without any substantive administrative experience, making her first achievement the act of taking charge of affairs in all the Habsburg dominions without any significant opposition within any of their governing bodies.

But the rest of Europe was not so compliant. The accession of an inexperienced twenty-three-year-old woman was the signal to several European powers to abandon the Pragmatic Sanction and subdivide the Habsburg inheritance. Prussian King Frederick II struck first in December, seizing the fertile and mineral rich province of Silesia, while Bavarian elector Charles Albert set his sights on the kingdom of Bohemia in concert with his ally Louis XV of France, events that began the War of the Austrian Succession (1740–1748).[5] Maria Theresa could have negotiated with her enemies, which her father's ministers and Francis Stephen had urged her to do, but she decided to stand firm and fight for her right to inherit all the Habsburg lands. Her immediate goals were getting Francis Stephen recognized as her co-ruler in all her territories, and to enhance his candidacy for the imperial throne, which was the cornerstone of the Habsburg inheritance. The motivation for this goes beyond her obvious love for her husband. A male consort can provide a powerful form of legitimacy for a ruling queen, by creating an image and perception of the royal family as a unit operating within prescribed gender norms in which the husband and father was the head of the household. In the first four years of her marriage Maria Theresa cultivated this image of a domestic patriarchal paradise, in which she played the role of and loving a submissive wife and mother, once she began to bear children in 1737.

But upon her accession she asserted herself, in Deborah-like fashion, as an autonomous female ruler. If Maria Theresa's queenship resembles any other early modern queenship, it was that of her Spanish ancestor Isabella of Castile. Both queens lacked a formal education in statecraft or military affairs while learning a female-gendered skill set of attributes prior to their accessions, which made both of their queenships a form of on-the-job training. Like Isabella, Maria Theresa married the man of her choice. She was also devotedly Catholic, having been raised by Jesuits, and considered religious uniformity a pillar of stability, practicing the *pietas austriaca*, an intense form of religious devotion first practiced by the seventeenth-century Holy Roman Empress Eleanora Gonzaga the Younger.[6] As Isabella achieved her accession without her husband by her side while retaining proprietary control of her kingdom within her marriage to Ferdinand, Maria Theresa also walked the fine line of honoring her husband and insisting on his position as her co-ruler while retaining control of her government and its policies.

Maria Theresa's ability to lead from the moment of her accession and her dogged refusal to surrender an inch of Silesia without a fight were astonishing as well as inspiring.[7] But she possessed other attributes. Pleasing in appearance, she was capable of great warmth and charm, frequently displaying a playful and sometimes exuberant spirit. At the same time, she deployed her anger against her ministers and councilors in Elizabethan fashion, as a political weapon to ward off obstructionism. While most scholars considered her a second-rate intellect, she viewed moral rectitude as the foundation of her authority, while possessing common sense, decisiveness, and a concern for her subjects that was considerably higher than her contemporaries as kings.

With the death of Emperor Charles Albert in 1745, Maria Theresa was in a much better position to get Francis Stephen elected emperor than she was in 1740, which occurred after Prussia threw their support behind him in exchange for recognition of their annexation of Silesia. But she declined to be crowned alongside him, as imperial consorts often were, preferring to stay in the background as her husband had during her Hungarian and Bohemian coronations. The reason for this is not quite clear, but she may not have wanted to be crowned a consort, which is why she underwent a sole crowning in Hungary and Bohemia. But it also conformed to the gender dynamics that were an integral part of her approach to queenship. Formally, it was her husband, not she, who had been elected Emperor, and she was more than happy to let him be the star of his imperial coronation, which went a long way to bolster public perceptions of a harmonious family life. This was also accomplished through portraiture, as both a husband and children provided the cloak of domesticity for Maria Theresa's body politic.[8]

Maria Theresa gave birth to a prodigious number of children, and she claimed she loved doing it. The bearing of heirs was the most tangible measure of queenly success, at least in Western and Central Europe. Kings usually make their reputations as military leaders, like Maria Theresa's arch-enemy Frederick II of Prussia, or as power brokers, lawgivers, symbolic fathers to their kingdoms, and representatives of God. But queenship demanded a different set of prestige-earning categories. First and foremost was the production of male heirs, the firmest of foundations for the establishment of dynastic legitimacy. But daughters came first. Her first child, Maria Elisabeth, was born in 1737, followed by two more daughters before the birth of a son and heir in 1741. Twelve more children followed over the next fifteen years, thirteen of whom survived to adulthood, although several succumbed to smallpox at an early age.

Playing the role of dutiful mother was another means of creating queenly prestige. While kings projected a sense of paternalistic protection and concern, queens often projected a more maternal image, as did Queen Anne in England, where she was perceived as the Hebrew prophet Isaiah's "nursing mother" to her people. Later, Maria Theresa herself would be remembered as *landesmutter*, the mother of her people. Not surprisingly, Maria Theresa took the role of mother quite seriously, striving to create an image of harmonious domesticity in numerous family portraits meant to create positive public perceptions. The reality was much different, and the approach to training and education differed sharply between sons and daughters and the less and the more favored within the royal family hierarchy.

Maria Theresa's role as a mother demonstrates the conflation of family and dynastic politics. As she raised her children, they were constantly appraised for their potential on the European marriage market. Affection and attention were doled out to those who were pleasing in appearance, like fourth daughter Maria Christina, later Duchess of Teschen, who enjoyed a formal education in letters that many of her sisters lacked, and, like her mother, married the man of her choice. As a child, Maria Christina was shunned by her siblings for the overt favor she enjoyed. In contrast, eldest surviving daughter Maria Anna, born with physical disabilities, was treated as a dynastic liability, although she was a favorite of her father and later emerged as an artist and a scientist before becoming the abbess of Klagenfurt.

While the younger sons, Leopold, Charles, and Ferdinand, received educations designed to prepare them for state service, the younger daughters, Maria Carolina and Marie Antoinette, were quite laxly raised and educated, which became a problem for the latter. Their childhoods occurred during the Seven Years War (1756–63), when their mother was preoccupied with retaking

Silesia. Both were saddled with incompatible marriages to kings they despised; and both developed reputations as adulteresses, which caused their mother, who spent much of her reign combatting moral laxity within her own realms, much consternation. But none of her children were exempt from criticism in the conduct of their private and public lives. While she may not have loved all her children equally, and later sacrificed several of them on the altar of her dynastic imperatives, she did her best to create a private space within the court for her husband and children, who all possessed myriads of musical and artistic talents and interests.

Maria Theresa's approach to her marriage remains among her more under-rated achievements. Her physical and emotional attachment to her husband was a major part of her public persona. Had he been more capable in state-craft, he might have been the kind of working partner Isabella of Castile enjoyed in her husband Ferdinand. But he did not possess the requisite politi-cal and military skills; Maria Theresa frequently dismissed him from policy meetings when she did not agree with him. Most scholars believe that Francis Stephen's influence upon Maria Theresa's government was marginal, although historian Derek Beales has recently offered a more nuanced assessment of his talents, noting that he ruled the Duchy of Tuscany in his own right, and left a fortune of 22 million gulden upon his death, which provided a needed bolster to the royal treasury in Vienna after his death.[9] But despite Francis Stephen's limited role in her administration, Maria Theresa was careful not to emascu-late her husband. Instead, she made sure he received all due honor as a sitting Holy Roman Emperor, even though within the Austrian monarchy he was a *de facto* male consort, while she played the role of devoted and adoring wife until he died in 1765 at the age of 56.

While Maria Theresa safeguarded her queenly reputation as a good wife and mother and a religious devotee, Francis Stephen was a noted philanderer. But Maria Theresa did not engage in public spats about her husband's infi-delities on the scale of Anne Boleyn or Marie de Medici. While Russian court culture tolerated their empresses' engaging in relationships with their male favorites (see Chapter 6), Maria Theresa recognized and reinforced the peren-nial double standard of royal sexuality, maintaining her own impeccable repu-tation for marital fidelity. Her sexual jealousy was undoubtedly sincere, but it was also a reflection of her female body politic; one of the ways to soften the perception of her possession of male gendered power was to tie it into her performance as a wife and mother who played by the rules of contemporary gendered expectations for women. Her daughters were instructed that they were "born to obey" their husbands.[10] As such, she advised Marie Christina to give her husband his sexual freedom with a minimum of fuss.

Jealousy was in fact an entirely conventional if not obligatory response. Similarly, Francis Stephen's philandering was also a means for him to demonstrate a measure of autonomy, and perhaps fortify himself against insinuations against his masculinity within the power structures of their inherently unequal marriage. The gender dynamics of their marriage were a delicate balancing act, with Francis Stephen being accorded all due respect and honor as her consort, but it worked for the duration of their twenty-nine-year marriage. With his death, Maria Theresa set aside the luxurious dress of a queen for widow's weeds and permanent exile from court festivities, free to reinvent her marriage in material culture as a harmonious and loving union, as both Catherine de Medici and Marie de Medici had done in France in the sixteenth and seventeenth centuries.

Maria Theresa's success was based upon her arsenal of traditional and conventional queenly strategies, most of which were followed by her predecessors as imperial consorts. The most successful ruling queens recognized that they were in fact serving a substitute form of kingship, a role they performed in the outwardly public role of queen. While they recognized that through the accident of birth they had come to possess sovereign power, they had no intention of challenging the patriarchal systems that dominated European monarchies. Maria Theresa succeeded because her queenship embodied a form of ultimate womanhood as a loving wife and mother and grieving widow. Like George III and Charlotte of Mecklenberg-Strelitz of Great Britain, Maria Theresa and Francis Stephen do not excite the historical imagination, but they knew how to play to contemporary expectations for a well-rounded royal family.

QUEENSHIP IN THE HOLY ROMAN EMPIRE

Maria Theresa was the inheritor of 200 years of precedent and experience surrounding Habsburg queenship. The Holy Roman Empire was in fact a nexus for the pan-European kinship network of royalty, consisting of hundreds of autonomous German and Italian states, whose nominal prince was an emperor elected by seven imperial electors. In practice, the post was held by the Habsburg family, who, as we have seen, also ruled several Central European states of their own, some of which, like Hungary, Croatia, and Transylvania, lay outside the boundaries of the Holy Roman Empire. In the sixteenth and seventeenth centuries, the Habsburgs attempted to bind the Empire into a more centralized pan-German state.[11] The Protestant Reformation complicated this process, with much of northern Germany becoming either Lutheran or Calvinist, creating a form of doctrinal iron curtain which required potential Catholic queen consorts to convert to Protestantism and vice versa. A number of queens challenged this dictum and got away with it, like Henrietta Maria of England and Christiane Eberhardine of Poland (discussed in Chapter 5), while Austrian Habsburgs were absolutely forbidden to marry Protestants unless they converted, as Maria Theresa's own mother had done prior to her marriage to Emperor Charles VI. Although the Thirty Years War (1617–1647) failed to unify the Holy Roman Empire, it did re-catholicize Bohemia, Silesia, and Moravia, while dynastic ties with the more prominent German Catholic states were continually reinforced by marriage alliances with the Habsburg family.[12]

Within this framework, the position of Holy Roman Empress emerged as a bastion for post-Tridentine Catholicism, drawing its candidates from Spain, Bavaria, Brunswick-Luneburg (or Hanover), Mantua, and Tuscany. As the preeminent position for a woman in Europe, Holy Roman Empresses followed a basic queenship model that combined intense religiosity with a privileged devotion to fecundity and family while playing an active role within the royal court and serving as marriage brokers for their children and their relatives. On many occasions also, Holy Roman Empresses wielded political power in conjunction with and on behalf of their husbands and sons. Much of Maria Theresa's success as a ruling queen reflects the collective experiences of her predecessors as Holy Roman Empresses.

This model for imperial queenship owes much to the queenship of Isabella of Castile, whose daughter and heir Juana had married Philip the Handsome of Burgundy, the son and heir of Holy Roman Emperor Maximilian I (r. 1493–1519), which joined the houses of Trastamara and Habsburg. As we have seen in Chapter 1, Isabella's reputation cast a powerful shadow over Spanish queenship, culminating in the queenship of her namesake grand-daughter, Isabel of Portugal, consort of Holy Roman Emperor Charles V, who emulated Isabella's piety, chastity, and moral probity, all within the confines of a companionate marriage. As regent for her husband in Spain, Isabel wielded a royal prerogative much in accordance with the precedent laid down by her grandmother Isabella. This powerful Iberian model was welded onto the Habsburg monarchy, as the dynasty split into two, with Charles V's brother Ferdinand succeeding him as Holy Roman Emperor in 1556, the same year his son Philip II was invested with the Spanish kingdoms and the Netherlands.

What followed, for the next century and a half, was the constant inter-breeding between the Spanish and Austrian Habsburgs, interrupted only by marriages to women from strategic parts of the Holy Roman Empire, in a policy of dynastic consolidation unparalled in the history of Early Modern Europe. This policy was reflective of the marriage patterns of Iberian monarchy, in which the royal houses of Portugal, Castile, Aragon, and Navarre continuously interbred among themselves, as well as those of Germany, in which princely and ducal houses constantly engaged in similar dynastic strategies, rearranging and consolidating Germanic states as dynastic possibilities played out generationally. If we look at the daughters of Juana and Philip, all of whom became queens, we can see how this form of dynastic imperialism was put into play as this first generation of Austro-Burgundian-Spanish Habsburg women were drafted for service around the continent in search of dynastic possibilities.

Charles V's sisters were all raised to be consorts. As Spanish *infantas* and Habsburg archduchesses, they ranked among the most eligible marriage partners of their day. Once they were married, they worked hard to get along with their husbands and create the perception that their marriage was companionate, to insinuate a pro-Habsburg policy into their marriages, to co-opt royal power when the opportunity arose, and to raise their children as Catholic Habsburg stalwarts. These lofty ambitions informed the marital career of eldest sister Eleanor (see Chapter 3): marriage in Portugal to the elderly Manual I, which produced a daughter, and then in France, to seal peace between her brother Charles V and Francis I, another dynastic disappointment because the marriage produced neither children nor political influence nor a companionate relationship, although Eleanor did do her best to gain the affection of and influence her stepchildren, with decidedly mixed results.

Sister Isabella (1501–1526) also endured much hardship as queen consort of Denmark and Sweden. Married at age fourteen in 1515 to Christian II of Denmark, who was twenty years her senior, she had to contend with her husband's long-standing mistress, Dyveke Sigbritsdatter, who died two years later, paving the way for what evolved into a more companionate marriage. Under these circumstances, Isabella did her best to fulfill the dynastic goals of her queenship. She bore six children and emerged as a major player in Danish politics, making her peace with Sigbritsdatter's mother, until her husband was deposed from his Swedish and Danish thrones in 1523 and forced into exile in the Netherlands. True to her Habsburg roots, Isabella remained devoted to her husband, but she died young (age twenty-five) of a lingering illness, allegedly receiving both Catholic and Protestant last rites. Of her six children, only two daughters survived to adulthood, including Christina, famously painted by Henry VIII's court painter Hans Holbein the Younger in 1539 as a teenaged widowed duchess of Milan. Later as duchess of Lorraine, Christina emerged as a powerful ruler on behalf of her underage son Duke Charles III, playing a key role in the negotiations that resulted in the Treaty of Cateau-Cambresis in 1559, which ended the Habsburg/Valois dynastic wars of the sixteenth century. As Duchess of Lorraine, she was also the ancestress of Francis Stephen, consort to Maria Theresa.

The other two Habsburg sisters, Mary and Catherine, played more substantial political roles than their sisters. Mary's role in the family business was first focused on Central Europe, where Habsburg ambitions included gaining the thrones of Hungary and Bohemia. When not quite ten years old, Mary married prince Louis Jagiellon, the son of King Ladislaus II of Hungary, in Vienna in July 1515. Mary's life epitomizes the range of Habsburg queenly experiences. True to form, Mary dutifully fell in love with her husband, who succeeded as king in 1516 at the age of ten. Although the consummation was delayed for a few years, Mary quite successfully created the perception that her marriage was happy and companionate, as she carved out for herself a position of political influence within her husband's court even as a teenager. Unfortunately for her, Louis's kingship was a disaster. Following the brazen execution of an Ottoman diplomat, Sultan Suleiman launched an invasion of Hungary that ended up dismembering the Hungarian state, culminating with Louis's death at the Battle of Mohács in 1526.

Although the marriage was childless, Mary nonetheless stepped into the political vacuum created by her husband's death, accepting the role of regent on behalf of her brother Ferdinand, who had married Louis's sister Anna, her brother's heir. Over the next year, Mary worked energetically to get Ferdinand elected King of Hungary and Bohemia, effectively bringing these kingdoms within the Habsburg orbit, where they remained until the end of World War One. Despite her power and her ability, Mary strove to cloak the power she wielded within contemporary expectations of womanhood. On the surface, she was a reluctant regent, downplaying her abilities and pointing out her womanly limitations in her letters and other writings. Quite unlike her sister Eleanor, who was reportedly eager to marry the physically imposing Francis I of France, Mary, based on the love she had felt for her husband, refused all marriage offers, including those of James V of Scotland and Duke Frederick of Bavaria.

But if she refused to be enlisted for further matrimonial duty, Mary fulfilled the political side of Habsburg queenship. Following the death in 1530 of her aunt Margaret of Austria, Duchess of Savoy, who had served as Charles V's regent in the Netherlands, Mary was prevailed upon to take up the post, which she held for the next twenty-five years.[13] All along, Mary made it known that she wielded power reluctantly. Despite her affection for her brother Charles, she frequently butted heads with him on matters of policy, as she placed Dutch and Flemish interests before those of the Habsburg Empire in its entirety. She also defended the interests of her nieces Dorothea and Christina, the daughters of her sister Isabella, delaying their inevitable dynastic marriages as long as possible, as her brother the emperor was eager to marry both off even as children.

Ruling the Netherlands was a tough assignment, especially while Reformation literature percolated through the northern states, the precursor of a Dutch Calvinist Reformation. Both Mary and her sister Isabella had reportedly been somewhat receptive or sympathetic to Protestant ideologies, but Charles V made it very clear to all his sisters that embracing the Reformation was a form of treason against the Habsburg dynasty.[14] This constituted a form of Habsburg orthodoxy that would outlive the early modern era and to which all Holy Roman Empresses and Habsburg archduchesses rigidly adhered.[15] Mary dutifully toed this Habsburg line, as a firm, no-nonsense administrator, who faced the challenges of Dutch and Flemish intransigence with remarkable ingenuity. For all her troubles, she received a Spanish retirement with her brother Charles and her sister Eleanor, and was later interred in the El Escorial, built by her nephew Philip II.

Youngest sister Catherine also proved adept at fulfilling the dynastic objectives of Habsburg queenship. Charles V held her in reserve for Portugal, another dynastic possibility as the Habsburgs embraced the type of Iberian dynastic interbreeding that bordered on the incestuous. The youngest of Juana and Philip's daughters, Catherine married John III of Portugal, her first cousin, the son of her aunt Maria of Aragon. They were married for thirty-two years and produced nine children, although only two survived, including a son, John Manual (1537–1554), who lived long enough to marry his own double first cousin, Joanna of Austria, the daughter of Charles V, and produce a son, Sebastian. With the death of John III in 1557, both Catherine and Joanna sought the regency for the underage Sebastian. Charles V decided in Catherine's favor, and Joanna received the consolation prize of the Spanish regency while Philip II was in England and the Netherlands.[16]

The male members of the Habsburg family also worked to fulfill dynastic goals. Charles V's younger brother Ferdinand, like youngest sister Catherine, had been raised in Spain, unlike his siblings Charles, Isabella, and Mary, who grew up in the Netherlands. Despite this, Ferdinand was enlisted for Central European service, marrying Anna Jagiellon, the sister of Louis II of Hungary and Bohemia, in 1516, according to the terms of the First Congress of Vienna of 1515. Following her father's death in 1516, as the ward of Emperor Maximilian I, Anna was groomed for Habsburg queenship. As a descendant of the kings of Poland, Hungary, and Bohemia, and the dukes of Lithuania on her father's side, and the counts of Foix and the queens of Navarre on her mother's side, she was a highly desirable dynastic catch for the Habsburg dynasty, the latest in a series of acquisitions that began with Mary of Burgundy and continued with Juana of Castile, that had greatly expanded Habsburg territories in Western Europe. Now the focus was Central Europe; when Anna's brother Louis II died without heirs, Ferdinand was elected king of Bohemia and a rump of Hungary, the rest going to John Zápolya, who ruled as a vassal to Ottoman Sultan Suleiman I.

Anna figures very little in the histories of her husband's reign as king of Hungary and Bohemia and later king of the Romans, and she did not live long enough to mount the imperial throne when Charles V retired in 1556. Like Charles V and Isabella of Portugal, Ferdinand and Anna were successful in creating the perception that their twenty-six-year marriage was companionate. Anna was superbly educated, learning Latin, German, Czech, and the Magyar (Hungarian) languages. She was also devoutly Catholic. Anna's close identification with both the Bohemian and Hungarian cultures and peoples is rarely mentioned in historical descriptions of Ferdinand's acquisition of those thrones, but it undoubtedly smoothed the way for his acceptance as king. Anna's devotion to her husband, her queenly piety and charity, and her fecundity, with fifteen children born, thirteen surviving to adulthood, all of whom were born in either Hungary or Bohemia, reinforced the Habsburg claims upon these thrones. In turn, Ferdinand was devoted to her; the absence of mention of any philandering on his part is quite telling. The pair spent most of their time together and personally raised their children, sending them to public school in Innsbruck rather than hiring private tutors. Like Isabel of Portugal, Anna's reign was a textbook example of a successfully managed Habsburg queenship. It is significant that she and Ferdinand were buried together in St. Vitus's Cathedral in Prague, a fitting place for an emperor and a queen who had brought so much to the Habsburg dynasty in terms of both territories and the reproduction of heirs.

Like so many queens before her, Anna sacrificed her life on the altar of dynastic security, the ultimate form of queenly martyrdom, dying from complications after giving birth to her youngest daughter Joanna at the age of forty-three. It is not clear what role she played in the marriage negotiations for her two eldest daughters, both of whom married before her death. The oldest, Elizabeth, was married to Sigismund II Augustus of Poland, an unhappy union that produced no issue. Sigismund later married Elizabeth's younger sister Catherine, another union that did not produce heirs either. Much more successful was second daughter Anna's marriage to Duke Albert V of Bavaria, the first of many marriage alliances between the Habsburgs and the ducal house of Wittlesbach. This marriage secured Albert's support for Charles V as the Emperor launched the Schmalkaldic Wars against the Protestant princes of the Empire. But the marriage was companionate and fruitful, with Anna and Albert having many mutual interests in art, music, and leisure activities; they were once painted playing chess as courtiers look on with serious intent. Anna also re-pollinated the Habsburg dynasty with the House of Wittlesbach, with Anna's brother archduke Charles, the former suitor of Elizabeth I of England, marrying Anna's daughter Maria Anna, whose son eventually succeeded to the imperial throne as Ferdinand II in 1619, and whose daughters Margaret, Anna, and Constance all married European kings.[17]

While his sister's marriages created a wide orbit of dynastic connections and possibilities, Ferdinand I and Anna Jagiellon's heir Maximilian united the Spanish and Austrian branches of the Habsburg dynasty with his marriage to Maria of Spain, elder daughter of Emperor Charles V, who was his first cousin. Raised in the Spanish courts of Toledo and Vallalodid, Maria was born into a family that frequently called upon women to be administrators and regents in the mold of Margaret of Austria and Mary of Hungary.[18] Maria never formally relinquished her rights to the Spanish throne, which made her perhaps the most eligible heiress of her day. She also had no intention of being a passive apolitical queen. Like her mother, Maria served as regent in Spain from 1548 to 1551 following her marriage to Maximilian. After moving to Austria in 1552, Maria returned for a solo stint as regent in 1558 for three years. Like her mother-in-law, Anna Jagiellon, Maria was remarkably fecund, giving birth to sixteen children, including two Holy Roman Emperors, with many of her children born in the core Habsburg territories of Austria, Bohemia, and Spain, although several of them, including the future emperor Rudolf II, were sent to be educated in Spain. Her eldest daughter, Anna, became Philip II's third queen in 1570 and the mother of his heir Philip III. Her daughter Elizabeth married Charles IX of France in 1570, the second Habsburg marriage with the royal houses of France, which, as we have seen in the previous chapter, emerged as a pattern for the remainder of the early modern era.

Nevertheless, Maria's achievements as empress were mixed. As was expected of Habsburg queens, the marriage was companionate, which allowed Maria to exert influence over her husband and exercise control over the raising of their children and the brokering of their marriages. But while Maria dutifully followed her peripatetic husband around Germany, she did not duplicate Anna Jageillon's policy of cultural immersion, resisting Germanization and remaining inordinately devoted to her Spanish household entourage of ladies and confessors. Proud of her lineage as a member of the senior Habsburg line, Maria maintained a private correspondence with her brother Philip II of Spain, who had a problematic relationship with Maximilian, and frequently spoke on her own initiative to the Spanish ambassadors resident in the imperial court.

The issue of religion also became a wedge between herself and her husband. Like all Habsburg queens, Maria took her religious obligations seriously, remaining a devoted Catholic like her brother Philip II, whose dogmatic views on religion did much to spur the revolt of the Dutch Protestants in the 1560s and the ill-conceived Armada against England in 1588. But both Maria's father-in-law Ferdinand I and her husband Maximilian II (r. 1564–1576) were much more pragmatic towards German and Bohemian Protestantism; Ferdinand had been primarily responsible for negotiating the Peace of Augsburg of 1555, which essentially divided Germany into Catholic and Protestant states.[19] But Maximilian's pan-German approach to religion was too much for Maria; while Maximilian lay on his deathbed, refusing Catholic last rites, Maria was at mass, praying for his soul. Maria returned to Spain in 1582, six years after Maximilian's death, so she could live in a country without heretics, settling in at the Convent of the Poor Clares at Las Descalzas Reales in Madrid, along with her daughter Margaret, who took holy orders as Margaret of the Cross. Ironically, as a dowager empress in Spain, she pushed a pro-Austrian foreign policy upon her nephew (and grandson) Philip III.[20]

Much in the tradition of Maria of Spain, seventeenth-century Habsburg queens provided a powerful bolster to imperial counter-Reformation orthodoxy. Not surprisingly, this went hand in hand with the Habsburg attempt to both catholicize and centralize control over the Holy Roman Empire during the Thirty Years War (1617–1647), the bloodiest conflict yet fought on the European continent, which inflicted untold damage and misery upon the peoples and lands of Germany. Anna of Tyrol, the consort of the Emperor Mattias (r. 1612–1619), was a granddaughter of Ferdinand I and the daughter of Anna Juliana Gonzaga of Mantua, an Italian imperial city that supplied several brides for Austrian archdukes. Matthias had remained unmarried for most of his life and was fifty-four when, in December 1611, he married the twenty-six-year-old Anna, who became the first crowned Holy Roman Empress since the fifteenth-century Eleanor of Portugal.

While the marriage was childless, Anna successfully embodied the roles of queen and empress. Superlatively educated in a post-Tridentine Renaissance fashion in letters, social graces, and musical and leisure training, Anna wielded great influence over her husband, in conjunction with his mistress Susana Wachter, while promoting her native Tyrolese in her husband's administration. Above all, she was a strict enforcer of Catholic orthodoxy, refusing to meet or speak to Protestant courtiers at the imperial court, which was moved from Prague to Vienna at her request. Her most enduring legacy was spearheading the building of the imperial crypt at a Capuchin monastery near the Hofburg palace in Vienna, a form of queenly legacy building that queens of France from Anne of Brittany to Marie de Medici had utilized at St. Denis and the Spanish Habsburgs at the El Escorial. For the next two centuries, Holy Roman Emperors and Empresses added to and embellished the tomb for their own legacies, creating their own monuments to Catholic orthodoxy and marital fidelity, such as the magnificent tomb Maria Theresa built for herself and Francis Stephen, in which their effigies gaze at each other for eternity. The tomb took fifteen years to complete, and Matthias and Anna were reinterred there in 1532 by Ferdinand II (r. 1619–1637) and his queen Eleanora Gonzaga.

Beginning with Ferdinand II, the age of Habsburg religious pragmatism was over, as he and all subsequent seventeenth-century Holy Roman Emperors embraced Orthodox, post-Tridentine Catholicism as a central facet of their reigns.[21] Their empresses followed suit. Eleanora Gonzaga was Ferdinand's second wife; his first, Anna of Bavaria, represented the cyclical cross-pollination with the Bavarian House of Wittlesbach, while Anna herself was a granddaughter of Ferdinand I. This marriage produced four children who survived to adulthood, all of whom made important dynastic marriages, with daughter Maria Anna marrying her brother Maximilian I, Elector of Bavaria, and daughter Cecilia Renate marrying Ladislaus IV of Poland. But Anna died in 1616, three years before her husband mounted the imperial throne. In 1622, after being on the Italian marriage market for some years, Eleanora wed Ferdinand II.

Eleanora built upon the queenship of Anna of Tyrol. Both were childless and compensated for this in similar ways. For Eleanora, the fact that Anna of Bavaria had borne Ferdinand several male and female heirs made her childlessness less of a liability. Quite unlike Maria of Spain, who clung to her Spanish identity through her marriage to Maximilian II, Eleanor began a rapid process of Germanization, swiftly learning the language, adopting the dress, and hiring the Austrian, Bohemian, and Hungarian attendants of her predecessor. The marriage was widely perceived as companionate, and Eleanor accompanied her husband all around the Holy Roman Empire. She also proved a loving and attentive stepmother to Ferdinand's children. But she was decidedly apolitical, focusing her energies on her religious devotions and patronage, such as the building of the monastery for Discalced Carmelites in Vienna, the perennial central role for Holy Roman Empresses. At the same time, she lavished cultural patronage on such Italian exports as baroque music, which took Vienna by storm, remaining a staple at the imperial court for the remainder of the early modern era.[22]

The importation of Italian culture continued during the reign of Emperor Ferdinand III (r. 1637–1657), who was married three times.[23] The geographic range of his queens represent Habsburg dynastic and strategic interests. His first wife, Maria Anna, daughter of Philip III and Margaret of Austria, represented another strong dynastic link between the Spanish and Austrian branches of the family. Ardently Catholic, she had earlier refused to marry the future Charles I of England because of his Protestantism and was scandalized when he visited the Spanish court incognito in 1623. She was a beautiful queen, a highly desirable asset of baroque queenship, and her marriage was companionate, as Ferdinand III remained entirely faithful to her. She brought Spanish taste in art and music with her to Vienna, which put her somewhat at odds with her Italian stepmother-in-law Eleanora Gonzaga. Nevertheless, she was a popular and well-liked queen, bearing six children, including the future Emperor Leopold I. She also served as Ferdinand's regent when he was in Bohemia in 1645, as Protestant armies circled Austria. She in fact died on the run from the Swedish army in Linz, pregnant with her final child in 1646.

Two years later, Ferdinand III married sixteen-year-old Maria Leopoldine of Austria-Tyrol, who died a year later, after giving birth to a son, Charles Joseph, who died at age fifteen. In 1651, Ferdinand married Eleanora Gonzaga the Younger, the niece of the dowager empress. The elder Eleanora had played a prominent role in arranging the marriage between the twenty-year-old heiress and the forty-two-year-old emperor. In many ways, the younger emulated the elder. Both fashioned companionate marriages, with the younger bearing several children. Both rapidly learned German, and enjoyed the affection of the imperial family, including their stepchildren. As the Scientific Revolution and the Enlightenment began to dawn upon European intellectual life, both Eleanora and Ferdinand were avid patrons of literature, and patrons of science. But most importantly, Eleanora continued the importation of Italian Baroque culture in all of its manifestations, further establishing it as a basis for imperial court culture for the remainder of the early modern period, while the Italian language itself emerged as a second tongue at the imperial court.

In many ways, Eleanora was the archetype seventeenth-century Habsburg queen, setting the model for the remainder of the early modern era. Extremely well-educated and cultured, with a particular interest in religious poetry, Eleanora literally conquered Vienna in the six years of her consortship. Eleanora gained the affection of her stepchildren, in particular Archduke Leopold, her husband's heir. She also accompanied her husband on his travels around the empire, all the while bearing four children, only two of whom, both daughters, survived to adulthood. But when her husband died in 1657, when she was twenty-seven, she retained her relevance in imperial politics. The first Holy Roman Empress to outlive her husband since Maria of Spain, Eleanora declined to remarry, despite her youth. Instead, embracing the role of devoted widow, she served as guardian for her stepchildren, enjoying the respect and attention of her stepson Leopold I (r. 1658–1705). Eleanora clearly enjoyed her widowhood, decorating the Favorita, Schönbrunn, and Laxenburg Palaces, the gift of the elder Empress Eleanora, in the Italianate style, with her home serving as a literary, artistic, and scientific salon for an increasingly cultured and educated Viennese civil society. What is notable about the two Eleanora Gonzagas is how they marshalled a cultural invasion of literally everything Italian all the while enjoying the trust and affection of the adoptive kingdoms without any kind of xenophobic reaction.

Eleanora's secular pursuits in music, arts, literature and science were balanced by her religious devotions, which went beyond the typical patronage of convents and monasteries to the founding of female religious orders, the Order of Virtuosity in 1662 and the Order of the Starry Cross in 1668, the latter of which was confined to noblewomen only. Eleanora served as the first Grand Mistress, and she was followed by nearly all subsequent Holy Roman and Austrian Empresses. She also reflected the tenets of the *pietas austriaca*, the Austrian piety, which personified the imperial court of her stepson Leopold I. In the nearly thirty years of her widowhood, she remained a serious power broker, negotiating marriages for the imperial royal family, including Leopold himself, who, like his father, also had three wives, and serving as a negotiator between Mantua and the papacy. She enjoyed all the trappings of dowager queenship, remaining a familiar and stabilizing figure within the imperial court until her death in 1686. In all facets, Eleanora's queenship created a model that would be replicated by her stepdaughter-in-law Eleonor Magdalene of Neuburg and her step-grand-daughter Maria Theresa.

Eleonor Magdalene was the third queen of Leopold I. Leopold's first wife, Margarita Theresa, was also his niece, the daughter of his sister Mariana and Philip IV of Spain. The marriage represented the final dynastic alliance with the Spanish Habsburgs, whose direct male line ended with Margarita's brother Charles II.[24] Escaping the debilitating effects of in-breeding that plagued her brother, Margarita was a beautiful child, painted by Spanish master Diego Velasquez in a series of portraits. She was also charming and vivacious, adored by both her father and her husband, whom she affectionately addressed as uncle. The actual marriage took place in December 1666, when the bride was fifteen and the groom was twenty-six. The celebrations for the marriage lasted for two years.[25]

It was a fateful marriage. Margarita faced enormous dynastic pressure to provide both Spanish and Austrian Habsburg heirs. She wilted in the spotlight, failing to follow the model laid down by her aunt Maria Anna, the first consort of Ferdinand III, refusing to learn German, and remaining unduly attached to her Spanish entourage. These attitudes did not endear her to the imperial court, and out of four pregnancies only one child, a daughter, Maria Antonia, later Electress of Bavaria, survived infancy. She reportedly blamed the Jews for her dynastic failure, a far cry from her more educated and rational predecessors. She died young, at age twenty-one in 1673.

In 1673, Leopold married Claudia Felicitas, the last descendant of the collateral Habsburg House of Tyrol, who died of tuberculosis at age twenty-two after a marriage that lasted less than three years. Her two daughters both died during infancy. Once again Leopold mourned, and once again he went in search of another dynastic match. This time the shift was to western and northern Germany, to the Palatinate of Neuburg, ruled by the Wittlesbach family, who were also closely connected dynastically to the Habsburg dynasty as Electors of Bavaria. As potential Spanish and other collateral Habsburg consorts dwindled away amid the cyclical wars with Louis XIV's France, Leopold was drawn to such stalwart Catholic dynasties as the Wittlesbachs, who would later be supportive of the Austrian claim during the War of the Spanish Succession.

The bride was twenty-one-year-old Eleonor Magdalene of Neuburg, who married Leopold in 1676 after undergoing a procedure to determine if she was fertile. Her grandparents came from the ducal and electoral houses of Bavaria, Saxony, and Hesse-Darmstadt. Over the course of her long career as consort and dowager, Eleonor Magdalene emerged as the most powerful of imperial consorts since Maria of Spain. Her path to queenly authority was entirely orthodox and appeared to be reflective of the deep historical roots that served to bind Habsburg queenship.[26]

As we have seen, the recipe for Habsburg queenly success was based on a fierce devotion to religiosity, fecundity, companionate marriage, the acquisition of political power through the distribution of patronage, and the ability to play the role of marriage broker and legacy builder. Eleanor Magdalene succeeded admirably in all these endeavors. While all early modern Holy Roman Empresses were quite publicly religious and observant, Eleanor Magdalene took queenly religiosity to new heights. From her early years to the end of her life she led a religiously observant life, ending her life as a *de facto* nun. She had not wanted to marry and had turned down several dynastically advantageous offers, including the future James II of England, before being compelled to marry Leopold by her father. But even after her marriage she led an ascetic life, mortifying her flesh, while building monasteries and hospitals, visiting and ministering to the sick herself, and actively practicing the *pietas austriaca* with an emphasis on the Marian cult. While it was established historical precedent for Habsburg queens to be publicly religiously observant, Eleonor's religious sincerity is without question, and was reflective of medieval queen-saints such as the thirteenth-century Elizabeth of Hungary, who also combined the functions of queenship with an ascetic life of serving the poor. Eleonor Magdalene's piety reinforced that of her husband, who remained sexually faithful to her, in marked contrast to his contemporaries the Stuart kings Charles II and James II and Louis XIV of France.

Like Saint Elizabeth of Hungary, Eleanor Magdalene took her queenly duties as seriously as she did her spiritual ones. Well educated and fluent in several languages, with an Elizabethan-like devotion to scholarship, she once translated the Bible from Latin to German. Armed with these skills she assumed a position in her husband's government comparable to a minister without portfolio, similar to that of Madame de Maintenon in France, translating diplomatic dispatches for her husband and running the royal household with an eye towards economy. At the same time, she rigorously enforced the formal Spanish etiquette at court, the most enduring legacy of Spanish Habsburg consorts. She was also a regular correspondent with all the ducal courts of Germany, commanding a nearly pan-European kinship-based diplomatic service that served both her husband's and her own interests.

The production of heirs remained paramount. Despite all her queenly activity, including fleeing the plague in 1679 and a Turkish invasion in 1683, Elenore Magdalene gave birth to ten children in twelve years, including two Holy Roman Emperors, although only five lived to adulthood, but her two sons resolved a temporary lack of male Habsburg heirs. She was very much a hands-on mother, in the tradition of Anna Jagiellon and Maria of Spain, while dutifully following her husband all over the Empire. While her more recent predecessors had worked hard to situate Italian culture within the imperial court, Eleonore Magdalene used her influence to orient the Habsburgs towards Rhineland Germany, where she engaged in high-level marriage brokering for her Wittlesbach and Hanoverian relatives, such as the marriage between her son the future Joseph I and Wilhelmine Amalia of Brunswick-Lüneburg in 1699, who was chosen not only for her filial relationship but because of her sobriety and religiosity, which it was hoped would temper Joseph's moral laxity. It is a curious twist of fate that neither Eleonor Magdalene nor Leopold were able to instill in their heir the Habsburg tradition of reverence for the institution of marriage, ending a long run of imperial monogamous marriages.

Eleonor Magdalene was understandably reluctant to part with such a formidable power base following Leopold's death (5 May 1705) and the accession of her eldest son Joseph I (r. 1705–1711). Both Joseph and his brother and successor Charles VI (r. 1711–1740) were resistant to female participation in politics and sought to curb both their mother and their wives in this area of their queenships. Both obviously felt threatened by the power wielded by their mother, whose ostentatious widow's weeds were a powerful reminder of her relationship with her dead husband. Joseph in fact represented a clear break with Habsburg precedent by engaging in extramarital affairs, eventually contracting a venereal disease, probably syphilis.

Under these circumstances, Wilhelmine Amalia did her best to fulfill the requirements of Habsburg queenship. Like her mother-in-law, whom she was close to, she had been trained to play her part well; she was educated, accomplished, and deeply religious. Both queens were scandalized by Joseph's licentious behavior, eventually appealing to the Pope. But with her husband's accession, all Wilhelmine Amalia could do was grin and bear it. It was a unique experience for a Holy Roman Empress; early modern Holy Roman Emperors were remarkably devoted to their consorts. After Joseph gave her syphilis, she initially thought she was to blame for her reproductive problems, although she did give birth to three children, two daughters, and a son who died in infancy, before the syphilis made her infertile. Despite this experience, she did her best to create the perception of a companionate marriage, participating in court ceremonials and hunting and other leisure activities and attending the opera. But after Joseph died of smallpox (April 17, 1711) it was Eleonor Magdalene, not Wilhelmine Amalia, who assumed the regency in Austria while Charles VI remained in Catalonia in Spain, endeavoring to gain the Spanish throne, which was also claimed by Louis XIV's grandson Philip of Anjou.

Charles VI was the last direct male Habsburg heir. For a dynasty that experienced a remarkable run of fecund queens, this created a succession crisis. Like the sixteenth-century Henry VIII of England, Charles VI had little choice but to contemplate a female succession.

The two dowager empresses resident at the imperial court were also closely invested in this process. Even before the death of their father, Leopold, Charles and his brother Joseph had agreed to a mutual pact of succession, which stated that in the event of a lack of male heirs, the daughters of Joseph would take precedence over those of Charles. Given Wilhelmine Amalia's reproductive issues, the pressure on Elisabeth-Christine to produce sons was immense. She had already gone through much to prepare herself for her role as empress. She had been raised in the Calvinist church and was reluctant to convert to Catholicism. But her family prevailed upon her, and the philospher Leibniz convinced her, so Eleonor Magdalene introduced her to the *pietas austriaca* and the Marian cult, before her proxy marriage to archduke Charles in 1708. Like her cousin Wilhelmine Amalia, she was well educated, fluent in languages, conversant in court etiquette and protocol, and a very good huntress. But her initial attempts to procreate were disappointing. She did not conceive right after her marriage, and she remained in Catalonia as regent after the death of Joseph I in 1711, remaining for two years, ruling with apparent competence.

But when Elisabeth-Christine returned to Vienna, Charles VI marginalized her politically, as he did his mother and sister-in-law. She still had problems conceiving and was prescribed rich foods and liquor to stimulate conception, which eventually rendered her obese. She finally conceived in 1715, producing a son who died several months later. Three daughters eventually followed, including Maria Theresa. For her last pregnancy in 1724, Charles VI had her bedchamber decorated with erotic male images, in the hope that this would spur the birth of a son. The son never materialized, and as we have seen, Charles promulgated the Pragmatic Sanction of 1713, which disinherited Wilhelmine Amalia's two daughters, who had to agree with its terms before they were allowed to marry.

Charles VI's ambivalence towards female power bound together the three empresses, who enjoyed each other's company and nursed each other through sickness, displaying their queenly attributes of caring personally for members of their imperial family. Despite conflicts over marriage alliances for their daughters, Eleonor Magdalene, Wilhelmine Amalia, and Elisabeth-Christine continued the traditions of Habsburg queenship, whose collective correspondence with the royal courts of Europe represented a formidable kinship and patronage network. Wilhelmine Amalia followed in Eleonor Magdalene's footsteps as a religiously devoted widow, and all three empresses served successive terms as grand mistress of the order of the starry cross. Like Wilhelmine Amalia before her, Elisabeth-Christine tolerated her husband's infidelities with queenly grace and dignity, maintaining the observance of the *pietas austriaca*. She apparently learned to exercise power and wield influence under the radar of her husband, as such forming part of the court circle that opposed the marriages of her daughters to the sons of Philip V of Spain. Later, during the reign of her daughter, the Prussian ambassador observed that she knew how to engage politically in an extremely subtle fashion. She remained devoted in true Habsburg fashion to her husband, who returned her affection in kind, despite his affairs. Like her two predecessors, she kept up a voluminous correspondence with the various ducal houses of Germany, while remaining on good terms with her sister-in-law and cousin Wilhelmine Amalia.

Elisabeth-Christine outlived her husband by a decade, but she did not enjoy the level of power and influence as had her predecessors Maria of Spain, Eleanora Gonzaga the younger, and Eleonor Magdalene of Neuburg in their widowhoods. The warmth that permeated her daughter Maria Theresa's correspondence with other family members did not extend to her mother, and their relationship appears to have been largely ceremonial. In the final year of her life, however, she created the order of Elisabeth and Theresa, to reward officers who served bravely in battle. This rather secular form of legacy building, which was continued by her daughter and subsequent Habsburg rulers, represented something of a break with the more religiously inspired means for Holy Roman Empresses to create their legacies.

CONCLUSION

In marked contrast to British and French queens, whose collective experiences reveal a heterogeneous variety of queenly strategies, Habsburg queenship developed and adhered to a rather uniform set of dynastic imperatives. The history of early modern queenship in the Holy Roman Empire represented a powerful historical model for Maria Theresa to draw from in the fashioning of her own queenship, in particular the consortship of her grandmother Eleonore Magdalene, the most powerful and influential of imperial consorts. Reaching all the way back to Anna Jagiellon, Austrian Habsburg queenship was predicated upon companionate marriage, fecundity, cultural assimilation, devotion to family, and a willingness to embrace political power in conjunction with husbands and sons, particularly as marriage brokers; in this sense, Maria Theresa had much in common with her predecessors as imperial consorts.

Religious conformity was also an integral facet of Habsburg queenship, a tradition that reached back to Isabella of Castile through to her granddaughter Maria of Spain.[27] The development of the *pietas austriaca* in the seventeenth century also served as a binding agent for Habsburg queenly conformity. Post-Tridentine Catholicism was also closely associated with Baroque art, which Spanish and Italian imperial consorts brought with them to Vienna in their roles as pan-European cultural pollinators. In turn, Habsburg archduchesses married the kings of France and Poland and into the princely houses of Catholic Germany, bringing their cultural tastes and religious beliefs with them. The Hofsburg Palace mausoleum is a testament to their collective tastes, celebrating the Habsburg dynasty in Baroque splendor.

The Holy Roman Empire was a powerful nexus for the market in European queens consort. As the most prestigious royal house in Europe, Habsburg archduchesses were the most highly desired royal brides in Early Modern Europe. Seen through the lens of European dynastic politics, the Habsburgs operated as a transcontinental conglomerate, drawing consorts from the cream of Spanish, Germanic, and Italian heiresses, while Habsburg archduchesses in turn married into the royal and princely houses of Germany, France, and Poland-Lithuania. These dynastic interests in turn insinuated the Habsburgs into the affairs of the kingdoms of Poland-Lithuania, Denmark-Norway, Sweden, and Prussia, all of which clamored for control of the lands surrounding the Baltic Sea.

5 Bona Sforza and Queenship in the Baltic Kingdoms

"Chicken War" painted in 1872 by Henryk Rodakowski (1823–1894)

Source: World History Archive/Alamy Stock Photo

In the National Museum in Warsaw hangs a painting titled *Chicken War* by artist Henryk Rodakowski, a romanticist who painted this scene in 1872, a time when Poland was not an independent nation but subject to the rulers of the Russia, Austria-Hungary, and Germany after it was partitioned out of existence at the end of the eighteenth century. In this painting the artist has invested Bona Sforza, Queen Consort of Poland (1494–1557), with an attitude completely different from all the other figures depicted in the painting.[1] While King Sigismund the Old (r. 1506–1549) sits dejected on the battlements of a fortress, surrounded by counselors and clerics all depicted in a state of alarm as they wait to face the nobility and their demands, Queen Bona appears resplendent, standing confidently behind the seated king looking off to her left with a smile on her face, as if she already knows the outcome of the revolt.[2] It is an image indicative of Bona's place in Polish history as a queen with a well-developed sense of confidence and autonomy.

It was these qualities that spurred the "Chicken War" (1537), a form of noble revolt or *rokosz*, which was the culmination of years of opposition to Sigismund and Bona's centralizing policies, the common pastime of Renaissance monarchy, which resulted in a diminution of noble power and influence. But much of the revolt's fury was specifically directed towards Queen Bona, who in the nearly thirty years of her consortship had become a substantial landowner in Poland as well as the Grand Duchy of Lithuania. In addition to calls prohibiting the queen from acquiring additional land, the nobility also objected to Bona's raising of her eldest son Sigismund II Augustus and for exercising power within the Polish state, which was not considered proper for a queen consort.[3] But divisions within the Polish nobility diluted the power of the revolt, which quickly dissipated, while Queen Bona continued to exercise substantial power in Poland for the remainder of her husband's reign. As we shall see in this chapter, Bona's expansive model of queenship was widely imitated by many of the queens of the Baltic kingdoms of Poland, Denmark, Sweden, and, in the eighteenth century, Prussia.

THE QUEENSHIP OF BONA SFORZA

While the Polish nobility were not ready for a queen who refused to play a purely domestic role, Bona Sforza was well prepared to expand the functions of Polish queenship.[4] A member of the dynasty that had ruled the Duchy of Milan since the mid-fifteenth century, Bona was Poland's most powerful early modern queen consort; as historian Katarzyna Kosior has observed, "the line between regnant and consort were blurred in the eyes of some of her subjects."[5] She was also Poland's first Italian queen, pollinating the Polish royal court with the artistic and intellectual sensibilities of the Italian Renaissance as well as an Italian understanding of statecraft. Bona's mother and paternal grandmother provided her with models upon which she constructed her own expansive version of Polish queenship.[6]

Her paternal grandmother and namesake, Bona of Savoy (1449–1503), once a contender for a dynastic marriage to Edward IV of England, was a battle-scarred survivor of the strife and violence surrounding the succession to the Duchy of Milan in the later fifteenth century. In terms of its geographic location within the pan-European kinship network, the territories of the Duchy of Savoy lay between Valois France and Northern Italy; supplying consorts to both sides of the Habsburg-Valois conflict as well as the rulers of the various Italian states. Married to Galeazzo Maria Sforza, Duke of Milan, in 1468 at the age of eighteen, Bona assumed the role of regent for her seven-year-old son Gian Galleazzo, after her husband was assassinated in 1476. She was opposed by her husband's younger brother Ludivico, whom she banished from the city, but he returned in 1479 to provide a powerful model for Richard III of England to follow by deposing his nephew and assuming the regency while imprisoning Bona in the Castle of Abbiategrasso. She later escaped to exile in France after the marriage of her son to Isabella of Naples in 1489. Despite the turmoil of her life, she cultivated a highly developed artistic aesthetic, commissioning the Sforza Book of Hours, a beautiful work of Renaissance artistry, which later came into the possession of Bona's niece, Margaret of Austria, Dowager Duchess of Savoy.[7]

Bona Sforza's mother, Isabella of Naples (1470–1524), also had to negotiate her way through the violent politics of early sixteenth-century Italy. Married to Bona of Savoy's son Gian Galleazzo, she lived much of her married life as a political prisoner during the ascendancy of her husband's uncle Ludovico, while her natal family in Naples were ejected from the kingdom by the French under Charles VIII in 1494. She later worked out a deal to salvage a portion of her inheritance by obtaining the Duchy of Bari and other territories in Italy, where she went to rule in 1500 after the death of her husband, where she remained for twenty-four years until her death. Only as a sovereign woman was Isabella able to chart her own destiny, and she lavished care and attention on her only surviving child, daughter Bona, who received a thoroughly humanist education, including history and law, that rivalled those enjoyed by the children of Henry VIII of England. For Bona, the experiences of her mother and grandmother were cautionary tales, which made her determined to turn her queenship into a bastion of political and economic power.

The Emperor Maximilian I had no idea what an indefatigable foe of the Habsburgs Bona would become when he placed her on his short list of brides for Sigismund the Old of Poland, whose first wife, Barbara Zápolya, died in 1515 after bearing two daughters. Sigismund was a member of the Jagiellon dynasty, originally founded in Lithuania, whose grand ducal crown merged dynastically with Poland with the 1385 marriage of Queen Jadwiga of Poland and the pagan Jogaila, Grand Duke of Lithuania, although the two states were drawn into a more formal union in 1569 during the reign of Sigismund II Augustus (r. 1548–1572). Sigismund the Old had inherited the grand ducal crown of Lithuania and was elected king of Poland in 1506 after the death of his childless brother Alexander. The Jagiellons were wary of Habsburg dynastic ambitions, which had proved successful in Burgundy and Spain, and did their best to compete with them dynastically in Central Europe. Barbara Zápolya, the daughter of a powerful Hungarian nobleman, whose brother would later rule a rump of Hungary as an Ottoman vassal, had been the anti-Habsburg candidate, but in 1518, faced with a war with an expansive Muscovite Russia, Sigismund embraced a Habsburg alliance.

By this time Sigismund was fifty-one years old. He was an unremarkable yet affable king, whose twenty-four-year-old bride came to Poland better prepared to exercise royal power than many of the women who ruled as female kings in Early Modern Europe. Isabella of Naples imparted to her daughter a powerful model of autonomous female rule, while Bona understood the necessity of securing royal power through the accumulation of wealth and property, so she and her children would not suffer the same fate as her grandmother and mother. Thus, Bona's objectives were the same as other Renaissance monarchs like Henry VII of England and Isabella of Castile, to maximize crown profits and to call in all alienated crown properties. In 1524, when her mother died, Bona became Duchess of Bari and other Italian territories in her own right, administering them at her own discretion without interference from her husband.

Like most other queens who aspire to political power, Bona's ability to create a companionate marriage was an integral facet of her queenly success. Sigismund was delighted with his young bride, who played the role of loving stepmother to Sigismund's two daughters with Barbara Zápolya. She also proved fecund herself, bearing one son and four daughters and continuing the Jagiellon dynasty, which continued to rule Poland and Lithuania until 1587. She was also adventurous; in 1527, when she was five months pregnant, Bona went bear hunting and had a riding accident, which caused her to miscarry and prevented her from having any more children. Ironically, the end of her childbearing cycle allowed Bona to focus more of her time on helping her husband rule Poland. Her ability to do so was a direct result of the affection that existed between her and her husband, who occasionally chastised his wife for her often-exuberant spirit.[8]

Over the course of their thirty-year marriage, as Sigismund grew into his dotage, Bona expanded her role in Polish government. But Bona refused to take any steps to obscure her power by maintaining the fiction of being an outwardly obedient wife, as did her counterpart in England, Catherine of Aragon. Instead, Bona wielded power in the public spaces of the court for all to see. She also developed a reputation for ruthlessness and unscrupulousness, such as the occasion when she told a blind archbishop who got in her way she wished he had lost his tongue too.[9] Bona's Machiavellian approach to statecraft offended the Polish nobility, who were apparently used to more

gender-conforming performances of queenship.[10] But by enjoying the confidence of the king, she was able to build her own Italian staffed secretariat,
to further both her domestic and her foreign policies. Fiscally astute, in 1545
Bona engineered a renegotiation of her dower that left her in control of the
Masovia region of Poland, which included Warsaw.

Bona's interests as queen reached far and wide. She engaged in foreign
policy, pursuing a correspondence with her Ottoman counterpart Hurrem
Sultan Roxelana, former slave and legal wife of Ottoman Sultan Suleiman
the Magnificent, who was ethnically Polish. Together, these queens did
much to ease Polish-Ottoman tensions and on one occasion prevented an
Ottoman invasion of Poland.[11] Bona also maintained her Italian connections, gaining the power from the papacy to appoint cathedral benefices in
Poland. Finally, like so many other powerful and influential queens, Bona
was a builder, refurbishing several palaces in the Lithuanian capital of Vilnius
in the Renaissance style. She also brought to Vilnius the books and manu-
scripts that formed the basis for Lithuania's first library. While aspects of
the Renaissance had begun to trickle into Poland prior to her queenship,
Bona gave it a quantum leap that reached fruition under the reign of her
son Sigismund II Augustus, when Poland enjoyed its own "Golden Age" of
Renaissance achievement.[12]

Like other ambitious and powerful queens, Bona controlled the raising and
schooling of her children, who all received humanist educations. But she was
less successful in brokering their marriages. The marriage of elder daughter
Isabella to John Zápolya in 1539 failed to achieve its objectives of obtaining
the Hungarian throne, although Bona's grandson John Sigismund Zápolya
became Prince of Transylvania and the small rump of Hungary as a vassal of
Suleiman the Great. But Bona's three younger daughters, Sophia, Anna, and
Catherine, remained unmarried and lived with their mother. Only in 1556,
when she was thirty-four, did second daughter Sophia marry sixty-seven-year-
old Duke Henry V of Brunswick-Wolfenbüttel, who was looking for another
male heir. Younger daughters Anna and Catherine remained unmarried at the
time of Bona's death in 1557, although it is not clear why this was the case;
princesses of a substantial European kingdom such as Poland should have carried a high value in the pan-European royal kinship network. But Sigismund
the Old and Sigismund II Augustus both failed to take an active role in marriage diplomacy. It is interesting that a queen who was so driven in other
aspects of her queenship failed to find royal matches for her daughters, which
draws a striking contrast with the Habsburg Elisabeth of Austria (1436–
1505), the mother of Sigismund the Old, who married her four daughters into
the German and Baltic nobility.[13]

Bona may also have wanted her daughters around for companionship, especially after her relationship with her son and heir soured. Bona's inability to get along with Sigismund II Augustus ultimately served to dismantle the power of her queenship. In 1543, Sigismund the Old negotiated his son's marriage to Elisabeth of Austria, the daughter of Ferdinand, King of the Romans and Anna Jagiellon. Bona was opposed to this marriage, and made Elisabeth's life miserable at the Polish court, while the Habsburg ambassador Giovanni Masurpino remarked in the same year that Sigismund II Augustus was afraid of his mother.[14] Sigismund II Augustus's long-standing sexual relationship with the Polish noblewoman Barbara Radziwill was also a source of conflict between mother and son. Two years after Elisabeth's death in 1545, Sigismund II Augustus married Barbara in secret, announcing it to his parents in February 1548. Sigismund the Old died two months later in April. For once, Bona found herself on the same side as the nobility: They protested a marriage between king and subject while Bona lost the opportunity to broker her son's second marriage and thus demonstrated the limits of her royal authority, which ultimately derived from the goodwill of her male kin.[15]

As her son solidified his rule and gained acceptance for Barbara Radziwill as queen, Bona withdrew to her dower lands in the Masovia region, taking with her her daughters, who all shared her love of sumptuous clothing, jewels, and growing their own gardens of medicinal herbs and salad greens. While Bona fostered the arts and instituted agricultural reforms during her Masovian exile, she grew increasingly dissatisfied with her life as a powerless dowager queen, resolving to return to Bari in 1556 after arranging the marriage of her daughter Sophia. The decision to return to Italy sparked Bona's final controversy, whether a dowager queen of Poland could leave the country, which was decided in her favor by her refusal to countenance any opposition to her travel plans. But Bona's life as a sovereign lady in Bari was cut short only a year after her return when she was poisoned by one of her own servants, allegedly on the orders of Philip II of Spain, who owed her money. Her daughter Anna, who later became the last Jagiellon to occupy the Polish throne, built a magnificent Renaissance basilica in Bari to honor Bona's memory.

Like Catherine de Medici in France, Bona Sforza occupies an ambivalent place in the history of Polish queenship, cursed with her own "black legend," which included accusations of witchcraft and the poisonings of her daughters-in-law.[16] She never created the reputation of a good queen who cared about her people, although in reality many of her political and economic reforms helped the Polish and Lithuanian peoples, which suggests a kind of rationalization reminiscent of Enlightenment queens of a later century, introducing salad and other greens and vegetables into the Polish diet and reforming and standardizing agricultural taxation. It was the nobility that had a problem with her cosmopolitan brand of queenship, rather than her subjects in Poland and Lithuania. Bona also never developed a reputation as a pious and charitable queen, one of the more conventional routes to earn queenly prestige. In fact, Bona was generally tolerant of Protestantism, in keeping with the spirit of toleration practiced by Sigismund the Old, who nonetheless remained Catholic, although both their daughter Sophia and their grandson John Sigismund Zápolya became notable converts to Protestantism.

Bona's true legacy was her ability to create a space for queenship that simply had not existed before in Poland in terms of the breadth of its activity. Bona did not talk about it, she simply exercised power, and made no effort to cloak it behind the authority of her husband. But she never made any efforts to control the narrative of her queenship with hagiographies or works of art depicting her as a mother, as Isabella of Castile and Catherine de Medici had done for their queenships, while her noble detractors reviled her for her alleged avarice and corruption. She was perceived as keen to acquire property for herself, not for the Polish or Lithuanian crowns, in order to endow the Jagiellons with the kind of economic power to resist the traditional rights of the Polish nobility represented in their parliament, or *sejm*, and create a hereditary Jagiellon dynasty in Poland, a policy many other European monarchs pursued in their drive towards absolutism. It was Bona who led the campaign to have her son Sigismund II Augustus crowned as his father's successor in 1529 at the age of nine, in the face of hostile noble reaction. But Bona succeeded in expanding the parameters of Polish queenship, as Bona's confidante Roxalana the Hurrem Sultan Roxelana noted, because her political program served the needs of her husband. Her daughters in turn were avid book, art, and jewel collectors, bringing Bona's expansive model of queenship to Germany, Sweden, and Hungary.[17]

The early modern queens of the Baltic kingdoms of Poland, Denmark, and Sweden replicated aspects of Bona Sforza's active and engaged brand of queenship in various degrees. As these kingdoms made war with one another over religion, territories, and dynastic possibilities, their queens often participated in the marriage negotiations that sought peaceful resolution to these issues. These kingdoms possessed a wide variety of political systems. Poland's elective crown was joined in a personal union with the Grand Duchy of Lithuania in an expansive state that included large areas of present-day Belorus and Ukraine, with the king possessing limited power in terms of his relationship with the landed aristocracy and gentry, who in their *sejm* elected their king, although several dynasties, such as the Jagiellon and the Vasa, were able to sustain *de facto* hereditary monarchies. As the closest northern kingdom to the Habsburg domains, Poland was perennially under pressure for its kings to marry Habsburg archduchesses, with French kings also eager to influence the choice of Polish consorts. In contrast, Denmark, which also incorporated Norway in its crown, developed a powerful absolute monarchy during the early modern period, which served the interests of several Danish queens quite well.[18] Sweden also had sustained periods of absolutist monarchy interrupted by an eighteenth-century "Age of Liberty" during the early modern era, building an expansive east Baltic Empire during the seventeenth century before its defeat in the Great Northern War (1700–1721) by an alliance of Peter the Great's Russia, Denmark, and Poland, whose early eighteenth-century kings were also Electors of Saxony.[19]

Denmark and Sweden also underwent the Protestant Reformation in the sixteenth century, adopting Lutheranism as their state religion and confiscating the lands and wealth of the Roman Catholic Church, processes which greatly increased the power and wealth of their crowns, while Poland remained Catholic, making marriage alliances with the Polish crown attractive to generations of early modern Habsburg archduchesses. But Poland represented the great crossroads of the Reformation, with toleration for Protestantism much more evident than in other parts of Catholic Europe. The emergence of the Kingdom of Prussia at the beginning of the eighteenth century coupled with the emergence of Peter the Great's Russian Empire added additional complications for the ways in which queens were recruited in the Baltic kingdoms.

QUEENSHIP IN POLAND AND LITHUANIA

Bona Sforza's immediate successors as queens were unable to build upon her expansive model of queenship. As we have seen, Bona's son, Sigismund II Augustus (r. 1548–1572), had married his cousin Elisabeth of Austria in 1543. Sigismund ignored Elisabeth, who was timid, shy, and decidedly unhealthy, while Bona treated her with notable disdain. Elisabeth died in 1545 after an epileptic fit. Sigismund then engaged in a practice that was much more common among the kings of the Baltic states than in other parts of Europe: he married for love. Sigismund's romance with Barbara Radziwill, a Lithuanian Calvinist, is one of the great love stories of Polish history, but it caused the king enormous problems with the *sejm*, which tried to force him to divorce her in 1548. But the king carried the day, and even his mother accepted the marriage before her self-imposed exile to Masovia, where she looked with obvious disdain upon Sigismund's marriage to his first wife's sister Catherine in 1553 after Barbara's death in 1551.

Sigismund's third marriage, to a Habsburg archduchess, continued a long-standing Polish practice, which in this case was a shotgun marriage as Ferdinand threatened an alliance with Muscovy against Poland unless Sigismund married his daughter. But Sigismund had a hard time following the rules of marrying for state reasons; he neglected to honor his queen in the public spaces of the court as his father had done with his queens. After an early miscarriage and a later illness, Sigismund abandoned her in 1562 and unsuccessfully petitioned the Pope for an annulment so he could marry a fourth time and obtain a male heir, as he was the last of the male Jagiellons. Catherine later returned to Austria to live in Linz until her death in 1565, tending to the greens and medicinal herbs she had learned to cultivate from her sisters-in-law, the daughters of Bona Sforza.

One of these daughters was Anna (1523–1596), who remained unmarried at the time of Sigismund II Augustus's death in 1572. Anna negotiated the Polish succession dilemma of 1573–1576 with a level of skill that has only recently come to the attention of historians, who have revised a more traditional image of Anna as a powerless mediocrity. Anna, in fact, enjoyed a type of singular queenship that has no analogue in European history, except for Mary II of England, who was also elected queen alongside her husband William III, and Ulrika Eleonora of Sweden (see below). But unlike Mary and Ulrika, Anna outlived her husband, Stephen Báthory, and successfully negotiated the transition in Poland from the Jagiellon to the Vasa dynasty within the structures of an elective monarchy.

But this history is overshadowed by her more well-known perception as a jilted spinster princess. Born in 1523, Anna was the third of four sisters and was well educated like all her siblings. But Anna, then age 34, was still unmarried at the time of her mother's death in 1557, despite a series of marriage proposals that simply never worked out for a variety of reasons. The closest Anna came to marriage during her brother's reign was the 1562 proposal of Duke John of Finland, the brother of Erik XIV of Sweden (see below). During the negotiations John expressed a preference for Anna's younger sister Catherine, working out a deal with Sigismund II Augustus in which Anna would marry John's younger brother. But when John showed up in Vilnius alone, he refused Polish and Lithuanian demands to marry Anna, marrying Catherine instead and humiliating Anna, who agreed to the arrangement for state reasons.

Anna suffered another yet another matrimonial humiliation after her brother's death. For the first time since the late fourteenth century, there was not a male Jagiellon to stand for election to the Polish crown. Because of this, Anna's position as the "last" Jagiellon possessed a form of dynastic significance. When the French prince Henri Duke of Anjou began negotiations as a candidate for the throne, Anne threw her support behind him after he signaled he would be willing to marry her. But the marriage clause was not included in the contract, and after arriving in Poland and being crowned in 1574, Anjou declined to marry Anna, humiliating her before abandoning the Polish throne upon the death of his brother, French king Charles IX (May 30, 1574).

At this juncture, Anna emerged as a frontrunner for the Polish crown, assuming the title *infanta*, and making it known that she wished to become queen of Poland. As one of the beneficiaries of the Jagiellon family fortune, so carefully nurtured by Bona Sforza, Anna stood to gain a considerable inheritance, which, like a daughter of Bona Sforza, she leveraged to obtain the position of queen, gaining the same dower as her mother, which guaranteed her considerable income and influence as queen. This created a curious constitutional situation; while both Poland and Lithuania were initially prepared to elect her as a *de jure* female ruler, it was later deemed necessary that she be married, even though, for all intents and purposes, she was, at fifty-one, past childbearing age. The choice landed upon Stephen Báthory, *Voivode* (or military commander) of Transylvania, who was elected king at the same time Anna was elected queen (December 5, 1575).[20]

However, much like Isabella of Castile did upon her accession in 1474, Anna did not wait for Báthory to arrive in Poland before making a triumphant entry into Kraków as Queen in February 1576. While Anna may have had hopes of a companionate marriage, which was consummated according to a long-standing Polish wedding night ritual, it evolved into a long-distance relationship, in which only the formal aspects of monarchy were performed jointly by the pair. Although Báthory exercised the political and military aspects of kingship, he spent much of his reign fighting the Livonian War against Ivan IV's Russia, allowing Anna considerable latitude to create the public face of their joint monarchy.

Anna's model was her mother's queenship, launching an ambitious building campaign by completing the reconstruction of Warsaw Castle, and building the decorative gateway to the Sigismund II Augustus Bridge in Warsaw, while in Kraków she built the Sigismund Chapel in Wawel Cathedral, including Renaissance tombs for both for herself and her brother that rivalled those in St. Denis in France for their artistic magnificence. She also built a magnificent baroque tomb for her mother, Bona Sforza, in Bari, Italy in the Church San Nicola, which also houses the remains of St. Nicholas. Infused with the spirit of the Renaissance that reached back to her great-grandmother Bona of Savoy, Anna's court continued to exhibit the cosmopolitan qualities of Bona

Sforza's queenship in terms of its artistic and intellectual patronage.[21] She also remained close to both of her sisters, Sophia, Duchess of Brunswick-Lüneburg, and Catherine, Queen of Sweden (see below). Anna was also noted as an embroiderer, with several of her works still extant in museums in Poland today.

With the death of Stephen Báthory in 1586, Anna declined to continue to rule alone but decided to groom the son of her sister Catherine, Queen of Sweden, to be elected Poland's next king, using her authority and prestige to secure his election in 1587 as Sigismund III Vasa. She spent the rest of her life in Poland as a dowager queen, growing close to her nephew and his Habsburg wife, Anna of Austria, the sister of Queen Margaret of Spain and the future Emperor Ferdinand II. Even as Poland maintained the outward form of elective monarchy, Anna in fact engineered the continuance of the Jagiellons on the Polish throne though the female line. In these actions she emulated her mother. She also created a precedent followed by several later European female monarchs who found collateral male heirs to succeed them on their thrones, such as Christina of Sweden (see below) and Anna Ivanovna and Elizabeth Petrovna of Russia (see Chapter 6). Anna was unique not only because she was Europe's first elected queen; she also was Europe's first early modern queen to voluntarily abdicate her throne and embrace the role of dowager queen, demonstrating her queenly historical agency by the way in which she negotiated and conducted the various phases of her queenship.

Anna's successor as queen of Poland was the Habsburg Archduchess Anna of Austria (1573–1598), who married Sigismund III Vasa over the vehement objections of his nobility, who feared Habsburg dynastic encroachments. As the eldest son of John III of Sweden, Sigismund was also heir to the Swedish throne, and was eager to engineer a personal union of the Swedish and Polish-Lithuanian thrones, which meant Habsburg support was vital. Like her husband, Anna was a devout Catholic. This proved a problem when Sigismund ascended the Swedish throne in 1592. Sigismund had no intention of becoming a resident king in Sweden, traveling there long enough to get himself and his queen crowned and his authority established before returning to Poland, seemingly oblivious to the potential conflicts of a Catholic ruling a Protestant country.

Anna also did not appear to be interested in embracing Swedish culture or language. She was dismissive of the Swedes, whom she considered heretics, showing herself only rarely in public, and engaging in a public spat with Protestant Dowager Queen Gunilla Bielke, accusing her of stealing valuables. Returning to Poland in 1694 before the birth of her son, Anna did little to create any positive feelings for her Swedish queenship. Few Swedes lamented her fate; she died in childbirth in early 1598. Sigismund was deposed in Sweden in 1599 by a revolt led by his uncle Charles, who served as regent in Sweden and later assumed the throne as Charles IX in 1604. The success of the revolt had much to do with fears of a possible Catholic succession, while Anna and Sigismund's high-profile support of the Jesuits in Poland and their intolerance of Protestantism did much to erode their support in Sweden.

While Sigismund never reconciled himself to losing Sweden, and spent much time and effort trying to regain his crown, he remarried in 1605, to a sister of his first wife, Constance Renata (1588–1631). Constance was a queen very much in the mold of Bona Sforza. As her husband set out to stamp out Protestantism in Poland, Constance was by his side in the tradition of Habsburg archduchesses. Like Bona before her, Constance learned how to be a Polish queen, learning the language, demonstrating her piety, and marrying her female attendants to Polish nobles, creating an affinity for herself independent of her husband. Armed with patronage, Constance was a powerful advocate for a pro-Habsburg foreign policy, which fit in with Sigismund's continued designs on the Swedish throne. Deeply religious, as well as a patron to artists, scholars, and musicians, she was also a builder, as well as a talented money manager in the running of her household and her estates. She also inserted herself in the Polish succession, working to get her son John Casimir recognized as successor instead of Sigismund's eldest son Ladislaus IV Vasa, even though he was her sister Anna's son. But she died a year before her husband in 1631. In her active and engaged queenship, Constance built upon the precedent of the active and engaged queenships of Bona Sforza and Anna Jagiellon.

At the time of Constance Renata's death, much of Europe was consumed in warfare which continued virtually unabated for the duration of the seventeenth century. These conflicts included the Thirty Years War (1618–1648), during which Sweden emerged as a major power at the expense of Denmark, while a series of wars between Poland-Lithuania, Sweden, and Russia did much to increase the power and prestige of Sweden and Russia at the expense of the Polish-Lithuanian commonwealth during what was known as the "Deluge" (1648–1667). During this period, Polish kings were increasingly subject to the pressures of both the Austrian Habsburgs and the French Bourbons to marry candidates of their choice. The Habsburgs won the first round with Ladislaus IV, who married Cecilia Renata (1611–1644), daughter of Emperor Ferdinand II and Maria Anna of Bavaria, in 1637. She behaved exactly as a Habsburg consort should behave. She was known as a gentle, sweet, polite consort, who swiftly gained her husband's affection. But behind the sweetness lay a smooth political operator. Cecilia Renate allied herself with the pro-Habsburg faction at court and successfully undermined royal favorite Adam Kazanowski. Her early success, however, was undercut by Habsburg reticence to help Ladislaus gain the Swedish throne, which eventually served to lessen her credibility in her husband's counsels. She was also unlucky in childbearing; her three pregnancies resulted in only one live birth, a son, who died age seven. Her last pregnancy, in 1644, which ended in a stillbirth, killed her. Nevertheless, the Poles appreciated her charity, piety, and goodness, which were always a winning combination in a queen consort.

Two years later, Ladislaus married again. By this time, relations with the Habsburgs had deteriorated, while in France, Cardinal Mazarin was determined that Ladislaus marry a French noblewoman, Marie Louise Gonzaga (1611–1667), daughter of Charles Gonzaga, Duke of Mantua and Montferrat. In a scenario reminiscent of Anne of Brittany's marriage to two successive kings of France, Marie Louise married John II Casimir after the death of Ladislaus IV in 1648. John II Casimir faced the Cossack Khmelnytsky uprising of 1648–1657, which was compounded by the Swedish and Russian "Deluge" invasions of 1655–1660, which devastated Poland, as armies pillaged art, destroyed cities, and caused a famine that reduced the Polish-Lithuanian commonwealth's population by one-third, ending Poland's big-power status in European affairs. To face these tumults, John II Casimir had a brave, stouthearted queen by his side. Much like Bona Sforza before her, Marie Louise made strengthening the monarchy the primary mission of her queenship.[22]

Like Bona, she did not go about it in a subtle fashion. In fact, Marie Louise, who found John II Casimir much more pliable than the stubborn Ladislaus IV, set out to establish her own political base in the Polish court, whether the Polish nobility liked it or not. They did not, but several were compelled to marry the French ladies Marie Louise had brought with her to Poland from France. What makes Marie Louise remarkable is that she made no attempt to adapt to Polish customs or dress. As Bona Sforza did for all things Italian in her court, Marie Louise remained French in her own tastes, which in turn began to orient the court towards the more flamboyant style that was developing during the reign of Louis XIX of France. Despite her domineering style, John II Casimir was devoted to her, even though their two children both died in infancy. Undeterred, Marie Louise pressed forward with ambitious plans to shore up the powers of the monarchy at the expense of the nobility, ready to take on the entire kingdom in her single-minded pursuit of strengthening the monarchy, no matter what steps needed to be taken, which included dissimulation, bribery, and threats.

Eventually, Marie Louise had to back down on her ambitious plan of monarchical reform and the succession, pinning her hopes on Marie Casimire de La Grange d'Arquien (1641–1716), one of her French ladies in waiting, who was reportedly in love with the Polish Hetman (or supreme military commander) John Sobieski despite her marriage to Polish nobleman Jan "Sobiepan" Zamoyski. But weakened by the incredible demands she placed upon herself, most of which went unrealized, Marie Louise died in May 1667, refusing to send word to her husband that she was dying because he was busy presiding over an important meeting of the *sejm*.

John II Casimir (r. 1648–1668), the last of the Vasa kings, could not handle ruling Poland without his wife and abdicated the throne in September 1668. His successor was Michael I, who swung the pendulum back to closer ties with the Habsburgs, marrying seventeen-year-old Eleanor Maria (1653–1697), the daughter of Emperor Ferdinand III and Eleonor Gonzaga, in 1670. Once again, a Habsburg archduchess went to work for her dynasty, learning Polish, capturing her husband's heart, and accompanying him in his travels around the commonwealth. As with Cecilia Renata, the last Polish Habsburg consort, Eleanor Maria had trouble bearing heirs, with two pregnancies, a stillbirth and a miscarriage over the course of a three-year marriage, which ended with Michael's death in 1673. Lacking a male heir, Eleanor Maria moved on with her life, after the *sejm* elected John III Sobieski king in 1674, marrying the landless Duke Charles V of Lorraine, a loyal servant of the Habsburg dynasty, in 1678. The ducal house of Lorraine had been replenished by Habsburg duchesses since the sixteenth century Christina, while Eleanor Maria was much more fortunate bearing children in her second marriage; her eldest son Leopold, Duke of Lorraine, was the father of Francis Stephen, consort of Maria Theresa of Austria.

The marriage of John III Sobieski and Marie Casimire was a love match, a rarity with dynastic marriages, with the couple marrying after the death in 1665 of Marie Casimire's first husband, Jan Zamoyski. Like Bona Sforza and Marie Louise Gonzaga before her, Marie Casimire was a proactive, business-minded queen, working behind the scenes to get her husband elected king in 1674. Sobieski was one of the more remarkable and able of early modern Polish kings, distinguishing himself as a military commander against Cossacks, Turks, and Swedes during the Deluge invasions, and aligning himself with the Francophone faction at the court of Queen Marie Louise Gonzaga. By this time, the court of Louis XIV at Versailles was reaching its apogee of brilliance and opulence. Marie Casimire worked extremely hard to gain patronage from the Sun King, with mixed results, while scheduling periodic visits to Paris, where her eldest son James was born in 1667. There is more known about this Polish queen than any other of the seventeenth century because of the remarkable correspondence between her and John Sobieski. John referred to his wife as "Marysieńka," which reveals the couple as very much in love, as Sobieski was a big fan of romantic literature, following literary tropes in his missives. Marie Casimire responded in kind. What makes their letters so accessible is their warmth, earthiness, and sense of humor as they lampooned their antagonists with pet names and vague terminology, much of whose meaning remains to be deciphered.[23]

Marie Casimire was also an energetic marriage broker for her children, looking to Germany for spouses for her son James, who married Hedwig Elisabeth of Neuburg of the Palatinate, and daughter Theresa Kunegunda, who married Maximilian II Emanuel, Elector of Bavaria, making her the grandmother of Emperor Charles VII. After Sobieski's death in 1696, Marie Casimire failed to get her son James elected his father's successor, which was indicative of how powerful outside influences had become in Polish monarchical elections. She had even contemplated marrying Hetman Stanisław Jabłonowski to help sway the election. Instead, with her power base evaporated, she chose life as an exiled queen, spending her days in Rome until her money ran out, when she moved to Blois in 1714, where she died two years later.

While seventeenth century Poland had a run of popular and capable queens, the eighteenth century opened with Poland's first Protestant Queen, Christiane Eberhardine of Brandenburg-Bayreuth (1671–1727), who was married to Augustus II of Poland. Although Sweden had stabilized following its defeat in the Great Northern War, Poland never recovered from the Deluge invasions of the 1660s. Despite the productive reign of John Sobieski, Poland was increasingly subject to foreign influences, eventually becoming completely dismembered by the end of the early modern era in a series of partitions between Russia, Prussia, and Austria. But at the beginning of the eighteenth century the Dukes of Saxony captured the Polish throne, with the election of the Elector Frederick Augustus I, "the Strong" as Sobieski's successor in 1697. During his and the reign of his successor Augustus III (r. 1734–1763), who married Maria Josepha of Austria, Poland's final two queens were reflective of the state of eighteenth-century queenship, both from a Protestant and a Catholic perspective.[24] Neither had any influence upon the deterioration of the Polish state. Instead, while their husbands dealt with Poland's myriad internal and external problems, they set up shop as paragons of Enlightenment thinking and religious virtue.

Coming from a minor branch of the Hohenzollerns, Christiane Eberhardine had made a good marriage with Frederick Augustus, who was a second son of the Elector of Saxony. But with the death of his elder brother Johann Georg IV in 1694, she became Electress of Saxony. She had been raised strictly as a Lutheran and was a practitioner of pietism, a form of Protestant analogue to the *pietas austriaca* (see Chapter 4), which allowed Germanic noblewomen to achieve equivalent forms of religious prestige. In contrast, Augustus was an extremely virile man, whose infidelities were a constant affront to her dignity. Christiane experienced one pregnancy, giving birth to her husband's heir in 1696. After this, she did not resume marital relations with Augustus and began creating a separate life for herself in Saxony. In the meantime, Augustus pursued numerous women, fathering dozens, if not hundreds, of Saxon bastards. But rather than manage his affairs, or pretend that they did not exist, as many other queens had done, Christiane maintained a silent, dignified protest, presiding at state occasions in Dresden, which was fast becoming a glittering cultural center, and occasionally visiting with her husband, but otherwise they lived apart.

When Augustus converted to Catholicism and made a successful bid to be elected King of Poland, he wanted Christiane to come to Krakow to be crowned Queen. In the contract Augustus signed with the *sejm*, he promised to try to convert her to Catholicism. But Christiane would have none of it, refusing to step foot in Poland unless she could openly practice her religion, which the Poles refused to do, making her the first uncrowned Polish queen since Helena of Moscow at the beginning of the sixteenth century. Even her father could not persuade her to go to Gdansk, which had a sizeable Protestant population. Instead, she remained in Saxony, spending her time between Dresden and her castle at Pretsch on the Elbe river. She also enjoyed a warm relationship with her mother-in-law, Anna Sophie of Denmark, who was raising her son. Augustus could have divorced her, as there was no affection or bond between them at all, but he surprised his contemporaries by remaining married to her.

A big part of the reason why was that Christiane was popular in Saxony. Her husband was also, for entirely different reasons, and he found it useful to have a Protestant stalwart in the heart of Lutheran Germany, whose court was characterized by impeccable moral values. Christine raised dozens of young women, the daughters she never had, in the strict pietism that defined her tenure as Electress of Saxony; cared for orphans; and was in the process of establishing a convent for Protestant women when she died in 1727. She was also interested in science and botany, building a glass factory and planting an orangery at Pretsch. She appeared to have lived a full life, although Protestant commentators cast her as the martyred Protestant queen to a renegade Catholic king.

Poland regained an in-residence queen consort in 1734 with the accession of Augustus III and his queen Maria Josepha (1699–1757), the eldest daughter of Emperor Joseph I. She had been removed from her place in the Austrian succession by her uncle Charles VI and the Pragmatic Sanction and was compelled to renounce her inheritance rights before her marriage in 1719. Like

her cousin and dynastic rival Maria Theresa, Maria Josepha was the benefi-
ciary of two centuries of precedent surrounding Habsburg queenship, and she
played her part to perfection. First, quite unlike the unhappy experience of
Christiane Eberhardine, Maria Josepha formed an emotional bond with her
husband, who remained faithful to her for the remainder of her life. Like so
many of her Habsburg forbears, she was remarkably fecund with fourteen
pregnancies, with eleven children surviving to adulthood. She was particularly
close to her children, encouraging them to write to her informally, while she
spent as much time with her husband as possible, creating a public image of
royal domestic harmony. Skilled in several languages, she swiftly learned
Polish, and became a major player in the governments of both Poland and
Saxony. As a marriage broker, she married her daughters into the royal houses
of Spain and France, and into the electoral house of Bavaria, while her eldest
son, Frederick Christian, married her niece Maria Antonia of Bavaria.

Quite unlike Christiane Eberhardine, who refused to step foot in Catholic
Poland, Maria Josepha was much more comfortable in Protestant Saxony,
and exhibited no prejudice towards Protestants, even as she built Catholic
churches and supported the Jesuits. In these attitudes, she reflected the
cosmopolitan attitudes of Habsburg queenship, which long had sought to represent and identify with several ethnicities, languages, and among the most
enlightened of them, of religions as well. While her cousin Maria Theresa
was intolerant towards Protestantism in her realms, Maria Josepha gave to
Catholic and Protestant charities alike. She founded hospitals, convents, and
orphanages, while the intensity of her devotions alarmed her Jesuit confessor.
She was also a practitioner of the *pietas austriaca*. She ended her days under
house arrest in Dresden after the city was occupied by the Prussian army
in 1757 during the Seven Years War, loyal to the end, writing her letters in
invisible ink to sneak them out of her palace. Like her cousin Maria Theresa,
she embodied the successful strategies of a long, grand tradition of Habsburg
queenship, from Isabel of Portugal to Eleonore Magdalene of Neuburg, which
exemplified companionate marriage, hands-on motherhood, and intense religiosity combined with an attention to Habsburg dynastic interests, particularly
as marriage brokers for their children and other relatives.

QUEENSHIP IN DENMARK

Like their counterparts in Poland, many of the queens of early modern
Denmark were capable and energetic women who followed in Bona Sforza's
footsteps to enjoy wide-ranging and occasionally autonomous queenships.

But unlike Habsburg and Polish queenships, Danish queens often faced formidable challenges to creating companionate marriages, which usually were a necessary condition for queens who aspired to political power and influence. A prime example was the marriage of Frederick I and Sophie of Pomerania (1498–1568) in 1514. From the first Sophie insisted on living on her dower lands, ruling them directly herself, rather than living within the royal court. This caused friction between the couple, and she lived apart from Frederick at Kiel, managing her fiefs independent of royal control after the death of her husband in 1533, until her stepson Christian III forced her to relinquish her sovereignty over these lands in 1540. Sophie's autonomous queenship was matched by her successor, Dorothea of Saxe-Luneburg (1511–1571), the queen of Christian III. It appears that there was a lack of emotional bonding here also, with the royal spouses spending considerable time apart from each other. Skilled as a gardener of medicinal plants, Dorothea had no interest in learning Danish and was quite severe with her ladies in waiting.

Denmark's next queen, Sophie of Mecklenburg-Güstrow (1557–1631), was able to create a companionate marriage, although under challenging circumstances.[25] Her marriage to Frederick II, twenty-three years her senior, was fruitful, with seven children living to adulthood. While Frederick did not allow her any political power, she kept control over the raising and education of her children, sending the older children to Güstrow in northern Germany, due to Frederick's indulgent lifestyle, which included riotous banquets, heavy drinking, and casual sexual affairs, which she endured with queenly dignity. When Frederick died in 1588, she threw a spectacular funeral for him, while she set out to carve for herself a political role during the minority of her son, Christian IV (r. 1588–1648).

Despite a rich tradition of female rulership in medieval Denmark, including several regents and one queen regnant, the minority council refused to grant her the regency or a place on the regency council.[26] Nevertheless, Sophie took charge of her own financial affairs, and those of her daughters, in defiance of the minority government. Barred from a place in this government, she nonetheless served as regent for her son in the duchy of Schleswig-Holstein until 1595, while she arranged for the marriage of her daughter Anne to James VI of Scotland, also in defiance of her son's council. In 1594, the council finally banished Sophie to Nykøbing Falster, where she lived out her life arranging the marriages of the rest of her children, managing her estates and other economic enterprises to great profits, and studying science. She died at the ripe old age of seventy-four as one of the most learned as well as richest women in Europe, while setting a benchmark for queenly power and prestige in Denmark.

Sophie's successor, Anna of Brandenburg (1575–1612), also dealt with serial infidelity within her marriage. Little is known about her queenship. She did bear her husband, Christian IV, seven children, including the future Frederick III, over the course of a fifteen-year marriage, which ended with her death in 1612 at age thirty-seven. Christian then contracted a morganatic union with Kirsten Munk, a seventeen-year-old noblewoman, in 1615. While it was a love match for Christian, Kirsten took control of several queenly prerogatives, bearing the king twelve children, many of whom survived to adulthood to be insinuated into the Danish nobility. But eventually, as the king matured, the marriage soured, with Kirsten taking a lover, cavalry captain Otto Ludwig of Salm-Kyrburg, who probably fathered several of her younger children. Christian divorced her in 1630, after taking up with Kristen's former servant Vibeke Kruse, who also bore him several children.

Denmark's next queen consort, Sophie Amalie of Brunswick-Lüneburg (1628–1685), who married the future Frederick III (r. 1648–1670) in 1643, was suitably appalled by the domestic arrangements of her father-in-law and developed a lifelong hatred for the children of Kirsten Munk. Sophie brought a decidedly francophone attitude towards court life, determined to live a lifestyle of conspicuous royal consumption like her counterparts in Western Europe, and commissioning as well as acting in plays and other entertainments at court, much as Henrietta Maria of England had done at the Caroline court. Taking advantage of the social reticence of her husband Frederick III, she emerged as a major player in Danish politics, and a prime mover in the war against Sweden in 1657. As she was acquisitive and frivolous, Sophie was not a particularly popular Danish queen, until the war with Sweden backfired and Denmark was invaded by Swedish forces, which laid siege to Copenhagen from 1658 to 1660. Both Sophie and Frederick put on an inspiring show of bravery during the ordeal, positioning them to push through constitutional changes that rendered Denmark an absolute monarchy. All of this was as much Sophie Amalie's legacy as it was her husband's.

Like Bona Sforza before her, Sophie Amalie played the role of domineering mother-in-law during the reign of her son Christian V and his queen Charlotte-Amalie of Hesse-Kassel (1650–1714). Sophie had arranged the match herself, looking for a daughter-in-law she could control, but Charlotte Amalie achieved queenly prestige and autonomy by following a traditional playbook. Twenty years old when she became queen in 1670, she remained devoted to her husband, despite a lack of commonality and Christian's penchant for sexual affairs. Instead, she maintained her dignity, and raised her brood of children, while embracing the Danish language and culture, apparently a first for early modern Danish queens, and creating a reputation for piety. At the same time, she was a queen who loved the social life of the court, enjoying a level of popularity that was beyond the reach of her more formidable mother-in-law. Charlotte Amalie also weighed in on foreign policy, supporting her relatives in Brandenburg in their alliance with Denmark against Sweden in the Scanian War.

Charlotte Amalie also declined to play the role of overbearing mother-in-law with her son Frederick IV's queen, Louise of Mecklenburg-Güstrow (1667–1721). Frederick was also a highly sexualized king who chose Louise for her beauty. Initially the pair were reported to be happy, but Frederick soon embarked on a series of high-profile love affairs with women of all social ranks. Like her mother-in-law, she did her best to play the role of a devoted wife and mother, bearing six children, although only two lived to adulthood, including her husband's successor Christian VI (r. 1730–1746). The fact that she had borne a son must account for why Frederick designated her as regent during his visit to Italy in 1708–1709, as Louise became enraged on several occasions over his mistresses. Nevertheless, despite her marginalization, she continued to preside over court functions and comport herself as a queen. The refuge of the neglected queen was always religiosity; Louise was a practitioner of pietism, and this devotion increased over the years as she endured the humiliation of her husband's liaisons with his bigamous wives. She died in 1721, age fifty-three, and unmourned by her husband.

The next day, Frederick married for the second time his morganatic wife, Anne Sophie Reventlow (1693–1743), a Danish commoner, officially making her queen. Well before Louise's death in 1711, Frederick had spied Anne Sophie at her parent's home, and the next year abducted her and committed bigamy by marrying her. Anne Sophie had much in common with Karin Månsdotter of Sweden as the only non-noble queen of Denmark. Aghast at the bigamy, most of the Danish royal family refused to accept Anne Sophie as queen. Her stepson, the future Christian VI, particularly despised her. But firmly possessed of the king's affection and confidence, Anne Sophie defied the opprobrium to establish herself and her family at the center of court life. She bore Frederick several children, all of whom died before adulthood, which contemporaries attributed to the sin of bigamy. Frederick obviously loved her, following a peculiarly Scandinavian predilection for kings to marry for love rather than reap the usual benefits of a foreign marriage. Her family, known as the "Reventlow gang," were installed at the center of court, while Sophie emerged as a powerful go-between in the distribution of royal patronage. Like Ulrika Eleonora of Sweden (see below), she was loved as a charitable queen, known as the "Protector of the Poor." But her popularity with the Danish people did not save her from the wrath of Christian VI, who banished her to her birthplace following his 1730 accession.

Christian VI (r. 1730–46) was quite the opposite of his father, embracing pietism, which influenced his choice of a queen, Sophie Magdalene of Brandenburg-Kulmbach (1700–1770). Raised at the court of Christiane Eberhardine, the uncrowned Queen of Poland and Electress of Saxony in Dresden (see above), she was from a relatively impoverished noble house and attracted Christian VI's attention with her intense piety. But her religiosity lacked a charitable component embraced by so many of her predecessors. She was, in fact, one of early modern Denmark's more unpopular queens, with little desire to adapt to Danish culture or to court favor with the Danish people, whom she considered inferior to Germans. In the age of Enlightenment, with contemporary queens like Caroline of Great Britain employing reason and rationality to improve the material condition of their kingdoms, Sophie Magdalene had a myopic view of her queenship. Despite her religiosity, she was fond of rich apparel and jewels, making the mission of her queenship to transform the Danish court into a Scandinavian Versailles. These pursuits were a considerable burden on the Danish economy, which included the commissioning of a new crown, because Sophie Magdalene refused to wear the one worn by Anne Sophie Reventlow.

Despite her unpopularity, she held the affection and confidence of her husband, who was uxorious in his devotion to her until he died, although on one occasion she accused her husband of having an affair with her sister. But they mostly presented a united front, living it up in royal style, despite Denmark's faltering economy. Possessed with a large family, and an even larger German entourage, Sophie Magdalene made sure they were all taken care of with marriages, sinecures, and military commissions, while encouraging her husband to pass laws compelling church attendance and forbidding rides on Sunday. In the words of one contemporary observer, Christian and Sophie Magdalene's court was "joyless."

Sophie Magdalene experienced a lengthy dowager queenship, outliving her husband by twenty-six years, but her power evaporated with her son Frederick V's accession in 1746. Frederick never absorbed the strict pietism that made his parent's court such a dreary place. In contrast to his monogamous father, and much like many of his predecessors, Frederick was a highly sexualized king, whose 1743 marriage to Princess Louise of Great Britain (1724–1751) was in part spurred to channel his sexual energies. Louise was the daughter of George II and Caroline of Great Britain, who were also the rulers of the electorate of Hanover in northern Germany, the usual recruiting grounds for Danish queen consorts.

While Sophie Magdalene was despised, Louise was adored. Louise had the advantage of having a mother who had mastered the art of queenly success. As her mother had immersed herself in English language and culture prior to her arrival in England (see Chapter 2), Louise embraced the Danish language and culture, and gained the affection of her husband, whose debauchery continued unabated after their marriage. But Louise pretended not to notice, probably on the advice of her mother, who managed George II's affairs as she did his government. Instead, she raised her children to speak Danish and to appreciate Danish court culture. She was an especially warm and approachable queen, noted for her sweetness and gentility, as well as her piety, which offered a contrast to her husband's infidelities. In fact, the royal couple's popularity was based much more on Louise's good qualities than her husband's. While she died young, at age twenty-seven in 1752, pregnant with her final child, she was widely mourned as a popular, beloved queen who had maintained a companionate marriage despite her husband's infidelities.

Denmark's final two early modern queens did not measure up to Louise. Six months after her death, Frederick V married Juliana Maria of Brunswick-Wolfenbüttel (1729–1796). Juliana Maria tried hard to fill Louise's shoes, but she was despised for marrying the king so soon after the death of his first consort. Her stepchildren also did not warm to her, so she poured her maternal energies into her own son, Prince Frederick, born in 1753. Over the course of her fourteen-year marriage she lived quietly at court, enduring Frederick's infidelities with queenly grace. But following his death in 1766, and the accession of Christian VII (r. 1766–1808), Juliana Maria found herself ignored at court by Christian and his consort, Caroline Matilda, the sister of George III of Great Britain, the second of Denmark's eighteenth-century British queens.

But Juliana Maria made a remarkable comeback after her stepdaughter-in-law embarked on a scandalous affair that derailed her queenship. Caroline Matilda is easily the most tragic of early modern Danish queens. The daughter of Frederick, Prince of Wales, she had been raised away from the British court and never really developed an appreciation for the rigid royal protocol that was very much in vogue at the Danish court. She was sweet, vivacious, and outgoing, enjoying a large measure of popularity initially, especially following the dour and humorless Juliana Maria. But Caroline Matilda was saddled to a king who was mentally unstable, emotionally distant, and completely self-centered. Christian took his time consummating the marriage, and when a male heir arrived, he returned exclusively to his favorites, whom Caroline Matilda despised, and his courtesans and prostitutes. When Christian returned from a European tour in 1769, he brought with him Johann Friedrich Struensee, a royal physician who possessed the ability to calm the king.

From this beachhead, Struensee made himself, Rasputin-like, indispensable to the king. At first Caroline Matilda resented Struensee, but she later dropped her resistance to his charms. By 1770, the pair had begun a sexual affair, as Struensee emerged as a *de facto* regent, eager to reform the Danish absolutist monarchy. Both Caroline Matilda and Struensee were influenced by the ideals of the Enlightenment and wished to implement them in Denmark. Despite their lofty ambitions, Caroline Matilda's scandalous behavior was unprecedented in Danish history, although most Danish kings were unfaithful to their queens. But the early modern sexual double standard for queens was fully operational in eighteenth-century Denmark, especially after Caroline Matilda's daughter was widely suspected of being Struensee's. Rumors made their way around the courts of Europe, prompting a visit in the summer of 1770 by Caroline Matilda's mother, Augusta, Dowager Princess of Wales, whose warnings failed to temper her daughter's behavior, who reportedly replied to her mother, "Pray, madam, allow me to govern my own kingdom as I please!"[27]

In the meantime, Juliana Maria plotted a coup to topple the pair, employing a disgruntled servant of Struensee's. The coup commenced without incident in January 1772, after which Struensee was executed and Carolina Matilda was divorced from the King and banished to Celle castle in Hanover. As the exiled mother of the next king, Caroline Matilda concocted a plot with the British government to return to Denmark and claim the regency on behalf of her son the crown prince. But before the plan could be put in motion Caroline Matilda died of scarlet fever in 1775, age twenty-five. She is the only early modern Danish consort to have a modern English language biography written about her, while her story has been fictionalized and filmed in Denmark in recent times.[28] In these works, Caroline Matilda's earthiness and rejection of traditional gender roles are seen through modern eyes; her impromptu walks in Copenhagen, wearing breeches while riding a horse, and her sexual freedom, behavior which scandalized her kingdom in her own day, have rendered her a vibrant and sympathetic historical figure today.

After disposing of Struensee and Caroline Matilda, Juliana Maria set about arranging the government to her liking. Backed by the cabal that had toppled Struensee, Juliana Maria installed her eighteen-year-old son, Prince Frederick, as regent for the unstable Christian VII. However, it soon became clear that Frederick was Juliana Maria's puppet, while she and chief minister Ove Høegh-Guldberg set about to reverse Struensee's reforms, which made her popular with the nobility. But she failed to gain the confidence or affection of the crown prince, the future Frederick VI, who achieved his majority in 1784, when he pulled off his own coup, sacking his stepuncle and step-grandmother from the regency, which he assumed himself. The same evening of the coup all parties attended a ball, pretending like nothing had happened, although the new regent reportedly had a fistfight with his half-uncle Frederick. Accepting defeat, Juliana Maria spent the rest of her life as a dignified, if marginalized, dowager queen, living discreetly at court, playing with her grandchildren, perhaps savoring the memories of her time as one of the most powerful and influential of Danish dowager queens.

QUEENSHIP IN SWEDEN

While the sixteenth-century Oldenburg kings of Denmark looked primarily to northern Germany for their queens, sixteenth-century Sweden experienced a succession of noble but native-born queens, as the Vasa kings prized beauty and sexual compatibility over the benefits of a foreign marriage. Like Denmark, Sweden also underwent the Protestant Reformation under Gustav I (r. 1523–1560), the founder of the Vasa dynasty. Gustav, a member of Swedish high nobility, gained his crown in 1523 after Sweden gained its independence, ending the Kalmar Union with Denmark. Like his contemporaries Henry VIII of England and Christian III of Denmark, Gustav directed a jurisdictional Reformation in Sweden, creating a state national church and confiscating the lands of the Roman Catholic Church. Under these circumstances, after being turned down by many royal houses as a parvenu usurper, Gustav found himself a Protestant queen, Catherine of Saxe-Lauenburg, a small duchy in the northern Germany just south of Holstein that was also a good source for mercenaries. Eighteen-year-old Catherine married Gustav in 1531. Very little is known about her or her queenship, although she did give birth to an heir, the future Erik XIV in 1533. But she died two years later, after falling while pregnant.

Catherine had little time to begin creating a model for queenship in a newly independent Sweden; this task was begun by her successor, Margaret Leijonhufvud, a native Swedish noblewoman who married Gustav in 1536 when she was twenty. Margaret was fecund, with ten pregnancies over the course of the fifteen-year marriage, with eight of her children reaching adulthood. Margaret created prestige for herself by serving as intercessor between her excitable husband and his subjects; her ability to calm Gustav down and get him to reduce the sentences of malefactors did much to create a reputation for herself as a good queen. She was also a good money manager, administering her dower estates herself and avoiding the charge of living an extravagant lifestyle. The king also employed her as a minister without portfolio, and in his will named her as regent should he die before his eldest son achieved his majority. The contemporary of Bona Sforza, Margaret emulated many aspects of Bona's wide-ranging queenship.

But Margaret's pregnancies ruined her health; she died of pneumonia in 1551 age thirty-five. Gustav, now fifty-five years of age, once again chose a Swedish noblewoman, a niece of Margaret's, seventeen-year-old Catherine Stenbock, whom he married in 1552. Gustav chose her principally to be step-mother to his brood of children. Even after a reign of over thirty years and much more secure on his throne, Gustav once again passed on the opportunity to marry a foreign princess. Catherine picked up where her aunt Margaret left off, endearing herself to her stepchildren, and serving as intercessor between them and their increasingly irascible father, such as the occasion when Princess Cecilia, who later made a high-profile visit to England to visit Elizabeth I, had an affair with her sister Catherine's brother-in-law in 1559.[29]

Following Gustav's death in 1560, Catherine began a sixty-one-year career as a dowager queen, living long enough to see her husband's grandson Gustav II Adolphus ascend the throne in 1611. Catherine got on well with Gustav's successor Erik XIV, the failed suitor of Elizabeth I. But Erik was mentally unstable, leading to the Sture murders of 1567, in which Erik went on a rampage, killing several members of the nobility, including members of Catherine's own family. Catherine served as intercessor between the king and the nobility, facilitating the negotiation of settlement packages to the families of the deceased. Despite the animosity between Erik and his half-siblings, Catherine remained above the strife, visiting Eric's imprisoned half-brother John, Duke of Finland, in prison while participating in Eric's marriage to Karin Månsdotter in 1568, Sweden's only early modern commoner queen.

Karin Månsdotter occupies a singular place in the history of Swedish queenship. While spending the early years of his reign unsuccessfully trying to arrange a foreign match, Erik XIV enjoyed the company of a harem of Swedish women, two of whom bore him children out of wedlock before settling on Karin in 1565. She was reportedly beautiful, and a calming influence upon the troubled king, who took the time to have her taught to read and write. Several contemporaries explained her rise as due to witchcraft, a common means to smear a queen's reputation. Erik entered a morganatic union with her in 1567, in accordance with the promise of his council in which he was assured he could marry the woman of his choice. But the next year, when he wanted to make Karin queen, following the tumult of the Sture murders, Eric's brothers deposed him, and imprisoned him and Karin, although Karin was forcibly separated from him in 1573 as she kept bearing legitimate children and was sent to exile in Finland. After Eric's death, she spent most of her time in Finland, but returned to the Swedish court on several occasions, enjoying respect as dowager queen that had been denied her during her brief consortship. Her story has been the source of numerous novels in the Swedish language, with Karin and Erik usually cast as a Cinderella-like queen and her troubled prince who were badly treated by the Swedish royal family.

Karin was not the only Swedish queen to accompany her husband into captivity. As we have seen earlier in this chapter, Erik XIV's brother and successor John III had married Catherine Jagiellon, the daughter of Sigismund the Old and Bona Sforza of Poland when he was Duke of Finland. Like her mother, Catherine Jagiellon recognized that the path to queenly power lay in developing a companionate relationship with her husband. Before their accession, Duke John and Catherine spent much time living in Finland, where they are still regarded fondly. In 1563, when Erik XIV imprisoned John, Catherine passed on the opportunity to return to Poland. Leaving behind most of her Polish entourage, she accompanied her husband to captivity, where she gave birth to her son Sigismund III Vasa, which ultimately served to minimize the severity of their conditions.

Catherine was Sweden's first foreign-born queen since Catherine of Saxe-Lauenburg, and, as a Catholic, the first to face the challenges of an interfaith dynastic marriage. Following Erik XIV's deposition, Catherine had no intentions of converting to Lutheranism, and worshipped privately as a Catholic in her own chapel, in marked contrast to her sister Sophia, who converted to Lutheranism after the death of her husband in 1570. Catherine made a spirited effort to bring the Counter-Reformation into Sweden, making her a champion among European Catholics, and she did her best to get her husband to convert. His response was the issuance of the Red Book, a mish-mash of Catholic and Protestant beliefs and practices that pleased no one. Stymied by her attempts at a Swedish Counter-Reformation, she nonetheless raised her children in the Catholic faith. She also sent the son of the deposed Erik XIV to Poland to be raised by the Jesuits.

None of these actions seems to have brought her the level of unpopularity that plagued the seventeenth-century Catholic queens of England, although the Church hierarchy was scandalized by the practice of her religion. But Catherine was a pragmatic queen. When asked in the first year of her reign to try to convert John III to Catholicism, she replied neither her husband nor the kingdom would permit it. Nevertheless, Catherine built a reputation based upon virtue and piety, which even her staunchly Protestant brother-in-law Charles grudgingly admitted. But following her death in 1583 John married again. Taking a cue from his father, John married a Swedish noblewoman,

Gunilla Bielke, rather than contracting a foreign match. He remarked that he wanted to be married to a beautiful woman, and, perhaps recalling the experience of Henry VIII and Anne of Cleves, that portraits of foreign women were not to be trusted.

Gunilla's marriage was as coldly received as Erik XIV's marriage to Karin Månsdotter, with none of the royal family attending the wedding, except for John's cash-strapped sister Sophia. But despite the initial hostility from the royal court, Gunilla made her queenship work, swinging the pendulum back to Protestantism as she and John developed a companionate marriage that allowed her to become a formidable power broker in her husband's court; even her royal brothers-in-law and sisters-in-law came around to employ her as a go-between between themselves and the king. Gunilla survived five years following John's death in 1592, finding favor with his successor Sigismund III Vasa, who had been elected king of Poland in 1587. In these actions, Gunilla, along with Margaret Leijonhufvud and Catherine Stenbock, demonstrated the advantages to their queenships of being native born and Lutheran.

Sigismund Vasa was deposed as king of Sweden in 1599 by his uncle, who later assumed the throne as Charles IX (r. 1604–1611) and was married to Christina of Holstein-Gottorp, a duchy in northern Germany that emerged as an ally of the Swedes against the Danes. While Charles IX was a particularly unscrupulous and ruthless, if effective, king, his queen was dour and severe, anxious for political power, and feared rather than loved. She was also famous for her thrift, which even extended to measuring out the thread her ladies used for sewing. While Charles IX kept her out of the political realm, he sought her advice, and demonstrated his trust in her by naming her regent in case of the minority of their son and heir Gustav II Adolphus (r. 1611–1632).

This was the role that Christina of Holstein Gottorp assumed when Charles IX died in 1611, when the new king was seventeen. She served briefly as regent but continued as a source of power and influence in the early years of her son's reign. Gustav II Adolphus was to Sweden what Henry V was to England, the ultimate warrior king. Soon after his accession, Gustav II Adolphus wished to follow in the footsteps of his Swedish Vasa predecessors, by marrying a Swedish noblewoman, Ebba Brahe, for love. But Christina would have none of it, deploying the historical narrative of Gunilla Bielke's "failed" queenship as a ploy to dissuade her son. Nevertheless, Gustav II Adolphus was determined to follow the Vasa custom of picking a beautiful bride with whom he could fall in love. He landed upon Maria Eleonora of Brandenburg, a noted beauty. The Hohenzollerns were not particularly interested in a dynastic match with Sweden, as Prussia was still a fief of Poland, and Sigismund Vasa still wanted back his Swedish throne. But once he had landed upon his choice, he pressed his case in person, charming both his future wife and her mother Anne, the dowager Electress of Brandenburg.

Although the courtship had a rather fairy-tale aspect, the marriage turned out to be a nightmare. It started off positively, with the queen creating a favorable image at the royal court. But the marriage eventually floundered. Gustav II Adolphus spent much of his marriage away from Sweden fighting on campaigns. While he was away, Maria Eleonora remained surrounded by her German ladies in waiting, resistant to adapting to Swedish language, customs, and royal society. She was initially unsuccessful in her efforts to produce children, and it became clear to Gustav and his court that the queen was mentally unstable; as time went on, her episodes of psychotic behavior became more frequent and pronounced. When she gave birth to her daughter Christina in 1626, the baby was covered in fleece, resulting in an initial determination that the child was male, which brought on a hysterical reaction from the queen, who rejected the child and later had to be confined because of her emotional instability. Because no additional children resulted from the marriage, Christina succeeded her father at the age of six following his death in 1632 while fighting in the Thirty Years War, with her minority regime run by Axel Oxenstierna, a highly respected general and diplomat who continued the war-like foreign policies of Gustav II Adolphus.

THE QUEENSHIP OF QUEEN CHRISTINA

Queen Christina (r. 1632–1654) is Sweden's most famous queen; like Elizabeth I of England, she is the subject of numerous histories, novels, and cinematic depictions. As Bona Sforza did for Polish queenship, Christina greatly expanded the parameters of what a Swedish queen could do, even though she never identified with the role of queen nor pursued the goals normally associated with queenship. Perhaps in the knowledge that Christina would be his last legitimate child as his queen became progressively more incapacitated, Gustav II Adolphus embraced his daughter as his heir, raising her as he would a boy and providing her with a first-class education that placed her among the most educated monarchs of Early Modern Europe; like Elizabeth I of England and Catherine II of Russia, Christina developed a lifelong love of learning.

But Christina was not trained to be a queen. In the Instrument of Government (1634), which established a form of minority government, Christina is referred to as a king, while in 1652 she was crowned as a king, much as Maria Theresa of Austria would be in the next century in her Hungarian coronation. With Christina's mother sidelined by mental illness, her first real role model was her father; she grew up a tomboy, idolizing Alexander the Great and never developing an appreciation for female adornment in clothing, accessories, and hairstyles. In contrast, she enjoyed such physical activities as riding and hunting, preferring breeches to dresses, and later remarked that "in women's words and occupations I showed myself to be quite incapable, and I saw no possibility of improvement in this respect."[30] In this sense, Christina may have conceptualized for herself an essentially male-gendered identity as Sweden's reigning monarch that lay outside the bounds of anything recognizing queenship.[31]

This rendered Christina radically different from all the other female rulers discussed in this volume. Like Elizabeth I of England, whom she greatly admired, the unmarried Christina was in effect both king and queen. As we have seen, ruling women from Isabella of Castile to Maria Theresa of Austria sought to exercise their kingly power through the prism of queenship, as did Elizabeth I, who represented herself as both the mother of her people and a virgin queen. Although Elizabeth wielded a kingly prerogative, she did so in the guise of a queen, with hairstyles, sumptuous clothing, accessories, and jewelry, while comporting herself in a queenly manner in the rituals of court culture, surrounded by her ladies in waiting as would a queen consort. In contrast, Christina was often presented in material culture as gendered male, such as in her coinage; her behavior was occasionally identified as vulgar, such as when she scandalized Louis XIV's court in Versailles with both her male dress and her habit of crossing her legs. While Elizabeth provided Christina with the model of an unmarried ruling queen, most ruling queens took husbands and had children if they could, which, besides satisfying the dynastic requirements of hereditary monarchy, allowed them to create the perception of enjoying a harmonious family life through portraiture and royal spectacle. They also found it useful to guard their chastity and moral probity while displaying their piety and religiosity in religious works and charities.

These were textbook strategies for queenly success, but Christina declined to follow any of them, most importantly the imperative to marry. She was equally unconventional in her approach to her kingly duties. While she was extremely well educated, in languages, philosophy, science, and statecraft, she had no practical examples of rulership to follow with her father dead and her mother deranged. Instead, she tried to model herself after the examples of exemplary kings found in the classical and Renaissance texts she devoured. While she had the example of the able Axel Oxenstierna, who stoutly defended her prerogatives during her minority (1632–1644), she turned against him and his aggressive foreign policy after attaining her majority. Singular in her distaste for perpetuating the warlike stance of her father and her minority government, and despite Swedish gains in Denmark and Pomerania in the final stages of the Thirty Years War, Christina favored a peace at any cost approach against the advice of Oxenstierna, who nonetheless continued to advise her for the rest of her reign.

In her quest to be a philosopher king, rather than a warrior queen, Christina lavished largesse on books, paintings, and sculptures, and she imported scientists and philosophers, including Rene Descartes, to Sweden in her desire to turn Stockholm into the "Athens of the North."[32] Christina spent much of her day devoted to her intellectual pursuits along with her duties as monarch, and she survived on just three or four hours' sleep per night. Torn between her duties as a monarch and a desire for intellectual and artistic fulfillment, which she thought was a proper path for an enlightened monarch to follow, she later suffered a complete breakdown in 1652 due to nervous exhaustion and a lack of sleep. She was certainly the most self-reflective monarch of the seventeenth century, as recounted in her memoirs, reportedly so devoted to her studies that she neglected her hair, hygiene, and apparel, items which were usually at the top of any other queen's daily maintenance schedule.[33] Instead, she frequently wore much more comfortable men's shoes and attire. Contemporaries also noted her manliness of expression, and lack of femininity, a quality she despised in herself and other women, as well as a brutal honesty that defied the social and political conventions of the day.

Christina was also intensely interested in religion. Despite her Enlightenment-like approach to knowledge and rationality, Sweden's state Lutheran religion did not satisfy her own spiritual needs, which for Christina included the majesty of ritual and the mystery of belief. She was drawn to Catholicism but also studied Islam and the Kabbala. These interests came into conflict with her duties as monarch, which included being the leader of the Lutheran Church hierarchy. But after her personal study and conversion to Catholicism in 1652, she also come to understand the difference between her body politic, which was required to be Lutheran, and her body natural, which desired to be a Catholic, a conceptual first for an Early Modern European ruler, which led to her decision to abdicate in 1654.

The only precedent for this in recent European history was the abdication of Anna Jagiellon in 1586, which paved the way for Sigismund III Vasa to succeed her on the Polish throne. Christina charted a similar path as she arranged for the Swedish succession. The decision to abdicate was not just based on her religious conversion. Perhaps foremost was her refusal to marry. Elizabeth I of England obviously was a model here, but their reasoning was widely divergent. In her commentary on her own marriage negotiations, Elizabeth always emphasized the need to find the right candidate but she was always explicit about her physical attraction to men, who in turn were attracted to her within the parameters of the dialogue of courtly love that was premised on Elizabeth's sexual allure as queen. No similar dialogue developed in Sweden around Christina, who did not appear to be interested in men except as counselors or as scholars. Instead, Christina's Robert Dudley was a woman, Ebba Sparre, a noted beauty who came to court in 1644, the year Christina achieved her majority. Historians in general are reluctant to discuss issues of homosexuality in royal history, both because explicit evidence is a rarity and because ideas about same-sex relations in the seventeenth century were radically different from our own.[34] As Elizabeth did with Dudley early in her reign, Christina spent much leisure time with Sparre, telling her contemporaries how much she loved her, how beautiful she was, and that she shared her bed.[35] While Christina embraced celibacy following her conversion to Catholicism, she remained devoted to Sparre, corresponding with her for the rest of her life.

Although Christina caused the Swedes anxiety by her refusal to marry and beget heirs, she did provide for an orderly succession. By 1649 Christina had already decided to arrange for her cousin Charles X Gustav (1622–1660), son of John Casimir, Count Palatine of Zweibrücken-Kleeburg and Catherine of Sweden, the sister of Gustav II Adolphus, to be her successor. But Christina had a difficult time persuading the nobility to accept her choice, as they were incensed by her rampant bestowing of noble titles and the alienation of crown lands, which seriously damaged the financial basis of the Swedish crown. This led to a rather tumultuous meeting of the Swedish Diet or *Riksdag* in 1650, in which the lower estates demanded that ennoblement be based upon merit alone. Christina displayed a splash of kingly leadership when she convinced the lower estates to accept her choice of heir, which compelled the nobility to follow suit. Two years later, in 1652, Christina was crowned, not as queen but as king, much like Maria Theresa, in full knowledge of who her successor would be.

Following her abdication on June 6, 1654, Christina ransacked Sweden of its treasures before she departed for Denmark dressed as a man. She lived for another thirty-five years, as a landless ex-queen, taking advantage of the largesse offered by the various royal courts of Europe. She died in Rome in 1689 and became one of only three women to be buried in the Vatican Grotto, despite the more provocative and sordid aspects of her picaresque life as an ex-queen, which included attempts to gain the thrones of Naples and Poland. While her contemporaries were shocked by her refusal to marry and her unconventional dress and mannerisms, she has been reborn in the modern world as a feminist icon, in histories and biographies applauding her intellect, individuality, and rejection of accepted gender roles. In more recent times, the trope of Christina the visionary had dominated modern interpretations of her life. Indeed, as the fabric of European unity frayed at the dawn of the twenty-first century, the image of Christina as a pan-European icon has developed. In 2011, French Academy member author Philippe Beaussant and Swedish conductor Mats Liljefors founded the "Queen Christina of Sweden, the European, a culture and tolerance project," celebrating Christina's achievements through a series of academic seminars and scientific conferences. They wrote on their website, "in the search for peace and harmony, Christina's values are also ours: tolerance, open borders, freedom of religion, female equality, freedom of expression."[36] Of all the queens of Early Modern Europe, it was Christina who saw most clearly the possibilities that the modern world would bring to Europe, rendering her the most visionary of European queens, whose performance as monarch in many ways lay outside the bounds of contemporary understandings of queenship.

LATER SWEDISH QUEENSHIP

While Christina set a benchmark for female intellectual achievement and gender advancement, her successor as Queen, Hedwig Eleonora of Holstein-Gottorp, reinvigorated Swedish queenship with a more traditional model based upon companionate marriage and motherhood. Hedwig Eleonora was particularly well educated by her father, Duke Frederick III of Holstein-Gottorp, in letters, fine arts, and financial management. Like his Vasa predecessors, Charles X Gustav wanted to marry a beautiful woman, choosing Hedwig over her elder sister Magdalene Sybilla based upon their portraits. Playing one of the more traditional roles of dowager queenship, ex-queen Christina brokered the marriage for her successor on her way to the Low Countries.

If Christina declined to play by a more traditional Swedish queenly playbook, Hedwig Eleonora embraced it wholeheartedly. In 1655, after she had given birth to a male heir, the future Charles XI, she joined her husband on campaign, as was often the custom of Swedish consorts. Hedwig Eleonora was the warrior queen Christina was not, accompanying Charles X Gustav on his Polish and Danish invasions, and earning contemporary praise for her bravery and devotion to her husband. In these actions, she was well positioned to become a major player in Swedish politics, following the untimely death of Charles X Gustav (February 13, 1660), and the accession of her five-year-old son Charles XI.

Like Catherine Stenbock before her, Hedwig Eleonora experienced a long (sixty-one years) dowager queenship, during which she remained a major player in Swedish politics. Her maneuvering to obtain her son's regency is highly reminiscent of Anne of Austria's successful efforts to enjoy the regency under her son Louis XIV. Quite unlike Louis XIII, who tried to limit the scope of Anne of Austria's regency, Charles X Gustav recognized Hedwig Eleonora's ability, stating in his will his desire that she should serve as regent as president of the regency council possessed with two votes. But despite a history of female regency under the Vasa kings, the council challenged her, removing her brother from his top military command position and questioning the propriety of a dowager queen attending meetings of the Diet. But she overrode the challenge when the Diet met, promising to stay out of council meetings, which satisfied the councilors. Hedwig Eleonora played a double game, seamlessly inserting herself into the center of the minority regime. She justified these actions by claiming to protect her son's prerogatives and inheritance, collapsing the personal and the political under the persuasive trope of motherhood. Similar to Bona Sforza, she also spent much time managing her own estates, to great profit, and mentoring several of her German female relatives.

For Hedwig Eleonora, the power of her dowager queenship trumped remarriage; despite her youth, she passed on a tempting offer from the newly restored Charles II of England. Instead, she chose to remain unmarried, which was a typical action for a dowager queen determined to remain influential in her adoptive kingdom. But after the prescribed period of mourning, she refused to wear widow's weeds for the rest of her life, as was typical of Catholic dowager queens, and settled back into a vibrant court life with herself at its center, which became renowned for its patronage of the arts.[37] She enjoyed a particularly close relationship with her son, who suffered from dyslexia, rendering him practically illiterate and ignorant of statecraft or foreign affairs, although he loved outdoor sports, including hunting. This, of course, made the king highly dependent upon his mother and other ministers, prolonging her influence into her son's majority reign, which began in 1672 when he was seventeen.

For the first time since Sweden gained its independence from Denmark 150 years earlier, a Swedish king married a Danish princess. Ulrika Eleonora, the daughter of Frederick III and Sophie Amalie of Brunswick-Lüneburg, married Charles XI in 1680, over the objections of Hedwig Eleonora and the Holstein-Gottorp faction at court. As Bona Sforza had done to her own daughters-in-law, Hedwig Eleonora refused to relinquish precedence to her daughter-in-law, the reigning queen. Charles IX did not challenge this situation, referring to Ulrika Eleonora as "his wife" and his mother as "the queen." Ulrika Eleonora never came to terms with this arrangement. At one point in the late spring of 1686 she went on strike, taking her children and her own court to Uppsala Castle. Both Hedwig Eleonora and her husband unsuccessfully tried to get her to return to Stockholm. Following another, solo visit by Hedwig Eleonora, Ulrika Eleonora returned to court, but the breach was never healed, and her husband continued to give his mother precedence over his wife. Hedwig Eleonora remained influential with her son, who forbade his wife to meddle in politics, for the rest of his life.

Despite these obstacles, Ulrika Eleonora made her queenship work. As the living embodiment of a fragile peace between Denmark and Sweden, and undoubtedly aware of the anti-Danish faction at court, she quickly fashioned herself into a Swedish queen, sending home her Danish attendants and swiftly working to establish a harmonious marriage and home life for her children, despite the interference of her mother-in-law. She was well known as a particularly charitable queen. Armed with considerable lands and income, as was common for Swedish queens, she built poorhouses, orphanages, and a tapestry-making school, financed purchases of grain for areas hit by famine, interceded with her husband on behalf of nobles who had property confiscated, and paid the medical bills for numerous residents of Stockholm. By the time of her death in 1693, about 17,000 people were being supported by her in one fashion or the other. Even Hedwig Eleonora must have had some admiration for her daughter-in-law's ability to play the role of a "good" queen without outwardly challenging her own queenly status.

Ulrika Eleonora's charitable enterprises reveal how secularized the strategies for creating the image of a good queen had become in Protestant Europe. While religious charities and patronage directed towards monastic houses remained a powerful prestige-building mechanism for the queens of Catholic Europe, Ulrika's charities benefitted people through an institutional structure of her own making, rather than through the channels of the state Lutheran religion and its religious foundations. She was particularly interested in the science of midwifery and financed research on the topic, which produced an influential study after her death. She died in 1693 at age thirty-six after a lingering illness, perhaps brought on by several rough pregnancies which took a toll on her health. Despite his relationship with his mother, which Ulrika Eleonora bitterly resented to her dying day, Charles XI mourned his wife deeply as did the rest of the kingdom and did not remarry for the remaining six years of his life.

Sweden did not have another queen until after the death of the unmarried Charles XII (r. 1699–1718), which resulted in a succession crisis. Charles had never designated a successor, but he had named his younger sister

Ulrika Eleonora regent during his absences on campaign. But her candidacy for the throne was opposed by her grandmother, Hedwig Eleonora, still alive and determined to see the son of her eldest granddaughter Hedwig Sophia, Charles, Duke of Holstein-Gottorp, as Charles XII's successor. Hedwig Eleonora in fact arranged the 1715 marriage of Ulrika Eleonora to Landgrave Frederick I of Hesse-Kassel (1676–1751) in the hopes that she would simply go live in Hesse.

Ulrika Eleonora had married Frederick for love, but he married her for a shot at becoming King of Sweden. Undoubtedly coached by her husband, when Charles XII died, she immediately asserted her rights to the succession over those of her nephew. In order to gain her title and vanquish her rival and the "Holstein" party, she agreed to end royal absolutist rule, as the *Riksdag* was determined to prevent another monarch like Charles XII from taking Sweden down the road of another disastrous war. In a scenario reminiscent of the English Glorious Revolution of 1688–1689, the estates elected Ulrika Eleonora queen on January 23, 1719 in place of the Duke of Holstein-Gottorp, whose claim was stronger by rule of primogeniture. The military backing that Frederick brought to the process also presaged the accession strategies of several of Russia's eighteenth-century female rulers.

As it turned out, Ulrika Eleonora was more interested in getting her husband recognized as co-ruler than ruling solely as a regnant queen with a male consort, in the manner of Queen Anne in Britain. However, dual rule had been outlawed in the fifteenth century, while the *Riksdag* was concerned that Ulrika was openly discussing state affairs with her husband as well as her confidante, Emerentia von Düben, both of whom were considered overly influential on the Queen. In a chain of events that was singular in Swedish history, Ulrika Eleonora agreed to abdicate the throne if the *Riksdag* would elect her husband as her successor. Sensing that Frederick would be a weak-willed ruler, the estates agreed. On March 24, 1721, her husband succeeded her as Frederick I, while she continued as queen consort and heir to the throne.

It is a curious coincidence that both of Sweden's early modern queens regnant resigned their crowns, for entirely different purposes. Christina had the knowledge and intelligence to rule, but Ulrika Eleonora was easily led, particularly by her husband, who eventually abandoned all pretense of devotion to his consort after his election as king. The marriage was ultimately childless, and Frederick soon commenced with a string of affairs before settling on an official mistress, Hedvig Taube, who bore the king several children. But Ulrika Eleonora was determined to make a success out of her consortship, a position she appeared to enjoy much more than her role as a regnant queen, an approach comparable to Anna Jagiellon of Poland and Mary II of England.

She remained devoted to Frederick, who lost the initiative as king after further reduction of royal power occurred in 1723. In contrast, Ulrika Eleonora was pious and charitable yet regal in appearance and behavior, presiding over a court that enjoyed music and theatrical productions. Her position as the last of the Palatinate-Zweibrücken monarchs descended from Gustav I Vasa also afforded her a reverence with the Swedish people that did not extend to her indolent and ineffective German husband. Aware of her influence, Ulrika Eleonora was able to weigh in on affairs when it suited her purpose, and she was taken seriously. Ulrika Eleonora only became publicly concerned about Hedvig Taube at the end of her life in 1741, confronting her husband on his adultery backed up by a *Riksdag* commission. She died later the same year, at age fifty-two, of smallpox.

Ulrika Eleonora's successor as queen, Louisa Ulrika (1720–1782), the daughter of Frederick William I of Prussia and his wife Sophia Dorothea of Hanover, played by a much different queenly playbook, one reflective of her Prussian outlook and upbringing.[38] She was a queen very much in the mold of Bona Sforza. In 1742, a year after the death of Ulrika Eleonora, the Swedish estates elected as the childless Frederick I's successor Adolph Frederick of Holstein-Gottorp, a duchy that had supplied several Swedish consorts. The election was part of a larger diplomatic agreement (following a disastrous war with Russia) that entailed a three-way alliance, between Russia, Sweden, and Prussia. The heir to the Russian throne married Sophie of Anhalt-Zerbst, the future Catherine II, while Adolph Frederick married Louisa Ulrika of Prussia, who duly converted to Lutheranism with a minimum of fuss, which was indicative of the increasingly secularized nature of royal dynastic politics.

Louisa Ulrika occupies an ambivalent place in the history of Swedish queenship. As eighteenth-century European queens increasingly participated in the intellectual world of the Enlightenment, with Hanover and Berlin emerging as highly refined centers of salon culture, Louisa Ulrika was superbly educated, as her father's favorite, and was well versed in Enlightenment ideologies, forming a lifelong friendship and correspondence with Voltaire. Like Bona Sforza before her, Louisa Ulrika was a cultural ambassador, bringing the latest in French and German styles, literature, art, and science to Sweden and presiding over a cultural and scientific renaissance. She was also a book and manuscript collector, with her collections forming the basis for the library in Drottningholm that is now housed in the Kungliga Biblioteket.[39] In these pursuits Louisa Ulrika emulated Queen Christina in her determination to make Sweden a center for Enlightenment culture and learning.[40]

But Louisa Ulrika's cultural and scientific achievements were overshadowed by her efforts to strengthen the Swedish monarchy, a pursuit very much in the mold of Bona Sforza. Louisa Ulrika's ability to play a political role was based upon the companionate marriage model; she and Adolph Frederick took to each other as Anne of England and Prince George of Denmark did upon their marriage. Like that duo, the power dynamics of this marriage consisted of Louisa Ulrika playing the role of dominant partner, with her passive husband, as the reigning king, playing the role of her political proxy. In this regard Louisa Ulrika also resembles Elisabeth Farnese of Spain, who disdained all thing Spanish, an attitude Louisa Ulrika felt for Swedish culture, which she made no effort to conform to. Instead, like Henrietta Maria of England, Louisa Ulrika saw her mission as queen as being to bring a superior culture with her to Sweden, which to her was not German but French. But while her marriage was companionate, and she delivered four children, including two future Swedish kings, Louisa Ulrika was an unpopular queen in an age fast approaching the outbreak of modernity unleashed by the French Revolution. While queens such as Charlotte of Great Britain and Maria Theresa of Austria cultivated the image of "good queens" as exemplary wives and mothers who were pious and charitable, Louisa Ulrika combined the intelligence and experience of Bona Sforza with the unscrupulousness of Elisabeth Farnese in her drive to reestablish royal absolutism in Sweden.

Most of Louisa Ulrika's contemporaries as queens in Western and Central Europe were aware of the power of print media and plebian culture to shape perceptions of themselves. Like Marie Antoinette of France, Louisa Ulrika did not put much energy into fashioning a positive narrative of her queenship, in works of literature or material culture, until it was too late to create a counternarrative. Contemporaries described her as haughty and without scruples, viewing the Swedish people, who held decisive power in the state, as the main obstacle to her pursuit of absolute power for her husband. There is no indication that this perception bothered Louisa Ulrika at all, despite a bustling Swedish civil society possessed with forms of media with which to critically evaluate their government.

But Louisa Ulrika was more forward looking in other aspects of her queenship. Scholar Marc Serge Rivière has argued that Louisa's deep understanding of European forms of monarchy made her keenly aware of Sweden's unique status as a parliamentary state with the king as little more than a figurehead.[41] Within the context of political instability wrought by the competition between Hats and Caps, proto-political parties heavily influenced by foreign interests, Louisa Ulrika viewed the restoration of monarchical power as vital to the stability of the state, a world view reflective of that of Bona Sforza. Her method of achieving these ends was also from the Bona Sforza school of queenship.[42] Even before Frederick I's death in 1751, Louisa Ulrika was at the center of plots and projected coups to return the Swedish monarchy to absolutism. The attempt at a palace revolution in 1756 was the most serious; her efforts at widescale bribery to achieve her aims caused her to pawn the royal jewels in secret. When she was compelled to physically produce them, it was like a scene out of Alexandre Dumas's swashbuckling novel *The Three Musketeers*.

The failure of the coup was a humiliation for Adolph Frederick, who was informed that he would be deposed if his queen tried it again. Forced to listen to a stern rebuke of her behavior, Louisa Ulrika, by her own admission to her brother Frederick II in a letter, stood in haughty silence, writing that the only thing she regretted was that the coup was a failure. So, in 1765 she followed the constitutional route, wooing both the Hats and the Caps, parties that came into existence at the beginning of the Age of Liberty, to change the constitution to reestablish absolute rule. But despite all her back-door channels, threats, and bribes, the only tangible result of the *Riksdag* was that the Caps were returned to power for the duration of the Age of Liberty. Adolph Frederick died in 1771, after literally eating himself to death. When his father died, his successor, Gustav III (r. 1771–1792), was in Paris and feared for his mother's safety because she was still that unpopular.

There was a long history of Swedish dowager queens wielding great influence, the most recent example being Hedwig Eleonora. Like her powerful predecessor, Louisa Ulrika was eager to play the role of marriage broker for her children. But Gustav's marriage had been arranged by the *Riksdag* in 1751, when he and the intended bride, Sophia Magdalena of Denmark, were only five years old. Virulently anti-Danish, Louisa Ulrika did all she could to break the engagement, conniving with her brother Frederick II of Prussia and Catherine II of Russia to come up with some face-saving means for Denmark to break the engagement, so she could marry Gustav to a Hohenzollern niece. Gustav, however, was eager to distance himself from his mother politically, arguing it was the will of the nation that he honor the engagement. But the marriage, celebrated in October 1766, turned out to be a disaster, and remained unconsummated for nearly a decade.

Like that of Louis Auguste and Marie Antoinette in France, this marriage was surrounded by innuendo, the product of salacious gossip emanating from the court and circulating in the popular and underground press in Sweden, which made its way into the correspondence networks that circulated within the royal courts over Europe. There were several facets of the royal family's public image in the popular consciousness. First, Sophia Magdalena was considered beautiful and charming but refined and distant; Gustav allegedly described her as being as cold as ice. She was terrified of her mother-in-law, who behaved abominably towards her while sowing mistrust between her and her son. The "public" supported Sophia Magdalena and blamed Louisa Ulrika for the problems in the royal marriage, while Gustav was rumored to have sexual abnormalities, including homosexual desires. Apparently, the couple asked Count Adolf Munck to provide instruction on copulation, and he guided them through the consummation process in 1775.

After the birth of a male heir in November 1778, rumors began to circulate that Munck had fathered the child. There is no proof for this, but the inability of the royal couple to create the perception of a companionate marriage, the frequent separations, and Sophia Magdalena's highly reserved attitude towards her duties as queen provided fodder for these rumors, which spread in both court circles and the public press. Louisa Ulrika apparently saw some gain from lending credence to the gossip and instructed her son Charles to interrogate Munck. When the King and Queen heard of this they were horrified. Gustav convened a meeting of the royal family, in which Louisa Ulrika was forced, one last time, to make a humiliating apology to restore the Queen's honor, before she was banished from court for the remaining six years of her life.

But Sophie Magdalene persevered, remaining close to Munck and later giving him a large sum of money, which alarmed the King, while living an increasingly distant and reclusive life from her husband, whom she outlived by twenty years after his assassination in 1792. Ironically, she had the opportunity to become an influential and powerful dowager queen during the reign of her son Gustav IV, but she preferred the quiet life, away from the public eye. She never gave any indication that she enjoyed being Queen of Sweden at all.

QUEENSHIP IN PRUSSIA

Over the course of the early modern era, the Hohenzollern rulers of Prussia constructed a Western and Central European state that reached its apogee in the later nineteenth century when they emerged as emperors of a unified Germany. They were just one of many early modern Germanic princely families such as the Wittlesbachs of Bavaria and the Palatinate, the Welfs (or Guelphs) of Brunswick-Lüneburg (or Hanover), and the Wettins of Saxony, which simultaneously subdivided family inheritances even as they sought dynastic consolidation through marriage alliances. Over the course of the seventeenth century, with the merging of two distinct lines of Hohenzollerns by the 1594 marriage of Anna of Prussia and Jülich-Cleves-Berg (1576–1625) to John Sigismund, Elector of Brandenburg, the Duchy of Prussia (or Brandenburg-Prussia) emerged as a form of quasi-feudal state. It encompassed territories within the Holy Roman Empire along the Rhine and in central-north Germany, and territories in Pomerania and the Duchy of Prussia (or East Prussia), which were held as fiefs of the Polish king. In 1657, during the reign of Frederick William, the "Great Elector" (r. 1640–1688), Prussia obtained its "feudal" independence from the Poles.[43] On a smaller scale, the Hohenzollerns replicated the strategies of dynastic consolidation of the Jagiellons and Habsburgs in their own conglomerations of Germanic, Baltic, and Central European territories.

Frederick William's consorts helped him achieve these goals. Prussian consorts were recruited almost exclusively from northern and Rhineland Germany, mainly to help consolidate the disparate Hohenzollern holdings and augment the Hohenzollern dynastic brand. Frederick William's first consort was Louise Henriette of Nassau (1627–1667), a marriage that helped in his quest to complete his takeover of Pomerania. Possessed with a sharp intellect, Louise and Frederick developed the kind of working relationship that developed into an emotional bond, reflective of their Calvinist beliefs, with Louise serving as a political advisor and proxy for her husband, following him around his territories, and negotiating the deal with Polish Queen Marie Louise Gonzaga which gained Prussian sovereignty. At the same time, she played the role of "good queen," raising her children, dispensing charity, and building orphanages. After Louise's death, Frederick William married again in 1668, to Dorothea of Schleswig-Holstein-Sonderburg-Glücksburg. Like so many other Baltic queens, Dorothea acquired land personally for her children to inherit, purchasing Brandenburg-Schwedt and other fiefs for her sons. She was also quite military minded in an increasingly militarized state, commanding her own regiment and equipping two fleets for Brandenburg in the Baltic Sea. These Electress-Duchesses reflected the Protestant version of the Habsburg queenly work ethic, serving as consorts to a wide-ranging group of Germanic and Slavic subjects scattered across Western and Central Europe.

With Frederick William's death in 1689, his eldest son, Frederick, became elector and duke and in 1701, assumed the title King in Prussia, a composite kingdom which combined the Electorate of Brandenburg, the Duchy of Prussia, and other Hohenzollern-ruled territories both within and outside the Holy Roman Empire. His consort was Sophia Charlotte of Hanover (1668–1705), whose brother, the Elector George Louis, inherited the British throne as George I in 1714. The Brunswick connection brought the type of intellectual and artistic stimulation to Berlin that Sophia Charlotte's granddaughter Louisa Ulrika would later bring to Sweden, a form of generational cultural ambassadorship for Prussian royal women. Sophia Charlotte was an enlightened queen, brought up in the brilliant court of her mother, Sophia, Electress of Hanover, and was extremely well educated in languages, literature, and science, bringing the culture and intellectualism of the Hanoverian court to Berlin.[44] Frederick was equally as cultured and reportedly in love with his queen, never using the services of his "official" mistress, but they never established a close personal attachment that was characteristic of the marriages of previous electress-consorts, even though they shared many of the same cultural and intellectual interests.

One of the byproducts of a lack of a companionate marriage was the lack of a large family; Sophia gave birth to only two children, sons, with only one surviving infancy, quite unlike her own mother, Sophia, who bore seven children who reached adulthood. Sophia Charlotte did inherit her mother's keen intellectual interests in science and philosophy, and she later earned a reputation as one of Europe's most educated women. Disliking the intrigue and the pomp of the Prussian court, she set out to create an autonomous place for her queenship at Lietzow Manor, west of Berlin, where she erected a baroque summer residence, renamed Charlottenburg Palace after her death, which the king was allowed to visit only by invitation. There, she fostered a salon-like atmosphere that attracted scientists, scholars, and artists, making her court a nexus for Enlightenment thinking and discourse.[45] She was also a lifelong devotee of philosopher and mathematician Gottfried Wilhelm Leibniz. Reputedly a formidable woman, Sophia Charlotte was so determined to meet Peter the Great of Russia when he was on his way to Holland in 1697 that she waylaid him in Hanover, compelling him to make a social visit and making the king nervous until she and her ladies disarmed him with their wit and charm.[46] Despite the lack of a companionate marriage, or perhaps because of it, Sophia Charlotte created a model for a culturally and intellectually autonomous Prussian queenship.

This model of queenship was not duplicated by Sophia Charlotte's immediate successor, Sophia Louise of Mecklenburg-Schwerin, who married Frederick I in 1708, but it resurfaced under the queenship of her niece, Sophia Dorothea (1687–1757), daughter of George I of Great Britain, who married the future Frederick William I in 1706. Like her aunt before her, Sophia Dorothea brought a Western European sensibility to her queenship, enjoying theatre, entertainments, and gambling. Like his father, Frederick William was enamored of his queen, who like her aunt did not return the sentiment. Nevertheless, Sophia Dorothea performed her duties as queen as both a consort and as a wife and mother. Physically and intellectually, she was a formidable woman, whom contemporaries referred to as "Olympia." In contrast, Frederick William was a cultural philistine, steeped in Prussian military culture, thrifty to a fault, and lacking any interest in art or refinement. He was a sound administrator of his kingdom, a virtue acknowledged even by his son and successor Frederick II, whom he terrorized with his sadistic temper that he also inflicted upon his wife and the rest of his children. Sophia Dorothea was perennially perturbed by her husband's avarice and lack of cultural appreciation, but she persevered in her queenship, waging a decades-long and ultimately unsuccessful effort, full of diplomatic intrigues, to marry her children into her natal family in Britain. She also crossed her husband repeatedly by taking her eldest son's side in his numerous conflicts with his father and doing her best to protect the rest of her children from his wrath.

When Frederick William I died in 1740, Sophia Dorothea's queenship took on a new life and meaning, and she enjoyed both status and autonomy in her role as dowager queen. Freed from an unsatisfactory marriage, Sophia reigned supreme in her son's court for the remaining seventeen years of her life. She remained influential and enjoyed the regard and affection of her eldest son, which he denied to his own wife, Elisabeth Christine of Brunswick-Wolfenbüttel-Bevern. Like Anne of Denmark, the consort of James I of England, Elisabeth Christine was married to a man who preferred love and sex with men. While it is an anachronism to use the term homosexual historically in the context of eighteenth-century Europe, Frederick II led a mostly homosocial life as king.[47]

While Frederick II was perturbed by a marriage forced upon him by his father, he violated the fundamental principle of hereditary monarchy, to perpetuate the dynasty. When James I of England felt the pressure to produce heirs of his body, he rose to the challenge. Frederick II did not, making no effort to create even the semblance of a companionate marriage, robbing his queen of the potential to be a mother and then later a marriage broker, something he allowed his own mother to do but not his wife. Frederick's mother and daughter-in-law did later develop the kind of amicable working relationship that eluded Hedwig Eleonora and Ulrika Eleonora of Sweden. Unlike his father and grandfather, who prided themselves on the dynastic luster of their Orange and Brunswick consorts, Frederick was much more comfortable with Prussia as a great power reliant upon military victories, not dynastic marriages; if the Habsburgs married for territory, the Hohenzollerns conquered for it. Fortunately, his mother's fecundity ensured the Prussian succession of male heirs, allowing Frederick II to essentially abandon his wife completely after his accession in 1740.

Elisabeth Christine had little choice but to create her own autonomous Prussian queenship, but for reasons completely different than those of her two Hanoverian predecessors. While Frederick always honored her, they met and appeared together only infrequently, leaving Elisabeth Christine free to create the face of her own queenship. This was not easy. Frederick was especially drawn to the rational side of Enlightenment thinking, considering an extravagant court to be a waste of state resources and criticizing his cultured grandfather Frederick I for his ostentatious court. Eventually Frederick retreated completely to his homosocial residence in Sanssouci at Potsdam, where his mother was welcomed but his queen was not. But back in Berlin, Elisabeth Christine, along with her mother-in-law and the rest of the Prussian royal family, conducted a royal court without a king in residence, throwing him birthday parties he never attended. Frederick had no patience for the more formal and ritualistic aspects of court life, which he left entirely to his queen to conduct. Her court functions were always well attended because there was no alternative in the capital while Frederick II ran his state from Potsdam. All foreign dignitaries paid their respects to the queen. Together with her mother-in-law and after her death, by herself, Elisabeth Christine was the public face of the Prussian monarchy.

Elisabeth Christine's experience has few analogues in the history of European queenship; she was a consort spurned both sexually and emotionally by her husband, who nonetheless supported aspects of her queenship that benefitted him politically. Of all the queens surveyed in this book, she most resembles Eleanor of Austria, the neglected second queen of Francis I of France. Both queens did their best to involve themselves in the affairs of the royal family and practice a high level of religious observance and dispense acts of charity. But with Elisabeth Christine in particular, the issue of religion was also a great contrast between her and her husband. While Frederick the Great was essentially an atheist, instituting complete religious toleration in his realm, Elisabeth Christine created prestige for herself as a pious and charitable Lutheran queen, which provided a contrast with her efficient yet parsimonious husband. She enjoyed popularity not only for her positive actions, such as her show of leadership and bravery during the sieges of Berlin during the Seven Years War, but also for her position as a neglected queen. In this latter respect, she is also comparable to Catherine of Braganza of England, who was pitied in Samuel Pepys' *Diary*.[48]

Because of her marginalization, Elisabeth Christine had a difficult time maintaining discipline within her court, while the lack of the king's presence in the capital contributed to the atomization of the Prussian royal family into a constellation of separate mini-courts. Yet she never gave up on Frederick; alone of the royal family and courtiers in general, she remained devoted to her ruthless and cantankerous husband, despite his lack of social graces, perhaps in realization that maintaining her tenuous hold on her queenship relied on the king's goodwill. In return, the king honored her at all required state and court functions and wrote letters to his nobles demanding they show his queen respect. As had happened for her mother-in-law, life also took on new meaning for Elisabeth Christine following Frederick II's death, in 1786. Free to follow the imperatives of queenship during the kingship of Frederick William II, she enjoyed influence at court, participating freely in court life until the end of her life, dispensing half her income in charity, and earning the sobriquet "the good queen."

Prussia's final early modern queen suffered from a completely different form of neglect, at the hands of Frederick II's successor, his nephew Frederick William II. Frederick William II had been married before his accession, to his double first-cousin Elisabeth Christine of Brunswick-Wolfenbüttel. She objected to his open philandering and engaged in some of her own, which ended in pregnancy by a court musician with whom she planned to run away to Italy. Despite the glaring double standard, Frederick William insisted upon a divorce from and imprisonment of Elisabeth Christine, the same fate meted out to Caroline Matilda of Denmark. Given that the marriage had been arranged specifically to ensure the succession, Frederick II ordered the crown prince married again as soon as possible, this time to Frederica Louisa of Hesse-Darmstadt, whom Frederick William married soon after his divorce in 1769.

Frederica proved much more pliable than her predecessor, enduring her husband's infidelities even as she bore several children in relative seclusion in Potsdam. When she became queen in 1786, Frederica was able to move to Berlin and perform the ceremonial aspects of queenship, even as her husband's mistresses co-opted many of the queenly functions. Like Sophia Dorothea before her, Frederica enjoyed the support and sympathy of her children through her decade-long consortship, which ended in 1797 with her husband's death. She lived another seven years in relative obscurity. It is instructive that Prussia's final queens were marginalized for completely different reasons. During the seventeenth century, as Brandenburg-Prussia consolidated its holdings, its electress-duchesses played a vital dynastic role in these processes. But as Thomas Biskup has argued, as the Prussian state increased its military power and efficiency, the forms of dynastic roles played by its queens swiftly evaporated in the Kingdom of Prussia, in which only the two Hanoverian queens, Sophia Charlotte and Sophia Dorothea, were able to stand up to their indomitable husbands.[49]

CONCLUSION

The wide-ranging queenship of Bona Sforza hovers over this chapter. Bona recognized no borders to her queenship, whether she was managing estates and business enterprises, reforming and rationalizing taxes, personally ruling her Italian territories, importing artists and works of art and music, building palaces, raising educated children, or playing the role of marriage broker, while appropriating the kingly role as her husband aged. No other early modern Western European consort had a reign comparable to the reach of Bona's queenship, which provided an expansive model for her successors as queens of Poland and the other Baltic kingdoms to emulate. Her daughter Anna Jagiellon brought a level of astuteness not noticed by previous historians to the way in which she obtained and conducted her queenship, while her other daughter, Catherine, negotiated her role as a Catholic queen of Lutheran Sweden with her reputation intact. But Bona's influence is most visible in three other queens: Constance Renata embraced Polish culture while also directing building churches and orphanages, operating as a superb money manager, and brokering marriages; Marie Louise Gonzaga, like Bona, made strengthening the monarchy her primary goal by replicating Bona's bold approach to appropriating political power; and Maria Josepha combined aspects of Bona's model with that of Habsburg queenship, ending Poland's run of early modern queens on a high note of queenly achievement. Overall, like Habsburg queenship, Polish queenship was strongly predicated on the companionate marriage model, with very few exceptions, such as the Habsburg consorts of Sigismund II Augustus and Christiane Eberhardine. In Denmark, many consorts were sound business managers, such as Sophie of Pomerania and Sophie of Mecklenburg-Güstrow.

Companionate marriage also formed a major part of Swedish queenship, partly because sixteenth-century Swedish kings often married for love or sought foreign consorts who were beautiful. Sweden's imperial objectives in its conflicts with Denmark required an infusion of foreign blood, provided in the seventeenth century by anti-Danish Holstein-Gottorp consorts, and in the eighteenth century, by Prussian and Germanic consorts. Periodic attempts at peace with Denmark were accompanied by the requisite dynastic marriages, which succeeded in the case of Ulrika Eleonora, whose queenship embraced Swedish culture and the Swedish people, but failed in the case of Louisa Ulrika, who was widely perceived as disdaining the Swedish people and their culture. But companionate marriage was more elusive in Prussian and Danish queenships, particularly in Denmark, whose kings had a higher propensity towards extramarital relationships than did monarchs in other regions of Europe. But while several Danish consorts endured marginalized queenships, Prussian queenship emerged in the eighteenth century as something much more autonomous than was the case in the rest of Europe, although this was not so much a pattern as it was the result of the peculiarities of the specific relationships between Prussian kings and their consorts.

Bona Sforza also paved the way for the increasing acculturation of the royal courts of the Baltic kingdoms; their queens served as importers of Renaissance artists, musicians, and architects, which in the seventeenth century gave way to Baroque and the intellectual processes of the Enlightenment and the Scientific Revolution. In all the Baltic kingdoms, queenship became much more cosmopolitan, as Versailles provided a model of court life that many Baltic queens from Sophie Magdalene of Denmark to Marie Louise Gonzaga of Poland to Louisa Ulrika of Sweden sought to recreate in their adoptive countries. These kingdoms are all dotted with palaces and other works of architecture commissioned by queens, such as Bona Sforza's Palace of the Grand Dukes on Vilnius, Sophia Charlotte's Charlottenburg Place in Berlin, and Louisa Ulrika's Drottningholm Palace in Sweden. Other queens, such as Hedwig Eleonora of Sweden, were great collectors of art who enriched the cultural legacy of their adoptive kingdoms with their acquisitions.

The Baltic kingdoms also experienced a high level of cross-confessional queenships, a factor that created additional stresses for queenship that did not exist in the late medieval world. Christiane Eberhardine put religion before her adoptive country, much like the Catholic queens of England and Scotland, which severely limited the scope of their queenships. Christina of Sweden abdicated her crown because her personal beliefs were not compatible with those of her country. This became a transcendent moment in the history of queenship, in which Christina's body politic and body natural were in fundamental disagreement on the issue of religion, a unique example of how theories of monarchical government reacted to the increasingly secularized Enlightenment ideas about state formation. But other queens, like Catherine Jagiellon of Sweden and Maria Josepha of Poland, remained true to their natal religions yet created such positive perceptions about their queenships that they transcended this potential pitfall of early modern queenship. The line between Protestant confessions was easier to cross, usually with a minimum of fuss, as Louisa Ulrika of Prussia freely converted from Calvinism to Lutheran when she moved to Sweden. Frederick the Great dispensed with religion completely in his public representations as king, rendering his queen Elisabeth Christine's religiosity an anachronism that nonetheless remained as potent a barometer of queenly success at the dawn of the modern era as it did at the end of the Middle Ages.

6 Catherine II "The Great" and Russian Queenship

On the evening of June 28, 1762, Empress and Tsarina Catherine II of Russia stood on the balcony of the Winter Palace in St. Petersburg, Russia, surveying the crowds gathered below who were celebrating her accession to the Russian imperial throne earlier that day. Only twenty-four hours earlier, the guards of her husband, Tsar Peter III, had arrested an officer privy to her plot to usurp the throne, prompting Catherine's co-conspirators, the diplomat Nikita Panin and her lover Gregory Orlov, to put their plans into action. A few hours later, Catherine was awakened by one of her female servants after the arrival of Alexis Orlov, Gregory's brother, who fetched her from Peterhof Palace and escorted her the twenty miles to St. Petersburg. By 9 p.m., she had reached the barracks of Count Kyril Razumovsky's Izmailovsky guards. Catherine claimed that both she and her son were in mortal danger, and the troops then wildly acclaimed Catherine as successor to her husband.[1]

During the morning, other armed regiments, the Semyonovsky and Preobrazhensky guards, pledged their allegiance to Catherine, as the entire capital appeared to enthusiastically embrace her accession. Catherine then proceeded to the Cathedral of Our Lady of Kazan, accompanied by all the armed regiments, where the archbishop of Novgorod proclaimed her the sovereign autocrat. From there she was escorted by wildly cheering crowds to the Winter Palace, where she met the members of the Senate and the Holy Synod. She presented to them an expanded manifesto for her usurpation, which included saving the Orthodox religion, reversing Peter III's disastrous foreign policy, and bowing to the will of divine providence manifested in the acclamations of the people, a classic *vox populi, vox dei* appeal for legitimacy.[2]

All that remained now was to secure the person of her husband and obtain his formal abdication. This was accomplished with little difficulty. As Frederick II of Prussia later remarked, "he allowed himself to be dethroned like a child being sent to bed."[3] Once seated on the throne, Catherine survived assassination attempts, pretenders to the throne, and a tumultuous peasant rebellion as she kept a firm grip on power over the course of a thirty-four-year reign, modernizing and Europeanizing the Russian Empire as she expanded its territories into the Black Sea and Eastern Europe.[4]

There is no other example in the history of Early Modern Europe of a foreign-born consort usurping her husband's throne, without any hereditary claim whatsoever. But in eighteenth-century Russia, an unprecedented series of *ad hoc* female successions created a body of precedent that made possible the accession of Catherine II.[5] Even before this time, under the final grand princes of Muscovy and the Tsars of the sixteenth and seventeenth centuries, Russian consorts enjoyed power and influence as both saintly queens and nursing mothers to their subjects. While Russia's eighteenth-century female rulers drew upon these precedents themselves, female autocracy did not depend upon emulating the female piety and modesty that was characteristic of their sixteenth- and seventeenth-century predecessors as consorts. In contrast, nearly all of Russia's ruling empresses practiced an astonishing level of sexual freedom that, for the most part, was completely divorced from any kind of effort to perpetuate the succession. Catherine II herself was the scandal of Western Europe for her series of lovers, but in autocratic Russia, her love life was no impediment to her ability to rule.[6] Ultimately Catherine's success as a queen was the combination of immersing herself in Russia's language, culture, and religion, even though she had been born German, while imposing her own European sensibilities and Enlightenment-oriented world view upon her efforts to modernize the Russian state, all the while deploying traditional Russian autocracy as a unique form of "enlightened" benevolence.

This book begins with a discussion of Isabella of Castile, whose reign bridged the medieval to the early modern. It ends with Catherine II, whose reign furthered Peter the Great's march to modernity as Russia emerged as a European nation endowed with an administrative system of government that persisted until the revolutions of 1917. Separated by three centuries of European history, Isabella and Catherine had little in common, except for their belief in the power of history to shape their reigns and their belief that scholarship could be a means for a queen to fashion herself into an autonomous female ruler capable of appropriating male-gendered political power. As Isabella set the stage for Spain's rise as a powerful and influential force in Europe in the next two centuries, Catherine furthered Russia's development as both a European nation and an empire. In this sense, Isabella and Catherine are both Janus-like figures, utilizing the past to propel themselves and their nations into the future.

QUEENSHIP IN TSARIST RUSSIA

In marked contrast to the quantity of English-language scholarship available on Catherine II, there is precious little available on early modern Russian queens. Nevertheless, Russian queenship, in terms of both consorts, or tsaritsas, and female rulers, or tsarinas, had much in common with its Western and Central European counterparts, although there were some regional differences. During the sixteenth and seventeenth centuries, the consorts of Russian tsars were exclusively Russian-born women, either drawn from the ranks of the minor nobility to prevent squabbling between Russian Boyar clans, the highest-ranking members of the nobility, or the daughters of elites in regions controlled by Russia and occasionally the daughters of wealthy merchants. Both the Rurik and Romanov tsars found their consorts through "bride shows" in which eligible Russian noblewomen would be paraded by the hundreds in front of the tsar for him to make his choice.[7] Bride shows were unique to Russia; they could only work in a country where the monarch chooses native-born wives exclusively, making them logistically impossible for Western and Central European monarchs. Such a method was considered scandalous in Western Europe; when Henry VIII of England suggested that Francis I assemble one for him in Calais in 1538, he received a biting retort from the French ambassador, appalled at Henry's lack of decency. As we have seen, most European kings had to settle for letters and paintings to help them decide on their choices of consorts.

One other major difference with the rest of Europe was that until after the reign of Catherine II, Russian consorts were not crowned, living relatively cloistered lives in what was called the *terem*, which segregated royal women in both public spaces and in private residences. Within this culture and unlike their Western and Central European counterparts, Russian consorts did not participate in public ceremonies, and when they did venture out in public, they were screened from public view.[8] Historian Isolde Thyrêt has argued that the social cloistering of the *terem* added to the prestige of Russian consorts, unsullied by contact with the male gender, which allowed consorts to enjoy reputations as pious and saintly queens, surpassing even the Habsburg *pietas austriaca* in their claims for queenly piety.[9] As the *terem* exalted the piety and purity of royal women, it also frequently served as a power base for ambitious and competent tsaritsas to influence patronage, intercede between subject and tsar, execute wills, and engage in marriage brokering for members of the imperial court.

In the sixteenth and seventeenth centuries, Russian consorts occasionally wielded autocratic power. Tsaritsa Elena Glenskaia, the consort of Vasili III

(r. 1505–1533), served as regent for her underage son Ivan IV "the Terrible" (r. 1533–1584) until her death in 1538, possibly by poison, in retaliation for her allegedly sexual relationship with a young boyar. During Ivan's long reign, Russian consortship developed the contours that remained in place until the eighteenth century.[10] Ivan eventually married seven times, but his first wife, Anastasia Romanovna (1530–1560), was his favorite. In 1552, Ivan readily acknowledged that his wife shared in the dignity of Russian tsardom – "I for prowess, and you for good deeds" – echoing earlier descriptions of the complementary roles of Isabella and Ferdinand in Spain, "she with her prayers, he with many armed men." Such good deeds including playing the role of intercessor, distributor of charity, and prayer in chief for both the tsar and his realm. In one of his earlier wills, Ivan nominated Anastasia to be his successor in the event of the deaths of his sons. Anastasia's reputation for saintliness, demonstrated in her religious pilgrimages, and her identification as the conveyer of divine blessings in the birth of her sons, elevated her to almost cult-like status after her death, especially after the Romanov family gained the throne in 1613.

Ivan IV was succeeded by his infirm son Feodor I (r. 1583–1598), whom he had married to Irina Godunovna, the sister of Boris Godunov, one of Ivan's principal advisors, whom he made a boyar upon the marriage. Feodor and Irina developed a companionate marriage, although they failed to produce living heirs. This close relationship allowed Irina to exercise a number of public roles associated with her husband's throne, such as receiving foreign delegations in the Tsaritsa's Golden Chamber in the Kremlin, which Irina completely refurbished with frescoes of Saints Helena and Theodora. This conflated her own authority with that of these orthodox queenly saints, much as Marie de Medici did in France with the Rubens panels in the Luxemburg Palace, which also drove home the message of the queen as co-ruler with her husband.

When Feodor died in 1598, the Zemsky Sobor elected Boris Godunov tsar, which brought an end to the Rurik dynasty. Upon his death in 1605, he was succeeded by his fourteen-year-old son, Feodor II, whose mother Maria Grigorievna Skuratova-Belskaya claimed the regency. Maria was likely the target of a historically misogynistic character assassination; she was described as an ugly overweight Jezebel, who carried on government in her own name, in place of the tsar. This was reportedly the reason she was murdered along with her son just a few months after his accession, which brought on the period known as the Time of Troubles, a succession crisis that was not finally resolved until the election of Michael Romanov as tsar in 1613.[11]

Michael was unmarried at the time of his accession. His mother, Xenia Shestova, had taken control of his marriage plans, objecting to his first bride-show choice and pressing him to marry Maria Dolgorukova, descended from the Rurik grand dukes, who died four months after the marriage in January 1625. For his next marriage, in 1626, Michael overrode the objections of his mother and married Eudoxia Streshnyova. Xenia nevertheless dominated the imperial court in the fashion of England's Margaret Beaufort, earning her own queenly prestige as mother to the tsar, a position particularly revered in Russian society. Xenia accompanied Eudoxia on all her pilgrimages to monasteries and convents, which were the only opportunities for these women to venture outside the confines of the *terem*.

The second Romanov, Tsar Alexis (r. 1645–1676), also had two wives. He met his first wife, Maria Miloslavskaya, who was noted for her beauty, in a typical bride show.[12] The marriage was a companionate one, with thirteen children born, including two future tsars. Maria followed a traditional model of queenship, creating a reputation for piety and charity even as she lived the semi-secluded life of a Russian tsaritsa. After her death in 1669, Alexis married another noted beauty, Natalya Naryshkina, who bore him three children, including the future Tsar Peter I. Following the death of her stepson, the infirm Fyodor III (r. 1676–1682), Natalya was instrumental in getting her ten-year-old son, Peter, recognized as tsar and herself as regent. But her glory was short lived; following the Streltsy uprising of May 1682, Natalya's step-daughter Sophia Alekseyevna, who had enjoyed a large measure of influence at court during Fyodor's reign, succeeded her as regent, installing her enfeebled younger brother Ivan V as co-tsar with Peter I.[13] The coup claimed the lives of two of Natalya's brothers and resulted in her father's banishment to a monastery, rendering it a blood feud between the Miloslavsky and Naryshkin clans. Despite his mental and physical disabilities, Ivan married, after choosing Praskovia Saltykova in a traditional bride show. Praskovia bore him five daughters, including the future empress Anna Ivanovna.

THE REIGNS OF SOPHIA ALEKSEYEVNA, CATHERINE I, ANNA IVANOVNA, AND ELIZABETH PETROVNA

Sophia's elevation to the regency, although accepted by the church leadership as well the nobility, was the first of a series of palace coups that came to define the Russian succession in the eighteenth century.[14] Even as a child, Sophia strove to create a singular identity for herself, breaking out of the *terem* to be educated alongside her brother Fyodor, inserting herself into politics and government, and attending his funeral without the traditional shielding screen, which caused a sensation among the mourners given that no woman had done this before her. As regent, she swiftly consolidated her hold on autocratic power. Sophia's willingness to operate openly in the all-male spaces of government was a revolution in of itself. Sophia also appropriated aspects of the tsaritsa's role, such as that of spiritual intercessor, a form of gender-role consolidation that all the eighteenth-century tsarinas who followed her emulated. Unmarried, as all the daughters of tsars, or tsarevnas, traditionally were, Sophia ruled in conjunction with Prince Vasily Golitsyn, who was both her partner and her lover, another precedent that would be repeated by all of Russia's eighteenth-century tsarinas. Sophia ruled firmly, deploying violence when neccessary, including executing her rival Prince Ivan Khovansky.

Sophia, Natalya, and Praskovia were representative and precursors of a move towards "westernization," a reaction to the insular nature of sixteenth- and seventeenth-century Russia, which did not participate in the cultural life or the religious and dynastic wars that bound together Western and Central Europe together. Nor was Russia a participating member of the pan-European royal kinship network. Church reform, which resulted in a schism between a reformed Orthodox Church and the "old believers," accompanied a greater exposure to the culture of Western Europe, which was reaching its apotheosis in the extravagant and cultured court of Louis XIV in Versailles.[15] Like Sophia, Natalya had been exposed to western ideas and culture in the westernized home of boyar Artamon Matveyev. After the death of Ivan V in 1696, Praskovia served as a *de facto* consort for Peter's imperial court while running her own court in a more western style, which endeared her to her brother-in-law, who later entrusted her with the education of his daughters. She also carried on a discreet relationship with the boyar Vassili Yushkov; as the rules of the Russian *terem* began to be loosened, Praskovia enjoyed a position of honor and respect in the Russian court. Although Peter had little love for Sophia, whom he exiled to a nunnery after ending his minority in 1689 when he was seventeen, he emulated her hard-boiled approach to rule.

With Sophia out of the way, Peter's mother, Natalya, experienced a renaissance of influence. Most importantly, Natalya played the role of marriage broker. In lieu of Peter attending a traditional bride show, Natalya chose Peter's first wife, Eudoxia Lopukhina, the last native-born Russian consort, who was from a family of the minor nobility. Eudoxia behaved like a traditional Russian tsaritsa, dutifully remaining within the spaces of the *terem*. Her family were also very conservative, which the progressive young tsar found abrasive. Although she bore Peter a son, Alexis, the marriage was not companionate, and Peter got rid of her in a traditionally Russian way by forcing her to enter a monastery in 1698, the usual fate for repudiated Russian wives.

There was nothing traditional about the way in which Peter found his second wife, Martha Samuilovna Skavronskaya. Peter had carried on a long-term affair with a Dutch merchant's daughter, Anna Mons, and came close to marrying her. But the relationship had cooled by 1703, when Peter's friend and advisor Alexander Menshikov introduced Peter to Martha, who was born a peasant in Swedish Livonia in 1684. Martha deployed her beauty and personality to make her way to Russia, where she came to the attention of Menshikov, who handed her off to Peter, initially as his mistress in 1703 and then in 1707 as his wife, after she had converted to Orthodoxy and took the name Catherine. Catherine gave birth to twelve children over a twenty-year period, although only two daughters survived to adulthood. Their marriage was highly companionate, something very important to Peter, who encouraged women to leave the *terem* and join their husbands downstairs. Peter's declaration that marriages should be voluntary reflected his unhappy arranged union with Eudoxia Lopukhina. This represented a form of social emancipation that fostered the acceptance of female rule in Russia.[16]

Peter's unconventional marriage was just one small facet of his attempt to turn Russia completely around, flouting its traditional culture and making Russia a forward-looking western-oriented nation.[17] In this light, Catherine lived a much less constrained existence than previous tsaritsas, accompanying Peter on his campaigns during the Great Northern War against Sweden.[18] The bond between Peter and Catherine was such that in 1712, Peter married her for a second time, and she assumed the formal title of tsaritsa. Together, Peter and Catherine expanded the role of the tsaritsa, seeking out foreign husbands for their surviving legitimized daughters Anna and Elizabeth, a first for Russian tsarvenas, who previously had always remained unmarried. In 1724 Peter took Ivan IV's recognition of his wife Anastasia as co-ruler and successor one step further by crowning Catherine as his co-ruler. Although they had quarreled for a few months prior to Peter's death in January 1725, he had not named his successor, something he had decreed was the right of the tsar to do in the Succession laws of 1722, which set into motion the wheels of a Russian female succession.

What all the tsarinas of the eighteenth century had in common is that they owed their accessions to the support of the armed regiments whose job it was to protect the tsar. Sophia had taken advantage of the frenzy of the Streltsy guards to achieve victory over the Naryshkins in 1682 and gain the regency. In 1725, the successors to the Streltsy, the Semyonovsky and Preobrazhensky guards, helped decide the contest between Peter I's grandson Peter Alexeevich, who was supported by the boyar aristocracy, tired of Peter's reforms, and Catherine, who, like Alexander Menshikov and Peter Tolstoy, was entirely Peter's creation. This "praetorian guard"-style form of accession was much more orderly and bloodless in 1725 than in 1682, but the effects were the same. Catherine's party justified her accession by citing her coronation as co-ruler, which suggested Peter wished her as his successor, given that he had praised her at the time for her "manly courage and deeds" and her ability to "throw off the weakness of a woman." With the support of the guards, both the Holy Synod and the Senate acknowledged her accession. It was the first of a series of precedents that made possible Catherine II's accession thirty-seven years later.

Catherine is commonly considered to be a figurehead for the pro-Petrine party at court. In many ways, she continued to exercise the functions of a tsaritsa, as the Petrine faction stabilized the country, which was not at war at the time. Catherine was intelligent and lively, but she was only semi-literate, which prevented her from taking a more active role in affairs. What she did do was dispense charity, keeping the affections of her Russian subjects, who appreciated her concerted efforts to reduce military expenditures, resulting in a tax break that was long remembered. She was also able to reunite with her family, bestowing honors upon them that Peter I was reluctant to do. But she died in 1727 after a reign of only two and a half years.[19] Instead of willing her crown to either of her two daughters (Anna, married to Charles Frederick of Holstein-Gottorp, and Elizabeth), she willed it to Peter I's grandson, thirteen-year-old Peter II, in accordance with the succession rules promulgated by Peter I in 1722. However, Peter II died three years later in 1730 without naming his heir, bringing the direct male Romanov line to an end.

This set the stage for the accession of Russia's second tsarina, Anna Ivanovna, the daughter of Ivan V and Praskovia Saltykova. Hers was a situation similar to that of Ulrika Eleonora of Sweden in 1718, who was induced by the Swedish parliamentary estates to consent to the end of royal absolutism in exchange for support for her title to the crown. What worked with Ulrika Eleonora did not with Anna. The differences were both personality and experience. Peter I had married Anna to Frederick William, Duke of Courland, in 1710 when she was seventeen, as part of his efforts to link the Romanovs into the pan-European royal kinship network. But before the honeymoon was over, Frederick William was dead. In previous Russian custom, Anna would have been sent to a convent, but Peter I ordered Anna to Courland as the figurehead of a Russian-backed government headed by Peter Bestuzhev-Ryumin, who became her lover at Peter's request and over the objections of her mother. Anna was never popular with her family; both Peter I and her own mother disliked her, while her desire to remarry was thwarted by both Peter I and Catherine I, who refused consent for Anna to marry Count Maurice of

Saxony. Forced to remain in Mitau, Livonia, under straitened economic conditions, Anna found her savior in Ernst Johann Biron, a Baltic German native to Courland, who supplanted Bestuzhev-Ryumin in her favors in 1726 after he was recalled to Russia. By 1728, Anna and Biron had removed Bestuzhev-Ryumin from power, as they forged a lifelong partnership and family unit that also included Biron's wife and their children (one of whom, Karl Ernst, may have been Anna's own natural son). Anna's career in Courland was a thorough tutelage in Petrine-era Russian politics.

With the death of Peter II in 1730, Anna became a front-runner for the Russian throne. Now, her unmarried status worked in her favor, as the Supreme Privy Council, a governing body first formed by Catherine I, selected Anna over her elder sister Catherine, whose complicated marriage to a German duke removed her from consideration. The Supreme Privy Council, viewing Anna as the tool of both Bestuzhev-Ryumin and Biron, anticipated her as a caretaker, like Catherine I before her, so they could preserve power for themselves. Anna had originally agreed to their "Conditions," which would have vastly curtailed her power, but after arriving in Moscow, and backed by a sizeable court faction and the noisy rumblings of the guard regiments, whom Anna had cultivated, she repudiated the Conditions and assumed full autocratic power in the manner of her male predecessors.[20] Quite unlike Catherine I, whose brief reign was more of an extension of her consortship, Anna's boldly asserted possession of female autocracy became a model for her female successors.

In the English-language scholarship on her reign, Anna is not highly regarded, nor is she given much direct credit for the policies enacted during her reign. Her reign was of great interest in Western Europe, as an increasingly literate and critical public sphere was eager for news about the Russian court as western governments sought trade and military alliances with post-Petrine Russia. Anna possessed a crude sense of humor, was fond of practical jokes, and liked to mete out humiliating forms of corporal punishments. She forced nobles to be her court jesters, and she surrounded herself with dwarfs and cripples.[21] She was also an avid hunter, keeping rifles positioned all over her palaces so she could shoot at birds or wild animals out the window whenever she wished. Her close relationship with Biron was also a subject of salacious gossip in the courts of Western Europe.

These character eccentricities aside, she was a strong-willed personality, fully cognizant of her power and informed about the direction of her government. She continued the processes of modernization and westernization begun under Peter the Great, as French tastes, Italian music, and ballet made their debut at her court. Her founding in 1731 of the Cadet Corps, a form of military training for boys, was fully in the Petrine tradition, while in 1732, she moved the capital back to St. Petersburg, a city she had enjoyed in her youth before her marriage. Her legacy consists of many architectural and engineering feats, including the cobbling of the streets of St. Petersburg, the building of the Peter and Paul Cathedral, and the casting of the largest bell ever in history. In many ways, her court was a hybrid of Petrine western court etiquette combined with old-school Muscovite forms. Perhaps because she endured a straitened economy during her time in Courland, she was overly fond of conspicuous extravagance; her court overflowed with personages derived from all social stations from all over her empire.

Nevertheless, her reign has conventionally been considered a dark time in Russian history and often is characterized as a period of German dominance in Russian affairs, led by her troika of ministers: Biron, Andrei Ivanovich Osterman, and Burkhard Christoph Münnich. In all fairness, the inner workings of her government, which consisted of a cabinet which replaced the disgraced supreme privy council, also featured high-ranking Russian noblemen. But the institution of her secret police (the Secret Office of Investigation) revealed her as an ultimately suspicious and cruel monarch, with over 1,000 executions, and 20,000 to 40,000 suspects arrested, many of whom were maimed. Often in histories of her reign, the blame is put squarely on Biron for the misery and violence of her reign, interpretations that tend to deny Anna the historical agency that she so richly deserves for such atrocities.

Age thirty-seven at her accession, the same age as Mary I when she became queen of England in 1553, Anna made no attempt to marry and bear heirs or to even name an heir until the end of her reign. The Russian aristocracy applied no pressure to her concerning the succession, and when a Portuguese infante showed up to woo her, he was laughed out of Russia. Instead, she arranged the marriage of her niece Anna Leopoldovna, the daughter of her elder sister Catherine, to Duke Anthony Ulrich of Brunswick, for the express purpose of producing a male heir to succeed her, furthering the process begun by Peter I of marrying the Russian imperial family into the kinship networks of Germany and the Baltic states. In 1740, the final year of her reign, Empress Anna recognized Anna Leopoldovna's infant son Ivan as her successor and she named Biron as regent during Ivan's minority. When Anna Ivanovna died a few weeks later, Ivan VI was two months old.

Anna Ivanovna was unable to grasp how hated Biron was; his regency lasted all of three weeks. Following the coup organized by Münnich, twenty-two-year-old Anna Leopoldovna was installed as regent, taking the title Grand Duchess and assuming autocratic powers. This elevation was in keeping with long-standing Russian custom, but Anna was decidedly not up to the task, in marked contrast to Maria Theresa of Austria, nearly the same age, who took charge of affairs swiftly and decisively in Austria upon her own 1740 accession. Anna Leopoldovna's husband, Anthony Ulrich, was a weak-willed man, and the marriage was not companionate. Instead, Anna carried on a rather torrid three-way relationship with the Saxon ambassador Court Mozritz zu Lynar, and one of her ladies in waiting, Julia von Mengden, at the expense of her duties as regent, and reportedly lay in bed all day while reading novels. Perhaps most importantly, she failed to court the favor of the guard regiments.

This inattention to detail led to her son's deposition and her own imprisonment. Into this breach stepped Peter I and Catherine I's daughter Elizabeth Petrovna (1709–1761), who had hovered in the background of court life since her mother's death. The family of Ivan V had little regard for Elizabeth, who remained unmarried at the time of Anna Ivanovna's death, on October 28, 1740. Elizabeth was a fabled beauty, full of charm, talent, and gaiety. She had a somewhat precarious existence under the distrustful eyes of Anna Ivanovna, who, as noted by a Chinese ambassador, was jealous of Elizabeth's charm and beauty. She was educated, but she was without any intellectual pursuits. Instead, her assets were physical and visceral. Following a decade of government dominated by Baltic Germans, Elizabeth provided a nativist alternative, much like Elizabeth I of England, who advertised herself as "mere English," as Catholic Europe rejected her dynastic legitimacy for that of Mary Queen of Scots.

Elizabeth Petrovna had in fact been schooled to be a consort. Her mother had arranged her betrothal to Charles Augustus of Holstein, a cousin of her sister Anna's husband. Charles Augustus had come to Russia to get to know Elizabeth, who had dutifully fallen in love with him, but he died of smallpox just days before their wedding was scheduled to take place, in 1727. By this time her mother had also died, along with her marriage prospects, as neither the regime of Peter II nor that of Anna Ivanovna had any real interest in marrying off a daughter of Peter I who could conceivably produce male heirs. Again, there are historical similarities with Elizabeth I of England, as Anna, like Mary I, found the marriage of a potential female heir to the throne problematical. So, Elizabeth remained unmarried, doing her best to avoid provoking Anna's distrust while experiencing relative sexual freedom. She eventually took as her lover Alexis Razumovsky, a Ukrainian Cossack peasant, who was originally in her choir but rose in her service, keeping her affection and confidence for the remainder of her life. This precedent for royal women keeping male lovers went all the way back to Elena Glenskaia and Sophia Alekseyevna, while Anna Ivanovna's relationship with Biron was yet another model for the unmarried tsarevna. While the old noble families despised her for her illegitimacy, Elizabeth built up relationships with the guard regiments, which Biron had augmented with a steady flow of peasant recruits and which later provided the military backing for Elizabeth's usurpation of the throne.

Nevertheless, Anna Ivanovna had no interest in recognizing Elizabeth's succession rights. By law, Anna had every right to disinherit Elizabeth and will the throne to her own nephew. Instead, Elizabeth simply sat back and watched the instability of the minority reign unfold, coupled with the inertia of Anna Leopoldovna, who was increasingly viewed as another prop for Baltic Germans like Osterman and Münnich who were running her government. Elizabeth's plot required great audacity; she was in fact committing treason by colluding with the French and Swedish ambassadors, who supplied cash to bribe the officers of the guards. Anna Leopoldovna refused to heed the rumors of Elizabeth's impending coup, failing to allow her ministers to arrest Elizabeth's doctor, Johann Herman Lestocq, who was at the center of her conspiracy. But when the regent confronted Elizabeth about the rumors of the plot, she simply denied it and went home. Twenty-four hours later she rode a sled from the Summer Palace to the barracks of the Preobrazhensky guards, who were more than delighted to set her plan into motion, cheering her on as their true natural sovereign whose throne had been stolen by foreign upstarts.

The deposition of Ivan VI was the first in Russia since the regime of the Polish Vasa Tsar Vladislas I was toppled in 1612. It also set a powerful precedent for that of Catherine II twenty-one years later. It unfolded with both audacity and simplicity. Riding at the front of the guards, Elizabeth led them to the Winter Palace, which the guards surrounded. Once inside, Elizabeth took possession of Anna Leopoldovna and her family, including the infant tsar, who submitted to arrest without offering any resistance. They were all later exiled within Russia, with the deposed tsar living a life of solitary confinement until his violent death during the reign of Catherine II, while Elizabeth set out to destroy any mention of the infant tsar and his reign. Her manifesto justifying her ascension to the throne was part bluster and part fabrication, claiming descent from both Peter I and Catherine I, who had willed her crown to her only surviving daughter, as well as complying with the will of the people, a justification that Catherine II later used to justify her own usurpation.

Fully confident of her authority, and perhaps aware of the sharp break with the past her accession represented, Elizabeth defied previous precedent to crown herself during her Kremlin coronation, sixty years before Napoleon Bonaparte would do the same for himself in Paris's Notre Dame Cathedral. In Western or Central Europe, the accession of an unmarried female monarch still of childbearing age would have been accompanied by calls for her to marry and bear heirs. This did not happen to Elizabeth Petrovna, as it did to Elizabeth I of England two centuries earlier. But Elizabeth Petrovna had Russian models to choose from in her decision to remain unmarried. Anna Ivanovna had ruled just fine with Biron by her side and without a formal male consort, and later designated a collateral male heir from her family to succeed her. Elizabeth followed her example, and together they engineered a conception of female autocracy that did not require formal male consorts or a direct male heir from their bodies.

Like Anna Ivanovna before her, performing the autocratic functions of a female tsar, Elizabeth enacted policies very much in the Petrine tradition, reviving the Senate, and staffing it with native Russian aristocrats. In Elizabeth's court, brilliant foreign policy was conducted by Aleksey Bestuzhev-Ryumin, a minister Elizabeth trusted completely until his fall from grace in 1758. She was virulently anti-Prussian, which endeared her to Maria Theresa of Austria, and led a coalition against Prussia in the Seven Years War (1756–1763) that had nearly defeated Frederick II at the time of her death in 1762. But because she was unmarried, Elizabeth was both tsaritsa and tsarina at the same time, presiding over a court that exhibited a level of extravagance unrivalled in the courts of Europe. While Anna Ivanovna had first set the example of an empress regnant directing all aspects of court life, Elizabeth Petrovna brought it to new heights of achievement. The extravagance and gaiety of her balls was legendary; the costumes, hairstyles, and exotic food, such as pineapples, both delighted and astonished foreign guests. Her vanity was legendary, far exceeding that of Elizabeth I of England, who operated under relatively tight financial circumstances in which parliament needed to consent to taxes.

The Empress Elizabeth operated under no such constraints. In an eighteenth-century setting her opulence was like Las Vegas-style megalomania to visiting dignitaries, who marveled at the heterogeneity of the peoples who mixed at Elizabeth's court. Russian law mandated that Elizabeth's wardrobe, hairstyles, and all manner of accessories be the most sumptuous at court.[22] Like the Virgin Queen, Elizabeth constructed an image of herself as an ageless beauty, despite the challenges of age and weight gain, a representational strategy that underpinned her authority as a female autocrat, unbeholden to anyone. Nevertheless, Elizabeth took her religious responsibilities seriously, assuming the traditional religious duties of Russian tsaritsas that conflated the role of tsar and consort in the person of a female autocrat. Because no one could play the role of intercessor for her, she was, in effect, her own intercessor, issuing a wide-ranging and permanent intercession by outlawing the death penalty during her reign, even as she sent her armies in wars of conquest against the Poles and the Turks in true tsarist fashion.[23]

The unfettered power of female autocracy allowed Russia's ruling empresses to transgress contemporary gender norms. Anna Ivanovna was fully aware that she was the reigning autocrat, capable of exercising male-gendered prerogatives. Like Christina of Sweden before her, Elizabeth Petrovna enjoyed dressing like a man when it suited her, often when on horseback, more for the relative comfort than any desire to engage in gender transgression, although her donning of a breastplate during her usurpation proved to be an effective representational strategy, echoing Elizabeth I's review of her troops at Tilbury on the eve of the Spanish Armada. Elizabeth also liked to throw cross-dressing balls, in which men dressed as women and vice versa, which provided other occasions for Elizabeth to be the best-dressed and best-coiffed attendee.

This freedom also extended to their sexuality. Anna, Elizabeth, and Catherine II, all of whom had male lovers prior to their accessions, appeared to believe that their possession of autocracy allowed them the same sexual license as their European contemporaries. This made Elizabeth's and Catherine II's sexual proclivities more along the lines of those of George II of England and Louis XV of France, kings who had mistresses, than those of their Catholic contemporary Maria Theresa, whose female body politic was bound up in her role as a chaste wife and mother. Their behavior was also in marked contrast to their male predecessors as tsars, whose sex lives remained within the sanctity of their marriage vows, much like the sixteenth- and seventeenth-century Holy Roman Emperors, who by and large remained sexually faithful to their wives. While the private lives of Russia's tsarinas were commented upon elsewhere in Europe, it did not cause problems for them within Russia. Russian society continued to produce pretenders to the throne throughout the eighteenth century, but none of these movements sought to depose any of these empresses because of their liberated expressions of sexuality. In contrast to Anna Ivanovna, Elizabeth was a popular monarch, with no taint of foreign influence in her government, while Russia's armies enjoyed success in their European wars against Sweden and Prussia. Elizabeth knew the value of positive public relations; she was affable and approachable, with decidedly plebian tastes, enjoying being sledded around St. Petersburg for all her subjects to see. At the same time, she took seriously the building of her legacy, with Tsarskoe Selo and the fourth version of the Winter Palace as her most enduring architectural achievements, continuing the importation of all things baroque that had begun with her father. Like Anna before her, her continued residence in St. Petersburg and continuous building projects there did much to further establish the city, Peter I's "window on the west," as Russia's permanent capital.

Like Anna before her, Elizabeth looked west to Europe to resolve her succession dilemma, particularly to the House of Holstein-Gottorp, which became as important dynastically to Russia as it had been for Sweden. Elizabeth had a special place in her heart for this house; her sister Anna Petrovna had married the reigning duke, while Elizabeth herself had been betrothed to his cousin. Not wishing to revive the claims of the deposed Ivan VI, Elizabeth found her own male heir in the person of Charles Peter Ulrich, Duke of Holstein-Gottorp, the son of her sister Anna Petrovna. Elizabeth brought the prince to Russia in 1742, renamed him Peter, made him a Grand Duke, converted him to Orthodoxy, and gave him Russian tutors. At the same time, Elizabeth cast about for a European consort for her heir.

CATHERINE AS GRAND DUCHESS AND EMPRESS CONSORT

The negotiations for Peter's consort reveal how far Russia had insinuated itself into the affairs of Central and Northern Europe. Elizabeth's designation of her nephew as her successor influenced the election of his cousin Adolf Frederick of Holstein-Gottorp as king of Sweden in 1743. The selection of Adolf's consort resulted in a tripartite alliance between Sweden, Prussia, and Russia: Louisa Ulrika of Prussia married Adolf Frederick, and fourteen-year-old Princess Sophie Friederike Auguste von Anhalt-Zerbst-Dornburg (born 1729) was brought to Russia to become Peter's wife. Her mother, Joanna Elizabeth of Holstein-Gottorp, was the sister of both Adolf Frederick and Elizabeth Petrovna's dead fiancé.

Sophie's father was Christian August, Prince of Anhalt-Zerbst, a stern Lutheran general who held the command of the Pomeranian port city of Stettin from the Prussians. It was a boring life for his wife, who had grown up at the intellectually stimulating and cosmopolitan ducal court at Brunswick. Sophie as a young girl traveled all around the ducal and princely courts of Germany with her mother, gaining a working knowledge of the pan-German kinship networks that later informed her understanding of European affairs as tsarina. Sophie gained experience interacting with many different types of people, from duchesses to servants, an invaluable form of experience that also served her well later in life. At the same time, she was intellectually precocious, with a love of learning and books. This set her apart from all of her female predecessors as tsarina, none of whom had any intellectual pursuits.

Sophie arrived in Russia in early 1744, when she was fifteen. Once in Russia, she swiftly converted to Orthodoxy, taking the name Catherine.[24] One year later she married her cousin the Grand Duke Peter. A common yet unfortunate byproduct of such arranged marriages is the complete antipathy of husband and wife towards each other. After an initial period in which Peter appeared to have affection for her, he soon made it clear he had no interest in Catherine; unlike Francis Stephen and Maria Theresa or George II and Caroline of Ansbach, they did not become friends. Instead, their marriage was much more like that of Marie Antoinette and Louis XVI of France, another royal husband who failed to connect emotionally or sexually with his wife; it would be years before Catherine and Peter consummated their marriage, if in fact they ever did. Instead, Peter pursued other women of the court and later took a mistress, Elizabeth Vorontsova. While European kings and their heirs were usually concerned with propagating their respective dynasties, Peter was not, nor did he accord his wife a level of honor and respect that even the most promiscuous of European kings routinely did for their queens. Instead, Catherine and Peter settled into separate lives at either end of their home at Oranienbaum, she with her books and he with his Germanic entourage and toy soldiers.[25]

In addition to their different temperaments and intellectual abilities, the most glaring difference between the couple was in their attitudes towards cultural Russification. Both had been raised as Germans, spoke the language, and were raised in the Lutheran Church. Peter never tried to create the perception that he identified with Russian culture and religion, openly stating his preference for Lutheranism and Holstein over Russia as the British Hanoverians preferred Lutheranism to Anglicanism and Hanover to London. He was also a devoted disciple of Frederick II of Prussia, Russia's enemy during the Seven Years War, and he never bothered to properly learn the Russian language, preferring to drill his regiment of Holsteiners at Oranienbaum rather than creating relationships with the officers of the Russian military and the guard regiments.

In contrast, as Russia's first foreign-born consort since the middle ages, Catherine early on realized that her future success in Russia depended on embracing all things Russian. As we have seen, this was always a winning strategy for a future consort. Much like Catherine de Medici did with Francis I in the sixteenth century, Catherine searched for ways around her marital neglect to build a relationship of trust and affection with Elizabeth Petrovna, who held absolute power over her life at court. This process of Russian cultural identification, perhaps more than any other factor, explained Catherine's popularity within the imperial court compared to her husband, who never gave a thought to endearing himself to any his xenophobic future subjects. But Catherine was already courting their favor. Having come from Central Europe, and possessing a mother well acquainted with the geopolitics of the Baltic world, Catherine knew the value of public relations as well as the power of the printed word, bringing this awareness to her future role as tsaritsa. From her chief lady in waiting, Praskovia Vladislavovna, she learned the genealogies of Russia's leading noble families, allowing her to develop a deep appreciation and understanding of the intricacies and loyalties of Russian noble culture.

At the same time, Catherine endeavored to educate herself, as Isabella of Castile had done 300 years previously, by studying history, such as Brantome's memoirs of Henri IV of France, a king who enjoyed a reputation in Europe as a model prince; pragmatic, charismatic, and concerned for the good of his subjects. In an ironic episode of role reversal, Catherine was the one preparing for her future rule, not Peter, who idled his time indulging in his own pastimes. Despite his loathing of her, Peter had come to depend on Catherine's expertise with governing his duchy of Holstein-Gottorp, calling her "Madame Resourceful" for her sage advice and growing expertise on the mechanics of rule. In her memoirs, Catherine described how she advised Peter to take his responsibilities seriously, to no avail.[26]

But while Catherine endeavored to turn herself into the perfect consort, she suffered the problem of Catherine de Medici, Anne of Austria, and Marie Antoinette in her failure to conceive after several years of marriage. The solution, however, was completely unorthodox. If both Catherine herself and her chamberlain Count Andrei Shuvalov are to be believed, Catherine, with Elizabeth's approval, conceived her son Paul in 1753 with the Russian nobleman Sergei Saltykov, who was descended from both the Romanov and Rurik tsars. There is no conclusive proof for this; Peter did acknowledge the child as his own, and many scholars have noted Paul's physical resemblance to Peter III. Whatever the truth, Catherine had succeeded with her part of the bargain, which resolved Elizabeth's succession dilemma. It appears that maintaining pure bloodlines was much less important to the eighteenth-century Romanov dynasty than it was to their Western and Central European counterparts. Instead, following the dictum laid down by Peter I, simply having a recognized designated heir was the means to settle the succession, regardless of the heir's blood relationship to the dynasty. Fortunately for Elizabeth, the "rising sun" of her nephew Peter was never an obstacle to her possession of autocratic power because he failed to build the kind of independent base of support that Catherine was slowly building for herself.

The production of a male heir failed to improve Catherine and Peter's marriage. In response, Catherine pursued a series of discreet lovers, starting in

1755 with the Polish nobleman Stanislaus Poniatowski, as she continued to study the major literary works of the European Enlightenment. As Catherine's marriage continued to deteriorate, Elizabeth Petrovna's health began to noticeably decline. With close ally Aleksey Bestuzhev-Ryumin, Catherine contemplated the next reign in which she would wield autocratic power with herself as regent for her son Paul. But Bestuzhev-Ryumin's fall from power in 1758 resulted in a serious rupture in Catherine's relationship with Elizabeth.

By this time Catherine had moved on to artillery officer Gregory Orlov, who provided Catherine with the means to form relationships with the guard regiments, as Elizabeth had done in Anna's reign. Catherine in fact was heavily pregnant with Orlov's child when Elizabeth died in January 1762, and she and her husband ascended the throne. Whereas Elizabeth I of England endured decades of unproven rumors of illegitimate pregnancies two centuries earlier, Catherine actually had them, giving birth to Poniatowski's daughter Anna in 1757. Peter did not acknowledge the child as his own, but Elizabeth Petrovna, who was not terribly bothered by issues of legitimacy, did, having the infant christened and bundled off to the royal nursery soon after her birth. The Orlov pregnancy, however, was kept secret and hidden with strategic modes of dress, including the billowy mourning dress Catherine wore for several months following Elizabeth's death. It is not known whether Peter was aware of the birth of Catherine's third child in April 1762, named Aleksey Grigorievich Bobrinsky, who was whisked away by Catherine's valet Vasily Shkurin to be raised in the countryside outside Tula. Later in her reign, Catherine openly acknowledged him as her son, the only instance of a female monarch formally acknowledging an illegitimate child in the history of Early Modern Europe.

Catherine's pregnancy may have been a key factor in why she declined to seize power upon Elizabeth's death, as some of her co-conspirators had urged her to do. However, Peter III lasted just three more months as Tsar after Catherine gave birth to her second son. In her self-serving memoirs, Catherine painted the picture of a stupid, mean-spirited, self-indulgent, childish man unable to shoulder responsibility and reluctant to study statecraft. In a revisionist work from the 1990s, historian Carole Leonard describes a more conscientious tsar than Catherine has described, some of whose policies she continued, such as the decree repealing Peter the Great's law requiring compulsory state service from the nobility and the alliance with Prussia.[27] Peter also granted religious freedom for Protestants, disbanded the secret police, fought corruption, built schools, and was in the process of modernizing the army when he was deposed.

Nevertheless, the nobility did not lift a finger to help Peter III during Catherine's coup. Peter's desire to fight a war with Denmark to recover territories in Schleswig for his duchy caused a complete reversal in foreign policy, as Peter yanked Russia out of the Seven Years War, just when her forces had Frederick II of Prussia prostrate. In addition to these unpopular measures, Catherine's relationship with Peter had completely unraveled, following a dinner party held in June 1762, in which he called her a fool in public in a manner precious few European queens were ever subjected to.

Privately, Peter talked of ending his marriage, so he could marry Elizabeth Vorontsova. Fully aware of her own popularity, confidence, education and training, and the historical examples of Anna Ivanovna and Elizabeth Petrovna, as well as the price of failure, Catherine set in motion her plans for usurpation, which went forward without a hitch over the course of June 28–29, 1762. The official justifications for the usurpation were to protect the Russian Church, to end Peter's impending Danish war, and to protect the rights of her son, a blend of justifications that held powerful sway over public opinion in St. Petersburg, which was backed up by her control of the guard regiments in the capital. Catherine also secured command of the Kronstadt Naval Fortress at the mouth of the River Neva and dispatched orders to Russian commanders in the field in Eastern Europe, ordering them to return to Russia.

The fate of Peter III was that of many deposed kings in the history of Europe; he died a violent death at the hands of his jailers just days after his deposition, although historians have largely absolved Catherine of complicity in the murder, which conveniently removed the only viable alternative to her rule.[28] Like Anna Leopoldovna before him, Peter made no effort to physically or militarily challenge his deposition and arrest, while offering a formal abdication that recognized Catherine's possession of the throne even though he had not designated her as his successor. In fact, Peter the Great's rule that the reigning tsar designate his successor had a rather dubious success rate; out of three formally designated male heirs, both Ivan VI and Peter III were deposed by female challengers, outcomes that had no analogue in the early modern history of Western and Central Europe. After Catherine's death, her son Tsar Paul ended the era of female autocrats in 1797 by instituting a Russian version of the Salic Law, which mandated a male-only line of succession whose success was secured by a plethora of nineteenth-century Russian male tsareeviches.

CATHERINE II AS TSARINA AND EMPRESS

Like so many queens before her who lacked administrative or executive experience, Catherine rose to the occasion upon her accession, consolidating her authority over Russia's government with little difficulty.[29] More than any of her female predecessors, Catherine had a command of history, a sense of destiny, and a good eye for talent. Even members of her ruling elite like Nikita Panin, who initially perceived of her as a caretaker until her son achieved his majority, considered her vastly more competent and concerned about Russia's interests than Peter III had been. Catherine distributed largesse to her followers, notably Gregory Orlov and his brothers, who had been so instrumental in the success of her usurpation; all of them received lands, titles, and offices. Catherine's generosity also extended to the guard regiments, which played such a large role in the accessions of Catherine I, Anna Ivanovna, and Elizabeth Petrovna. Because Peter III had no following of consequence in Russia, Catherine only had to make her appeal to Russia's nobility and gentry, which received more than adequate compensation for their support. For those elements of Russian society who still preferred a male tsar, Catherine reinstituted the secret police of Anna Ivanovna and Elizabeth Petrovna to root out dissidents. Catherine also forbade the publication of any Russian accounts of her usurpation.

Besides her competence and her charisma, Catherine offered a nativist alternative to Peter III, as Elizabeth Petrovna had to Anna Leopoldovna and her family. The Russian people, by and large, accepted Catherine, after seventeen years in Russia, as a *Russian* successor to a husband who was never able to shake the perception that he was a foreigner. In addition to these factors, Catherine's acceptance as monarch was undoubtedly bolstered by the fact that for the previous thirty-two years, both Anna Ivanovna and Elizabeth Petrovna had succeeded in gendering Russian autocracy to the reality of an unmarried female tsar. Russia had not experienced a competent male tsar since the death of Peter I in 1725, in contrast to the female autocrats Anna and Elizabeth, who both died in their beds still wearing their crowns. In the eyes of most Russians, the notion of a female tsar was already ingrained into their collective understanding of the Russian monarchy. In addition, Catherine proved to be a hard-working monarch, devoted to statecraft and keeping a firm grasp on policy, much more so than her three predecessors as tsarina. She also devoted considerable energy to public relations both within the Russian Empire and in the rest of Europe.

Much of Catherine's public relations efforts were consumed in creating forms of legitimacy for herself. Catherine's grip on autocratic power required a deft combination of pressure and conciliation, humor and toughness, and an eye for creating positive forms of public appearances and ritualized forms of imperial splendor. Foremost was the coronation. Peter III never got around to planning his own, thus losing the opportunity for a type of national bonding that conferred a powerful form of legitimacy, which was every bit as important for Russian tsars as it was for the kings and queens of

Western and Central Europe. The religious aspects of ceremony, in which the bishop of Novgorod proclaimed that "the Lord has placed the crown on your head," went a long way to further legitimize Catherine's possession of the throne. Recognizing that her accession was ushering in a new age for Russia, Catherine commissioned a new imperial crown, quartered in gold and silver, and encrusted with pearls, diamonds, and other precious stones, that remains one of the artistic treasures of the Russian nation today. Weighing over five pounds, it remained on Catherine's head throughout the lengthy ceremony, in which she proved, as Maria Theresa had done at her own Hungarian coronation in 1741, that she was able to bear the weight of male-gendered power. To drive the point home, following Elizabeth Petrovna's example, she crowned herself, a symbolic gesture that recognized the role of personal agency in both empresses' acquisition of the throne. Catherine's subsequent pilgrimages to the Troitsa Monastery northeast of Moscow, a tradition begun by Ivan IV, also established her as an outwardly traditional Russian monarch.

Catherine also sought to create legitimacy for herself in the benevolence of her rule, maintaining, until the end of her life, that her *purpose* was to rule for the good of the Russian people, a form of legitimacy that was not dynastic but tapped into the deep historical functions of tsardom, to act faithfully as God's agent on earth.[30] At the same time, this form of legitimacy was also tied to both the classical ideal of the philosopher king, which Catherine explicitly wished to emulate, and Enlightenment theories concerning the proper role of a monarch. Like Maria Theresa, Catherine pursued the modernization and rationalization of autocratic rule, with an eye towards education, including for women. In 1764, she founded the Smolny Institute in St. Petersburg, an academic school for noble and gentry women that was the first of its kind in Europe. Like Elizabeth I of England before her, for whom she expressed great admiration, Catherine wished to be perceived as a learned queen, devoting several hours daily to both reading and writing. Literacy and learning in fact had long been effective tools for female rulers to combat their "natural" female inadequacies; Catherine knew this because she was an avid reader of histories.

Another primary means for queens to earn prestige was by creating a religious identity. Within Russia, Catherine wished to be known as a religious queen, even as she sought to despoil the Church of its wealth and property. While Catherine began her reign in defense of the Russian Orthodox Church against the predations of Peter III, she eventually reasserted firm control over the Church, eventually directing a complete overhaul of its wealth, status, and independence and crushing the voice of her one challenger, Rostov Metropolitan Arseniy Matseyevich. Nonetheless, the confiscations, which furthered Peter I's goal of turning the Orthodox Church into an arm of the state like the army, was couched in Christian terms, as Catherine maintained her motivation was to improve the material and spiritual lives of her subjects. Catherine's actions brought Russia much more in line with other European states, Catholic and Protestant alike, which exercised control over their respective national churches.

While it was Catherine the Tsar who exercised control over the Church, it was Catherine the Tsaritsa who followed in the tradition of Russian queenship in her devotions, charity work, and ritualistic pilgrimages. But despite her outward show of piety, behind the scenes she was as much a secularist as her favorite European correspondent, Voltaire. Catherine in fact walked a religious tightrope similar to that of Maria Theresa, whose devotion to the *pietas austriaca* co-existed with a firm grasp over ecclesiastical appointments and fiscal control of the Catholic Church in Austria. Continuing to exercise the intercessory role of Russian tsaritsas, Catherine outlawed the use of torture and used capital punishment very sparingly. Following Elizabeth Petrovna's example, Catherine was generally a merciful tsarina, in keeping with her religious obligations and her identity as a benevolent ruler, unless her authority or the security of the state was challenged. Like Maria Theresa, Catherine often wept when the decision was made to go to war, as was expected from the gentler and more merciful sex. She also endeavored to play another traditionally female role, peacemaker, as she did in the War of the Bavarian Succession (1778–79).

Catherine also cultivated her popularity among the masses of her subjects. Most Russians were illiterate, while the Russian government exercised a monopoly over works published in Russia, so Catherine was not subject to the kind of literary abuse in Russia that was heaped upon her in Western Europe. Like Elizabeth I of England, Catherine knew the power of the royal progress. She enjoyed showing herself to her people on countless occasions during her reign, attired in traditional Russian dress, and attending long and tedious church services in cities and towns all over Russia, all the while chatting with the locals, an effective form of engaging with her subjects. Examples included her voyage down the Volga in 1767 which brought her to Kazan, and her Tauride tour of 1787, when she met Joseph II of Austria. Catherine also emulated Elizabeth I when she brought ambassadors and diplomats from Europe and Asia with her on progress, so they could see firsthand the charismatic effect Catherine had upon her subjects.

Catherine faced a different press reaction to her rule in Europe than she did in Russia, a nation lacking a robust civil society. The absence of domestic commentary regarding the suitability of female rule, which had become entrenched in Russian political reality, offers a stark contrast with Western Europe, whose political cultures had grappled with the issue since the 1558 publication of John Knox's *First Blast of the Trumpet Against the Monstrous Regiment of Women*. Much more than any other eighteenth-century monarch, Catherine can be seen to have created multiple personas – one for her Russian subjects, in which she performed many of the traditional functions of Russian tsars and tsaritsas to establish herself as a legitimate Russian ruler, and one for the rest of Europe, in which she worked to construct an image of herself as both legitimate and enlightened, the true successor to Peter the Great and his efforts to modernize Russia. Catherine was the primary architect of her own public relations campaign. As a diligent correspondent, Catherine conducted an official discourse with her contemporaries through the normal diplomatic channels, but she was also a prodigious letter writer, especially to French philosophes such as Voltaire, Denis Diderot, and Friedrich Melchior, Baron von Grimm, whose literary circle was a pan-European form of elite social media, which did much to shape perceptions of Catherine in pre-revolutionary French salon society.[31]

Catherine's efforts to modernize Russia's legal system can also be interpreted as a strategy for creating a sense of legitimacy for herself in the eyes of Europe. In 1766, she called together a national consultative commission to rationalize and overhaul Russia's antiquated legal system along the lines of Enlightenment principles, drawing representatives from all the Russian estates. When they assembled, Catherine presented to the delegates the *Nakaz*, or Instruction, a statement of Enlightenment legal principles, which she compiled herself. While Catherine's summoning of the commission was the closest Russia would come to representative government until the nineteenth-century reforms of Alexander II, she concluded that she could not liberalize Russia without imperiling her grip on power.

As her reign wore on, despite her desire to create the perception of benevolent rule over all her subjects, Catherine's most important source of support were the noble and gentry classes, who owned the bulk of the land in Russia. These classes also staffed the ranks of the military, which also grew exponentially during her reign. While Catherine had long expressed a willingness to her Western European correspondents to eradicate serfdom, which also supplied men for Russia's armies, serfdom's maintenance was much too ingrained in her relationship with the Russian ruling classes, as well as in the maintenance of her own imperial estate; Catherine herself owned 500,000 serfs. This *quid pro quo* was a permanent feature of her rule, undergirding her authority for the remainder of her reign. However, it was a top-down form of political consolidation, as was typical in Early Modern European polities; despite her protestations of ruling on behalf of all of her subjects, serfdom, which tied serfs and their families to property owners and not the land, was the most glaring evidence of Russia's backwardness in Western Europe.

Small-scale peasant rebellions were a constant occurrence in the vast Russian countryside, often stirred up in the name of a royal pretender. In 1774, the perfect storm of a peasant rebellion came together in southeastern Russia, galvanizing serfs, Cossacks, and other marginalized peoples led by Yemelyan Pugachev, a disaffected cavalry officer, who claimed he was Peter III. Playing the role of royal pretender was a time-honored custom in Russian history; Pugachev pulled together a rag-tag army that at one point reached 30,000 men. Catherine's government was unprepared for the rebellion, which engulfed large swathes of Russian territory and captured the city of Kazan before it was finally put down at the end of 1774. Despite her assurances to Voltaire that the revolt was of little consequence, Catherine had been caught off guard; for the rest of her reign, Catherine worked methodically to ensure greater control over her empire, further strengthening the military and authorizing a program of administrative reforms that saw the Russian Empire divided into provinces that formed the administrative structure of Russian government until the October Revolution of 1917. Always playing to her base, Catherine turned over control of provincial administration to the noble classes.

Catherine's sensibilities were also shaken to the core by the outbreak of the French Revolution in 1789. It must have been an existential blow to a monarch who had long been devoted to the study of the political and economic philosophies of the Enlightenment. Catherine's opposition to Britain supported the American colonists by default in their war of independence, the first occasion when a republican form of government put Enlightenment principles into action. But Catherine's support had been commercial and strategic; the actual overthrow of monarchical government itself brought out Catherine's conservative impulses. The year after the outbreak of the French Revolution, reform-minded intellectual Alexander Radischev anonymously published *The Journey from St. Petersburg to Moscow*, a scathing social critique of autocracy and serfdom, which to Catherine signaled the arrival of Jacobin ideas into Russia, labelling Radischev another Pugachev.[32] The book was indicative of the development of enlightened thinking and discourse among a growing Russian intelligentsia that Catherine had encouraged for much of her reign. The Enlightenment had always looked good on paper to her, and she thoroughly supported the development of institutions of higher learning in Russia that attracted foreign scholars and artists, who themselves contributed to the development of the Russian Enlightenment. But the overthrow of the French monarchy in 1792 and the violent deaths of Louis XVI and Marie Antoinette the next year shook Catherine to her core. The result was typically Russian; Radischev was exiled to Siberia and nearly all copies of his work (which was not published in Russia until 1905) were eradicated, while Catherine herself circled her autocratic wagons, railing against the spread of revolutionary ideas in Europe until her death in 1796.

CATHERINE THE DYNASTY BUILDER

Like Anna Ivanovna and Elizabeth Petrovna before her, Catherine reigned unmarried without an officially recognized male consort. Of fifteen queens (and empresses) regnant in Early Modern Europe, nine married. Of these nine, only three, Isabella of Castile, Anne of Great Britain, and Maria Theresa, could boast of companionate marriages that did not challenge their authority. For the rest, such as Mary I of England, Juana of Castile, Anna Jagiellon of Poland, and Mary Queen of Scots, marriage was a complication that brought neither companionship nor stability to their reigns. In the history of Early Modern Europe, it appears that remaining unmarried was a viable alternative for ruling queens such as Elizabeth I of England, Christina of Sweden, and the eighteenth-century Russian tsarinas. While Catherine II's accession was a unique event, with no connection to Russia's previous dynastic history, she spent her entire reign creating the image of herself as a traditional Russian mother to her subjects, while many of Catherine's later portraits display a kind and endearing expression, full of matronly appeal.

But Catherine's popular image as the mother of her people was at odds with her performance as a mother to her two sons. Like many other Early Modern European monarchs, Catherine was ambivalent about the "rising sun" of her heir, refusing to integrate Paul into her government or grant him a post in the military commensurate with his rank. This was another way in which Catherine followed in the footsteps of Peter the Great, who was outright hostile to his only surviving son, the Tsarevich Alexis. She also deprived Paul of his Duchy of Holstein-Gottorp, his father's patrimony, preventing him from forming a foreign and independent power base. Catherine rarely had herself painted with her heir, in marked contrast to almost every other queen in eighteenth-century Europe, who were eager to broadcast their dynastic achievements.

But Catherine's long-term legitimacy as Russia's ruler was based upon factors other than dynastic legitimacy, while her memoirs hint at the notion that Paul was not Peter III's son. This was in marked contrast to her contemporary

Maria Theresa, who actively promoted her eldest son Joseph as both his father's and her own heir, having him crowned as Holy Roman Emperor during her lifetime, despite her difficult relationship with him. Ultimately, Catherine adhered to the dictum laid down by Peter the Great, that the autocrat should choose his or her own successor.

It is perhaps a sign of how much Russian royal marriages had become westernized that less than 100 years previously Russian tsars and tsareeviches found their native-born wives in traditional bride shows. But in the Europe from which she sprang, playing the role of pan-European marriage broker was the pinnacle of queenly achievement. Catherine relished playing this role for Paul, arranging his marriage to Wilhelmina Louise, a daughter of Ludwig IX, Landgrave of Hesse-Darmstadt in 1773, who died three years later in childbirth. Catherine went back to Germany in search of her replacement, deciding upon Sophia Dorothea of Württemberg, who received the new Orthodox name Maria Feodorovna. While Elizabeth Petrovna gave no thought to compatibility in arranging Catherine's marriage to the Grand Duke Peter, Catherine did for Paul's second marriage; the couple had the chance to meet in Berlin at a state dinner, hosted by Frederick II, at which Maria revealed her determination to be an agreeable and supportive wife. Despite Paul's difficult personality, the marriage turned out to be entirely companionate. Catherine was initially delighted with her new daughter-in-law, but as mother and son continued to disagree, Maria sided with her husband and later shared his political isolation at their manor of Gatchina outside of St. Petersburg.

Catherine was equally as ambivalent about her illegitimate son with Gregory Orlov, born three months before her accession, who had been given the name Aleksey Grigorievich Bobrinsky. He was raised in Tula away from her court, and Catherine did not formally acknowledge him until 1781, when he was nineteen. It is curious that Catherine did not allow Bobrinsky to spend his teenage years preparing for roles in either the military or the church that other bastard sons of monarchs had performed in many of the states of Early Modern Europe. He certainly was an unwelcome reminder of Catherine's sexual past, especially because within Russia she took her traditional religious responsibilities seriously. But after Catherine's death, Paul I allowed Bobrinsky to enjoy the kind of status that royal bastards often enjoyed in the rest of Europe, creating him a count of the Russian Empire and a major-general in the army and brokering his marriage to a Baltic German heiress, Anna Dorothea von Ungern-Sternberg, whose descendants survive to this day in Russia.

Catherine was much less ambivalent about the next generation of her dynasty. Paul and Maria were quite effective in replenishing the Holstein-Gottorp-Romanov line, with four sons and six daughters surviving to adulthood. While Catherine had done a superlative job of creating the image of herself as a truly Russian monarch, her approach to marriage brokering revealed her deep Germanic roots. It is ironic that as Catherine railed against Elizabeth Petrovna in her memoirs for taking possession of her children as soon as they were born, she did the exact same thing with Paul's eldest sons, Alexander and Constantine. Catherine was as delighted with her grandsons as she was reticent about her son, personally arranging the grandsons' upbringing and educations.

All her grandchildren received superlative educations, and the grand-daughters also were taught the usual array of female-gendered social graces, music, and dancing. Perhaps sensing that her days were numbered, Catherine arranged in 1793 the marriage of her eldest grandson, fifteen-year-old Alexander, to fourteen-year-old Louise of Baden, who took the name Elizabeth Alexeievna. Two and a half years later, sixteen-year-old Constantine married another German heiress, Juliane of Saxe-Coburg-Saalfeld. Ever the imperialist, Catherine long dreamed of retaking Constantinople and placing Constantine on the long-dormant Byzantine throne. Constantine even had a Greek nurse as an infant for good measure. After serving as Tsar for three weeks in 1825 before abdicating the throne, he returned to his role as viceroy in Russian-occupied Poland.

Catherine also set her sights on Northern Europe. In the summer of 1796, age sixty-seven, and in ill health, she brokered the marriage between a cousin, the not quite eighteen-year-old Gustav IV of Sweden, and her granddaughter Alexandra. Just as her son Paul had the chance to meet his second wife before the marriage negotiations were concluded, she was adamant about making sure that Gustav and Alexandra were also compatible. When Gustav arrived in St. Petersburg in September, he and Alexandra appeared to get along splendidly, but Gustav derailed the marriage by refusing to consent to Catherine's demand that Alexandra would not be required to convert to Lutheranism after becoming Queen of Sweden. This was the deal breaker; Sweden had not had a non-Protestant queen since Catherine Jagiellon in the late sixteenth century, and the Swedish estates had made it clear that they would not accept one in 1796.

But Catherine's refusal to budge on the religious issue speaks volumes to her conflicting attitudes towards her role as a marriage broker. She championed her own Russification in her first years in Russia; one might assume that she would have counseled her granddaughter of the advantages of queenly accul-turation to the adoptive kingdom. Instead, she appeared to be imitating the attitude of Ivan III, Grand Prince of Muscovy (r. 1462–1505), the last Russian ruler to marry his daughter into a European royal house, who refused to allow his daughter Helena of Moscow to convert to Catholicism. Such policy was also consistent with the stipulations of Habsburg and Bourbon monarchs that their daughters remain Catholic after their marriages, reflective of their dynastic stature on the European stage. But Robert Massie has argued that Catherine did not want to subject her granddaughter to the same conversion trauma that she had gone through when she first arrived.[33] In all likelihood, Catherine was conflicted about her role as a tsar, determined to maintain and extend Russia's prestige and influence in the affairs of Europe, and as a grandmother, not wanting Alexandra subject to the same dynastic pressures inflicted upon her in her youth. The shock of the broken treaty, with the spectacle of an aged autocratic empress being snubbed by a teenaged monarch, acutely embarrassed Catherine and caused her to have a mini-stroke, which brought on the final decline that hastened her death two months later following another stroke.

As a dynast, Catherine completely integrated the Romanovs into the pan-European kinship network, a process begun with Peter the Great's efforts to marry his daughters into the royal houses of Europe. After Catherine's death, her granddaughter Anna Pavlovna married William, Prince of Orange, later William II of the Netherlands, while Alexandra became the only Romanov to marry a Habsburg archduke. For the rest of the nineteenth century, Russian tsars and their male heirs married almost exclusively into the various royal houses of Germany. While the Rurik and seventeenth-century Romanov tsars and their wives were by and large ethnically Russian, by the dawn of the twentieth century Nicholas II had precious little native blood in his veins, a trait he shared with the rest of Europe's hereditary monarchs. This Germanification of the Romanov family is also part of Catherine's dynastic legacy.

CATHERINE II AND SEXUALITY

Catherine's sexuality, like that of Marie Antoinette, was the subject of endless curiosity among her contemporaries in Europe and generations of historians and biographers ever since.[34] While Catherine's literary partisans did their best to create positive impressions of Catherine as an enlightened ruler, she was nonetheless the subject of a robust and salacious press in the west concerning her many male lovers and her allegedly voracious sexual appetite. Women who exercised power in Early Modern Europe have often been subject to inordinate speculation concerning their sexuality, which is perhaps why queens from Isabella of Castile to Maria Theresa worked hard to build up spotless reputations as chaste wives and doting mothers. In contrast, unmarried and dowager queens, from Elizabeth I of England to the widowed Mary of Guise and Anne of Austria, endured rumors of their alleged sexual infidelities, the easiest means to besmirch the reputation of a female ruler. While most of these accusations were unsupported by evidence, they betray the levels of misogyny that served as a filter to contemporary observations of how these women wielded male-gendered power.

What makes Catherine different from all these other queens was that some of the stories about her were in fact true. By her own admission, she craved love, sex, intimacy, and male companionship. By nature, she was also a very social woman, who loved to talk to people, whether face to face or in epistolary form, and enjoyed mixing informally behind closed doors with friends all her life. Emotional connections were especially important to Catherine, especially considering the lack of affection of her youth and the abomination of her marriage. In her memoirs, she lambasted the antipathy of Elizabeth Petrovna, who commanded that she not weep so much at the death of her father because he was not a king.[35]

But while Catherine nursed her intellect and her ambition, she never subjugated the desire for physical intimacy, as most queens elsewhere in Europe routinely did in the face of sexless marriages. It is perhaps instructive to note that female infidelity carried high penalties in Western and Central Europe. George Ludwig, Elector of Hanover imprisoned his wife Sophia Dorothea in Celle Castle for her infidelities, while he brought his two mistresses with him from Germany when he became King of Great Britain in 1714. In contrast, George's great-granddaughter Queen Caroline Matilda of Denmark was divorced and exiled for her infidelities and her lover was executed (see Chapter 5).

It appears, however, that the social mores developing at the imperial court of Elizabeth Petrovna were those of the sexually licentious Versailles of Louis XV, rather than the strait laced Vienna of Maria Theresa, in which sexual infidelity, both men's and women's, had become normalized behavior. But Catherine's choice of sexual partners also reflected a specific set of aesthetic and sexual concerns; Catherine preferred her lovers to be handsome, manly, and possessing sexual prowess, while also possessing wit and the ability to converse with her. Sergei Saltyov had all these attributes, in addition to being descended from the Romanovs. But on a more personal level, her lovers were friends, companions, and occasionally talented politicians and military leaders. For Catherine, the sexual was collapsed into the political; Saltyov gave her Paul, Orlov helped her gain her throne, and her most famous lover, Gregory Potemkin, was a brilliant statesman and general.

Saltyov's successor was Stanislaus Poniatowski, a Polish nobleman in the entourage of British diplomat Charles Hanbury Williams, who met Catherine in 1755, the year after she gave birth to her son.[36] Catherine's relationship with Poniatowski was not just about physical intimacy; they were both bibliophiles, enjoying each other's company on both an intellectual and a sexual level. For Catherine, the price of an active and unrestrained sex life was pregnancy; Poniatowski impregnated Catherine before he left Russia in August 1758. According to Catherine, her husband the Grand Duke Peter reportedly remarked, "God knows where my wife gets her pregnancies. I really do not know if this child is mine and if I ought to recognize it." As we have seen, Elizabeth Petrovna's official attitude was that Catherine's daughter Anna, who lived less than two years, was legitimate. After Catherine became Empress and Tsarina, Poniatowski proposed marriage, which Catherine declined, although she supported him as a pro-Russian candidate for the Polish throne when Augustus III died in 1763.

Catherine also declined to marry her next lover, Gregory Orlov, who participated in the construction of a sexualized political culture in which there was always an officially recognized male favorite. A similar form of culture had also developed around Elizabeth I of England, a queen Catherine greatly admired. But Elizabeth I's political culture was framed primarily in language, in which courtiers yearned for an unattainable queen in metaphorical and allegorical ways. In Catherine's political culture, in contrast, the queen was attainable, while the sexual element was physical and intimate. Many of her favorites wielded forms of power and influence similar to French royal mistresses, who frequently co-opted some of the functions of the queen consort, such as turning their access to Catherine into forms of informal patronage networks. Like French kings from Francis I to Louis XV (including Catherine's favorite Henri IV, a particularly licentious king), who provided for their mistresses once they tired of them with lands, wealth, and advantageous marriages, Catherine pursued a similar policy with her series of male favorites, remaining friends with them and mourning them when they died.

This pattern was set after Catherine tired of Orlov in 1774; while he was good company and reportedly an ardent lover, he was not a statesman nor was he sexually faithful. Alexander Vasilchikov, an ensign in the Chevalier Guard Regiment, succeeded Orlov, who swiftly faded into obscurity. This was Catherine's first lover after she became tsarina, and the power dynamics between Catherine and her lovers shifted accordingly. Catherine kept Vasilchikov on a short leash, on call day and night for his services, and he was not allowed to leave the palace without Catherine's permission. Catherine found his tenderness a bit cloying, and after she replaced him with Gregory Potemkin, Vasilchikov complained that he had been used like a gigolo. But Catherine pensioned him off, and like all the others, remained friends with him.

Potemkin was easily the most distinguished and powerful of Catherine's favorites, remaining an important and influential member of Catherine's administration long after he ceased to be her lover.[37] He had come to her attention during her usurpation, and she recognized his abilities, advancing him through the ranks of the military as well as her government. Potemkin was brilliant, creative, and charismatic and shared Catherine's imperial vision of an expansive Russian state. While their sexual relationship did not last long, their intimate relationship continued to blossom; as several of her letters to Potemkin suggest, she might have contracted a secret, morganatic marriage with him in 1774.[38] She later made him a virtual viceroy in the newly won southern territories, where he built up the Black Sea fleet, as well as leading Russia's armies in the Russo-Turkish Wars that added so much new territory to the Russian Empire.

Potemkin was well versed in the niceties of Catherinian political culture, finding his own replacement according to Catherine's exact specifications. But while Catherine's string of male lovers continued, Potemkin retained an intimate and intellectual relationship with Catherine that remained unbroken until his death in 1791.[39] Potemkin remained adept at regulating the flow of men who served as Catherine's lovers, existing at times in a form of ménage à trois with Catherine and her current lover, much as many queens adjusted to the reality of a royal mistress placed within their households.

Similar to Elizabeth I, as Catherine got older, her male favorites became progressively younger. Following Potemkin in 1776 was Alexander Dmitriev-Mamonov, who in turn was succeeded by Pyotr Zavadovsky, a particularly delightful and attentive lover, who received 50,000 rubles, a pension of 5,000 rubles, and 4,000 peasants in Ukraine after her affair with him ended in 1779. There were ten more male favorites before Catherine took her final lover, Prince Platon Alexandrovich Zubov, who was 40 years her junior, in 1789. Even Potemkin underestimated Zubov, who came to dominate Catherine's government, amassing a huge fortune from an ever-grateful Catherine, who showered him with offices and military commands. By the time of her death, Zubov held the imperial court in his thrall as he regulated access to Catherine, even snubbing the Tsarevich Paul. Zubov was on campaign in Persia when Catherine died in October 1796, and Tsar Paul I recalled him to Russia. His fate was that of Diane de Poitiers and Madame du Barry, losing all the benefits of a favorite upon the death of their royal patron.

Catherine's sexual history was much more reflective of the behavior of male kings rather than the queens regnant of Early Modern Europe, who usually prioritized their queenly chastity. Catherine, however, along with Anna Ivanovna and Elizabeth Petrovna, more properly belongs in the historical category of philandering kings, who mitigated the impact of their sexual proclivities by their strict and punctual religious observances. Such behavior suggests a shrewd exploitation of the gendered differences between men and women, with Anna Ivanovna, Elizabeth Petrovna, and Catherine playing the role of libertine tsar and pious tsaritsa simultaneously. In fact, the conflation of the masculine and the feminine within Catherine's persona as empress ranks among her more underrated achievements. Both Anna Ivanovna and Elizabeth Petrovna were perceived as women lacking the discipline or the intellectual ability to hold the actual reins of government, but Catherine, well before she seized power, was determined to overcome these gendered stereotypes. In her memoirs, she recounted that as a child, she was not interested in playing with dolls but in competing with the boys, boasting that she was just as good, if not better, at boyish outdoor activities.[40] She was also physically robust; after arriving in Russia and enduring a debilitating attack of pleurisy, she was bled multiple times over several weeks, yet she made a full recovery. Her daily schedule, starting at 5 a.m. at the height of her reign, revealed her as a hardworking monarch who made time daily for reading, writing letters, and fully engaging in the social life of her court.

Much like Christina of Sweden, whom she also admired for her intellect, Catherine enjoyed wearing male attire, especially while riding. Both Elizabeth Petrovna and Catherine donned male clothing on the day of their usurpations, leading armed soldiers as no Russian woman had done before. When Catherine donned a Preobrazhensky guard uniform, she was tapping into a long-established European custom of extraordinary women able to transgress the gendered limitations of female military leadership, one that extends from Joan of Arc to both Isabella of Castile and Elizabeth I of England donning armor as a representational strategy. She was frequently painted wearing medals from the orders she belonged to. Like Anna Ivanovna and Elizabeth Petrovna, she was also frequently painted in equestrian pose, astride a horse like a man, which was both symbolic and representative of their appropriation of male-gendered power. This was a first in Early Modern European history; even Maria Theresa, who was aware of the value of knowing how to ride a horse, preferred to be painted seated, usually surrounded by her family, or by her crowns, in a traditional queenly pose.[41]

CONCLUSION

Catherine the Great left Russia a far different nation than when she arrived. Above all she was a modernizing tsarina, building schools, encouraging mining and industrial production, expanding agriculture, and modernizing the armed forces. More than any other ruler until the Bolshevik Revolution, she presided over the secularization of Russian society, reducing the Orthodox

Church to an adjunct of the state. Catherine was also an avid art collector and built the Hermitage, a neoclassical monument for her vast collection of paintings and sculpture, which opened as a museum just prior to her death.[42] Catherine continued the ostentatious extravagance of her predecessors in her court life, and music and theater flourished as St. Petersburg emerged as a first-class European capital. While the liberalism of the French Revolution influenced the evolution of European monarchies and their aristocracies over the course of the nineteenth century, Catherine's reign inaugurated the golden age of the Russian nobility, whose support was essential to the maintenance of her power, as enunciated in her 1785 Charter to the Nobility.[43] She was every bit as imperialist as Peter the Great and nearly completed the territorial advance of the Russian Empire begun by the sixteenth-century Rurik tsars. While she kept Russia's serfs subjugated, she nonetheless paved the way for the emergence of the Russian Enlightenment and a Russian intelligentsia, educated at Russian universities, who began the process of building a nineteenth-century Russian civil society. Despite her adventurous sex life and her lack of dynastic legitimacy, Catherine garnered the respect of her fellow European monarchs and earned the sobriquet "the Great" even before her death.

Finally, Catherine expanded the definition and range of queenship more than any other Early Modern European queen. While most other European queens, both consort and regnant, built their reputations on the solid foundations of piety, marriage, and motherhood, Catherine side-stepped this well-worn path to queenly success to blaze her own trail, deposing her husband and assuming his place on the throne without any hereditary title. Like Elizabeth I of England, and to a lesser degree, Christina of Sweden, Catherine balanced the masculine and the feminine in her queenly persona. Contemporary observers often praised Catherine's positive traits as masculine, such as her coolness under pressure and her regal bearing, while criticizing other traits, such as her vanity and love of flattery and her desire for male lovers, which were all considered decidedly feminine characteristics.

For most of Europe's early modern queens, we have precious little knowledge of what they thought of their role as queen or how they felt about the demands of their queenships. But Catherine knew exactly how she wished to be remembered. At the end of her life, Catherine was consumed in both the study of history and the contemplation of her place in it, revising her memoirs and waxing philosophical in her letters to her still voluminous list of correspondents.[44] In this process of contemplating her own legacy, Catherine summed up herself up in her own epitaph, written several years before her death. Beyond the curious reference to her being a republican, it rings remarkably true as it outlines her winning strategy for queenly success.[45]

"Catherine II rests here. She came to Russia in 1744 to marry Peter III. At the age of 14 she took a three-sided decision: to enchant her husband, Empress Elizabeth and the people of Russia. And she used every single chance to succeed in this. Eighteen years of loneliness and boredom made her read many books. As she mounted to the Russian throne she did her best to give her people happiness, freedom and wellbeing. She forgave people easily and hated nobody. She was charitable, good-tempered and loved life. She was a true republican in her politics and was kind-hearted. She had friends. She worked easily. She loved social life and the arts."[46]

Notes

1 INTRODUCTION TO EARLY MODERN EUROPEAN QUEENSHIP

1. See Elena Woodacre, "Early Modern Queens on Screen: Victors, Victims, Villains, Virgins, and Viragoes," *Premodern Rulers and Postmodern Viewers*, Janice North, Karl C. Alvestad and Elena Woodacre, eds. (New York: Palgrave Macmillan, 2018), 27–50.
2. This study does not include an analysis of Ottoman queenship, even though the Ottomans ruled most of the Balkan Peninsula during the early modern era, as it is focused on the transregional kinship networks that the Muslim Ottomans did not participate in. For the standard study of the Ottoman version of queenship, see Leslie Penn Peirce, *The Imperial Harem: Women and Sovereignty in the Ottoman Empire* (Oxford: Oxford University Press, 1993).
3. See Helen Watanabe-O'Kelly, "Cultural Transfer and the Eighteenth-Century Queen Consort," *German History*, Vol. 34, No. 7 (2016), 279–292; *Early Modern Dynastic Marriages and Cultural Transfer*, Joan-Luís Palos and Magdalena S.Sánchez, eds. (Surrey: Ashgate Publishing Limited, 2016).
4. Clarissa Campbell Orr, "Introduction," *Queenship in Europe 1660–1815: The Role of the Consort*, Clarissa Campbell Orr, ed. (Cambridge: Cambridge University Press, 2004), 1–11.
5. Theresa Earenfight, "Preface – Partners in Politics," *Queenship and Political Power in Early Modern Spain*, Theresa Earenfight, ed. (Aldershot, Hamps: Ashgate, 2005), xiii–xxviii.
6. Studies of kingship include Henry A. Myers, *Medieval Kingship* (New York: St. Martin's Press, 1982); *Kings and Kingship in Medieval Europe*, Anne Duggan, ed. (London: Kings College London Centre for Late Antique and Medieval Studies, 1993); Paul Kleber Monod, *The Power of Kings: Monarchy and Religion in Europe* (New Haven, Conn: Yale University Press, 1999); and Glenn Richardson, *Renaissance Monarchy, the Reigns of Henry VIII, Francis I and Charles V* (London: Arnold, 2002).
7. Theresa Earenfight, "Without the Persona of the Prince: Kings, Queens and the Idea of Monarchy in Late Medieval Europe," *Gender & History*, Vol. 19, No. 1 (Apr. 2007), 1–21.
8. Alice Hunt, *The Drama of Coronation: Medieval Ceremony in Early Modern England* (Cambridge: Cambridge University Press, 2011).
9. Nadine Akkerman and Birgit Houben, *The Politics of Female Households: Ladies-in-Waiting Across Early Modern Europe* (Leiden: Brill, 2014).

10. See "The Queen as Intercessor," in *Three Medieval Queens*, Lisa Benz St. Johns, ed. (New York: Palgrave Macmillan, 2012), 33–64.
11. Joseph F. O'Callaghan, "The Many Roles of the Medieval Queen: Some Examples from Castile," *Queenship and Political Power in Early Modern Spain*, 21–32.
12. Marc Serge Rivière, "The Pallas of Stockholm: Louisa Ulrica of Prussia and the Swedish Crown," *Queenship in Europe 1660–1815: The Role of the Consort*.
13. Cinzia Recca, "Queenship and Family Dynamics through the Correspondence of Queen Maria Carolina of Naples," *Queenship in the Mediterranean*, Elena Woodacre, ed. (New York: Palgrave Macmillan, 2013).
14. Katherine Crawford, *Perilous Performances: Gender and Regency in Early Modern France* (Cambridge, Mass: Harvard University Press, 2004).
15. Charles Beem, *The Lioness Roared: The Problems of Female Rule in English History* (New York: Palgrave Macmillan, 2006), 1–12.
16. Kantorwicz, Ernst Kantorwicz, *The King's Two Bodies: A Study in Medieval Theology* (Princeton: Princeton University Press, 1957); Marie Axton, *The Queen's Two Bodies: Drama and the Elizabethan Succession* (London: Royal Historical Society, 1977).
17. Paula Louise Scalingi, "The Sceptre or the Distaff: The Question of Female Sovereignty, 1516–1607," *Historian*, Vol. 41 (Nov, 1978), 59–75; Constance Jordan, "Women's Rule in Sixteenth Century British Thought," *Renaissance Quarterly*, Vol. 40, Autumn (1987), 421–451.
18. Joseph Nye, *Soft Power: The Means to Success in World Politics* (New York: Public Affairs, 2005).
19. Adam Morton, "Introduction: Politics, Culture, and Queens Consort," *Queens Consort, Cultural Transfer and European Politics, c.1500–1800*, Helen Watanabe-O'Kelly and Adam Morton, eds. (London: Routledge, 2016), 1–14.
20. John Knox, *First Blast of the Trumpet Against the Monstrous Regiment of Women* (Geneva, 1558).
21. For a recent study, see Carolyn Harris, *Queenship and Revolution in Early Modern Europe: Henrietta Maria and Marie Antoinette* (New York: Palgrave Macmillan, 2016).
22. Theresa Earenfight, *Queenship in Medieval Europe* (New York: Palgrave Macmillan, 2013).
23. Agnes Strickland, *Lives of the Queens of England, from the Norman Conquest* (8 vols.) (London: Longmans, Green, 1864).
24. Joan Wallach Scott, "Gender: A Useful Category of Historical Analysis?" *American Historical Review*, Vol. 91, No. 5 (Dec, 1986), 1053–1075.
25. Peggy Liss, *Isabel the Queen* (Oxford: Oxford University Press, 1992), 69–70.
26. Beem, *The Lioness Roared*, 98, n.152.
27. Theresa Earenfight, "Two Bodies, One Spirit: Isabel and Fernando's Construction of Monarchical Partnership," *Queen Isabel I of Castile: Power, Patronage, Persona*, Barbara F. Weissberger, ed. (Woodbridge: Boydell and Brewer Press, 2008), 3–18.
28. Liss, *Isabel the Queen*, 121–126.

29. Peggy Liss, "Isabel of Castile (1451–1504) Her Self-Representation and its Context," *Queenship and Power in Early Modern Spain*, 120–144.
30. Cristina Guardiola-Griffiths, *Legitimizing the Queen: Propaganda and Ideology in the Reign of Isabel I of Castile* (Lewisburg, Pa: Bucknell University Press, 2011).
31. Maria Hayward, *Dress at the Court of Henry VIII* (Leeds: Maney, 2007).
32. Marvin Lunenfeld, "Isabella of Castile and the Company of Women in Power," *Historical Reflections*, Vol. 4, No. 2 (1977), 207–229.
33. Quoted in Liss, *Isabel the Queen*, 1.

2 MARY QUEEN OF SCOTS AND EARLY MODERN BRITISH QUEENSHIP

1. *Tudors and Stuarts on Film: Historical Perspectives*, Susan Doran and Thomas Freeman, eds. (New York: Palgrave Macmillan, 2008).
2. For a classic example, see Alison Plowden, *Two Queens in One Isle: Deadly Relationship of Elizabeth I and Mary Queen of Scots* (Totowa, NJ: Barnes & Noble Books, 1984).
3. For a brief discussion of these sources see Jayne Elizabeth Lewis, *The Trial of Mary Queen of Scots: A Brief History with Documents* (New York: Bedford St. Martin's, 1999).
4. Mary has been the subject of several modern scholarly biographies, including Antonia Fraser, *Mary, Queen of Scots* (New York: Delacorte Press, 1978); John Guy, *'My Heart is My Own': The Life of Mary Queen of Scots* (London: Mariner, 2004); and Retha Warnicke, *Mary Queen of Scots* (New York: Routledge, 2006).
5. Alexander F. Mitchell, *The Scottish Reformation – Its Epochs, Episodes, Leaders, and Distinctive Characteristics* (Minneapolis, MN: Fili-Quarian Classics, 2010); Gordon Donaldson, *The Scottish Reformation* (Cambridge: Cambridge University Press, 1972).
6. John Knox and Robert M. Healey, "Waiting for Deborah: John Knox and Four Ruling Queens," *Sixteenth Century Journal*, Vol. 25, No. 2 (Summer, 1994), 371–386. For a recent study of Knox, see Jane Lawson, *John Knox* (New Haven, CT: Yale University Press, 2015).
7. Kristen Post Walton, *Catholic Queen, Protestant Patriarchy: Mary, Queen of Scots, and the Politics of Gender and Religion* (New York: Palgrave Macmillan, 2006).
8. See Charles Beem, "Dynastic Loyalty and the 'Queenships" of Mary Queen of Scots," *Royal Women and Dynastic Loyalty*, Elizabeth Carney and Caroline Dunn, ed. (New York: Palgrave Macmillan, 2018), 111–121.
9. Elizabeth Lehfeldt, "Ruling Sexuality: The Political Legitimacy of Isabel of Castile," *Renaissance Quarterly*, Vol. 53, No. 1 (2000), 31–56.
10. This is often the subject of popular biographies. See Alison Weir, *Mary Queen of Scots and the Murder of Lord Darnley* (London: Pimlico, 2003).

11. A.E. MacRobert, *Mary Queen of Scots and the Casket Letters* (New York: Palgrave Macmillan, 2002).
12. Francis Edwards, *The Marvellous Chance: Thomas Howard, Fourth Duke of Norfolk, and the Ridolphi Plot, 1570–1572* (London: Hart Davis, 1968).
13. Jenny Wormald, *Mary Queen of Scots: A Study in Failure* (London: George Philip, 1988).
14. Fraser, *Mary Queen of Scots*, 555.
15. For a recent study, see Michael Hicks, *The Wars of the Roses* (New Haven, CT: Yale University Press, 2010).
16. Arlene Naylor Okerlund, *Elizabeth of York* (New York: Palgrave Macmillan, 2009), 203–211.
17. Retha Warnicke, *Elizabeth of York and her Six Daughters-in-Law* (New York: Palgrave Macmillan, 2018), 97–132.
18. Ilana Ben-Amos, *The Culture of Giving: Informal Support and Gift Exchange in Early Modern England* (Cambridge: Cambridge University Press, 2008). See also Felicity Heal, *The Power of Gifts: Gift-Exchange in Early Modern England* (Oxford: Oxford University Press, 2014).
19. See Retha Warnicke, "Margaret Tudor, Countess of Richmond and Elizabeth of York: Dynastic Competitors or Allies?", *Unexpected Heirs in Early Modern Europe*, Valerie Schutte, ed. (New York: Palgrave Macmillan, 2017), 35–62.
20. Warnicke, *Elizabeth of York*, 242.
21. Glenn Richardson, *The Field of Cloth of Gold* (New Haven: Yale University Press, 2013).
22. Warnicke, *Elizabeth of York*, 100.
23. Miles F. Shore, "Henry VIII and the Crisis of Generativity," *The Journal of Interdisciplinary History*, Vol. 2, No. 4, Psychoanalysis and History (Spring, 1972), 359–390.
24. For a recent study, see Susan Bordo, *The Creation of Anne Boleyn: A New Look at England's Most Notorious Queen* (Boston, MA: Houghton Mifflin Harcourt, 2013).
25. Greg Walker, "Rethinking the Fall of Anne Boleyn," *Historical Journal*, Vol. 45, No. 2 (2002), 1–29.
26. A major exception is George Bernard's *Anne Boleyn: Fatal Attractions* (New Haven, CT: Yale University Press, 2010).
27. Retha Warnicke, *The Marrying of Anne of Cleves: Royal Protocol in Early Modern England* (Cambridge: Cambridge University Press, 2000).
28. Linda Porter, *Mary Tudor: The First Queen* (London: Piatkus, 2007), 256–261.
29. For a recent, sympathetic study, see Gareth Russell, *Young and Damned and Fair: The Life of Catherine Howard, Fifth Wife of King Henry VIII* (New York: Simon and Schuster, 2017).
30. Linda Porter, *Katherine the Queen: The Remarkable Life of Katherine Parr, the Last Wife of Henry VIII* (New York: St. Martin's Press, 2011).
31. John Foxe, *The Acts and Monuments of the Christian Church* (London, 1563), https://www.exclassics.com/foxe/foxe212.htm

32. Howard Nenner, *The Right to Be King* (Chapel Hill, NC: University of North Carolina Press, 1995).

33. See various essays in *Virtuous or Villainess? The Image of the Royal Mother From the Early Medieval Era to the Early Modern Era*, Carey Fleiner and Elena Woodacre, eds. (New York: Palgrave Macmillan, 2016).

34. Mortimer Levine, *Tudor Dynastic Problems 1460–1571* (London: George Unwin, 1973).

35. Jeri L. McIntosh, *From Heads of Household to Heads of State: The Preaccession Households of Mary and Elizabeth Tudor, 1516–1558* (Gutenberg-e) (New York: Columbia University Press, 2008).

36. Charles Beem, "Have Not Wee a Noblye Kinge?: The Minority of Edward VI," *The Royal Minorities of Medieval and Early Modern England* (New York: Palgrave Macmillan, 2008), 211–248.

37. John Knox, *First Blast of the Trumpet Against the Monstrous Regiment of Women* (Geneva, 1558). For a discussion of these works, see Constance Jordan, "Women's Rule in Sixteenth Century Thought," *Renaissance Quarterly*, Vol. 40 (Autumn 1987), 436–443.

38. John Strype, *Ecclesiastical Memorials* (London: J. Nichols, 1823), Vol. 3 pt. 2. 537–550.

39. See Ernst Kantorwicz, *The King's Two Bodies: A Study in Medieval Theology* (Princeton, NJ: Princeton University Press, 1957), and Marie Axton, *The Queen's Two Bodies: Drama and the Elizabethan Succession* (London: Royal Historical Society, 1977).

40. For a brief discussion of Marian historiography, see Retha Warnicke, "Mary I, Queen of England: Historiographical Essay, 2006 to Present," *The Birth of a Queen: Essays on the Quincentenary of Mary I* (New York: Palgrave Macmillan, 2016), 255–272.

41. G.R. Elton, *Reform and Reformation* (London: Edward Arnold, 1977); John Guy, *Tudor England* (Oxford: Oxford University Press, 1988); David Loades, *The Reign of Mary Tudor* (London: Longmans, 1977). For a concise analysis of recent Marian historiography, see Retha Warnicke, "Mary I, Queen of England: Historiographical Essay, 2006 to Present," in *The Birth of a Queen: Essays on the Quincentenary of Mary I* (New York: Palgrave Macmillan, 2016), 255–272.

42. Judith M. Richards, "Mary Tudor as a 'Sole Quene'?: Gendering Tudor Monarchy", *The Historical Journal*, Vol. 40, No. 4 (1997), 895–924.

43. Sarah Duncan, *Mary I: Gender, Power, and Ceremony in the Reign of England's First Queen* (New York: Palgrave Macmillan, 2012), 111–126.

44. Charles Beem, *The Lioness Roared: The Problems of Female Rule in English History* (New York: Palgrave Macmillan, 2006), 63–99.

45. Alice Hunt, "The Monarchical Republic of Mary I," *The Historical Journal*, Vol. 52, No. 3 (2009), 557–572.

46. Sarah Duncan, "'He to Be Intituled Kinge': King Philip of England and the Anglo-Spanish Court," in *The Man Behind the Queen: Male Consorts in History*, Charles Beem and Miles Taylor, eds. (New York: Palgrave Macmillan, 2014), 55–80.

47. Anna Whitelock, "'A queen, and by the same title, a king also': Mary I: Queen in Parliament," in *Birth of a Queen*, 89–112.
48. See Charles Beem, "The Pastimes of George Ferrers: Reconstructing the Life and Career of a Tudor Renaissance Gentleman," *Explorations in Renaissance Culture*, Vol. 37, No. 1 (2011), 157–174.
49. Alexandra Briscoe, "Elizabeth I: An Overview," *BBC Online*, http://www.bbc.co.uk/history/british/tudors/elizabeth_i_01.shtml
50. William Camden, *The History of the Most Renowned and Victorious Princess Elizabeth, Late Queen of England*, Wallace McCaffery, ed. (Chicago, IL: University of Chicago Press, 1970), J.E. Neale, *Queen Elizabeth I* (New York: Anchor Books, 1957) (orig. pub. 1934).
51. Carole Levin, *The Heart and Stomach of a King* (Philadelphia: University of Pennsylvania Press, 1994); Susan Doran, *Monarchy and Matrimony*, (London: Routledge, 1996).
52. Wallace McCaffery, *Elizabeth I* (London: Edward Arnold, 1993), 27.
53. Sir John Harington, *Nugae Antiquae*, Thomas Park, ed. (London: 1804).
54. Guy, *Tudor England*, 250–330.
55. Nabil Matar, "Elizabeth through Moroccan Eyes," *The Foreign Relations of Elizabeth I*, Charles Beem, ed. (New York: Palgrave Macmillan, 2011), 145–167.
56. Charles Beem and Carole Levin, "Why Elizabeth Never Left England," in *The Foreign Relations of Elizabeth I*, 3–26.
57. Queen Elizabeth I. Elizabeth I to King Eric XIV of Sweden. February 25, 1560. National Archives. http://www.nationalarchives.gov.uk/education/resources/elizabeth-monarchy/elizabeth-i-to-king-eric-xiv-of-sweden/
58. Doran, *Monarchy and Matrimony*, 73–194.
59. "Golden Speech", 30 November 1601. National Archives. (SP 12/282 ff.137r-141v), http://www.nationalarchives.gov.uk/education/resources/elizabeth-monarchy/the-golden-speech/
60. Elaine Kruse, "A Network of Honor and Obligation: Elizabeth as Godmother," in *Queens Matter in Early Modern Studies*, Anna Rielh Bertolet, ed. (New York: Palgrave Macmillan, 2018), 181–198.
61. Levin, *Heart and Stomach of a King*, 66–90.
62. Katherine Crawford, *European Sexualities 1400–1800* (Cambridge: Cambridge University Press, 2007), 11–54.
63. Edmund Spenser, *The Fairie Queene*, A.C. Hamilton, ed. (London: Routledge, 2017).
64. Franky Wardell, "Queen Elizabeth I's Progress to Bristol–An Examination of Expenses," *Smugglers' City Special Field Project* (2009/10), http://www.bris.ac.uk/Depts/History/Maritime/Sources/2009sfpwardell.pdf
65. Robert Devereux, *To Plead My Faith* http://www.theotherpages.org/poems//dever01.html
66. Gascoigne, George, *Princelye Pleasures at the Courte of Kenelwoorth* (London, 1576).

67. David M. Bergeron, "The 'I' of the Beholder: Thomas Churchyard and the 1578 Norwich Pageant," in *The Progresses, Pageants, and Entertainments of Queen Elizabeth I*, Jayne Elisabeth Archer, Elizabeth Goldring and Sarah Knight, eds. (Oxford: Oxford University Press, 2014), 142–166.

68. Zillah Dovey, *An Elizabethan Progress: The Queen's Journey Into East Anglia, 1578* (Florham Park, N.J: Fairleigh Dickinson University Press, 1996).

69. Susan Frye, "The Myth of Elizabeth at Tilbury," *Sixteenth Century Journal*, Vol. 23, No. 1 (Spring, 1992), 95–114.

70. Donatella Montini, "Behold me Thy Handmaiden: The Pragmatics and Politics of Queen Elizabeth's Prayers," in *Elizabeth I in Writing*, Donatella Montini and Iolanda Plescia, eds. (New York: Palgrave Macmillan, 2018), 83–108.

71. Janet Green, "Queen Elizabeth I's Latin Reply to the Polish Ambassador," *Sixteenth Century Journal*, Vol. 31, No. 4 (Winter 2000), 987–1008. See also Linda Shenk, *Learned Queen: The Image of Elizabeth I in Politics and Poetry* (New York: Palgrave Macmillan, 2010).

72. Catherine Howey, "Dressing a Virgin Queen: Court Women, Dress, and Fashioning the Image of England's Elizabeth I," *Early Modern Women*, Vol. 4 (2009), 201–208.

73. Anna Riehl, *The Face of Queenship: Early Modern Representations of Elizabeth I* (New York: Palgrave Macmillan, 2010).

74. Catherine Loomis, *The Death of Elizabeth I: Remembering and Reconstructing the Virgin Queen* (New York: Palgrave Macmillan, 2010).

75. Rosalind Marshall, *Scottish Queens, 1034–1714* (Edinburgh: Birlinn, 2019).

76. There are several modern scholarly works on Margaret Tudor, who is often studied in conjunction with other royal women, including Nancy Lenz Harvey, *The Rose and the Thorn: The Lives of Mary and Margaret Tudor* (New York: Macmillan, 1975); Patricia Hill Buchanan, *Margaret Tudor: Queen of Scotland* (London: Scottish Academic Press, 1985); Maria Perry, *The Sisters of Henry VIII: The Tumultuous Lives of Margaret of Scotland and Mary of France* (New York: St. Martin's Press, 1999); and Michelle L. Beer, *Queenship at the Renaissance Courts of Britain: Catherine of Aragon and Margaret Tudor, 1503–1533* (Suffolk, UK: The Boydell Press, 2018).

77. Andrea Thomas, *Glory and Honour: The Renaissance in Scotland* (Edinburgh: Birlinn, 2013); Norman Macdougall, *James IV* (Edinburgh: John Donald, 2015).

78. Amy Blakeway, *Regency in Sixteenth Century Scotland* (Woodbridge, Suff: Boydell and Brewer, 2015).

79. Richard Glen Eaves, *Henry VIII and James V's Regency 1524–1528: A Study in Anglo-Scottish Diplomacy* (Lanham, MD: University Press of America, 1987).

80. There are two modern scholarly studies of Mary of Guise, Rosalind Marshall, *Mary of Guise* (Edinburgh: NMS, 2001), Pamela E Ritchie, *Mary of Guise in Scotland 1548–1560: A Political Career* (East Linton, Scotland: Tuckwell, 2002).

81. A. Thomas, *Princelie Majestie: The Court of James V of Scotland, 1528–1542* (Edinburgh: John Donald, 2005).

82. Stuart McCabe, *Let the Wolves Devour: War, Religion and Espionage During the Minority of Mary Queen of Scots, 1542–1560* (Cirencester: Mereo, 2015).

83. There are several modern studies of Anne of Denmark, including Leeds Barroll, *Anna of Denmark, Queen of England: A Cultural Biography* (Philadelphia, PA: University of Pennsylvania Press, 2001); Clare McManus, *Women on the Renaissance Stage: Anna of Denmark and Female Masquing in the Stuart Court (1590–1619)* (Manchester: Manchester University Press, 2002); and Susan Dunn-Hensley, *Anna of Denmark and Henriette Maria: Virgins, Witches, and Catholic Queens* (New York: Palgrave Macmillan, 2017).

84. David Stevenson, *Scotland's Last Royal Wedding: The Marriage of James VI and Anne of Denmark* (Edinburgh: John Donald, 1997).

85. Maria Hayward, "In Fine Style: The Art of Tudor and Stuart Fashion," *Renaissance Studies*, Vol. 28, No. 5 (Nov. 2014), 777–781.

86. Mark Brayshay, "Long-distance Royal Journeys: Anne of Denmark's Journey from Stirling to Windsor in 1603," *Journal of Transport History*, Vol. 25, No. 1 (Mar. 2004), 1–21.

87. Anna Whitelock, "Reconsidering the Political Role of Anna of Denmark," in *Queenship and Counsel in Early Modern Europe*, Helen Matheson Pollock, Joanne Paul and Catherine Fletcher, eds. (New York: Palgrave Macmillan, 2018), 237–258.

88. Barbara Keifer Lewalski, "Anne of Denmark and the Subversions of Masquing," *Criticism*, Vol. 35, No. 3 (Summer 1993), 341–355.

89. Alan Stewart, *The Cradle King* (New York: St. Martin's Press, 2003).

90. Alexandra Halasz, *The Marketplace of Print: Pamphlets and the Public Sphere in Early Modern England* (Cambridge: Cambridge University Press, 1997).

91. Michelle Ann White, *Henrietta Maria And the English Civil Wars* (Burlington, VT: Ashgate, 2006).

92. Other recent scholarly studies of Henrietta Maria include Karen Britland, *Drama at the Court of Henrietta Maria* (Cambridge: Cambridge University Press, 2006); and Carolyn Harris, *Queenship and Revolution in Early Modern Europe: Henrietta Maria and Marie Antoinette* (New York: Palgrave Macmillan, 2016).

93. Andrew Morton, "Sanctity and Suspicion: Catholicism, Conspiracy and the Representation of Henrietta Maria of France and Catherine of Braganza, Queens of Britain," *Queens Consort, Cultural Transfer and European Politics, c.1500–1800*, Helen Watanabe-O'Kelly and Adam Morton, eds. (New York: Routledge, 2017), 172–201.

94. Malcom Smuts, "Religion, Politics, and Henrietta Maria's Circle, 1625–1641," in *Henrietta Maria: Piety, Politics and Patronage*, Erin Griffey, ed. (New York: Routledge, 2016), 13–38.

95. Sarah Wolfson, "The Female Bedchamber of Henrietta Maria: Politics, Familiar Networks, and Policy, 1629–1640," in *The Politics of Female Households: Ladies-In-Waiting Across Early Modern Europe*, Nadine Akkerman and Birgit Houben, eds. (Leiden: Brill, 2014), 311–341.

96. Lorraine Madway, "Rites of Deliverance and Disenchantment: The Marriage Celebrations for Charles II and Catherine of Braganza 1661–62," *The Seventeenth Century*, Vol. 27, No. 1 (Spring 2012): 79–103B. See also Gertrude Z. Thomas, *Richer than Spices: How a Royal Bride's Dowry Introduced Cane, Lacquer, Cottons, Tea, and Porcelain to England, and So Revolutionized Taste, Manners, Craftsmanship, and History in both England and America* (New York: Knopf, 1965).

97. Edward Corp, "Catherine of Braganza and Cultural Politics," in *Queenship in Britain, 1660–1837: Royal Patronage, Court Culture, and Dynastic Politics*, Clarissa Campbell Orr, ed. (Manchester: Manchester University Press, 2002), 53–73.

98. Peter Leech, "Musicians in the Catholic Chapel of Catherine of Braganza, 1662–92," *Early Music*, Vol. 29, No. 1 (Nov. 2001), 570–587.

99. Mary of Modena lacks a modern scholarly biography. The most recent was Mary Hopkirk, *Queen Over the Water: Mary Beatrice of Modena, Queen of James II* (London: John Murray, 1953).

100. Andrew Barclay, "Mary Beatrice of Modena: The 'Second Bless'd of Womankind'?", in *Queenship in Britain 1660–1837 Royal Patronage, Court Culture and Dynastic Politics*, Clarissa Campbell-Orr, ed. (Manchester: Manchester University Press, 2002), 74–93.

101. Linda Colley, *Britons: Forging the Nation (1707–1837)* (New Haven: Yale University Press, 1992).

102. Mary II still awaits a modern scholarly biography of her own. The most recent is Nellie M. Waterson, *Mary II Queen of England, 1689–1694* (Durham NC: Duke University Press, 1928). More recently she is the subject of biographies of herself and her husband, see Henri and Barbara Van Der Zee, *William and Mary* (New York: Knoft, 1973), and John Van Der Kriste, *William and Mary: Heroes of the Glorious Revolution* (London: Stroud, 2008).

103. Beem, *The Lioness Roared*, 117–128.

104. Lois Schowerer, "Images of Queen Mary II, 1689–95," *Renaissance Quarterly*, Vol. 42, No. 4 (Winter 1989), 717–748.

105. Rachel Weil, *Political Passions: Gender, the Family, and Political Argument in England, 1680–1714* (Manchester: Manchester University Press, 1999), 110–116.

106. Richard Price, "An Incomparable Lady: Queen Mary's Share in the Government of England, 1689–1694," *Huntington Library Quarterly*, Vol. 75, No. 3 (2012), 307–326.

107. Sarah Churchill, Duchess of Marlborough, *An Account of the Conduct of the Dowager Duchess of Marlborough* (London, 1742).

108. See George Macaulay Trevelyan's multivolume *The Reign of Queen Anne* (London: Longman's Green and Co, 1930–34).

109. Anne also lacks a recent scholarly biography. The most recent include David Green, *Queen Anne* (London: Collins, 1970); and Edward Gregg, *Queen Anne* (London: Routledge and Kegan Paul, 1980).

110. Charles Beem, "'I Am Her Majesty's Subject': Prince George of Denmark and the Transformation of the English Male Consort," *Canadian Journal of History*, Vol. 34, No. 3 (Dec. 2004), 457–487.

111. Charles Beem, "Why Prince George of Denmark did not Become a King of England," in *The Man Behind the Queen*, 81–92.
112. Robert O. Bucholz, "Queen Anne: Victim of her Virtues?" in *Queenship in Britain 1660–1837*, 94–129.
113. Jeremy Black, *George II: Puppet of the Politicians?* (Exeter: Exeter University Press, 2007).
114. Recent scholarly studies of Caroline include Joanna Marschner, *Queen Caroline of Ansbach: Cultural Politics at the Eighteenth-century Court* (New Haven, CT: Yale University Press, 2014); and Matthew Dennison, *The First Iron Lady: A Life of Caroline of Ansbach* (Glasgow: HarperCollins, 2017).
115. Andrew Hanham, "Caroline of Brandenburg-Ansbach and the 'Anglicization' of the House of Hanover," in *Queenship in Europe 1660–1815*, Clarissa Campbell Orr, ed. (Cambridge: Cambridge University Press, 2004), 276–299.
116. Christine Gerrard, "Queens-in-Waiting: Caroline of Ansbach and Augusta of Saxe-Coburg as Princess of Wales," in *Queenship in Britain 1660–1837*, 142–161.
117. Emma Jay, "Queen Caroline's Library and its European Contexts," *Book History*, Vol. 9 (2006), 31–55.
118. Hannah Smith, *Georgian Monarchy: Politics and Culture, 1714–1760* (Cambridge: Cambridge University Press, 2006).
119. R. L. Arkell, *Caroline of Ansbach* (Oxford: Oxford University Press, 1939), 149.
120. Clarissa Campbell Orr, "Marriage in a Global Context: Charlotte of Mecklenburg-Strelitz, Queen of Great Britain and Ireland," in *Queens Consorts, Cultural Transfer*, 106–131.
121. Clarissa Campbell Orr, "Queen Charlotte, Scientific Queen," in *Queenship in Britain 1660–1837*, 236–266, and "Charlotte of Mecklenburg-Strelitz, Queen of Great Britain and Electress of Hanover: Northern Dynasties and the Northern Republic of Letters," in *Queenship in Europe 1660–1815*, 368–402.
122. Anna-Marie Linnell, "Becoming a Stuart Queen Consort: Nuptial Texts for Henrietta Maria of France and Catherine of Braganza, Queens of Britain," in *Queen Consorts, Cultural Transfer*, 153–171.

3 ANNE OF AUSTRIA AND FRANCO-IBERIAN QUEENSHIP

1. Mark de Vitis, "The Queen of France and the Capital of Cultural Heritage," *Early Modern Dynastic Marriages and Cultural Transfer*, Joan-Lluis Palos and Magdalena S. Sanchez, eds. (New York: Routledge, 2017), 45–65.
2. Abbey Zanger, *Scenes from the Marriage of Louis XIV: Nuptial Fictions and the Making of Absolutist Power* (Palo Alto: Stanford University Press, 1997).
3. The sole modern scholarly biography is Ruth Kleinman, *Anne of Austria: Queen of France* (Columbus, OH: Ohio State University Press, 1985). More recently, Anne of Austria received a modern feminist perspective in Katherine Crawford, *Perilous*

Performances: Gender and Regency in Early Modern France (Cambridge: Harvard University Press, 2004).

4. Eleanor Hoffman, *Raised to Rule: Educating Royalty at the Court of the Spanish Habsburgs, 1601–1634* (Baton Rouge, LA: Louisiana State University Press, 2011).

5. See the various essays in *Dynastic Marriages, 1612/1615: A Celebration of the Habsburg and Bourbon Unions*, Margaret M. McGowan, ed. (Burlington, VT: Ashgate, 2013).

6. Recent studies on Richelieu include Anthony Levi, *Cardinal Richelieu and the Making of France* (New York: Carroll & Graf, 2000); Jean-Vincent Blanchard, *Éminence: Cardinal Richelieu and the Rise of France* (New York: Walker & Co., 2011); and Robert Knecht, *Richelieu* (New York: Routledge, 2014).

7. See the various essays in *The Portrayal of Anne of Austria in Modern French Literature: Spanish Infanta or French Queen?*, Michael G Paulson, Tamara Alvarez-Detrell and Maria Galli Stampino, eds. (Lewiston, PA: Edwin Mellon Press, 2010).

8. Oliver Mallick, "Clients and Friends: The Ladies in Waiting at the Court of Anne of Austria, (1615–66)," in *The Politics of Female Households: Ladies in Waiting Across Early Modern Europe*, Vol. 4, Nadine Akkerman and Birgit Houben, eds. (Leiden: Brill, 2013), 231–264.

9. Geoffrey Treasure, *Richelieu and Mazarin* (London: Routledge, 1998).

10. Michael D. Slaven, "The Mirror Which Flatters Not: Anne of Austria and Representations of the Regency During the Fronde," *Proceedings of the Western Society for French History*, Vol. 24 (Oct. 1997), 451–461.

11. Jeffrey Merrick, "The Cardinal and the Queen: Sexual and Political Disorders in the Mazarinades," *French Historical Studies*, Vol. 18, No. 3 (Spring 1994), 667–699.

12. Derek Croxton, *Peacemaking in Early Modern Europe: Cardinal Mazarin and the Congress of Westphalia, 1643–1648* (Selinsgrove, NJ: Susquehanna University Press, 1999).

13. Modern studies of Anne of Brittany include Pauline Matarasso, *Queen's Mate: Three Women of Power in France on the Eve of the Renaissance* (Burlington, VT: Ashgate, 2001); and Cynthia J. Brown, *The Queens' Library: Image Making at the Court of Anne of Brittany, 1477–1514* (Philadelphia, PA: University of Pennsylvania Press, 2011).

14. Hélène M. Bloem, "The Processions and Decorations at the Royal Funeral of Anne of Brittany," *BibliothÃ¨que d'Humanisme et Renaissance*, T. 54, No. 1 (1992), 131–160.

15. James J. Rorimer, "The Unicorn Tapestries Were Made for Anne of Brittany," *The Metropolitan Museum of Art BulletinNew Series*, Vol. 1, No. 1 (Summer 1942), 7–20.

16. See the various essays in *The Cultural and Political Legacy of Anne de Bretagne: Negotiating Convention in Books and Documents*, Cynthia J. Brown, ed. (Woodbridge: Boydell & Brewer, 2010).

17. Nicole Hochner, "Imagining Esther in Early Modern France," *Sixteenth Century Journal*, Vol. 41, No. 3 (Fall 2010), 757–787.

18. There are three modern scholarly studies of Juana: Bethany Aram, *Juana the Mad: Sovereignty and Dynasty in Renaissance Europe* (Baltimore, MD: Johns Hopkins, 2005); *Juana of Castile, History and Myth of the Mad Queen*, Maria Gomez, Santiago Juan-Navarro and Phylis Zatlin, eds. (Lewisburg, PA: Bucknell University Press, 2008); and Gillian Fleming, *Juana I: Legitimacy and Conflict in Sixteenth-Century Castile* (New York: Palgrave Macmillan, 2018).

19. Bethany Aram, "Philip the Handsome (1478–1506), Duke of Burgundy and King of Castile: Voyages from Burgundy to Castile: Cultural Conflict and Dynastic Transitions, 1502–06," in *Early Modern Dynastic Marriages and Cultural Transfer*, 90–112.

20. Salvatore Poeta, "The Hispanic and Luso-Brazilian World: From Mad Queen to Martyred Saint: The Case of Juana La Loca Revisited in History and Art on the Occasion of the 450th Anniversary of Her Death," *Hispania*, Vol. 90, No. 1 (Mar. 2007), 165–172.

21. Matasarro, *Queen's Mate: Three Women of Power in France on the Eve of the Revolution* (New York: Routledge, 2001); Kathleen Wellman, *Queens and Mistresses in Renaissance France* (New Haven, CT: Yale University Press, 2013).

22. Catherine Fletcher, "The Ladies' Peace Revisited: Gender, Counsel, and Diplomacy," in *Queenship and Counsel in Early Modern Europe*, 111–133.

23. Wellman, *Queens and Mistresses in Renaissance France*; Matasarro, *Queens' Mate: Three Women of Power in France on the Eve of the Revolution*.

24. D. Potter, "Politics and Faction at the Court of Francis I: The Duchesse D'Etampes, Montmorency and the Dauphin Henri," *French History*, Vol. 21, No. 2 (2007), 127–146.

25. Jose Sebastian Lozano, "Choices and Consequences: The Construction of Isabel de Portugal's Image," in *Queenship and Political Power in Medieval and Early Modern Spain*, 145–162.

26. Mary Tiffany Ferer, "Queen Juana, Empress Isabel, and Musicians at the Royal Courts of Spain (1505–1556)," *Tijdschrift van de Koninklijke Vereniging voor Nederlandse Muziekgeschiedenis*, Deel 65, No. 1/2 (2015), 13–36.

27. There are many scholarly biographies of Catherine de Medici. See the select bibliography for a sampling of these titles.

28. Susan Broomhall, "Fit for a King? The Gendered Emotional Performances of Catherine de Medici as Dauphine of France, 1536–1547," in *Unexpected Heirs in Early Modern Europe: Potential Kings and Queens*, Valerie Schutte, ed. (New York: Palgrave Macmillan, 2017), 85–111.

29. K. Crawford, "Catherine de Médicis and the Performance of Political Motherhood," *Sixteenth Century Journal*, Vol. XXXI/3, (2000), 643–673.

30. Susan Broomhall, "'My Daughter, My Dear': The Correspondence of Catherine de Médicis and Elisabeth de Valois," *Women's History Review*, Vol. 24, No. 4 (2015), 548–569.

31. Una Mcilvenna, "'A Stable of Whores'?: The 'Flying Squadron' of Catherine de Medici," in *The Politics of Female Households: Ladies-In-Waiting Across Early Modern Europe*, 178–208.

32. Elaine Kruse, "The Blood-Stained Hands of Catherine de'Medici," in *Queens and Power in Medieval and Early Modern England*, Carole Levin and Robert O. Bucholz, eds. (Lincoln, NE: University of Nebraska Press, 2009), 39–155.

33. N.M. Sutherland, "Catherine de' Medici: The Legend of the Wicked Italian Queen," *The Sixteenth Century Journal*, Vol. 9, No. 2 (1978), 45–56.

34. The sole modern study of Marguerite in the English language is E.R. Chamberlin, *Marguerite of Navarre* (New York: Dial Press, 1974).

35. Marguerite de Valois, *Memoirs of Marguerite de Valois* (McLean, VA: IndyPublish. com, 2003).

36. There are no recent biographical studies of Marie de Medici in the English language. There are studies of her artistic patronage, all from the 1980s. See Susan Saward, *The Golden Age of Marie de' Medici* (Ann Arbor, MI: UMI Research Press, 1982); Deborah Marrow, *The Art Patronage of Maria de' Medici* (Ann Arbor, MI: UMI Research Press, 1982); Ronald Forsyth Millen and Robert Erich Wolf, *Heroic Deeds and Mystic Figures: A New Reading of Rubens' Life of Maria de' Medici* (Princeton, NJ: Princeton University Press, 1989).

37. Toby Osborne, "A Queen Mother in Exile: Marie De Médicis in the Spanish Netherlands and England, 1631–41," *Monarchy and Exile: The Politics of Legitimacy from Marie de Médicis to Wilhelm II*, P. Mansel and T. Riotte, eds. (New York: Palgrave Macmillan, 2011), 17–43.

38. Geraldine A. Johnson, "Pictures Fit for a Queen: Peter Paul Rubens and the Marie de' Medici Cycle," *Art History*, Vol. 16, No. 3 (Sept. 1993), 447–469.

39. Sarah R. Cohen, "Rubens's France: Gender and Personification in the Marie de Médicis Cycle," *The Art Bulletin. College Art Association*, Vol. 85, No. 3 (2003), 490–522.

40. Estelle Paranque, *Elizabeth I Through Valois Eyes* (New York: Palgrave Macmillan, 2019), 36.

41. J.H. Elliot, "The Court of the Spanish Habsburgs: A Peculiar Institution?" *Politics and Culture in Early Modern Europe: Essays in Honour of H. G. Koenigsberger*, Phyllis Mack and Margaret C. Jacob, eds. (Cambridge: Cambridge University Press, 1987), 5–24; Magdalena S. Sanchez, *The Empress, The Queen, and the Nun: Women and Power at the Court of Philip III of Spain* (Baltimore, MD: Johns Hopkins Press, 1998).

42. Magdalena S. Sánchez, "Melancholy and Female Illness: Habsburg Women and Politics at the Court of Philip III," *Journal of Women's History*, Vol. 8, No. 2 (1996), 81–102.

43. Laura Oliván Santaliestra, "Isabel of Borbón's Sartorial Politics: From French Princess to Habsburg Regent," *Early Modern Habsburg Women: Transnational Contexts, Cultural Conflicts, Dynastic Continuities*, Anne J Cruz and Maria Galli Stampino, eds. (London: Routledge, 2013), 225–242.

44. Steven N. Orso, "Praising the Queen: The Decorations at the Royal Exequies of Isabella of Bourbon," *The Art Bulletin*, Vol. 72, No. 1 (March 1990), 52–73; Emilia Montaner, "The Last Tribute to Isabella of Bourbon at Salamanca," *Journal of the Warburg and Courtauld Institutes*, Vol. 60 (1997), 164–193.

45. Mariana has been the subject of a recent diplomatic biography. See Sylvia Z. Mitchell, *Mariana of Austria and Imperial Spain: Court, Dynastic, and International Politics in Seventeenth-Century Europe* (Miami: University of Miami, 2013).

46. Silvia Z. Mitchell, "Habsburg Motherhood: The Power of Mariana of Austria, Mother and Regent for Carlos II of Spain," in *Early Modern Habsburg Women*, 175–195.

47. Eleanor Goodman, "Conspicuous in Her Absence: Mariana of Austria, Juan Jose of Austria, and the Representation of Her Power," in *Queenship and Political Power in Medieval and Early Modern Spain*, 163–184.

48. Mark Bryant, "Partner, Matriarch, and Minister: Mme de Maintenon of France, Clandestine Consort, 1680–1715," in *Queenship in Europe 1660–1815: The Role of the Consort*, 77–106.

49. Charles C. Noel, "Barbara Succeeds Elizabeth . . . The Feminization and Domestication of Politics in the Spanish Monarchy, 1701–1759," in *Queenship in Europe 1660–1615: The Role of the Consort*, 155–185.

50. María de los Ángeles Pérez Samper, "Elisabetta Farnese (1692–1766), Queen of Spain: A Queen between Three Worlds: Italy, Spain, and France," in *Early Modern Dynastic Marriages and Cultural Transfer*, 66–88.

51. Sharon L. Jansen, "Luisa de Guzmán, Regent of Portugal," https://www.monstrousregimentofwomen.com/2015/10/luisa-de-guzman-regent-of-portugal.html

52. Robert Oresko, "Maria Giovanna Battista of Savoy-Nemours (1644–1724): Daughter, Consort, and Regent of Savoy," in *Queenship in Europe 1660–1815: The Role of the Consort*; Clarissa Campbell Orr, ed. (Cambridge: Cambridge University Press, 2004), 17–23.

53. Maria Beatriz Nizza da Silva, *Reis de Portugal: D. João V* (in Portuguese) (Lisbon: Temas & Debates, 2009), 33.

54. Steven Saunders, *Cross, Sword, and Lyre: Sacred Music at the Imperial Court of Ferdinand II of Habsburg (1619–1637)* (Oxford: Clarendon Press, 1995).

55. Jennifer Roberts, *The Madness of Queen Maria: The Remarkable Life of Maria I of Portugal* (London: Templeton Press, 2009).

56. Daniel Alves, "Ferdinand II of Portugal: A Conciliatory King in an Age of Turmoil," in *The Man Behind the Queen: The Male Consort in History*, Charles Beem and Miles Taylor, eds. (New York: Palgrave Macmillan, 2014), 163–176.

57. Timothy J. Peters, "Mental Health Issues of Maria I of Portugal and Her Sisters: The Contributions of the Willis Family to the Development of Psychiatry," *History of Psychiatry*, Vol. 24, No. 3 (2013), 292–307.

58. John Rogister, "Queen Marie Leszczynska and Faction at the French Court 1725–1768," in *Queenship in Europe, 1660–1815: The Role of Consort*, 186–220.

59. Jennifer Germann, *Picturing Marie Leszczinska (1703–1768): Representing Queenship in Eighteenth-Century France* (New York: Routledge, 2016).

60. Marie Antoinette is the subject of numerous scholarly studies. In addition to the titles cited below, see the select bibliography for a sampling of studies.

61. Nancy N. Barker, "'Let Them Eat Cake': The Mythical Marie Antoinette and the French Revolution," *Historian*, Vol. 55, No. 4 (Summer 1993), 709–725.
62. *Maria Theresa.*, Karl A. Roider, ed. (Englewood Cliffs, NJ: Prentice-Hall, 1973), 88–90.
63. Desmond Hosford, "The Queen's Hair: Marie-Antoinette, Politics, and DNA," *Eighteenth-Century Studies*, Vol. 38, No. 1, Hair (Fall 2004), 183–200.
64. For a recent study of the affair, see Jonathan Beckman, *How to Ruin a Queen: Marie Antoinette and the Diamond Necklace Affair* (Boston, MA: De Capo Press, 2014).
65. Elizabeth Colwill, "Just Another 'Citoyenne'? Marie-Antoinette on Trial, 1790–1793," *History Workshop*, No. 28 (Autumn 1989), 63–87.
66. Carolyn Harris, *Queenship and Revolution in Early Modern Europe: Henrietta Maria and Marie Antoinette* (New York: Palgrave Macmillan, 2016).
67. Katharine Binhammer, "Marie Antoinette was 'One of Us': British Accounts of the Martyred Wicked Queen," *Eighteenth Century: Theory & Interpretation* (Texas Tech University Press), Vol. 44, No. 2/3 (Summer/Fall 2003), 233–255.
68. John Watkins, "Marriage a la Mode 1559: Elisabeth Valois, Elizabeth I, and the Changing Practice of Dynastic Marriage", *Queens and Power in Early Modern England*, Carole Levin and Robert O. Bucholz, eds. (Lincoln, NE: University of Nebraska Press, 2009), 77–96.

4 THE EMPRESS MARIA THERESA AND QUEENSHIP IN THE HOLY ROMAN EMPIRE

1. Christina Strunck, "The 'Two Bodies' of the Female Sovereign: Awkward Hierarchies in Images of Empress Maria Theresia, Catherine the Great of Russia and their Male Consorts," in *Queens Consort, Cultural Transfer and European Politics, c. 1500–1800*, 64–83.
2. Although well studied over the first half of the twentieth century, Maria Theresa has been woefully understudied in the English language for the past forty years. See the select bibliography for a sampling of scholarly studies of Maria Theresa. For an overview of her place in Habsburg history, see Andrew Wheatcroft, *The Habsburgs: Embodying Empire* (London: Penguin, 1995), and Charles W. Ingrao, *The Habsburg Monarchy, 1618–1815* (Cambridge: Cambridge University Press, 2000). For a brief online annotated bibliography of Maria Theresa titles from the history department of King's College, Cambridge, see http://departments.kings.edu/womens_history/mariatheres.html
3. Charlotte Backerra, "For Empire or Dynasty? Empress Elisabeth Christine and the Brunswicks," in *Royal Women and Dynastic Loyalty*, 165–180.
4. Maria Theresa, "Maria Theresa's Political Testament (1749–50)," in *German History in Documents, Volume 2. From Absolutism to Napoleon, 1648–1815*. http://ghdi.ghi-dc.org/pdf/eng/3_AustrianHabsburgEmpire_Doc.1_English.pdf

5. Reed Browning, *The War of the Austrian Succession* (Stroud: Alan Sutton, 1994).
6. Anna Coreth, *Pietas Austriaca: Austrian Religious Practices in the Baroque Era*, trans by William D. Bowman and Anna Maria Leitgeb (West Lafayette, IN: Purdue University Press, 2004).
7. The French philosophe and wit Voltaire described Europe's astonishment at Maria Theresa's ability to take the reins of the Habsburg inheritance. See *Maria Theresa*, Roider, ed. 92–93.
8. Michael Elia Yonan, *Empress Maria Theresa and the Politics of Habsburg Imperial Art* (University Park, PA: Pennsylvania State University Press, 2011).
9. Derek Beales, "Francis Stephen of Lorraine (Emperor Francis I, 1745–65), Consort of Maria Theresa, Ruler of the Austrian Monarchy from 1740," *The Man Behind the Queen*, 125–144.
10. *Maria Theresa*, Roider, ed. 81–83.
11. Joachim Whaley, *Germany and the Holy Roman Empire, Volume I: Maximilian I to the Peace of Westphalia, 1493–1648* (Oxford: Oxford University Press, 2012).
12. See the various essays in *A Constellation of Courts: The Courts and Households of Habsburg Europe, 1555–1665*, Rene Vermier, Dries Raeymaekers and Jose Eloy Hortal Munoz, eds. (Leuven: Leuven University Press, 2014).
13. Daniel R. Doyle, "The Sinews of Habsburg Governance in the Sixteenth Century: Mary of Hungary and Political Patronage," *Sixteenth Century Journal*, Vol. 31, No. 2 (Summer 2000), 349–360.
14. B.J. Spruyt, "'En bruit d'estre bonne luteriene': Mary of Hungary (1505–58) and Religious Reform," *English Historical Review*, Vol. 109, No. 431 (April 1994), 275–303.
15. Dieter A. Binder, "Pietas Austriaca? The Imperial Legacy in Interwar and Postwar Austria," *Religions* (August 29, 2017), https://www.mdpi.com/2077-1444/8/9/171
16. Anne J. Cruz, "Juana of Austria: Patron of the Arts and Regnant of Spain, 1554–59," in *The Rule of Women in Early Modern Europe*, 103–122.
17. Paula S. Fichtner, "Dynastic Marriage in Sixteenth-Century Habsburg Diplomacy and Statecraft: An Interdisciplinary Approach," *The American Historical Review*, Vol. 81, No. 2 (Apr. 1976), 243–265.
18. Joseph Patrouch, *Queen's Apprentice: Archduchess Elizabeth, Empress María, the Habsburgs, and the Holy Roman Empire, 1554–1569* (Leiden: Brill, 2010).
19. Paula S. Fichtner, *Ferdinand I of Austria: The Politics of Dynasticism in the Age of the Reformation* (Boulder, CO: East European Monographs, 1982).
20. Magdalena S. Sanchez, *The Empress, The Queen, and the Nun: Women and Power at the Court of Philip III of Spain* (Baltimore, Maryland: John Hopkins University Press, 1998)
21. Robert Bireley, *Ferdinand II, Counter-Reformation Emperor, 1578–1637* (Cambridge: Cambridge University Press, 2014).
22. Stephen Saunders, *Cross, Sword, and Lyre: Sacred Music at the Imperial Court of Ferdinand II of Habsburg (1619–1637)* (Oxford: Clarendon Press, 1995).

23. Mark Hengerer, *Making Peace in an Age of War: Emperor Ferdinand III (1608–1657)* (West Lafayette, IN: Purdue University Press, 2019).
24. Rocío Martínez López, "'The Infanta will Marry the Person who Provides the Peace or the One who Gives us the Means to Continue the War'. The Negotiations for the Marriage between Infanta María Teresa of Austria and Emperor Leopold I (1654–1657)," *Royal Studies Journal*, Vol. 3, No. 1, 6–27. DOI: http://doi.org/10.21039/rsj.v3i1.108
25. Gladys Taylor, *The Little Infanta* (London: Phoenix House, 1960).
26. See John P. Spielman, *Leopold I of Austria* (London: Thames and Hudson, 1997).
27. Charles W. Ingrao and Andrew L. Thomas, "Piety and Power: The Empress-Consort of the High Baroque," in *Queenship in Europe, 1660–1815 The Role of Consort*, 107–130.

5   BONA SFORZA AND QUEENSHIP IN THE BALTIC KINGDOMS

1. The most recent scholarly study of Bona Sforza is Adam Darowski, *Bona Sforza* (London: Kessinger, 2010).
2. Henryk Rodakowski, *Chicken War*, https://en.wikipedia.org/wiki/Chicken_War#/media/File:Rodakowski_Chicken_War.png
3. Katarzyna Kosior, *Becoming a Queen in Early Modern Europe: East and West* (New York: Palgrave Macmillan, 2019), 157.
4. Ibid.
5. Kosior, *Becoming a Queen*, 127.
6. Frieda, Leonie, *The Deadly Sisterhood: A Story of Women, Power and Intrigue in the Italian Renaissance* (New York: Harper Perennial, 2014).
7. "Sforza Book of Hours," British Library Add MS 34294, http://www.bl.uk/onlinegallery/ttp/sforza/accessible/pages7and8.html#content
8. Andrzej Wyczanski, "The Problem of Authority in Sixteenth-Century Poland," in *A Republic of Nobles: Studies in Polish History to 1864*, J.K. Fererowicz, Maria Bogucka and Henryk Samsonowicz, eds. (Cambridge: Cambridge University Press, 1982), 91–108.
9. Sharen Jansen, *The Monstrous Regiment of Women: Female Rulers in Early Modern Europe* (New York: Palgrave Macmillan, 2002), 168.
10. Katarzyna Kosior, "Bona Sforza and the Realpolitik of Queenly Counsel," in *Queenship and Counsel in Early Modern Europe*, Helen Matheson Pollock, Joanne Paul and Catherine Fletcher, eds. (New York: Palgrave Macmillan, 2018), 15–34.
11. Leslie Peirce, *Empress of the East. How a Slave Girl Became Queen of the Ottoman Empire* (Cambridge: Icon Books, 2017).
12. Richard Butterwick, ed., *The Polish-Lithuanian Monarchy in European Context, c. 1500–1795* (New York: Palgrave Macmillan, 2001).

13. Joseph Patrouch, "'*Bella gerant alii*.' Laodamia's Sisters, Habsburg Brides: Leaving Home for the Sake of the House," in *Early Modern Habsburg Women*, Anne J. Cruz and Maria Galli Stampino, eds. (London and New York: Routledge, 2016), 25–40.
14. Katarzyna Kosior, "Outlander, Baby Killer, Poisoner? Rethinking Bona Sforza's Black Legend," in *Virtuous or Villainess? The Image of the Royal Mother From the Early Medieval to the Early Modern Era*, Carey Fleiner and Elena Woodacre, eds. (New York: Palgrave Macmillan, 2016), 209.
15. See Charles Beem, "Introduction," in *The Lioness Roared: The Problems of Female Rule in English History* (New York: Palgrave Macmillan, 2006), 1–12.
16. Kosior, "Outlander," 199–224.
17. Almut Bues, "Art Collections as Dynastic Tools: The Jagiellonian Princesses Katarzyna, Queen of Sweden, and Zofia, Duchess of Braunschweig-Wolfenbüttel," in *Queens Consort, Cultural Transfer and European Politics, c.1500–1800*, Helen Watanabe-O'Kelly and Adam Morton, eds. (London and New York: Routledge, 2017), 15–36.
18. S. Olden-Jørgensen, "State Ceremonial, Court Culture and Political Power in Early Modern Denmark, 1536-1746," *Scandinavian Journal of History*, Vol. 27, No. 2 (2002), 65–76; Michael Bregnsbo, "Danish Absolutism and Queenship: Louisa, Caroline Matilda, and Juliana Maria," in *Queenship in Europe: 1660–1815*, 344–367.
19. Michael Roberts, *The Age of Liberty: 1719-1772* (Cambridge: Cambridge University Press, 1986); Gary Dean Peterson, *Warrior Kings of Sweden: The Rise of an Empire in the Sixteenth and Seventeenth Centuries* (Jefferson, NC: McFarland & Co., 2007).
20. Katarzyna Kosior, "Anna Jagiellon: A Female Political Figure in the Early-Modern Polish-Lithuanian Commonwealth," in *A Companion to Global Queenship*, Elena Woodacre, ed. (Leeds: Arc Humanities Press, 2018), 67–78.
21. Maria Bogucka, "The Court of Anna Jagiellon: Size, Structure and Functions," *Acta Poloniae Historica*, Vol. 99 (2009), 91–105.
22. R. I. Frost, "The Ethiopian and the Elephant? Queen Louise Marie Gonzaga and Queenship in an Elective Monarchy, 1645-1667," *The Slavonic and East European Review*, Vol. 91, No. 4 (2013), 787–817.
23. Helena Widaka, "Astrea and Celadon, or the Letters of Jan Sobieski and Marysieńka," Passage to Knowledge: Museum of King Jan III's Palace at Wilanow, http://www.wilanow-palac.pl/astrea_and_celadon_or_the_letters_of_jan_sobieski_and_marysienka.html
24. Helen Watanabe-O'Kelly, "Religion and the Consort: Two Electresses of Saxony and Queens of Poland (1697–1757)," in *Queenship in Europe, 1660–1815 The Role of Consort*, 252–275.
25. "Anna Sophia, Queen of Denmark," The Royal Danish Collection at Rosenborg Castle, http://www.kongernessamling.dk/en/rosenborg/person/anna-sophie/
26. William Layher, *Queenship and Voice in Medieval Northern Europe* (New York: Palgrave Macmillan, 2010).

27. Barbara Clay Finch, *Lives of the Princess of Wales* (London: Remington, 1883), 38–39.

28. William Henry Wilkins, *A Queen of Tears: Caroline Matilda, Queen of Denmark and Norway and Princess of Great Britain and Ireland* (London: Forgotten Books, 2017); C. F. Lachelles Wraxall, *Life and Times of Her Majesty Caroline Matilda* (3 vols.) (London: Forgotten Books, 2015); Hester Chapman, *Caroline Matilda, Queen of Denmark* (New York: Coward, McCann & Geoghegan, 1972).

29. Nathan Martin, "Princess Cecilia's Visitation to England," in *The Foreign Relations of Elizabeth I*, Charles Beem, ed. (New York: Palgrave Macmillan, 2011), 27–44.

30. Sven Stolpe, *Christina of Sweden* (New York: Macmillan, 1966), 40.

31. Sarah Walters, "'A Girton Girl on a Throne': Queen Christina and Versions of Lesbianism, 1906–1933", *Feminist Review*, No. 46, Sexualities: Challenge & Change (Spring 1994), 41–60.

32. Susanna Kristina Akerman, *Queen Christina of Sweden and her Circle: The Transformation of a Seventeenth-Century Philosophical Libertine* (Leyden: Brill, 1992).

33. Henry Woodhead, *Memoirs of Christina, Queen of Sweden* (2 vols.) (London: Forgotten Books, 2017).

34. Crawford *European Sexualities*, 57–60.

35. Louis Crompton, *Homosexuality and Civilization* (Cambridge, MA: Harvard University Press, 2009), 357–360.

36. Queen Christina-Culture and Peace: The European Initiative, http://queenchristina.eu/

37. Lis Granlund, "Queen Hedwig Eleonora of Sweden: Dowager, Builder, Collector," in *Queenship in Europe: 1660–1815*, 56–76. See also the various essays in *Queen Hedwig Eleonora and the Arts: Court Culture in Seventeenth-Century Northern Europe*, Kristoffer Neville and Lisa Skogh, eds. (Abingdon, Oxon: Routledge, 2016).

38. Elise M. Dermineuer, *Gender and Politics in Eighteenth-century Sweden: Queen Louisa Ulrika* (New York: Routledge Taylor & Francis Group, 2017).

39. Marc Serge Riviere, "'The Pallas of Stockholm': Louisa Ulrica of Prussia and the Swedish Crown," in *Queenship in Europe: 1660–1815*, 322–343.

40. Merit Laine, "An Eighteenth-Century Minerva: Lovisa Ulrika and Her Collections at Drottningholm Palace, 1744–1777," *Eighteenth-Century Studies*, Vol. 31, No. 4 (1998), 493–503.

41. Ibid.

42. Elise Dermineur and Svante Norrhem, "Luise Ulrike of Prussia, Queen of Sweden, and the Search for Political Space," in *Queens Consort, Cultural Transfer and European Politics*, 84–108.

43. For a recent study, see Christopher Clark, *Iron Kingdom: The Rise and Downfall of Prussia, 1600–1947* (Cambridge: Belknap Press, 2009).

44. Beatrice H. Zedler, "The Three Princesses," *Hypatia*, *The History of Women in Philosophy*, Vol. 4, No. 1 (Spring 1989), 28–63.

45. George MacDonald Ross, "Leibniz's Exposition of His System to Queen Sophie Charlotte and Other Ladies," in *Leibniz in Berlin*, H. Poser and A. Heinekamp, eds. (Stuttgart: Franz Steiner, 1990), 61–69.
46. Robert K. Massie, *Peter the Great* (New York: Knopf, 1980), 176.
47. This is the conclusion of a recent scholarly biography. See Tim Blanning, *Frederick the Great* (New York: Random House, 2016).
48. *The Diary of Samuel Pepys: Daily Entries from the Seventeenth Century London Diary: Catherine of Braganza (Queen)*, https://www.pepysdiary.com/encyclopedia/2381/
49. Thomas Biskup, "The Hidden Queen: Elisabeth Christine of Prussia and Hohenzollern Queenship in the Eighteenth Century," in *Queenship in Europe: 1660–1815*, 300–321.

6 CATHERINE II "THE GREAT" AND RUSSIAN QUEENSHIP

1. Isabel de Madariaga, *Russia in the Age of Catherine the Great* (New Haven: Yale University Press, 1981), 21–37.
2. Ruth Dawson, "Perilous Royal Biography: Representations of Catherine II Immediately After the Seizure of Her Throne," *Biography*, Vol. 27, No. 3 (2004), 517–534.
3. Quoted in Robert K. Massie, *Catherine the Great* (New York: Random House, 2011), 265–266.
4. Madariaga, *Russia in the Age of Catherine the Great*, 187–236.
5. Eugenii V. Anisimov, *Five Empresses: Court Life in Eighteenth Century Russia*, Kathleen Carroll, trans. (Westport, CT: Praeger, 2004).
6. John T. Alexander, *Catherine the Great: Life and Legend* (New York: Oxford University Press, 1988). Alexander devoted considerable space to discussing the political implications of Catherine's sex life.
7. Russell Martin, *A Bride for the Tsar: Bride-shows and Marriage Politics in Early Modern Russia* (DeKalb: Northern Illinois University Press, 2011).
8. See Chapter 3, Massie, *Peter the Great*.
9. Isolde Thyrêt, *Between God and Tsar: Religious Symbolism and the Royal Women of Muscovite Russia* (DeKalb: Northern Illinois University Press, 2001).
10. See Chapters 1–3, Isabel de Madariaga, *Ivan the Terrible* (New Haven, CT: Yale University Press, 2006).
11. Chester S.L. Dunning, *Russia's First Civil War: The Time of Troubles and the Founding of the Romanov Dynasty* (Philadelphia, PA: Penn State University Press, 2001).
12. J.T. Fuhrmann, *Tsar Alexis: His Reign and His Russia* (Gulf Breeze, FL: Academic International Press, 1981).
13. Lindsey Hughes, "Sofiya Alekseyevna and the Moscow Rebellion of 1682," *The Slavonic and East European Review*, Vol. 63, No. 4 (Oct. 1985), 518–539.

14. Lindsey Hughes, *Sophia: Regent of Russia, 1657–1704* (New Haven, CT & London: Yale University Press, 1990).

15. V.O. Kliuchevskii, *A Course in Russian History: The Seventeenth Century* (New York: Routledge, 1994).

16. Orel Beilinson, "Female Rule in Imperial Russia: Is Gender a Useful Category of Historical Analysis?", *A Companion to Global Queenship*, 79–96.

17. Russell E. Martin, "The Petrine Divide and the Periodization of Early Modern Russian History," *Slavic Review*, Vol. 69, No. 2 (Summer 2010), 410–425.

18. Lindsey Hughes, "Catherine I of Russia, Consort to Peter the Great," *Queenship in Europe, 1660–1815: The Role of the Consort*, 131–154.

19. Walther Kirchner, "The Death of Catherine I of Russia," *The American Historical Review*, Vol. 51, No. 2 (Jan. 1946), 254–261.

20. "The 'Conditions' of Anna Ivanovna's Accession to the Throne, 1730," Daniel Field, trans.http://academic.shu.edu/russianhistory/index.php/ The_%22Conditions%22_of_Anna_Ivanovna%27s_Accession_to_the_ Throne,_1730

21. Nina Curtiss, *A Forgotten Empress: Anna Ivanovna and her Era 1730–1740* (New York: Frederick Unger, 1974).

22. Liv Berdnikov, "Empress Elizabeth," *Russian Life*, Vol. 52, No. 6 (Nov./Dec. 2009), 54–59.

23. Cyril Bryner, "The Issue of Capital Punishment in the Reign of Elizabeth Petrovna," *The Russian Review*, Vol. 49, No. 4 (Oct. 1990), 389–416.

24. Peter Petschauer, "Catherine the Great's Conversion of 1744," *Jahrbücher für Geschichte Osteuropas* Neue Folge, Bd. 20, H. 2 (June 1972), 179–193.

25. Frank T. Brechka, "Catherine the Great: The Books She Read," *The Journal of Library History* (1966–1972) Vol. 4, No. 1 (Jan. 1969), 39–52.

26. *The Memoirs of Catherine the Great*, Markus Hoogenboomeds Cruse, ed. (New York: Modern Library, 2005).

27. Carol S. Leonard, *Reform and Regicide: The Reign of Peter III of Russia* (Bloomington, IN: Indiana University Press,1993).

28. In a letter to her former lover Stanislaus Poniatowski, Catherine explained her version of peter III's death. See Massie, *Catherine the Great*, 276–276.

29. Brenda Meehan-Water, "Catherine the Great and the Problem of Female Rule," *The Russian Review*, Vol. 34, No. 3 (July 1975), 293–307.

30. Cynthia Whitaker, "The Reforming Tsar: The Redefinition of Autocratic Duty in Eighteenth- Century Russia," *Slavic Review*, Vol. 51, No. 1 (Spring 1992), 77–98.

31. *Voltaire and Catherine the Great: Selected Correspondence*, A. Lentin, ed. (Cambridge: Cambridge University Press, 1974).

32. Aleksandr Radishchev, *A Journey From St. Petersburg to Moscow* (Cambridge, MA: Harvard University Press, 1958).

33. Massie, *Catherine the Great*, 566–569.

34. Virginia Rounding, *Catherine the Great: Love, Sex and Power* (London: Hutchinson, 2006).

35. *Memoirs of Catherine the Great*, Mark Cruse and Hilde Hoogenboom, eds. (New York: Modern Library, 2003).
36. Richard Butterwick, *Poland's Last King and English Culture: Stanisław August Poniatowski, 1732–1798* (Oxford: Clarendon, 1998).
37. Simon Sebag Montefiore, *Catherine the Great and Potemkin: The Imperial Love Affair* (New York: Vintage, 2016).
38. *Love and Conquest: Personal Correspondence of Catherine the Great and Prince Grigory Potemkin*, Douglas Smith, ed. and trans. (DeKalb: Northern Illinois University Press, 2004).
39. Ibid.
40. *Memoirs of Catherine the Great* 35.
41. Yonan, *Maria Theresa*.
42. Katia Dianina, "Art and Authority: The Hermitage of Catherine the Great," *The Russian Review*, Vol. 63, No. 4 (Oct. 2004), 630–654; Susan Jacques, *The Empress of Art: Catherine the Great and the Transformation of Russia* (New York: Pegasus, 2016).
43. Madariaga, *Russia in the Age of Catherine the Great*, 295–299.
44. Monika Greenleaf, "Performing Autobiography: The Multiple Memoirs of Catherine The Great (1756–96)," *The Russian Review*, Vol. 63, No. 3 (July 2004), 407–426.
45. David M. Griffiths, "Catherine II: The Republican Empress," *Jahrbücher für Geschichte Osteuropas*, Neue Folge, Bd. 21, H. 3 (1973), 323–344.
46. Quoted in Massie, *Catherine the Great*, 573.

Select Bibliography

Åkerman, Susanna Kristina. *Queen Christina of Sweden and her Circle: The Transformation of a Seventeenth-Century Philosophical Libertine.* Leiden: Brill, 1992.

Akkerman, Nadine and Houben, Birgit. *The Politics of Female Households: Ladies-in-Waiting Across Early Modern Europe.* Leiden: Brill, 2014.

Alexander, John T. *Catherine the Great: Life and Legend.* New York: Oxford University Press, 1988.

Anisimov, Eugenii V. *Five Empresses: Court Life in Eighteenth Century Russia.* Kathleen Carroll, trans. Westport, CT: Praeger, 2004.

Aram, Bethany. *Juana the Mad: Sovereignty and Dynasty in Renaissance Europe.* Baltimore, MD: Johns Hopkins, 2005.

Axton, Marie. *The Queen's Two Bodies: Drama and the Elizabethan Succession.* London: Royal Historical Society, 1977.

Barroll, Leeds. *Anna of Denmark, Queen of England: A Cultural Biography.* Philadelphia, PA: University of Pennsylvania Press, 2001.

Bassnet, Susan. *Elizabeth I: A Feminist Perspective.* Oxford: Berg, 1988.

Beckman, Jonathan. *How to Ruin a Queen: Marie Antoinette and the Diamond Necklace Affair.* Boston, MA: De Capo Press, 2014.

Beem, Charles. *The Lioness Roared: The Problems of Female Rule in English History.* New York: Palgrave Macmillan, 2006.

Beer, Michelle L. *Queenship at the Renaissance Courts of Britain: Catherine of Aragon and Margaret Tudor, 1503–1533.* Suffolk, UK: The Boydell Press, 2018.

Bell, Ilona. *Elizabeth I: The Voice of a Monarch.* New York: Palgrave Macmillan, 2010.

The Birth of a Queen: Essays on the Quincentenary of Mary I, Sarah Duncan, Valerie Schutte, eds. New York: Palgrave Macmillan, 2016.

Blakeway, Amy. *Regency in Sixteenth Century Scotland.* Woodbridge, UK: Boydell and Brewer, 2015.

The Body of the Queen: Gender and Rule in the Courtly World, 1500–2000, Regina Schulte, ed. New York: Berghahn, 2006.

Brown, Cynthia. *The Queens' Library: Image Making at the Court of Anne of Brittany, 1477–1514.* Philadelphia: University of Pennsylvania Press, 2011.

Buchanan, Patricia. *Margaret Tudor Queen of Scots.* Edinburgh: Scottish Academy Press, 1985.

Bucholz, Robert O. *The Augustan Court: Queen Anne and the Decline of Court Culture.* Stanford, CA: Stanford University Press, 1993.

Catherine the Great: A Profile. Marc Raeff, ed. New York: Macmillan, 1972.

Chamberlin, E.R. *Marguerite of Navarre.* New York: Dial Press, 1974.

Chantal, Thomas. *The Wicked Queen: The Origins of the Myth of Marie-Antoinette*. New York: Zone, 1999.

Cole, Mary Hill. *The Portable Queen: Elizabeth I and the Politics of Ceremony*. Amherst: University of Massachusetts Press, 1999.

A Companion to Global Queenship. Elena Woodacre, ed. Leeds: Arc Humanities Press, 2018.

A Constellation of Courts: The Courts and Households of Habsburg Europe, 1555–1665. Rene Vermier, Dries Raeymaekers and Jose Eloy Hortal Munoz, eds. Leuven: Leuven University Press, 2014.

Coreth, Anna. *Pietas Austriaca: Austrian Religious Practices in the Baroque Era*. William D. Bowman and Anna Maria Leitgeb, trans. West Lafayette, IN: Purdue University Press, 2004.

Coughlan, Robert. *Elizabeth and Catherine: Empresses of all the Russias*. London: MacDonald and Jane's, 1974.

Crankshaw, Edward. *Maria Theresa*. London: Longman, 1969.

Crawford, Katherine. *Perilous Performances: Gender and Regency in Early Modern France*. Cambridge, MA: Harvard University Press, 2004.

———. *European Sexualities 1400–1800*. Cambridge: Cambridge University Press, 2007.

Cronin, Vincent. *Catherine, Empress of All the Russias*. London: Collins, 1978.

The Cultural and Political Legacy of Anne de Bretagne: Negotiating Convention in Books and Documents. Cynthia J. Brown, ed. Woodbridge: Boydell & Brewer, 2010.

Curtiss, Nina. *A Forgotten Empress: Anna Ivanovna and her Era 1730–1740*. New York: Frederick Unger, 1974.

Darowski, Adam. *Bona Sforza*. London: Kessinger, 2010.

De Madariaga, Isabel. *Russia in the Age of Catherine the Great*. New Haven, CT: Yale University Press, 1981.

———. *Catherine the Great: A Short History*. New Haven, CT & London: Yale University Press, 1990.

Dennison, Matthew. *The First Iron Lady: A Life of Caroline of Ansbach*. Glasgow: HarperCollins, 2017.

Denny, Joanna. *Anne Boleyn: A New Life of England's Tragic Queen*. Cambridge, MA: Da Capo Press, 2004.

Dermineuer, Elise M. *Gender and Politics in Eighteenth-Century Sweden: Queen Louisa Ulrika*. New York: Routledge Taylor & Francis Group, 2017.

Dixon, Simon. *Catherine the Great*. London: Profile Books, 2009.

Doran, Susan. *Monarchy and Matrimony*. London: Routledge, 1996.

Downey, Kirstin. *Isabella: The Warrior Queen*. New York: Anchor, 2014.

Duindam, Jeroen. *Dynasties: A Global History of Power, 1300–1800*. Cambridge: Cambridge University Press, 2015.

Duncan, Sarah. *Mary I: Gender, Power, and Ceremony in the Reign of England's First Queen*. New York: Palgrave Macmillan, 2012.

Dunn-Hensley, Susan. *Anna of Denmark and Henriette Maria: Virgins, Witches, and Catholic Queens*. New York: Palgrave Macmillan, 2017.

Earenfight, Theresa. *Queenship in Medieval Europe*. New York: Palgrave Macmillan, 2013.

Early Modern Dynastic Marriages and Cultural Transfer. Joan-Lluis Palos and Magdalena S. Sanchez, eds. New York: Routledge, 2017.

Early Modern Habsburg Women: Transnational Contexts, Cultural Conflicts, Dynastic Continuities. Anne J Cruz and Maria Galli Stampino, eds. London: Routledge, 2013.

Edwards, John. *The Spain of the Catholic Monarchs 1474–1520*. Oxford: Wiley-Blackwell, 2000.

———— *Ferdinand and Isabella (Profiles in Power)*. Harlow, UK: Taylor & Francis, 2005.

Elizabeth I: Collected Works. Leah S. Marcus, Janel Mueller and Mary Beth Rose, eds. Chicago, IL: University of Chicago Press, 2000.

The English Court: From the Wars of the Roses to the Civil War. David Starkey, ed. London and New York: Longman, 1987.

Fleming, Gillian B. *Juana I: Legitimacy and Conflict in Sixteenth-Century Castile*. New York: Palgrave Macmillan, 2018.

The Foreign Relations of Elizabeth I. Charles Beem, ed. New York: Palgrave Macmillan, 2011.

Fraser, Antonia. *Mary, Queen of Scots*. New York: Delacorte Press, 1978.

————. *The Warrior Queens*. New York: Knopf, 1988.

————. *Marie Antoinette: The Journey*. New York: Anchor, 2002.

Freida, Leonie. *Catherine de Medici: Renaissance Queen of France*. New York: Harper Perennial, 2003.

————. *The Deadly Sisterhood: A Story of Women, Power and Intrigue in the Italian Renaissance*. New York: Harper Perennial, 2014.

Germann, Jennifer G. *Picturing Marie Leszczinska (1703–1768): Representing Queenship in Eighteenth-Century France*. London: Routledge, 2016.

Green, David. *Queen Anne*. London: Collins, 1970.

Gregg, Edward. *Queen Anne*. London: Routledge and Kegan Paul, 1980.

Guardiola-Griffiths, Cristina. *Legitimizing the Queen: Propaganda and Ideology in the Reign of Isabel I of Castile*. Lewisburg, PA: Bucknell University Press, 2011.

Guy, John. *'My Heart is My Own': The Life of Mary Queen of Scots*. London: Mariner, 2004.

Hackett, Helen. *Virgin Mother, Maiden Queen: Elizabeth I and the Cult of the Virgin Mary*. New York: St. Martin's Press, 1995.

Haigh, Christopher. *Elizabeth I*. New York: Longman, 1988.

Harris, Carolyn. *Queenship and Revolution in Early Modern Europe: Henrietta Maria and Marie Antoinette*. New York: Palgrave Macmillan, 2016.

Hayward, Maria. *Dress at the Court of Henry VIII*. Leeds: Maney, 2007.

Heal, Felicity. *The Power of Gifts: Gift-Exchange in Early Modern England*. Oxford: Oxford University Press, 2014.

Hedley, Olwen. *Queen Charlotte*. London: J. Murray, 1975.

Hoffman, Eleanor. *Raised to Rule: Educating Royalty at the Court of the Spanish Habsburgs, 1601–1634*. Baton Rouge: Louisiana State University Press, 2011.

Hopkins, Lisa. *Women Who Would Be Kings: Female Rulers of the Sixteenth Century*. New York: St. Martin's Press, 1991.

Hopkirk, Mary. *Queen over the Water: Mary Beatrice of Modena, Queen of James II*. London: John Murray, 1953.

Hughes, Lindsey. *Sophia: Regent of Russia, 1657–1704*. New Haven, CT & London: Yale University Press, 1990.

Hunt, Alice. *The Drama of Coronation: Medieval Ceremony in Early Modern England*. Cambridge: Cambridge University Press, 2011.

Hunt, Lynn. *The Family Romance of the French Revolution*. Berkeley: University of California Press, 1992.

Isabel la Católica, Queen of Castile: Critical Essays. David A. Boruchoff, ed. New York: 2003.

Jacques, Susan. *The Empress of Art: Catherine the Great and the Transformation of Russia*. New York: Pegasus, 2016.

Jansen, Sharon L. *The Monstrous Regiment of Women*. New York: Palgrave Macmillan, 2002.

———. *Anne of France: Lessons for My Daughter*. Cambridge: Boydell and Brewer, 2004.

Juana of Castile, History and Myth of the Mad Queen. Maria Gomez, Santiago Juan-Navarro and Phylis Zatlin, eds. Lewisburg, PA: Bucknell University Press, 2008.

Kantorwicz, Ernst. *The King's Two Bodies: A Study in Medieval Theology*. Princeton, NJ: Princeton University Press, 1957.

Kleinman, Ruth. *Anne of Austria: Queen of France*. Columbus: Ohio State University Press, 1985.

Knecht, R.K. *Catherine de' Medici*. New York: Longman, 1998.

Kosior, Katarzyna. *Becoming a Queen in Early Modern Europe*. New York: Palgrave Macmillan, 2019.

Lever, Evelyn. *Marie Antoinette, The Last Queen of France*. New York: St. Martin's Griffin, 2001.

Levin, Carole. *The Heart and Stomach of a King: Elizabeth I and the Politics of Sex and Power*. Philadelphia, PA: University of Pennsylvania Press, 1994.

———. *The Reign of Elizabeth I*. New York: Palgrave Macmillan, 2002.

Lewis, Brenda Ralphs. *Monarchy: The History of an Idea*. Stroud: Sutton, 2003.

Lewis, Jayne Elizabeth. *The Trial of Mary Queen of Scots: A Brief History with Documents*. New York: Bedford St. Martin's, 1999.

Liss, Peggy. *Isabel the Queen*. Oxford: Oxford University Press, 1992.

Loades, David. *Mary Tudor: A Life*. London: Basil Blackwell, 1989.

Longworth, Philip. *The Three Empresses: Catherine I, Anna, and Elizabeth of Russia*. New York: Holt, Rinehart, and Winston, 1973.

Love and Conquest: Personal Correspondence of Catherine the Great and Prince Grigory Potemkin. Douglas Smith, ed. and trans. DeKalb: Northern Illinois University Press, 2004.

MacRobert, A.E. *Mary Queen of Scots and the Casket Letters*. New York: Palgrave Macmillan, 2002.

Mahoney, Irene. *Madame Catherine*. New York: Coward, McCann & Geoghegan, 1975.

The Man Behind the Queen: Male Consorts in History. Charles Beem and Miles Taylor, eds. New York: Palgrave Macmillan, 2014.

Marie Antoinette: Writing on the Body of the Queen. Dena Goodman, ed. New York: Routledge, 2000.

Marschner, Joanna. *Queen Caroline of Ansbach: Cultural Politics at the Eighteenth-Century Court*. New Haven, CT: Yale University Press, 2014.

Marshall, Rosalind. *Scottish Queens, 1034–1714*. East Linton, Scotland: Tuckwell Press, 2003.

Martin, Russell. *A Bride for the Tsar: Bride-Shows and Marriage Politics in Early Modern Russia*. DeKalb: Northern Illinois University Press, 2011.

Massie, Robert K. *Catherine the Great: Portrait of a Woman*. New York: Random House, 2011.

Matarasso, Pauline. *Queen's Mate: Three Women of Power in France on the Eve of the Renaissance*. Burlington, VT: Ashgate, 2001.

McCaffery, Wallace. *Elizabeth I*. New York: Edward Arnold, 1993.

McGowan, M. M. *Dynastic Marriages 1612/1615: A Celebration of the Habsburg and Bourbon Unions*. Farnham: Ashgate, 2013.

McIlvenna, Una. *Scandal and Reputation at the Court of Catherine de Medici*. London: Routledge, 2016.

Mattingly, Garret. *Catherine of Aragon*. London: Jonathan Cape, 1963.

McManus, Clare. *Women on the Renaissance Stage: Anna of Denmark and Female Masquing in the Stuart Court (1590–1619)*. Manchester: Manchester University Press, 2002.

Medieval Queenship, John Carmi Parsons, ed. New York: St. Martins, 1993.

The Memoirs of Catherine the Great. Markus Cruse and Hilde Hoogenboom, eds. and trans. New York: Modern Library, 2005.

Mitchell, Silvia Z. *Mariana of Austria and Imperial Spain: Court, Dynastic, and International Politics in Seventeenth-Century Europe* (dissertation). Miami, FL: University of Miami, 2013.

Monter, William. *The Rise of Female Kings in Europe, 1300–1800*. New Haven, CT: Yale University Press, 2012.

Montefiore, Simon Sebag. *Catherine the Great and Potemkin: The Imperial Love Affair*. New York: Vintage, 2016.

Mulgan, Catherine. *The Renaissance Monarchies: 1469–1558 (Cambridge Perspectives in History)*. Cambridge: Cambridge University Press, 1998.

Neale, J.E. *Queen Elizabeth I*. Chicago: Academy Chicago Publishers, 1992.

Okerlund, Arlen Naylor. *Elizabeth of York*. New York: Palgrave Macmillan, 2009.

Paranque, Estelle. *Elizabeth I Through Valois Eyes*. New York: Palgrave Macmillan, 2019.

Patrouch, Joseph F. *Queen's Apprentice: Archduchess Elizabeth, Empress María, the Habsburgs, and the Holy Roman Empire, 1554–1569*. Leiden: Brill, 2010.

Paulson, Michael G. *Catherine de' Médici: Five Portraits*. New York: P. Lang, 2002.

Peirce, Leslie. *The Imperial Harem: Women and Sovereignty in the Ottoman Empire.* Oxford: Oxford University Press, 1993.

Perry, Maria. *The Sisters of Henry VIII.* Cambridge, MA: Da Capo Press, 2000.

Plowden, Alison. *Two Queens in One Isle: Deadly Relationship of Elizabeth I and Mary Queen of Scots.* Totowa, NJ: Barnes & Noble Books, 1984.

Porter, Linda. *Katherine the Queen: The Remarkable Life of Katherine Parr, the Last Wife of Henry VIII.* New York: St. Martin's Press, 2011.

The Portrayal of Anne of Austria in Modern French Literature: Spanish Infanta or French Queen? Michael G Paulson, Tamara Alvarez-Detrell and Maria Galli Stampino, eds. Lewiston, PA: Edwin Mellon Press, 2010.

Premodern Rulers and Postmodern Viewers. Janice North, Karl C. Alvestad and Elena Woodacre, eds. New York: Palgrave Macmillan, 2018.

The Princely Courts of Europe, 1500–1750. John Adamson, ed. London: Seven Dials, 2000.

Queen Hedwig Eleonora and the Arts: Court Culture in Seventeenth-Century Northern Europe. Kristoffer Neville and Lisa Skogh, eds. Abingdon, Oxon: Routledge, 2016.

Queen Isabel I of Castile: Power, Patronage, Persona. Barbara Weissberger, ed. Suffolk: Boydell and Brewer, 2008.

Queens and Power in Medieval and Early Modern England. Carole Levin and Robert O. Bucholz, eds. Lincoln: University of Nebraska Press, 2009.

Queens Consort, Cultural Transfer and European Politics, c. 1500–1800. Helen Watanabe-O'Kelly and Adam Morton, eds. Abingdon, Oxon: Routledge, 2017.

Queenship and Counsel in Early Modern Europe. Helen Matheson-Pollock, Joanne Paul and Catherine Fletcher, eds. New York: Palgrave Macmillan, 2018.

Queenship and Power in Medieval and Early Modern Spain. Theresa Earenfight, ed. Burlington, VT: Ashgate, 2005.

Queenship in Britain 1660–1837. Clarissa Campbell Orr, ed. Manchester: Manchester University Press, 2002.

Queenship in Europe 1600–1815: The Role of the Consort. Clarissa Campbell Orr, ed. Cambridge: Cambridge University Press, 2004.

Queenship in the Mediterranean. Elena Woodacre, ed. New York: Palgrave Macmillan, 2013.

Recca, Cinzia. *The Diary of Queen Maria Carolina of Naples, 1781–1785.* New York: Palgrave Macmillan, 2017.

Richards, Judith M. "Mary Tudor as a 'Sole Quene'? Gendering Tudor Monarchy", *The Historical Journal*, 40, 4 (1997), 895–924.

———. "To Promote a Woman to Beare Rule: Talking of Queens in Mid-Tudor England, *Sixteenth Century Journal* 28 (1997), 101–121.

Riehl, Anna. *The Face of Queenship: Early Modern Representations of Elizabeth I.* New York: Palgrave Macmillan, 2010.

The Rituals and Rhetoric of Queenship: Medieval to Early Modern. Liz Oakley Brown and Louise Wilkinson, eds. Dublin: Four Courts, 2009.

Ritchie, Pamela E. *Mary of Guise in Scotland, 1548–1560: A Political Career*. East Linton: Scotland: Tuckwell Press, 2002.

Roberts, Jennifer. *The Madness of Queen Maria: The Remarkable Life of Maria I of Portugal*. London: Templeton Press, 2009.

Roider, Karl A. *Maria Theresa*. Englewood Cliffs, NJ: Prentice-Hall, 1973.

Rounding, Virginia. *Catherine the Great: Love, Sex and Power*. London: Hutchinson, 2006.

Royal Women and Dynastic Loyalty, Caroline Dunn and Elizabeth Carney, eds. New York: Palgrave Macmillan, 2018.

Rubin, Nancy. *Isabella of Castile*, New York, 1991.

The Rule of Women in Early Modern Europe, Anne J. Cruz and Sukuki Mihoko, eds. Urbana: University of Illinois Press, 2009.

Sanchez, Magdalena S. *The Empress, The Queen, and the Nun: Women and Power at the Court of Philip III of Spain*. Baltimore, MD: Johns Hopkins Press, 1998.

Saunders, Stephen. *Cross, Sword, and Lyre: Sacred Music at the Imperial Court of Ferdinand II of Habsburg (1619–1637)*. Oxford: Clarendon Press, 1995.

Saward, Susan. *The Golden Age of Marie de' Medici*. Ann Arbor, MI: UMI Research Press, 1982.

Shenk, Linda. *Learned Queen: The Images of Elizabeth I in Politics and Poetry*. New York: Palgrave Macmillan, 2010.

Spellman, W.M. *Monarchies, 1000–2000*. London: Reaktion, 2001.

Starkey, David. *Six Wives: The Queens of Henry VIII*. New York: Harper Collins, 2004.

———. *Monarchy: From the Middle Ages to Modernity*. New York: Harper, 2007.

Stolpe, Sven. *Christina of Sweden*. New York: Macmillan, 1966.

Strage, Mark. *Women of Power: The Life and Times of Catherine de' Medici*. New York: Harcourt Brace Jovanovich, 1976.

Strickland, Agnes. *Lives of the Queens of England, From the Norman Conquest* (8 vols.). London: Longmans, Green, 1864.

Taylor, Gladys. *The Little Infanta*. London: Phoenix House, 1960.

Thyrêt, Isolde. *Between God and Tsar: Religious Symbolism and the Royal Women of Muscovite Russia*. DeKalb: Northern Illinois University Press, 2001.

Tittler, Robert. *The Reign of Mary Tudor*. London: Longman, 1991.

Tremlett, Giles. *Catherine of Aragon*. New York: Walker, 2010.

Trevelyan, George Macaulay. *The Reign of Queen Anne* (3 vols.). London: Longmans and Green, 1930–34.

Tudor Queenship: The Reigns of Mary and Elizabeth. Alice Hunt and Anna Whitelock, eds. New York: Palgrave Macmillan, 2010.

Tudors and Stuarts on Film: Historical Perspectives. Susan Doran and Thomas Freeman, eds. New York: Palgrave Macmillan, 2008.

Unexpected Heirs in Early Modern Europe: Potential Kings and Queens. Valerie Schutte, ed. New York: Palgrave Macmillan, 2017.

Van Der Kiste, John. *William and Mary: Heroes of the Glorious Revolution*. London: Stroud, 2008.

Van Der Zee, Henri and Barbara. *William and Mary*. New York: Alfred A. Knopf, 1973.

Virtuous or Villainess? The Image of the Royal Mother from the Early Medieval Era to the Early Modern Era. Carey Fleiner and Elena Woodacre, eds. New York: Palgrave Macmillan, 2016.

Lentin, A., ed. and trans. *Voltaire and Catherine the Great: Selected Correspondence*. Cambridge: Cambridge University Press, 1974.

Walton, Kristen Post. *Catholic Queen, Protestant Patriarchy: Mary, Queen of Scots, and the Politics of Gender and Religion*. New York: Palgrave Macmillan, 2006.

Warnicke, Retha. *The Rise and Fall of Anne Boleyn*. Cambridge: Cambridge University Press, 1989.

———. *Elizabeth of York and her Six Daughters-In-Law*. New York: Palgrave Macmillan, 2017.

Weber, Carolyn. *Queen of Fashion: What Marie Antoinette Wore to the Revolution*. New York: Picador, 2007.

Weil, Rachel. *Political Passions: Gender, the Family, and Political Argument in England, 1680–1714*. Manchester: Manchester University Press, 1999.

Weissberger, Barbara F. *Isabel Rules: Constructing Queenship, Wielding Power*. Minneapolis: University of Minnesota Press, 2004.

Wellman, Kathleen, *Queens and Mistresses in Renaissance France*. New Haven, CT: Yale University Press, 2013.

Wheatcroft, Andrew. *The Habsburgs: Embodying Empire*. London: Penguin, 1995.

White, Michelle Ann. *Henrietta Maria and the English Civil Wars*. Burlington, VT: Ashgate, 2006.

Whitelock, Anna. *Mary Tudor: England's First Queen*. London: Bloomsbury, 2010.

Wilkins, William Henry. *A Queen of Tears: Caroline Matilda, Queen of Denmark and Norway and Princess of Great Britain and Ireland*. London: Forgotten Books, 2017.

Williamson, David. *Debrett's Kings and Queens of Europe*. Topsfield, MA: Salem House, 1988.

Woodacre, Elena. *The Queens Regnant of Navarre*. New York: Palgrave Macmillan, 2013.

Woodhead, Henry. *Memoirs of Christina, Queen of Sweden* (2 vols.). London: Forgotten Books, 2017.

Wormald, Jenny. *Mary, Queen of Scots: Politics, Passion and a Kingdom Lost*. London: Taurus, 2001.

Wraxall, C. F. Lachelles. *Life and Times of Her Majesty Caroline Matilda* (3 vols.). London: Forgotten Books, 2015.

Yonan, Michael Elia. *Empress Maria Theresa and the Politics of Habsburg Imperial Art*. University Park, PA: Penn State University Press, 2011.

Zanger, Abbey. *Scenes from the Marriage of Louis XIV: Nuptial Fictions and the Making of Absolutist Power*. Palo Alto, CA: Stanford University Press, 1997.

Zweig, Stefan, *Marie Antoinette: The Portrait of an Average Woman*. New York: Grove, 2002.

Index

Printed by Printforce, the Netherlands